Luann 2

Dates and Other Disasters

by Greg Evans

Andrews McMeel
Publishing

Kansas City

04 05 06 07 08 BBG 10 9 8 7 6 5 4 3 2 1

ISBN: 0-7407-4664-2

Library of Congress Control Number: 2004105604

www.LUANNSROOM.com

—— **ATTENTION: SCHOOLS AND BUSINESSES** ——

Andrews McMeel books are available at quantity discounts with bulk purchase for educational, business, or sales promotional use. For information, please write to: Special Sales Department, Andrews McMeel Publishing, 4520 Main Street, Kansas City, Missouri 64111.

WHEN MEN WATCH TV
©2001 GEC Inc. Dist. by United Feature Syndicate, Inc. www.LuannsRoom.com
WHEN WOMEN WATCH TV
Silver Polish

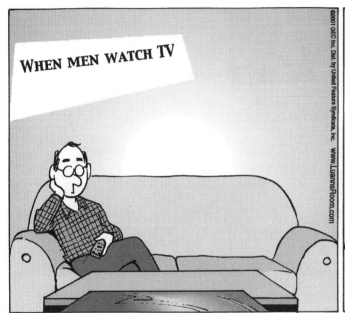

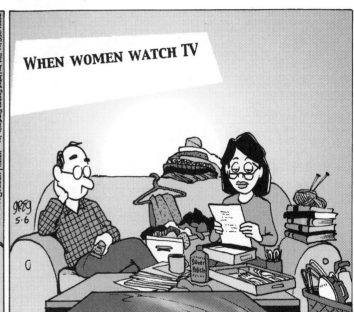

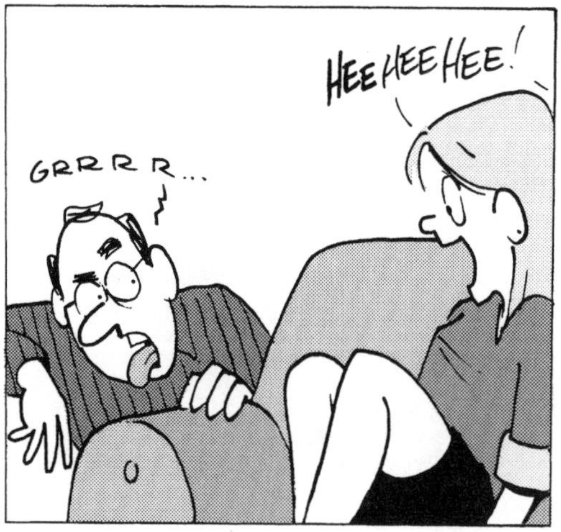
HEE HEE HEE!
GRRRR...

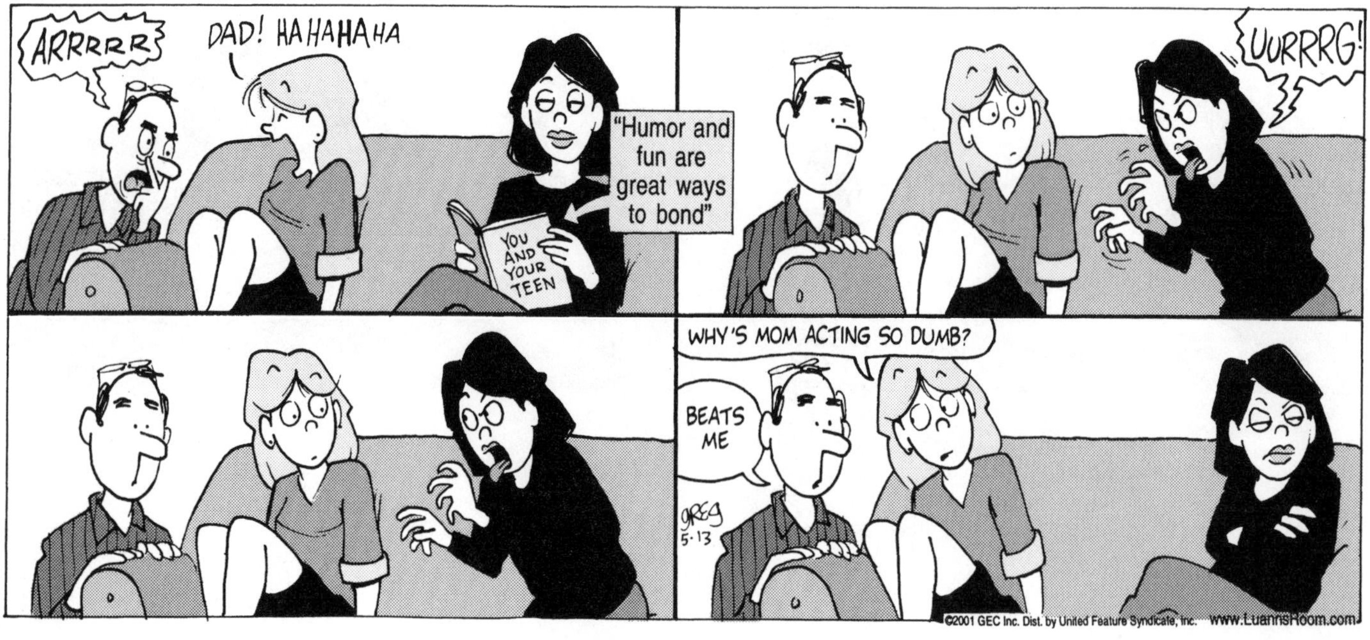
ARRRRR
DAD! HAHAHAHAHA
"Humor and fun are great ways to bond"
YOU AND YOUR TEEN
UURRRG!
WHY'S MOM ACTING SO DUMB?
BEATS ME
GREG 5-13
©2001 GEC Inc. Dist. by United Feature Syndicate, Inc. www.LuannsRoom.com

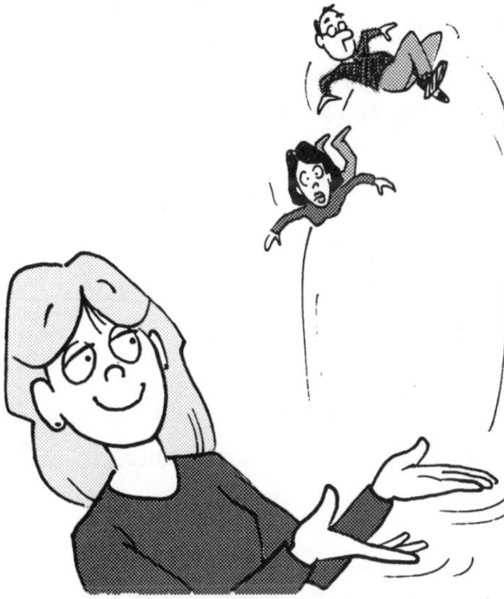

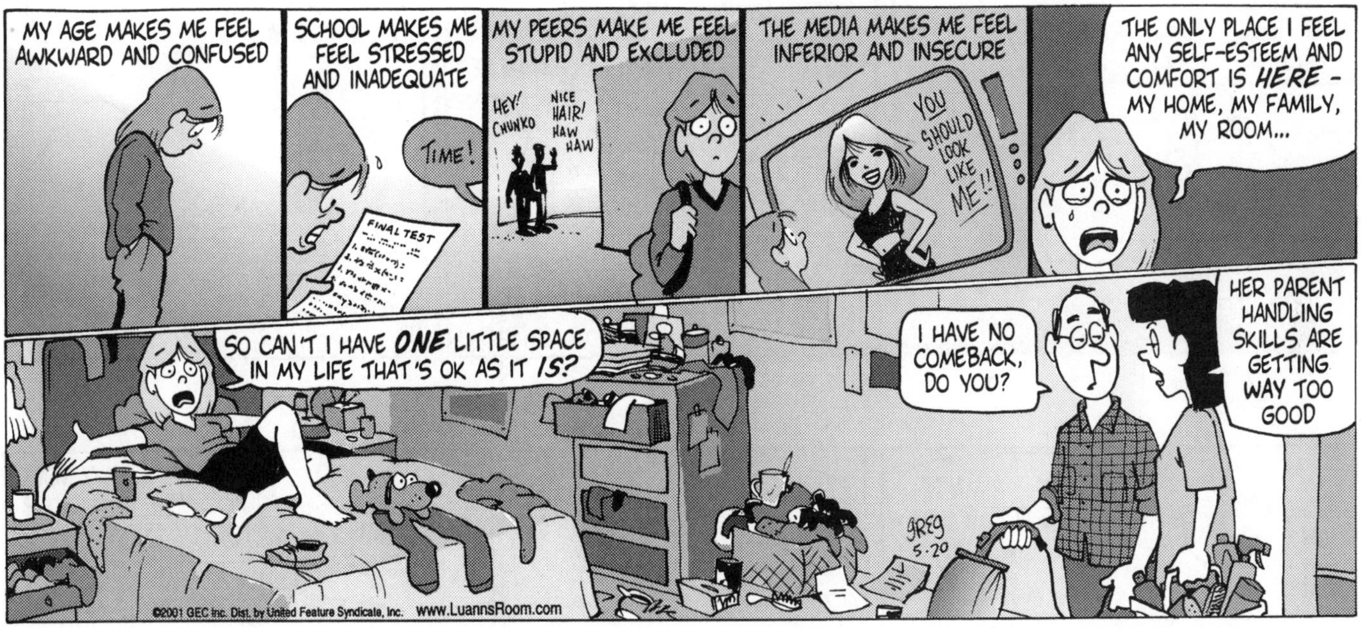
MY AGE MAKES ME FEEL AWKWARD AND CONFUSED
SCHOOL MAKES ME FEEL STRESSED AND INADEQUATE
TIME!
FINAL TEST
MY PEERS MAKE ME FEEL STUPID AND EXCLUDED
HEY! CHUNKO
NICE HAIR! HAW HAW
THE MEDIA MAKES ME FEEL INFERIOR AND INSECURE
YOU SHOULD LOOK LIKE ME!!
THE ONLY PLACE I FEEL ANY SELF-ESTEEM AND COMFORT IS HERE - MY HOME, MY FAMILY, MY ROOM...
SO CAN'T I HAVE ONE LITTLE SPACE IN MY LIFE THAT'S OK AS IT IS?
I HAVE NO COMEBACK, DO YOU?
HER PARENT HANDLING SKILLS ARE GETTING WAY TOO GOOD
GREG 5-20
©2001 GEC Inc. Dist. by United Feature Syndicate, Inc. www.LuannsRoom.com

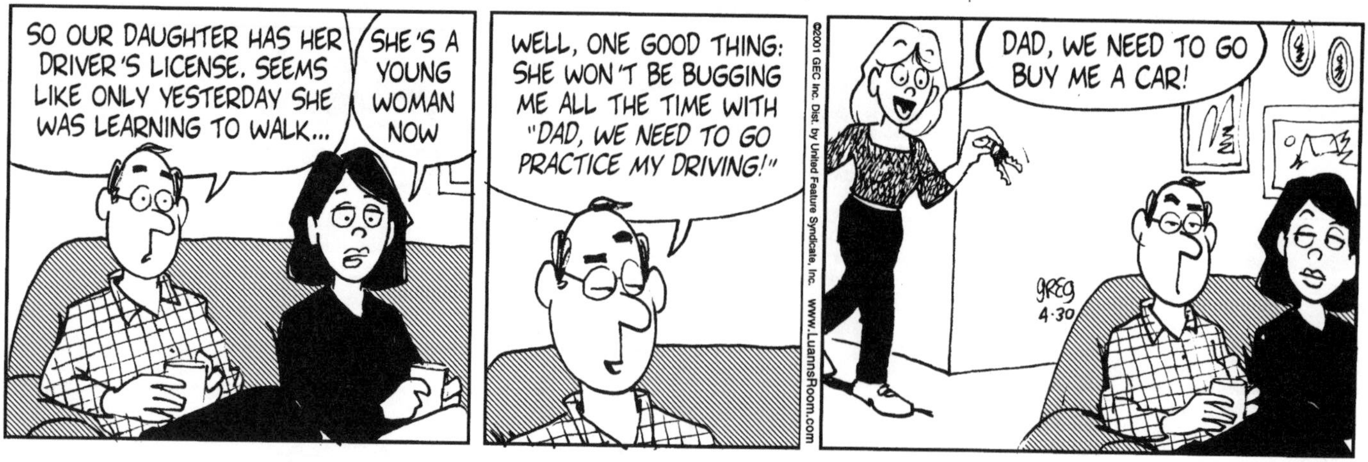
SO OUR DAUGHTER HAS HER DRIVER'S LICENSE. SEEMS LIKE ONLY YESTERDAY SHE WAS LEARNING TO WALK...
SHE'S A YOUNG WOMAN NOW
WELL, ONE GOOD THING: SHE WON'T BE BUGGING ME ALL THE TIME WITH "DAD, WE NEED TO GO PRACTICE MY DRIVING!"
©2001 GEC Inc. Dist. by United Feature Syndicate, Inc. www.LuannsRoom.com
DAD, WE NEED TO GO BUY ME A CAR!
GREG 4·30

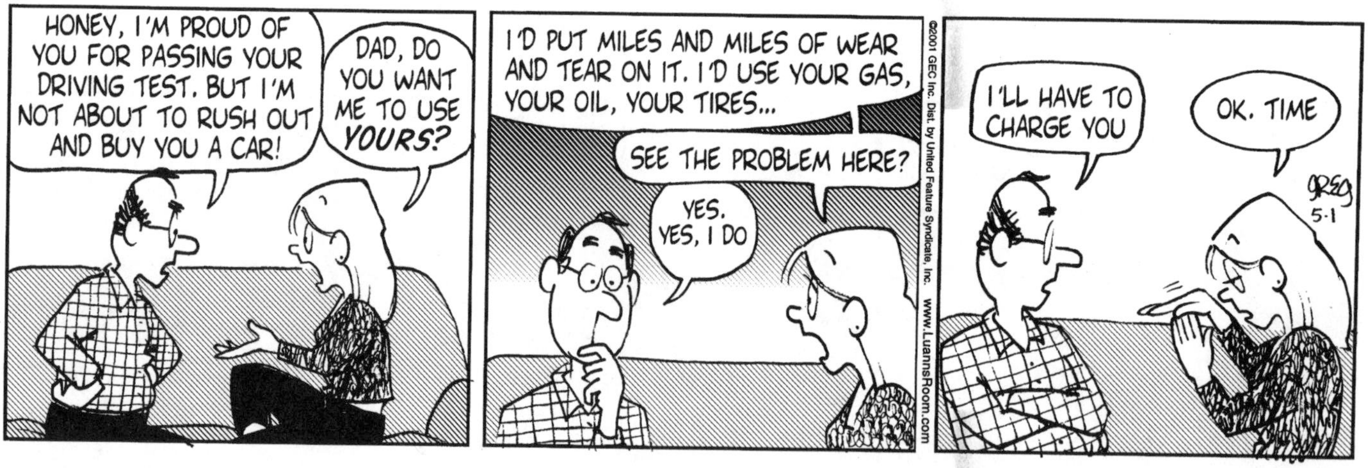
HONEY, I'M PROUD OF YOU FOR PASSING YOUR DRIVING TEST. BUT I'M NOT ABOUT TO RUSH OUT AND BUY YOU A CAR!
DAD, DO YOU WANT ME TO USE ***YOURS?***
I'D PUT MILES AND MILES OF WEAR AND TEAR ON IT. I'D USE YOUR GAS, YOUR OIL, YOUR TIRES...
SEE THE PROBLEM HERE?
YES. YES, I DO
©2001 GEC Inc. Dist. by United Feature Syndicate, Inc. www.LuannsRoom.com
I'LL HAVE TO CHARGE YOU
OK. TIME
GREG 5·1

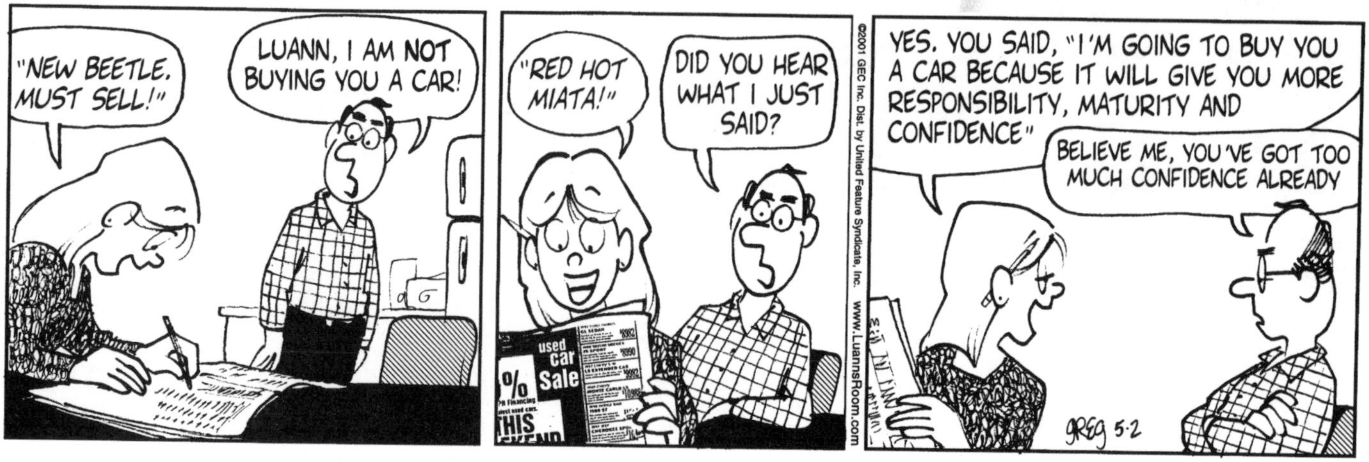
"NEW BEETLE. MUST SELL!"
LUANN, I AM **NOT** BUYING YOU A CAR!
"RED HOT MIATA!"
DID YOU HEAR WHAT I JUST SAID?
used car Sale
©2001 GEC Inc. Dist. by United Feature Syndicate, Inc. www.LuannsRoom.com
YES. YOU SAID, "I'M GOING TO BUY YOU A CAR BECAUSE IT WILL GIVE YOU MORE RESPONSIBILITY, MATURITY AND CONFIDENCE"
BELIEVE ME, YOU'VE GOT TOO MUCH CONFIDENCE ALREADY
GREG 5·2

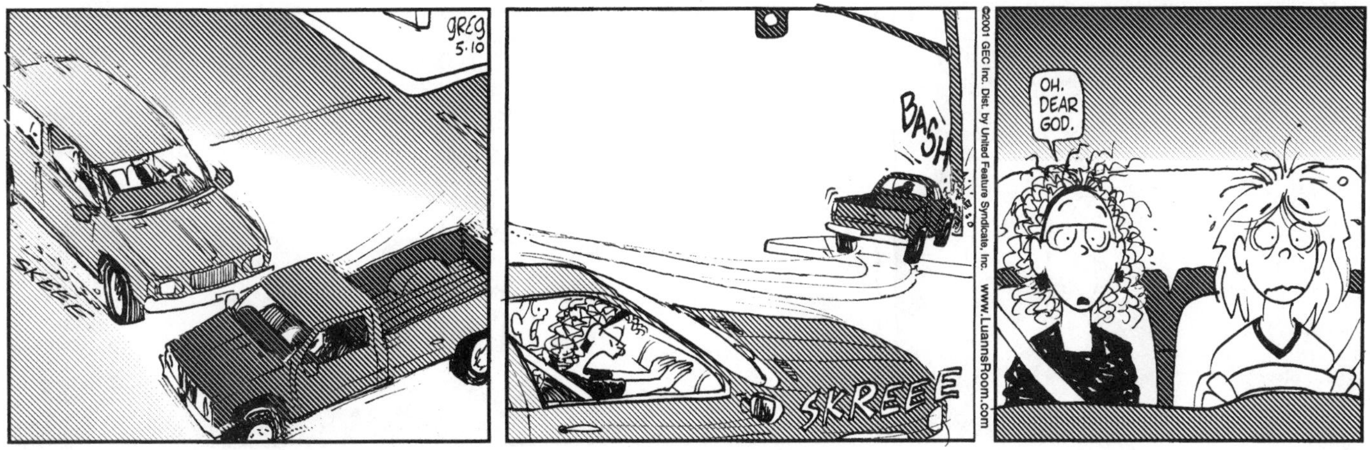
GREG 5·10
SKEEE
BASH
SKREEE
©2001 GEC Inc. Dist. by United Feature Syndicate, Inc. www.LuannsRoom.com
OH. DEAR GOD.

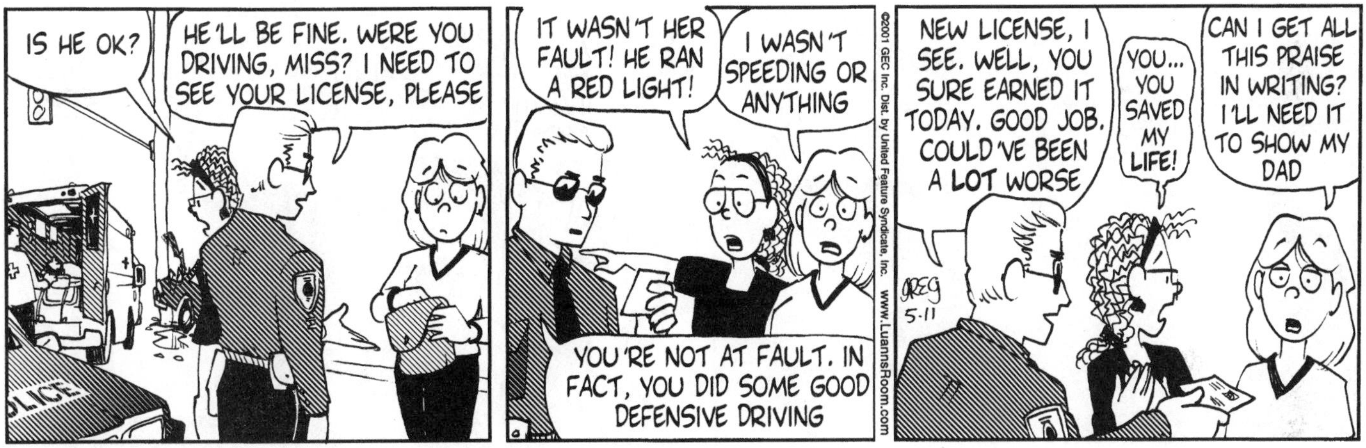
IS HE OK?
HE'LL BE FINE. WERE YOU DRIVING, MISS? I NEED TO SEE YOUR LICENSE, PLEASE
POLICE
IT WASN'T HER FAULT! HE RAN A RED LIGHT!
I WASN'T SPEEDING OR ANYTHING
YOU'RE NOT AT FAULT. IN FACT, YOU DID SOME GOOD DEFENSIVE DRIVING
©2001 GEC Inc. Dist. by United Feature Syndicate, Inc. www.LuannsRoom.com
NEW LICENSE, I SEE. WELL, YOU SURE EARNED IT TODAY. GOOD JOB. COULD'VE BEEN A **LOT** WORSE
YOU... YOU SAVED MY **LIFE!**
CAN I GET ALL THIS PRAISE IN WRITING? I'LL NEED IT TO SHOW MY DAD
GREG 5·11

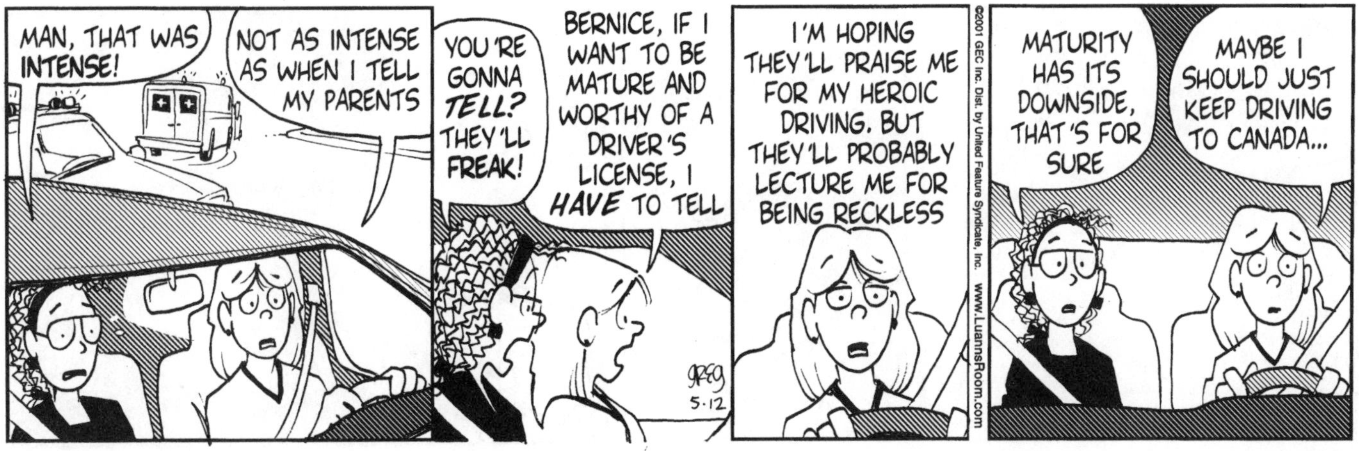
MAN, THAT WAS **INTENSE!**
NOT AS INTENSE AS WHEN I TELL MY PARENTS
YOU'RE GONNA ***TELL?*** THEY'LL **FREAK!**
BERNICE, IF I WANT TO BE MATURE AND WORTHY OF A DRIVER'S LICENSE, I ***HAVE*** TO TELL
GREG 5·12
I'M HOPING THEY'LL PRAISE ME FOR MY HEROIC DRIVING. BUT THEY'LL PROBABLY LECTURE ME FOR BEING RECKLESS
©2001 GEC Inc. Dist. by United Feature Syndicate, Inc. www.LuannsRoom.com
MATURITY HAS ITS DOWNSIDE, THAT'S FOR SURE
MAYBE I SHOULD JUST KEEP DRIVING TO CANADA...

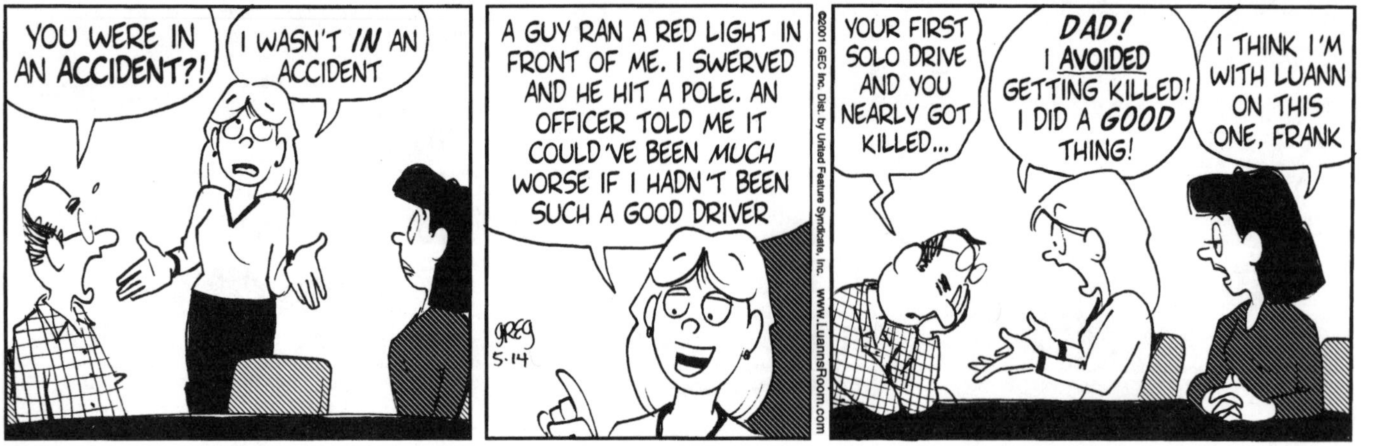
YOU WERE IN AN **ACCIDENT?!**
I WASN'T ***IN*** AN ACCIDENT
A GUY RAN A RED LIGHT IN FRONT OF ME. I SWERVED AND HE HIT A POLE. AN OFFICER TOLD ME IT COULD'VE BEEN *MUCH* WORSE IF I HADN'T BEEN SUCH A GOOD DRIVER
GREG 5·14
©2001 GEC Inc. Dist. by United Feature Syndicate, Inc. www.LuannsRoom.com
YOUR FIRST SOLO DRIVE AND YOU NEARLY GOT KILLED...
DAD! I AVOIDED GETTING KILLED! I DID A ***GOOD*** THING!
I THINK I'M WITH LUANN ON THIS ONE, FRANK

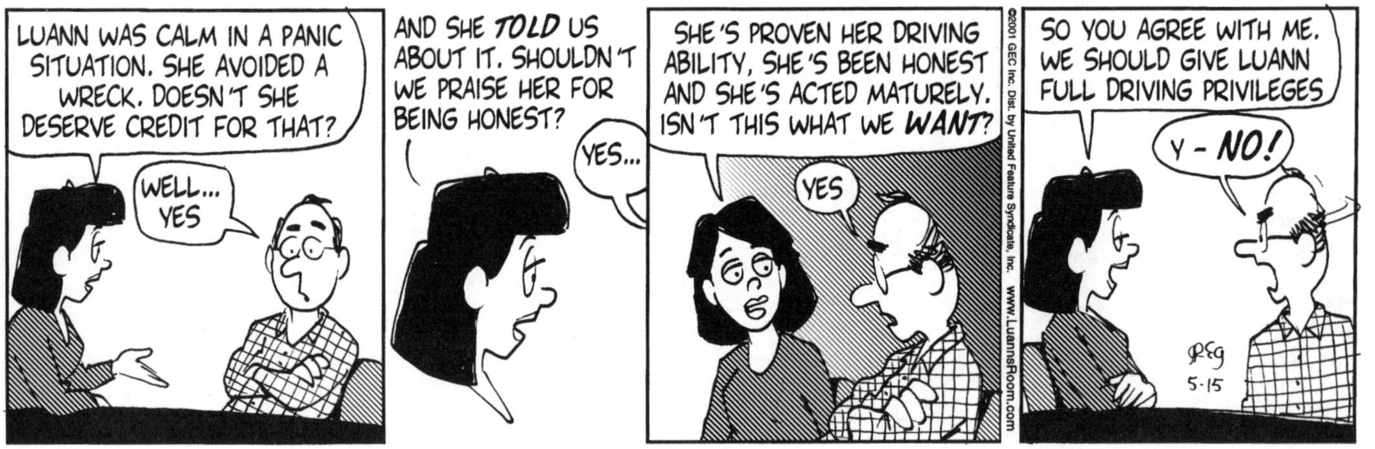
LUANN WAS CALM IN A PANIC SITUATION. SHE AVOIDED A WRECK. DOESN'T SHE DESERVE CREDIT FOR THAT?
WELL... YES
AND SHE ***TOLD*** US ABOUT IT. SHOULDN'T WE PRAISE HER FOR BEING HONEST?
YES...
SHE'S PROVEN HER DRIVING ABILITY, SHE'S BEEN HONEST AND SHE'S ACTED MATURELY. ISN'T THIS WHAT WE ***WANT?***
YES
©2001 GEC Inc. Dist. by United Feature Syndicate, Inc. www.LuannsRoom.com
SO YOU AGREE WITH ME. WE SHOULD GIVE LUANN FULL DRIVING PRIVILEGES
Y - ***NO!***
GREG 5·15

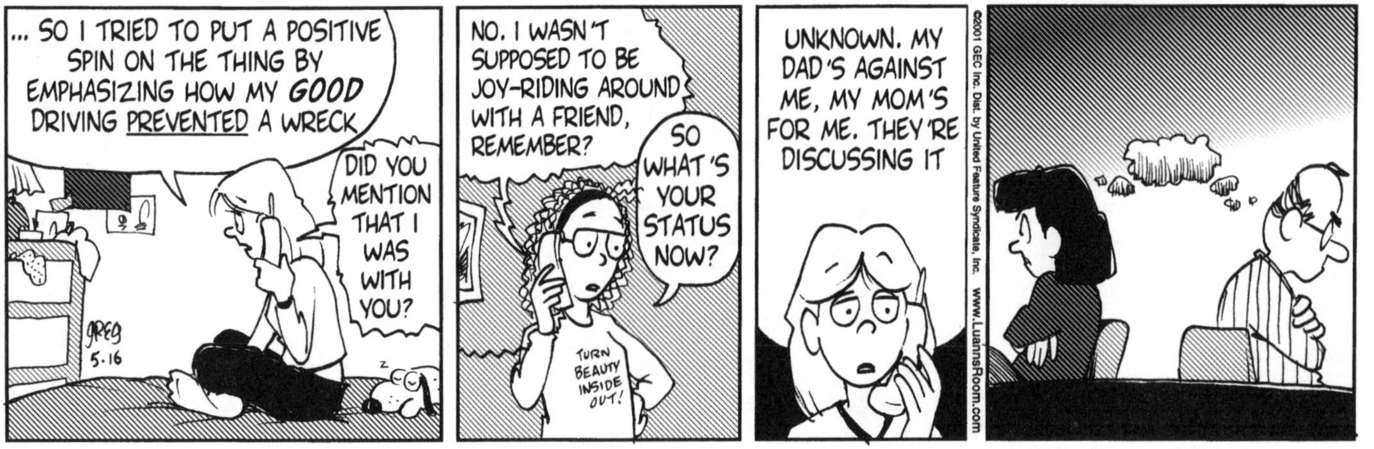
... SO I TRIED TO PUT A POSITIVE SPIN ON THE THING BY EMPHASIZING HOW MY ***GOOD*** DRIVING PREVENTED A WRECK
DID YOU MENTION THAT I WAS WITH YOU?
GREG 5·16
NO. I WASN'T SUPPOSED TO BE JOY-RIDING AROUND WITH A FRIEND, REMEMBER?
SO WHAT'S YOUR STATUS NOW?
TURN BEAUTY INSIDE OUT!
UNKNOWN. MY DAD'S AGAINST ME, MY MOM'S FOR ME. THEY'RE DISCUSSING IT
©2001 GEC Inc. Dist. by United Feature Syndicate, Inc. www.LuannsRoom.com

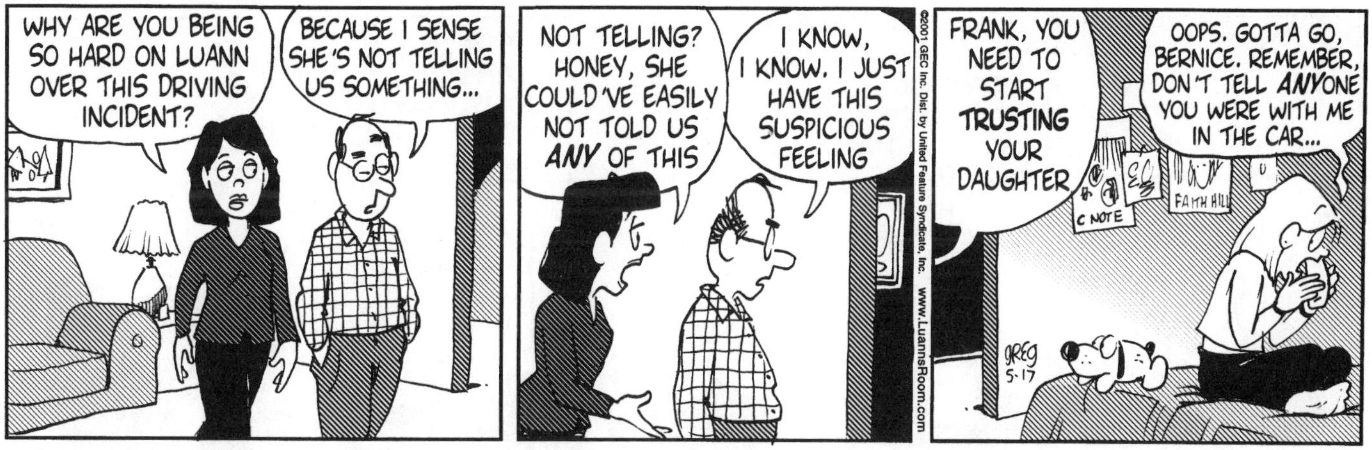
WHY ARE YOU BEING SO HARD ON LUANN OVER THIS DRIVING INCIDENT?
BECAUSE I SENSE SHE'S NOT TELLING US SOMETHING...
NOT TELLING? HONEY, SHE COULD'VE EASILY NOT TOLD US ANY OF THIS
I KNOW, I KNOW. I JUST HAVE THIS SUSPICIOUS FEELING
©2001 GEC Inc. Dist. by United Feature Syndicate, Inc. www.LuannsRoom.com
FRANK, YOU NEED TO START TRUSTING YOUR DAUGHTER
OOPS. GOTTA GO, BERNICE. REMEMBER, DON'T TELL ANYONE YOU WERE WITH ME IN THE CAR...
C NOTE
FAITH HILL
GREG 5·17

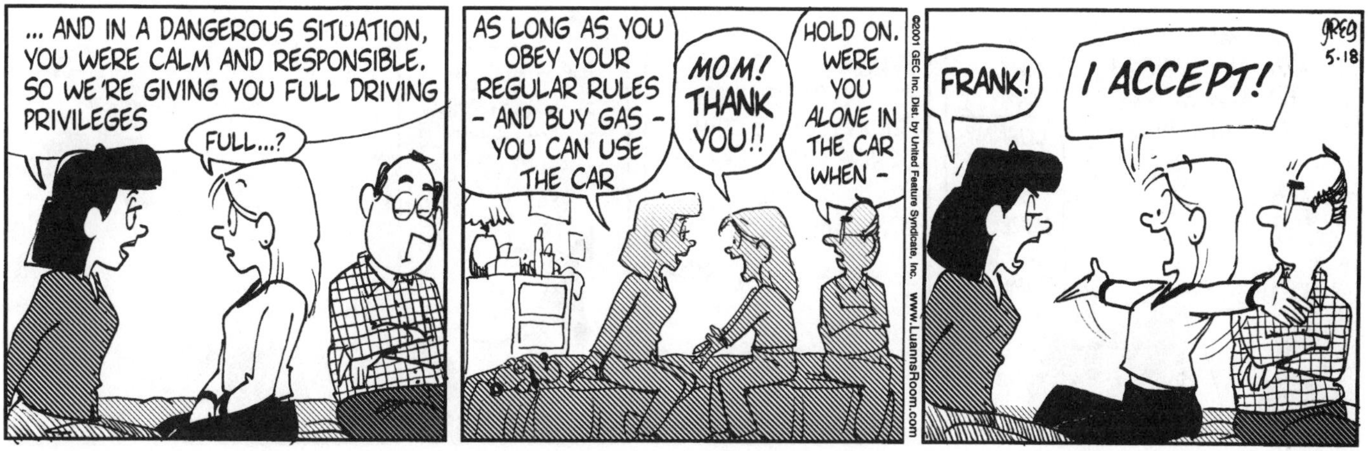
... AND IN A DANGEROUS SITUATION, YOU WERE CALM AND RESPONSIBLE. SO WE'RE GIVING YOU FULL DRIVING PRIVILEGES
FULL...?
AS LONG AS YOU OBEY YOUR REGULAR RULES - AND BUY GAS - YOU CAN USE THE CAR
MOM! THANK YOU!!
HOLD ON. WERE YOU ALONE IN THE CAR WHEN -
©2001 GEC Inc. Dist. by United Feature Syndicate, Inc. www.LuannsRoom.com
GREG 5·18
FRANK!
I ACCEPT!

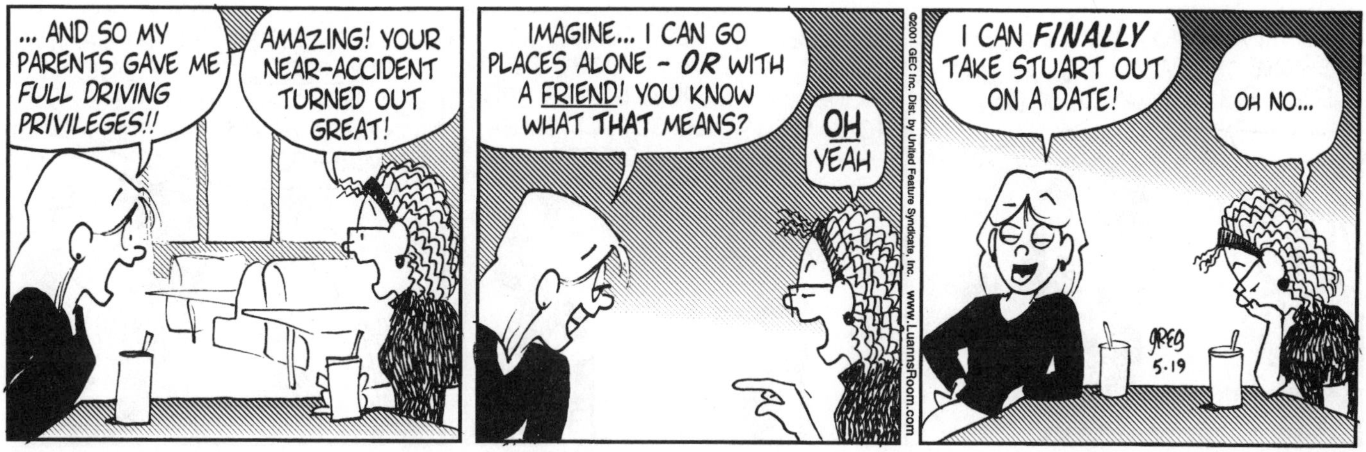
... AND SO MY PARENTS GAVE ME FULL DRIVING PRIVILEGES!!
AMAZING! YOUR NEAR-ACCIDENT TURNED OUT GREAT!
IMAGINE... I CAN GO PLACES ALONE - OR WITH A FRIEND! YOU KNOW WHAT THAT MEANS?
OH YEAH
©2001 GEC Inc. Dist. by United Feature Syndicate, Inc. www.LuannsRoom.com
I CAN FINALLY TAKE STUART OUT ON A DATE!
OH NO...
GREG 5·19

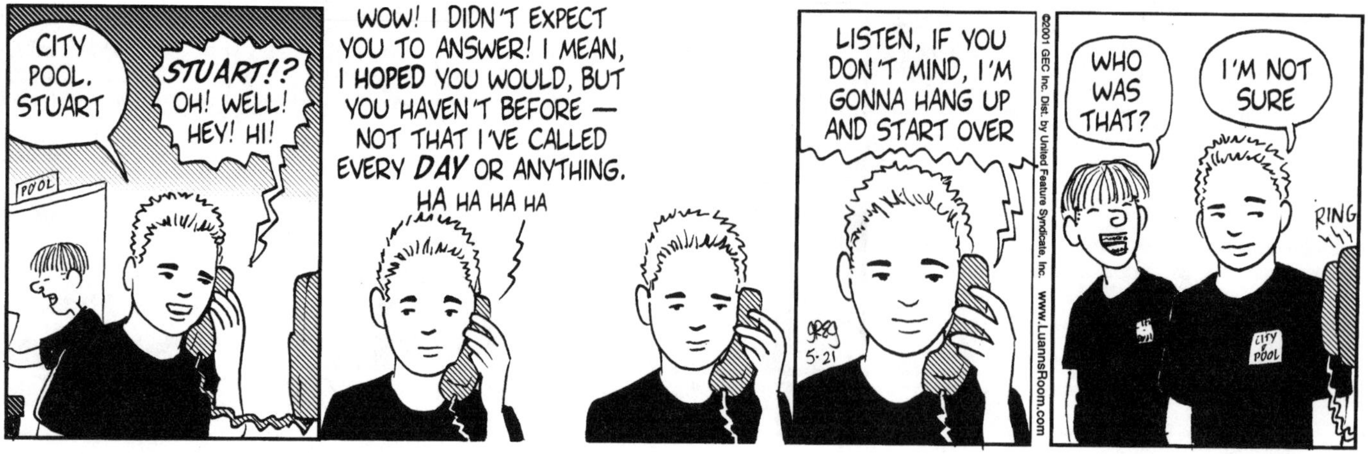
CITY POOL. STUART
STUART!? OH! WELL! HEY! HI!
POOL
WOW! I DIDN'T EXPECT YOU TO ANSWER! I MEAN, I HOPED YOU WOULD, BUT YOU HAVEN'T BEFORE — NOT THAT I'VE CALLED EVERY DAY OR ANYTHING.
HA HA HA HA
LISTEN, IF YOU DON'T MIND, I'M GONNA HANG UP AND START OVER
GREG 5-21
©2001 GEC Inc. Dist. by United Feature Syndicate, Inc. www.LuannsRoom.com
WHO WAS THAT?
I'M NOT SURE
RING
CITY POOL

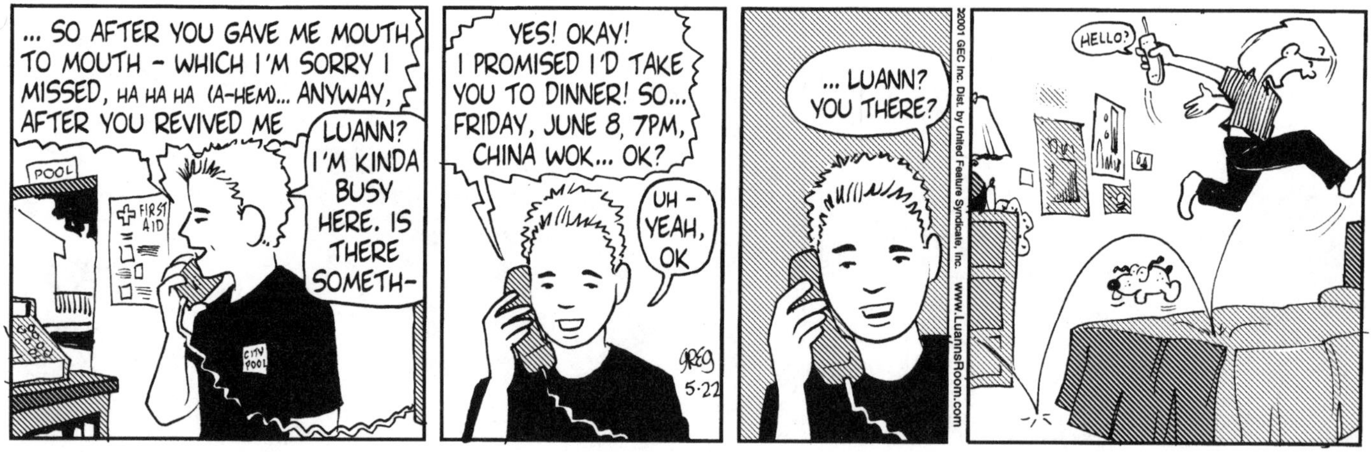
... SO AFTER YOU GAVE ME MOUTH TO MOUTH - WHICH I'M SORRY I MISSED, HA HA HA (A-HEM)... ANYWAY, AFTER YOU REVIVED ME
LUANN? I'M KINDA BUSY HERE. IS THERE SOMETH-
POOL
FIRST AID
CITY POOL
YES! OKAY! I PROMISED I'D TAKE YOU TO DINNER! SO... FRIDAY, JUNE 8, 7PM, CHINA WOK... OK?
UH - YEAH, OK
GREG 5-22
... LUANN? YOU THERE?
©2001 GEC Inc. Dist. by United Feature Syndicate, Inc. www.LuannsRoom.com
HELLO?

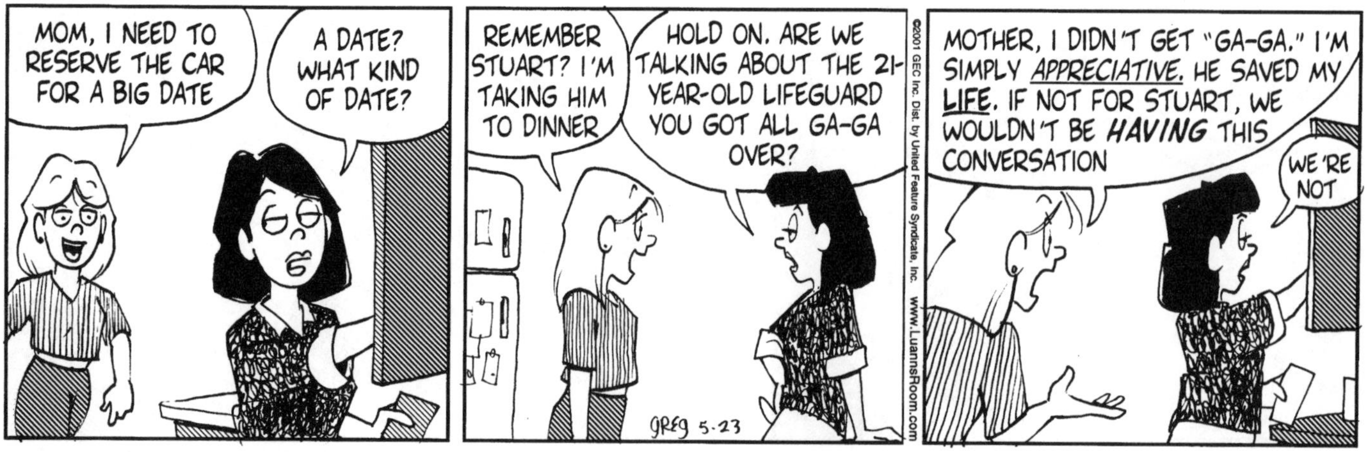
MOM, I NEED TO RESERVE THE CAR FOR A BIG DATE
A DATE? WHAT KIND OF DATE?
REMEMBER STUART? I'M TAKING HIM TO DINNER
HOLD ON. ARE WE TALKING ABOUT THE 21-YEAR-OLD LIFEGUARD YOU GOT ALL GA-GA OVER?
GREG 5-23
©2001 GEC Inc. Dist. by United Feature Syndicate, Inc. www.LuannsRoom.com
MOTHER, I DIDN'T GET "GA-GA." I'M SIMPLY APPRECIATIVE. HE SAVED MY LIFE. IF NOT FOR STUART, WE WOULDN'T BE HAVING THIS CONVERSATION
WE'RE NOT

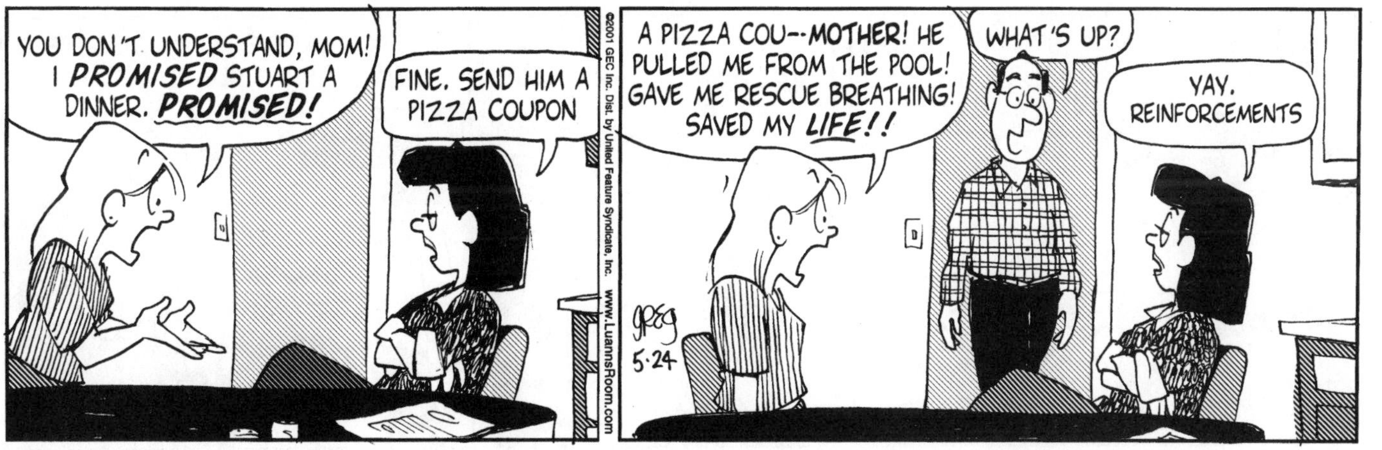
YOU DON'T UNDERSTAND, MOM! I **PROMISED** STUART A DINNER. ***PROMISED!***
FINE. SEND HIM A PIZZA COUPON
©2001 GEC Inc. Dist. by United Feature Syndicate, Inc. www.LuannsRoom.com
A PIZZA COU--**MOTHER**! HE PULLED ME FROM THE POOL! GAVE ME RESCUE BREATHING! SAVED MY ***LIFE!!***
WHAT'S UP?
YAY. REINFORCEMENTS
GREG 5·24

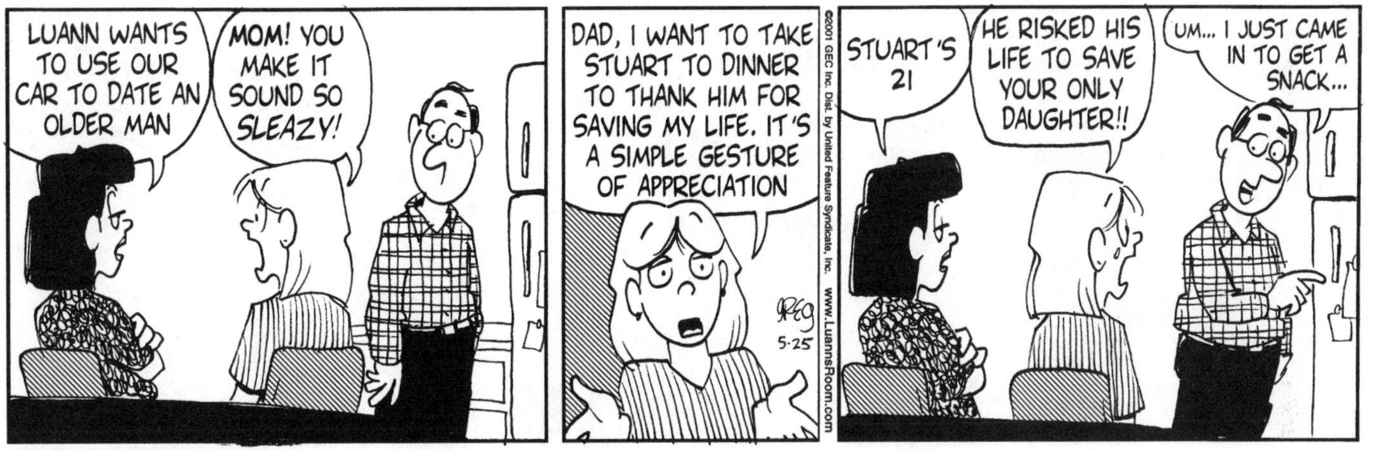
LUANN WANTS TO USE OUR CAR TO DATE AN OLDER MAN
MOM! YOU MAKE IT SOUND SO *SLEAZY!*
DAD, I WANT TO TAKE STUART TO DINNER TO THANK HIM FOR SAVING MY LIFE. IT'S A SIMPLE GESTURE OF APPRECIATION
GREG 5·25
©2001 GEC Inc. Dist. by United Feature Syndicate, Inc. www.LuannsRoom.com
STUART'S 21
HE RISKED HIS LIFE TO SAVE YOUR ONLY DAUGHTER!!
UM... I JUST CAME IN TO GET A SNACK...

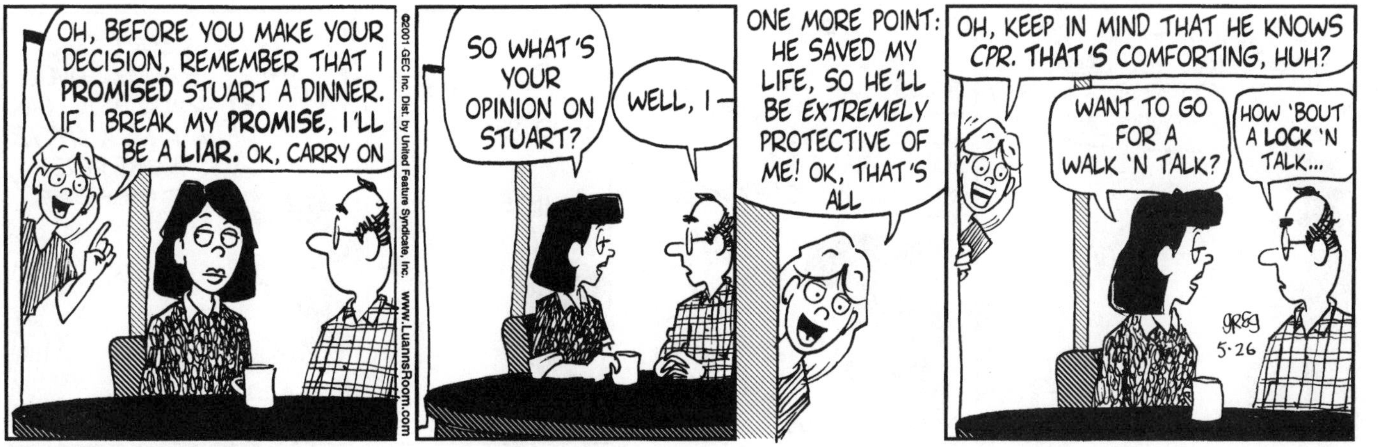
OH, BEFORE YOU MAKE YOUR DECISION, REMEMBER THAT I **PROMISED** STUART A DINNER. IF I BREAK MY **PROMISE**, I'LL BE A **LIAR.** OK, CARRY ON
©2001 GEC Inc. Dist. by United Feature Syndicate, Inc. www.LuannsRoom.com
SO WHAT'S YOUR OPINION ON STUART?
WELL, I—
ONE MORE POINT: HE SAVED MY LIFE, SO HE'LL BE *EXTREMELY* PROTECTIVE OF ME! OK, THAT'S ALL
OH, KEEP IN MIND THAT HE KNOWS *CPR.* **THAT'S** COMFORTING, HUH?
WANT TO GO FOR A WALK 'N TALK?
HOW 'BOUT A **LOCK** 'N TALK...
GREG 5·26

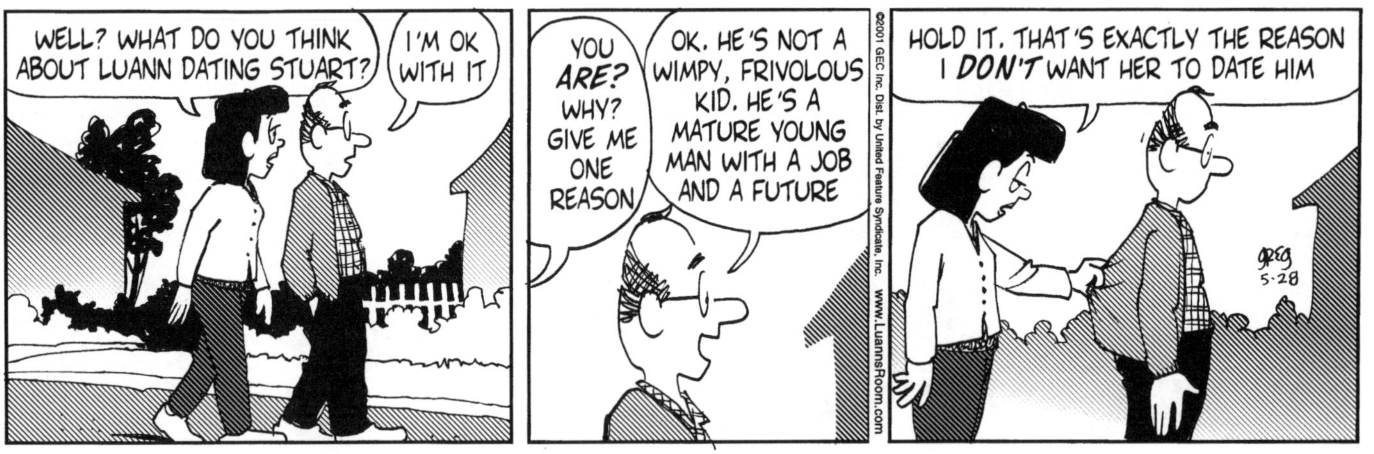
WELL? WHAT DO YOU THINK ABOUT LUANN DATING STUART?
I'M OK WITH IT
YOU *ARE?* WHY? GIVE ME ONE REASON
OK. HE'S NOT A WIMPY, FRIVOLOUS KID. HE'S A MATURE YOUNG MAN WITH A JOB AND A FUTURE
©2001 GEC Inc. Dist. by United Feature Syndicate, Inc. www.LuannsRoom.com
HOLD IT. THAT'S EXACTLY THE REASON I *DON'T* WANT HER TO DATE HIM
GREG 5-28

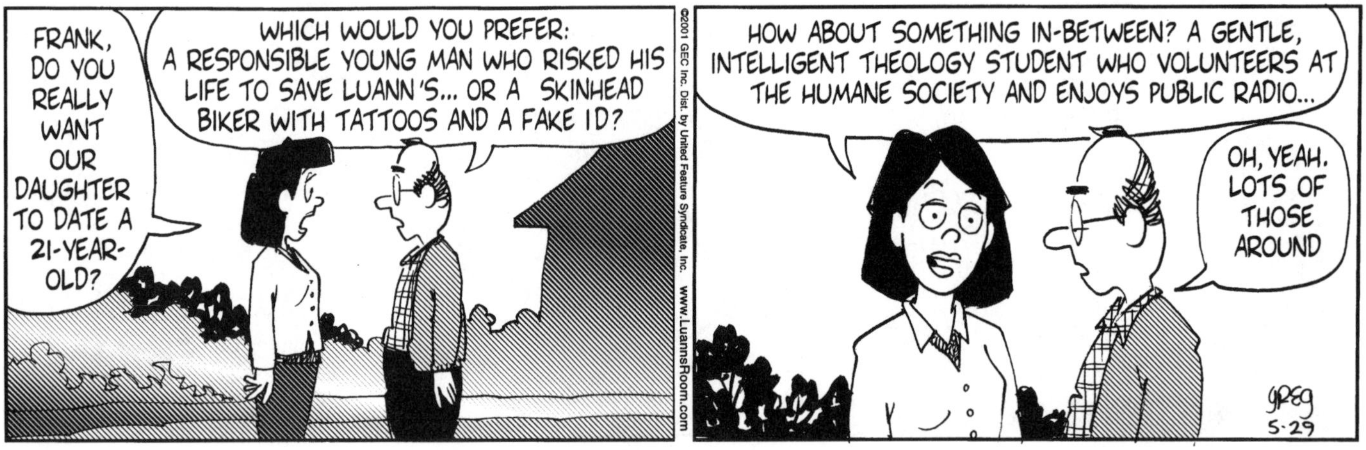
FRANK, DO YOU REALLY WANT OUR DAUGHTER TO DATE A 21-YEAR-OLD?
WHICH WOULD YOU PREFER: A RESPONSIBLE YOUNG MAN WHO RISKED HIS LIFE TO SAVE LUANN'S... OR A SKINHEAD BIKER WITH TATTOOS AND A FAKE ID?
©2001 GEC Inc. Dist. by United Feature Syndicate, Inc. www.LuannsRoom.com
HOW ABOUT SOMETHING IN-BETWEEN? A GENTLE, INTELLIGENT THEOLOGY STUDENT WHO VOLUNTEERS AT THE HUMANE SOCIETY AND ENJOYS PUBLIC RADIO...
OH, YEAH. LOTS OF THOSE AROUND
GREG 5-29

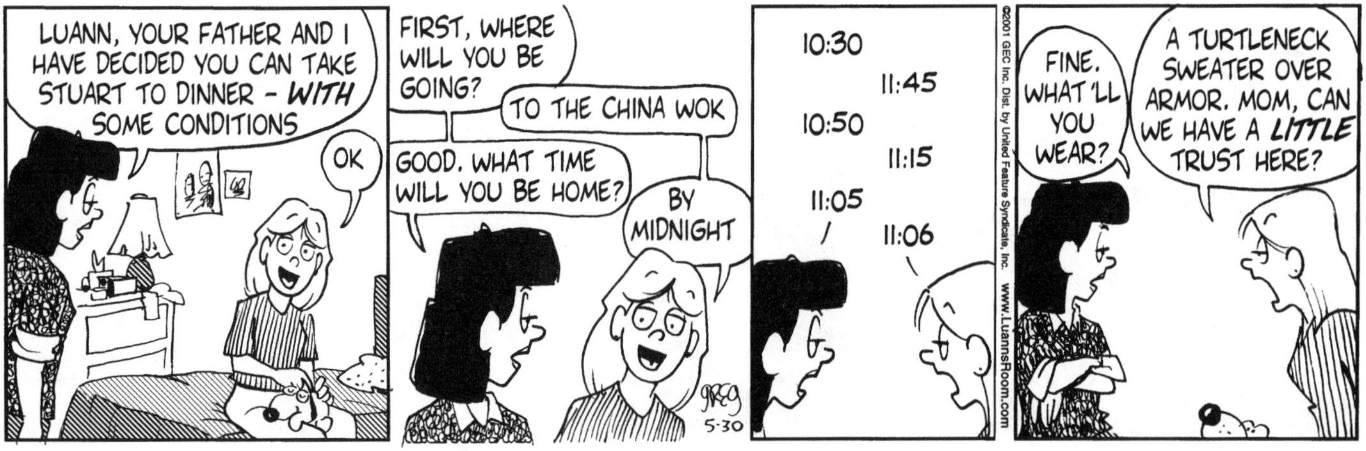
LUANN, YOUR FATHER AND I HAVE DECIDED YOU CAN TAKE STUART TO DINNER - *WITH* SOME CONDITIONS
OK
FIRST, WHERE WILL YOU BE GOING?
TO THE CHINA WOK
GOOD. WHAT TIME WILL YOU BE HOME?
BY MIDNIGHT
GREG 5-30
10:30
11:45
10:50
11:15
11:05
11:06
©2001 GEC Inc. Dist. by United Feature Syndicate, Inc. www.LuannsRoom.com
FINE. WHAT'LL YOU WEAR?
A TURTLENECK SWEATER OVER ARMOR. MOM, CAN WE HAVE A *LITTLE* TRUST HERE?

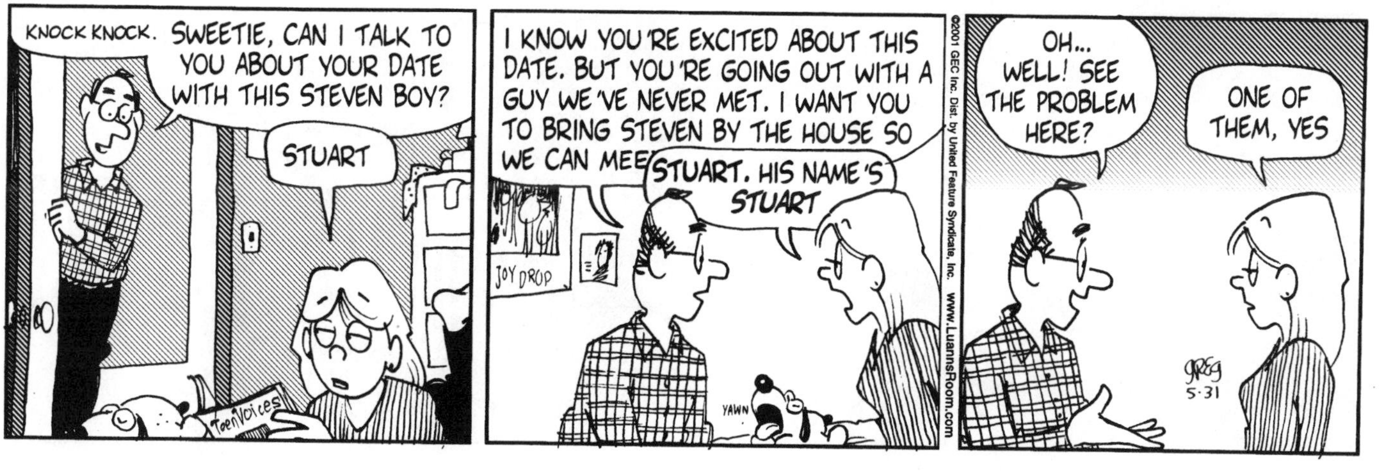
KNOCK KNOCK.
SWEETIE, CAN I TALK TO YOU ABOUT YOUR DATE WITH THIS STEVEN BOY?
STUART
TeenVoices
I KNOW YOU'RE EXCITED ABOUT THIS DATE. BUT YOU'RE GOING OUT WITH A GUY WE'VE NEVER MET. I WANT YOU TO BRING STEVEN BY THE HOUSE SO WE CAN MEE
STUART. HIS NAME'S *STUART*
JOY DROP
YAWN
©2001 GEC Inc. Dist. by United Feature Syndicate, Inc. www.LuannsRoom.com
OH... WELL! SEE THE PROBLEM HERE?
ONE OF THEM, YES
GREG 5·31

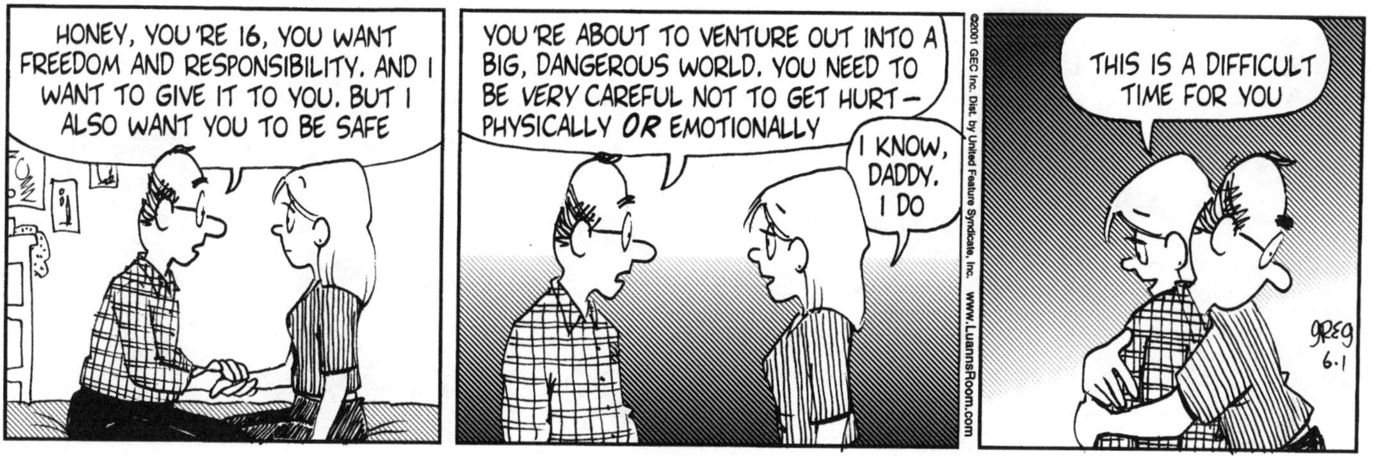
HONEY, YOU'RE 16, YOU WANT FREEDOM AND RESPONSIBILITY. AND I WANT TO GIVE IT TO YOU. BUT I ALSO WANT YOU TO BE SAFE
YOU'RE ABOUT TO VENTURE OUT INTO A BIG, DANGEROUS WORLD. YOU NEED TO BE *VERY* CAREFUL NOT TO GET HURT— PHYSICALLY ***OR*** EMOTIONALLY
I KNOW, DADDY. I DO
©2001 GEC Inc. Dist. by United Feature Syndicate, Inc. www.LuannsRoom.com
THIS IS A DIFFICULT TIME FOR YOU
GREG 6·1

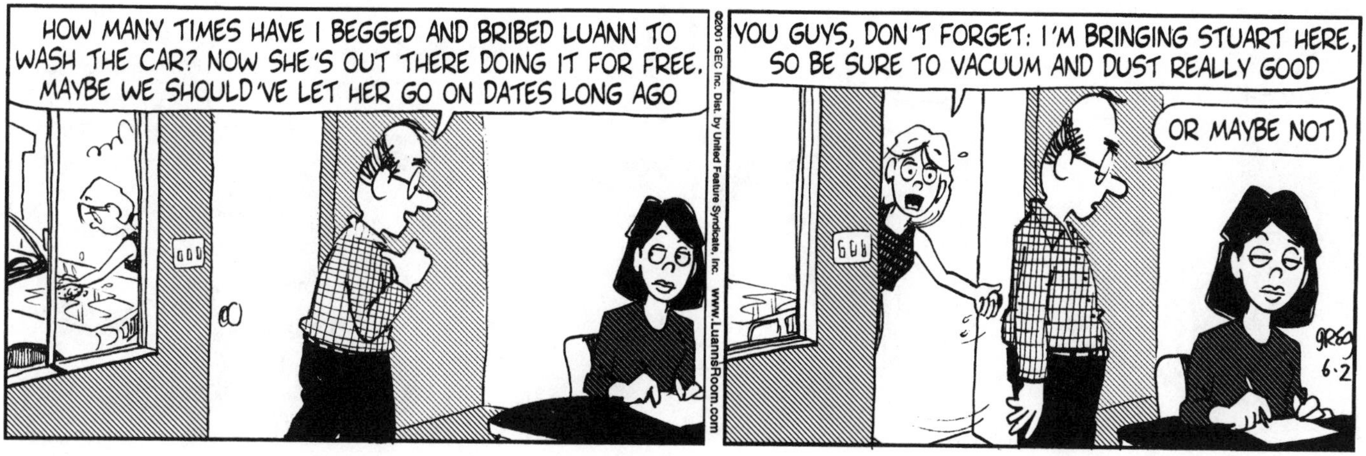
HOW MANY TIMES HAVE I BEGGED AND BRIBED LUANN TO WASH THE CAR? NOW SHE'S OUT THERE DOING IT FOR FREE. MAYBE WE SHOULD'VE LET HER GO ON DATES LONG AGO
©2001 GEC Inc. Dist. by United Feature Syndicate, Inc. www.LuannsRoom.com
YOU GUYS, DON'T FORGET: I'M BRINGING STUART HERE, SO BE SURE TO VACUUM AND DUST REALLY GOOD
OR MAYBE NOT
GREG 6·2

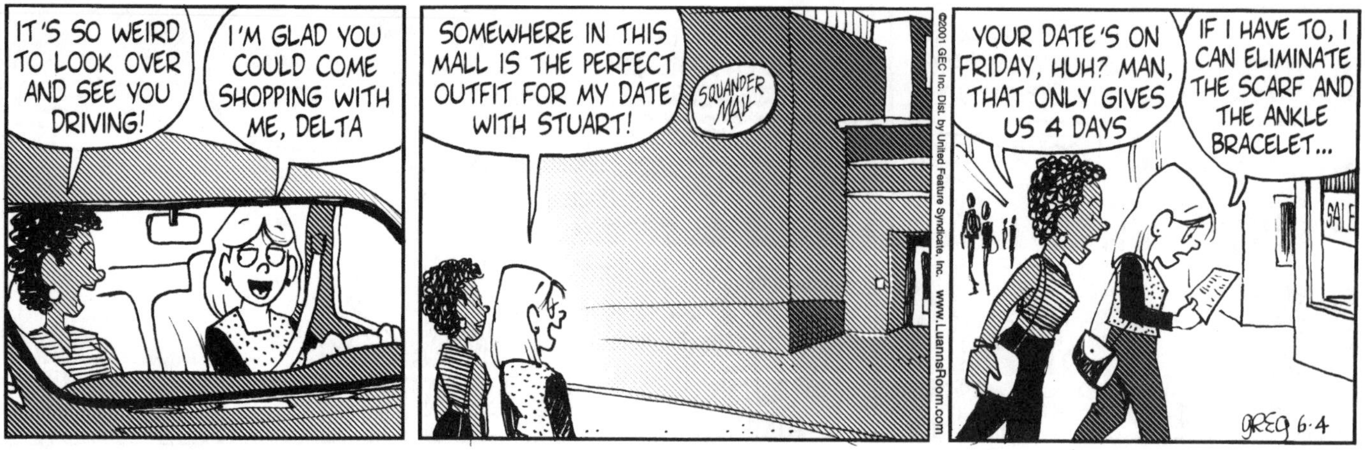
IT'S SO WEIRD TO LOOK OVER AND SEE YOU DRIVING!
I'M GLAD YOU COULD COME SHOPPING WITH ME, DELTA
SOMEWHERE IN THIS MALL IS THE PERFECT OUTFIT FOR MY DATE WITH STUART!
SQUANDER MALL
©2001 GEC Inc. Dist. by United Feature Syndicate, Inc. www.LuannsRoom.com
YOUR DATE'S ON FRIDAY, HUH? MAN, THAT ONLY GIVES US 4 DAYS
IF I HAVE TO, I CAN ELIMINATE THE SCARF AND THE ANKLE BRACELET...
SALE
GREG 6·4

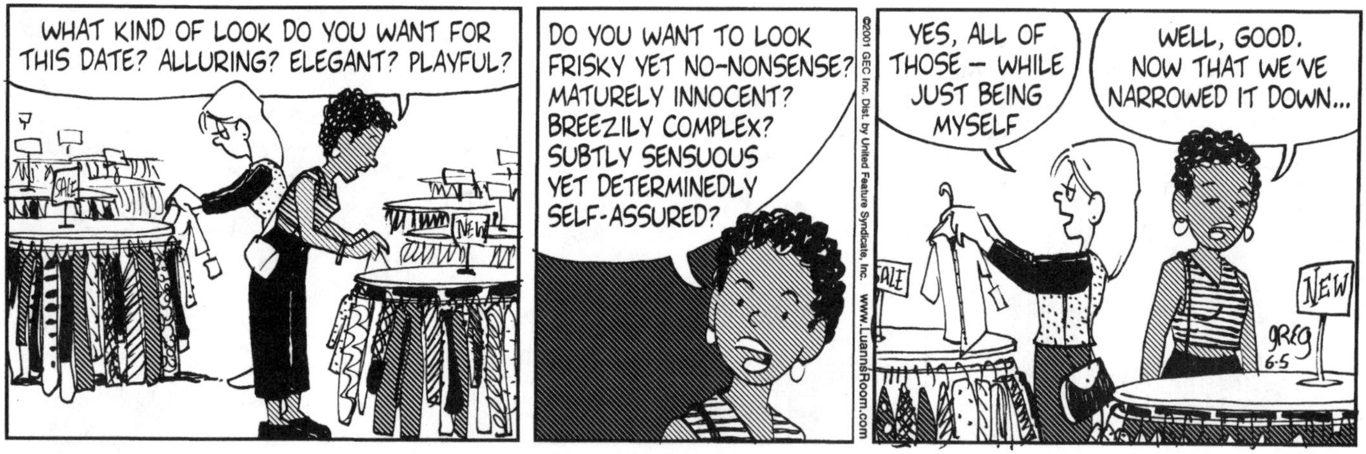
WHAT KIND OF LOOK DO YOU WANT FOR THIS DATE? ALLURING? ELEGANT? PLAYFUL?
SALE
NEW
DO YOU WANT TO LOOK FRISKY YET NO-NONSENSE? MATURELY INNOCENT? BREEZILY COMPLEX? SUBTLY SENSUOUS YET DETERMINEDLY SELF-ASSURED?
©2001 GEC Inc. Dist. by United Feature Syndicate, Inc. www.LuannsRoom.com
YES, ALL OF THOSE — WHILE JUST BEING MYSELF
WELL, GOOD. NOW THAT WE'VE NARROWED IT DOWN...
SALE
NEW
GREG 6·5

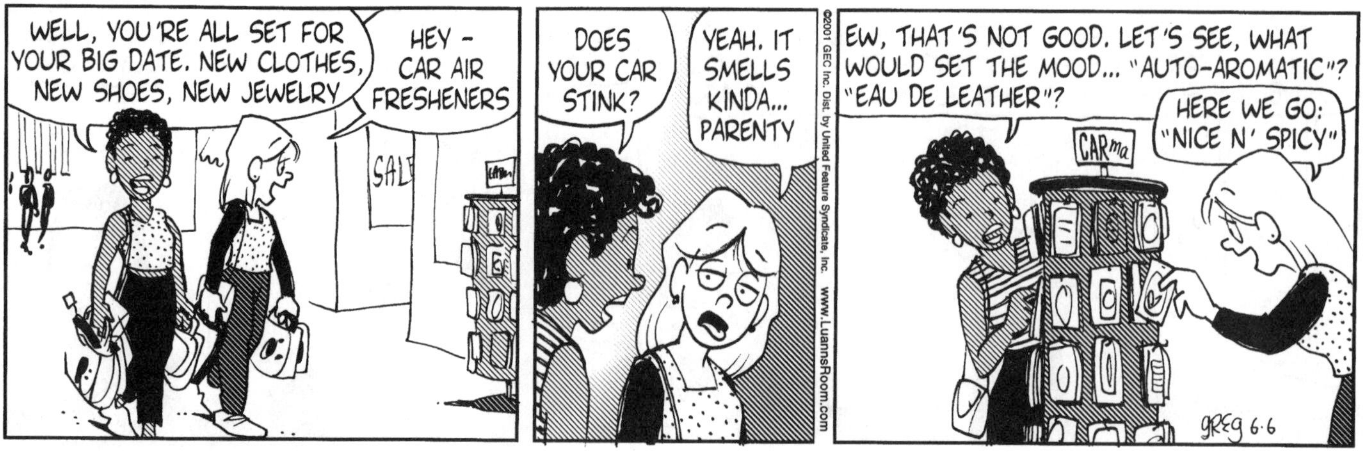
WELL, YOU'RE ALL SET FOR YOUR BIG DATE. NEW CLOTHES, NEW SHOES, NEW JEWELRY
HEY – CAR AIR FRESHENERS
SALE
DOES YOUR CAR STINK?
YEAH. IT SMELLS KINDA... PARENTY
©2001 GEC Inc. Dist. by United Feature Syndicate, Inc. www.LuannsRoom.com
EW, THAT'S NOT GOOD. LET'S SEE, WHAT WOULD SET THE MOOD... "AUTO-AROMATIC"? "EAU DE LEATHER"?
CARma
HERE WE GO: "NICE N' SPICY"
GREG 6·6

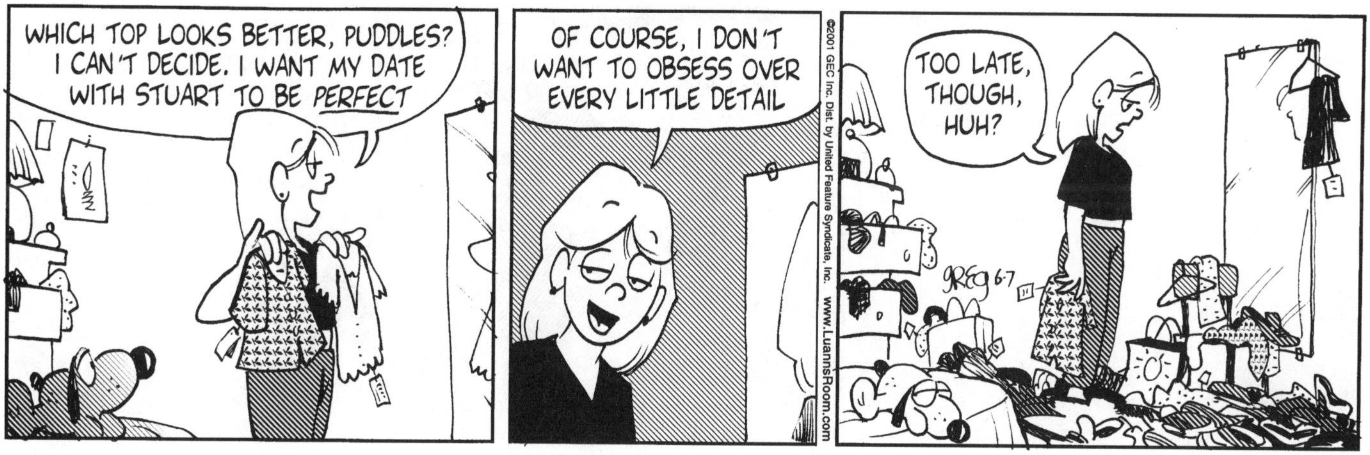
WHICH TOP LOOKS BETTER, PUDDLES? I CAN'T DECIDE. I WANT MY DATE WITH STUART TO BE PERFECT
OF COURSE, I DON'T WANT TO OBSESS OVER EVERY LITTLE DETAIL
©2001 GEC Inc. Dist. by United Feature Syndicate, Inc. www.LuannsRoom.com
TOO LATE, THOUGH, HUH?
GREG 6-7

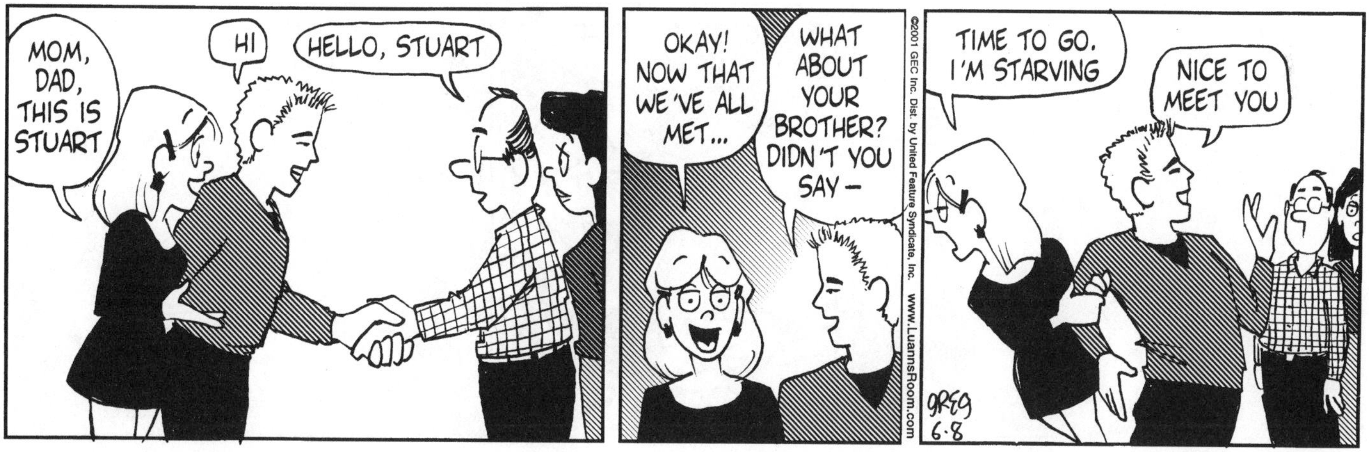
MOM, DAD, THIS IS STUART
HI
HELLO, STUART
OKAY! NOW THAT WE'VE ALL MET...
WHAT ABOUT YOUR BROTHER? DIDN'T YOU SAY—
©2001 GEC Inc. Dist. by United Feature Syndicate, Inc. www.LuannsRoom.com
TIME TO GO. I'M STARVING
NICE TO MEET YOU
GREG 6·8

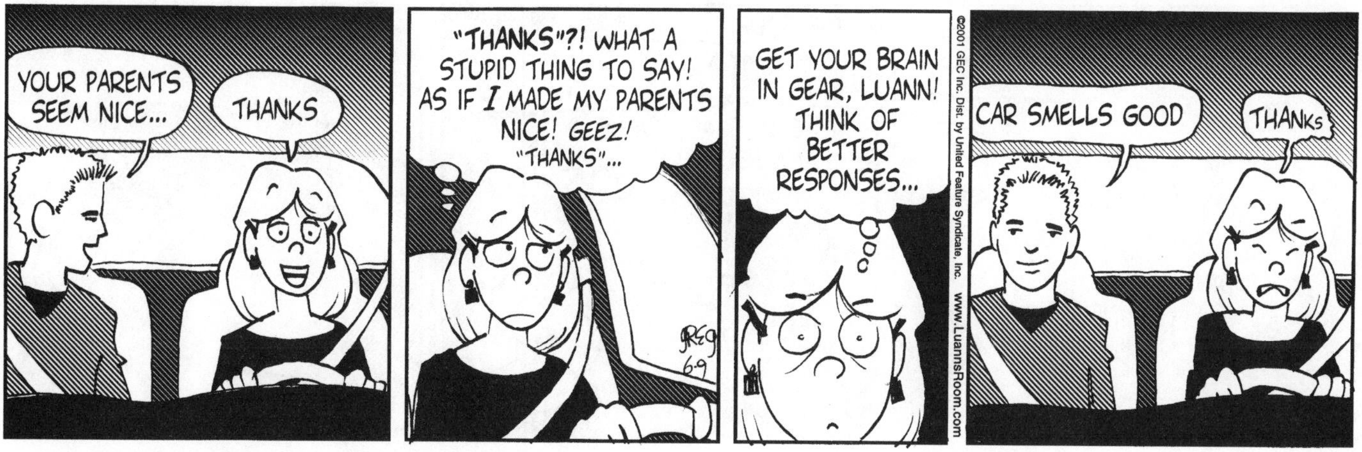
YOUR PARENTS SEEM NICE...
THANKS
"THANKS"?! WHAT A STUPID THING TO SAY! AS IF I MADE MY PARENTS NICE! GEEZ! "THANKS"...
GREG 6-9
GET YOUR BRAIN IN GEAR, LUANN! THINK OF BETTER RESPONSES...
©2001 GEC Inc. Dist. by United Feature Syndicate, Inc. www.LuannsRoom.com
CAR SMELLS GOOD
THANKs

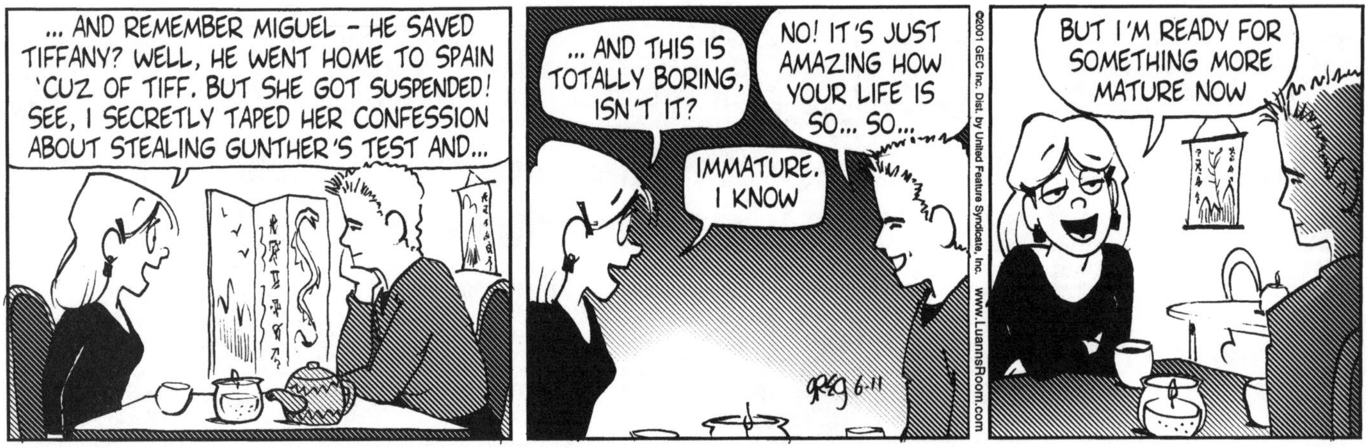
... AND REMEMBER MIGUEL – HE SAVED TIFFANY? WELL, HE WENT HOME TO SPAIN 'CUZ OF TIFF. BUT SHE GOT SUSPENDED! SEE, I SECRETLY TAPED HER CONFESSION ABOUT STEALING GUNTHER'S TEST AND...
... AND THIS IS TOTALLY BORING, ISN'T IT?
NO! IT'S JUST AMAZING HOW YOUR LIFE IS SO... SO...
IMMATURE. I KNOW
GREG 6-11
©2001 GEC Inc. Dist. by United Feature Syndicate, Inc. www.LuannsRoom.com
BUT I'M READY FOR SOMETHING MORE MATURE NOW

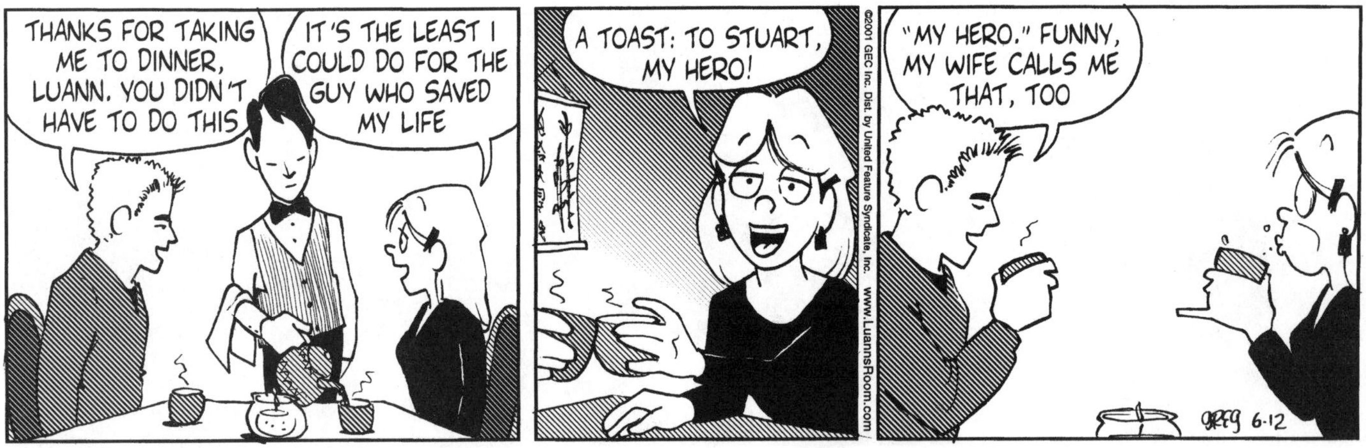
THANKS FOR TAKING ME TO DINNER, LUANN. YOU DIDN'T HAVE TO DO THIS
IT'S THE LEAST I COULD DO FOR THE GUY WHO SAVED MY LIFE
©2001 GEC Inc. Dist. by United Feature Syndicate, Inc. www.LuannsRoom.com
A TOAST: TO STUART, MY HERO!
"MY HERO." FUNNY, MY WIFE CALLS ME THAT, TOO
GREG 6-12

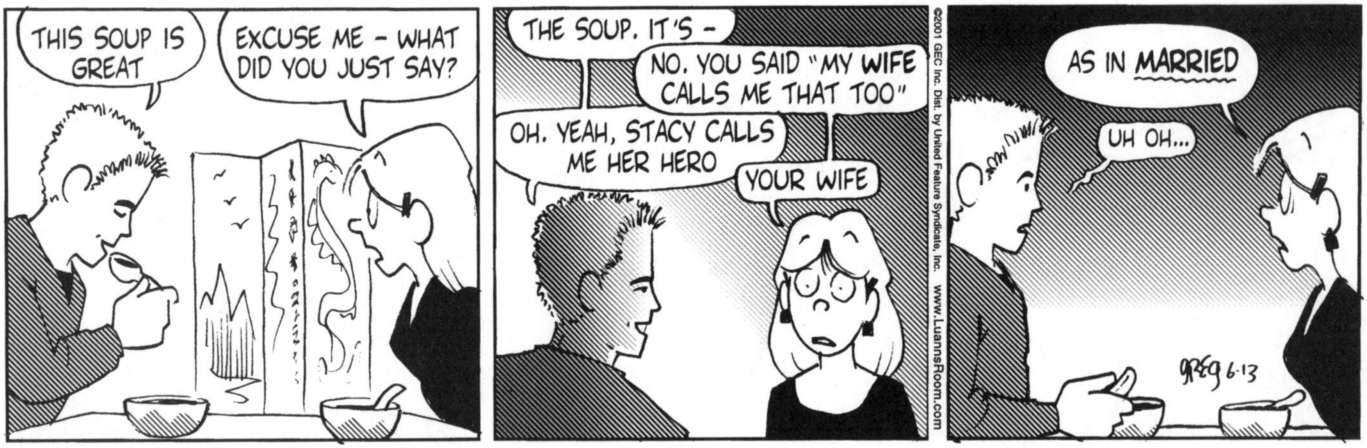
THIS SOUP IS GREAT
EXCUSE ME – WHAT DID YOU JUST SAY?
THE SOUP. IT'S –
NO. YOU SAID "MY **WIFE** CALLS ME THAT TOO"
OH. YEAH, STACY CALLS ME HER HERO
YOUR WIFE
©2001 GEC Inc. Dist. by United Feature Syndicate, Inc. www.LuannsRoom.com
AS IN MARRIED
UH OH...
GREG 6-13

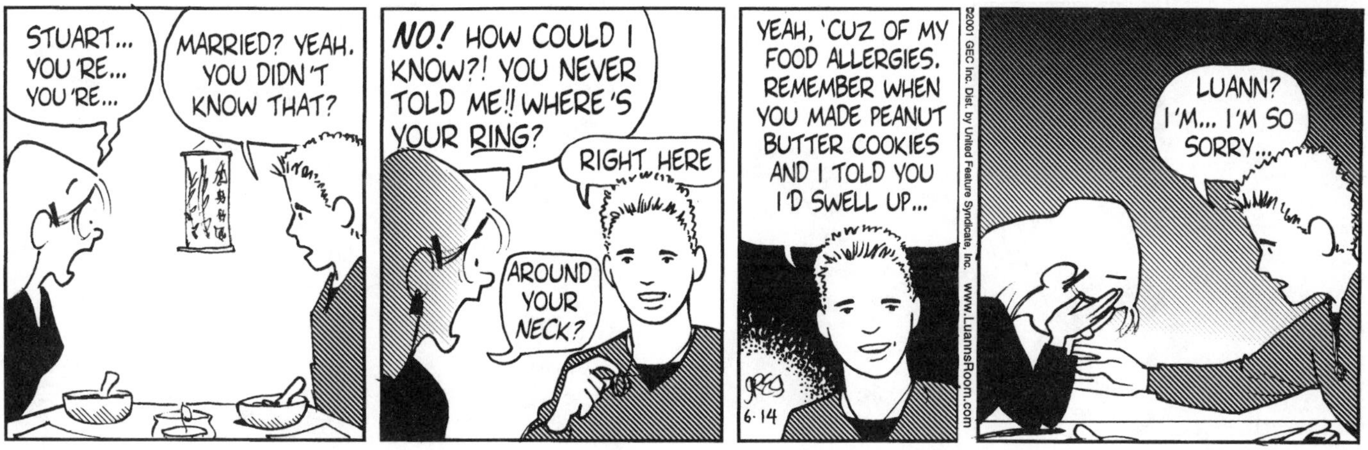
STUART... YOU'RE... YOU'RE...
MARRIED? YEAH. YOU DIDN'T KNOW THAT?
NO! HOW COULD I KNOW?! YOU NEVER TOLD ME!! WHERE'S YOUR RING?
RIGHT HERE
AROUND YOUR NECK?
YEAH, 'CUZ OF MY FOOD ALLERGIES. REMEMBER WHEN YOU MADE PEANUT BUTTER COOKIES AND I TOLD YOU I'D SWELL UP...
GREG 6·14
©2001 GEC Inc. Dist. by United Feature Syndicate, Inc. www.LuannsRoom.com
LUANN? I'M... I'M SO SORRY...

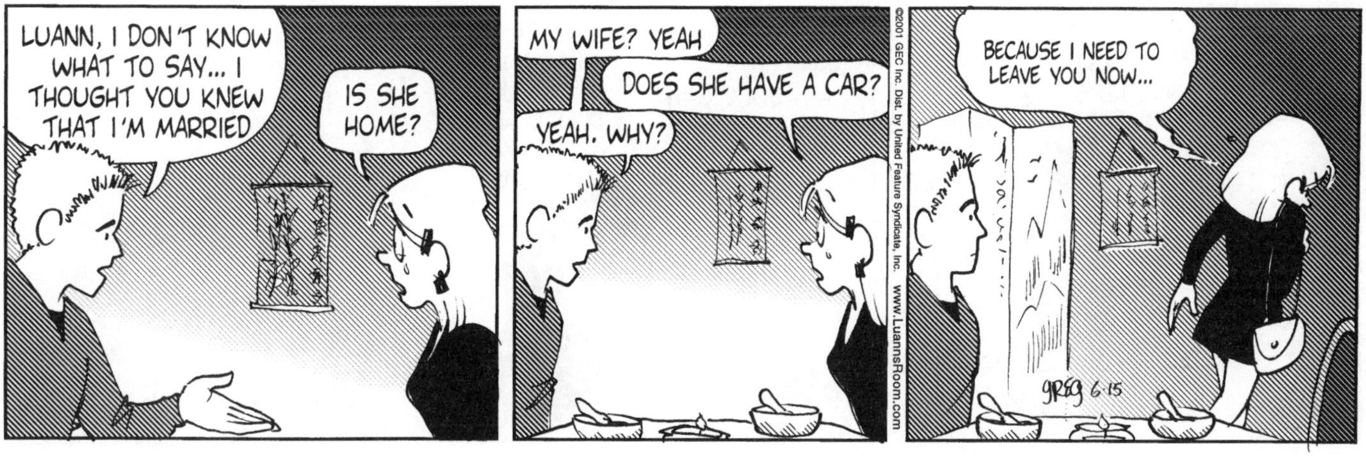
LUANN, I DON'T KNOW WHAT TO SAY... I THOUGHT YOU KNEW THAT I'M MARRIED
IS SHE HOME?
MY WIFE? YEAH
DOES SHE HAVE A CAR?
YEAH. WHY?
©2001 GEC Inc. Dist. by United Feature Syndicate, Inc. www.LuannsRoom.com
BECAUSE I NEED TO LEAVE YOU NOW...
GREG 6·15

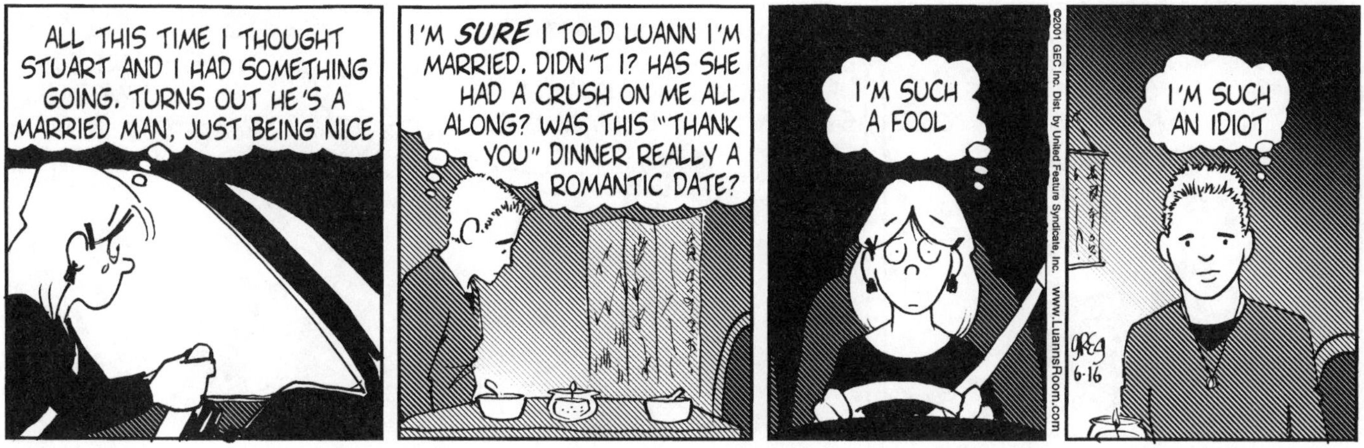
ALL THIS TIME I THOUGHT STUART AND I HAD SOMETHING GOING. TURNS OUT HE'S A MARRIED MAN, JUST BEING NICE
I'M SURE I TOLD LUANN I'M MARRIED. DIDN'T I? HAS SHE HAD A CRUSH ON ME ALL ALONG? WAS THIS "THANK YOU" DINNER REALLY A ROMANTIC DATE?
I'M SUCH A FOOL
©2001 GEC Inc. Dist. by United Feature Syndicate, Inc. www.LuannsRoom.com
GREG 6·16
I'M SUCH AN IDIOT

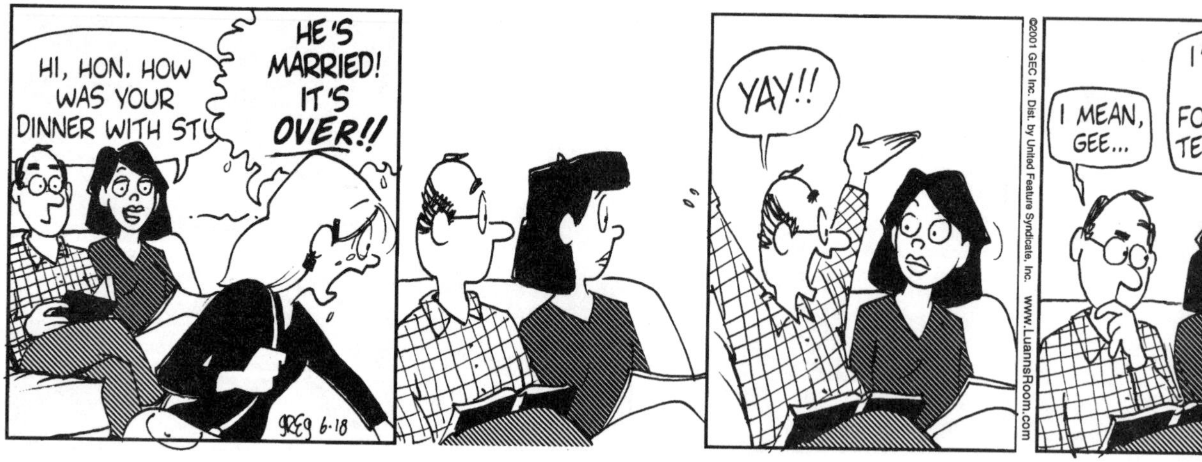
HI, HON. HOW WAS YOUR DINNER WITH ST
HE'S MARRIED! IT'S OVER!!
YAY!!
I MEAN, GEE...
I'M STARTING TO THINK FONDLY OF HER TERRIBLE TWOS
©2001 GEC Inc. Dist. by United Feature Syndicate, Inc. www.LuannsRoom.com

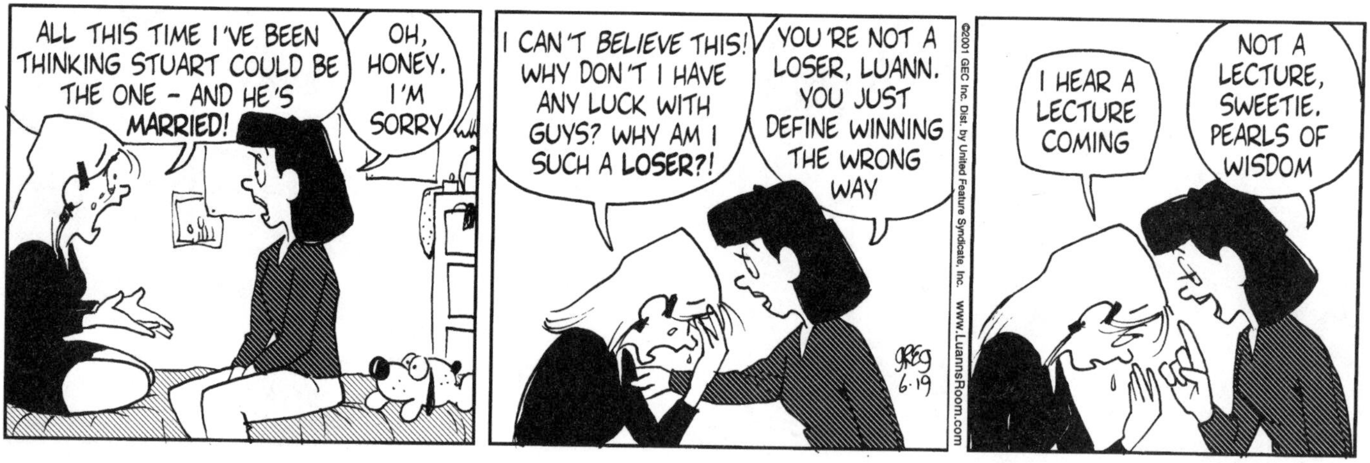
ALL THIS TIME I'VE BEEN THINKING STUART COULD BE THE ONE – AND HE'S MARRIED!
OH, HONEY. I'M SORRY
I CAN'T BELIEVE THIS! WHY DON'T I HAVE ANY LUCK WITH GUYS? WHY AM I SUCH A LOSER?!
YOU'RE NOT A LOSER, LUANN. YOU JUST DEFINE WINNING THE WRONG WAY
I HEAR A LECTURE COMING
NOT A LECTURE, SWEETIE. PEARLS OF WISDOM
©2001 GEC Inc. Dist. by United Feature Syndicate, Inc. www.LuannsRoom.com

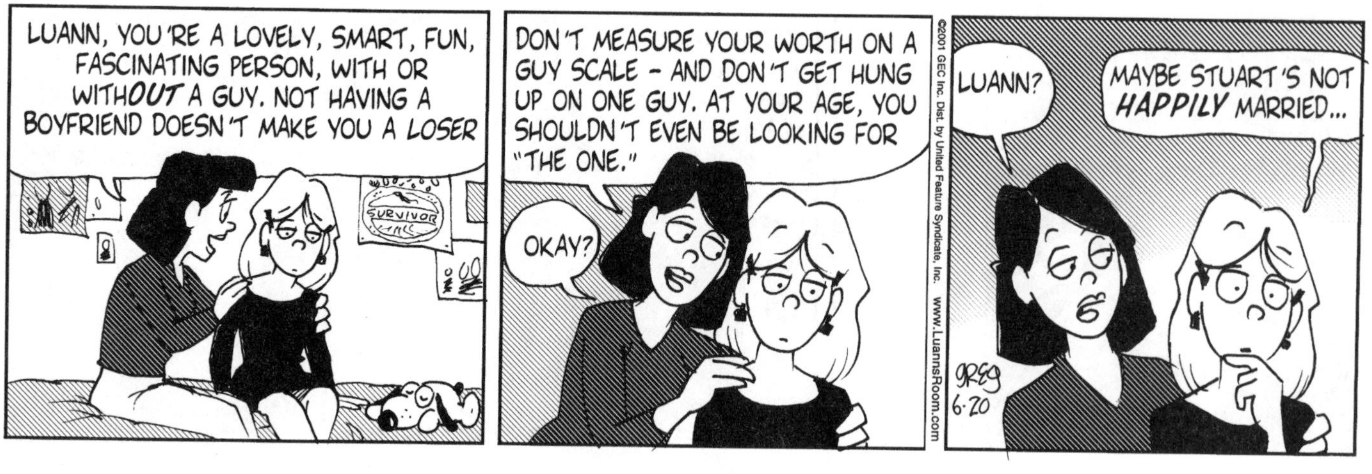
LUANN, YOU'RE A LOVELY, SMART, FUN, FASCINATING PERSON, WITH OR WITHOUT A GUY. NOT HAVING A BOYFRIEND DOESN'T MAKE YOU A LOSER
SURVIVOR
DON'T MEASURE YOUR WORTH ON A GUY SCALE – AND DON'T GET HUNG UP ON ONE GUY. AT YOUR AGE, YOU SHOULDN'T EVEN BE LOOKING FOR "THE ONE."
OKAY?
LUANN?
MAYBE STUART'S NOT HAPPILY MARRIED...
©2001 GEC Inc. Dist. by United Feature Syndicate, Inc. www.LuannsRoom.com

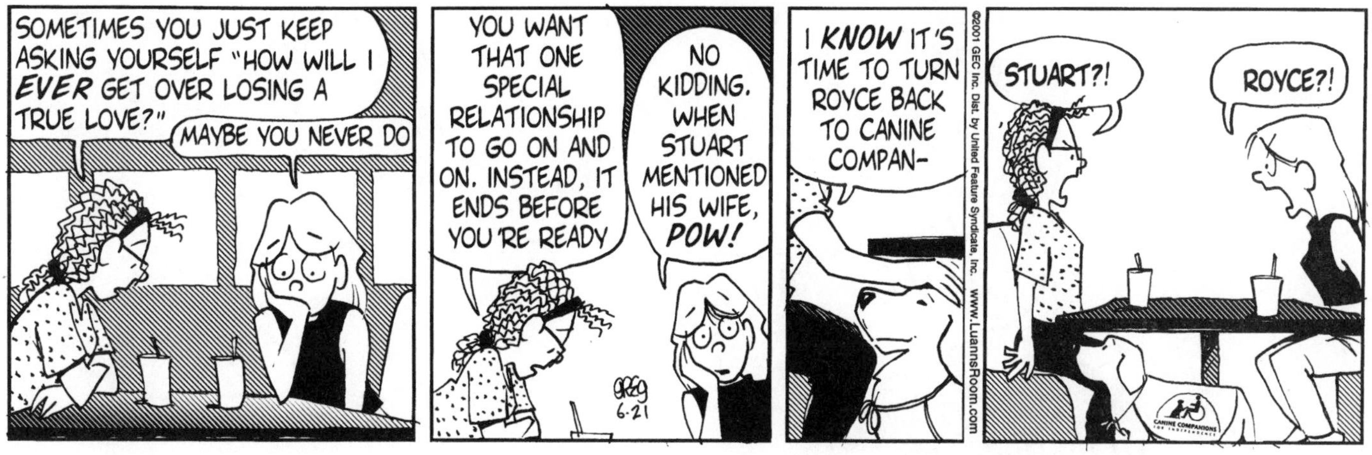
SOMETIMES YOU JUST KEEP ASKING YOURSELF "HOW WILL I *EVER* GET OVER LOSING A TRUE LOVE?"
MAYBE YOU NEVER DO
YOU WANT THAT ONE SPECIAL RELATIONSHIP TO GO ON AND ON. INSTEAD, IT ENDS BEFORE YOU'RE READY
NO KIDDING. WHEN STUART MENTIONED HIS WIFE, *POW!*
GREG 6·21
I ***KNOW*** IT'S TIME TO TURN ROYCE BACK TO CANINE COMPAN–
©2001 GEC Inc. Dist. by United Feature Syndicate, Inc. www.LuannsRoom.com
STUART?!
ROYCE?!

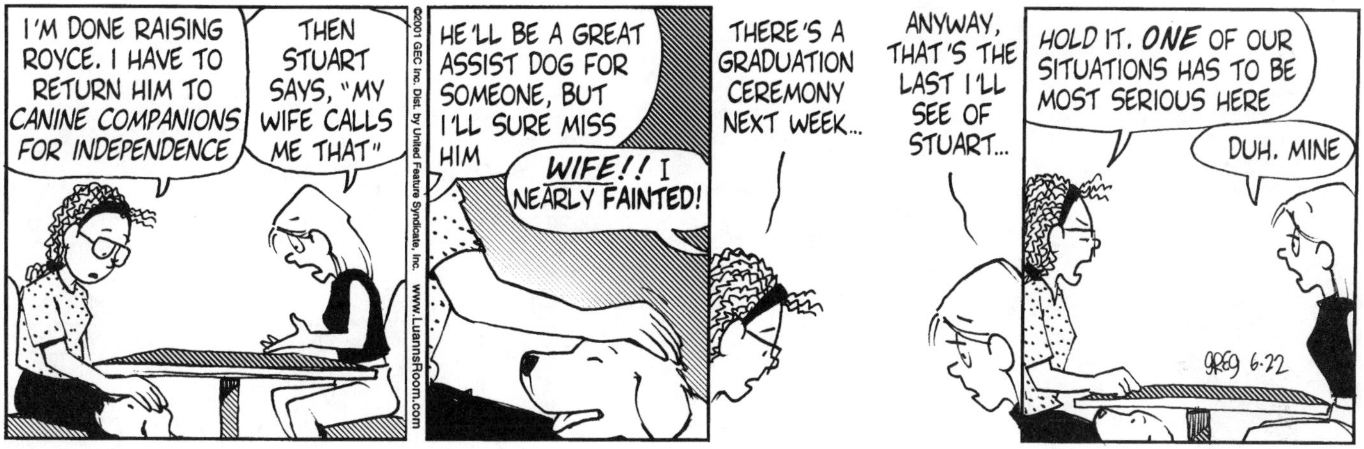
I'M DONE RAISING ROYCE. I HAVE TO RETURN HIM TO *CANINE COMPANIONS FOR INDEPENDENCE*
THEN STUART SAYS, "MY WIFE CALLS ME THAT"
©2001 GEC Inc. Dist. by United Feature Syndicate, Inc. www.LuannsRoom.com
HE'LL BE A GREAT ASSIST DOG FOR SOMEONE, BUT I'LL SURE MISS HIM
WIFE!! I NEARLY **FAINTED!**
THERE'S A GRADUATION CEREMONY NEXT WEEK...
ANYWAY, THAT'S THE LAST I'LL SEE OF STUART...
HOLD IT. ***ONE*** OF OUR SITUATIONS HAS TO BE MOST SERIOUS HERE
DUH. MINE
GREG 6·22

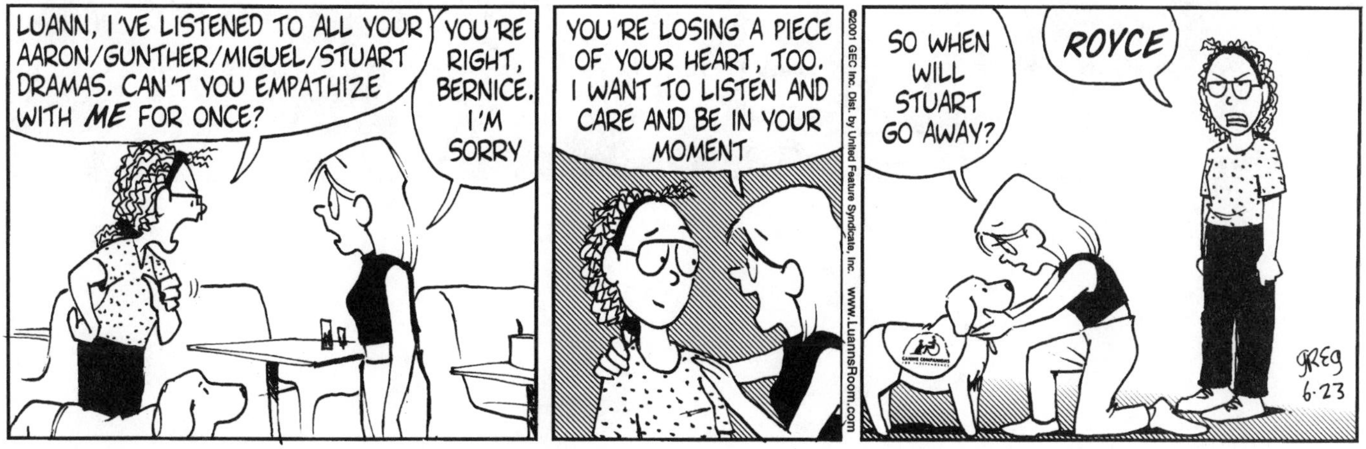
LUANN, I'VE LISTENED TO ALL YOUR AARON/GUNTHER/MIGUEL/STUART DRAMAS. CAN'T YOU EMPATHIZE WITH ***ME*** FOR ONCE?
YOU'RE RIGHT, BERNICE. I'M SORRY
YOU'RE LOSING A PIECE OF YOUR HEART, TOO. I WANT TO LISTEN AND CARE AND BE IN YOUR MOMENT
©2001 GEC Inc. Dist. by United Feature Syndicate, Inc. www.LuannsRoom.com
SO WHEN WILL STUART GO AWAY?
ROYCE
GREG 6·23

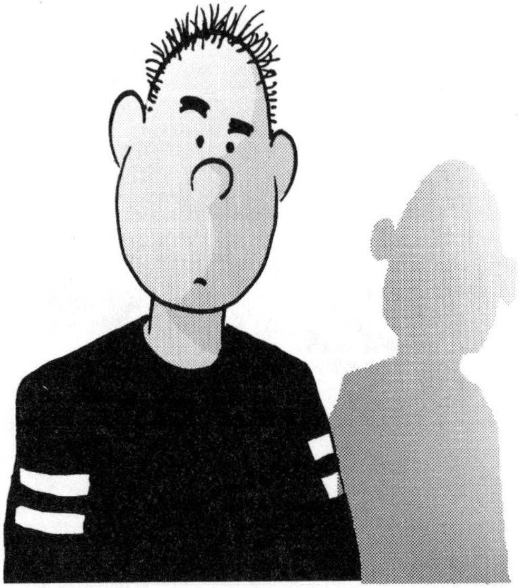

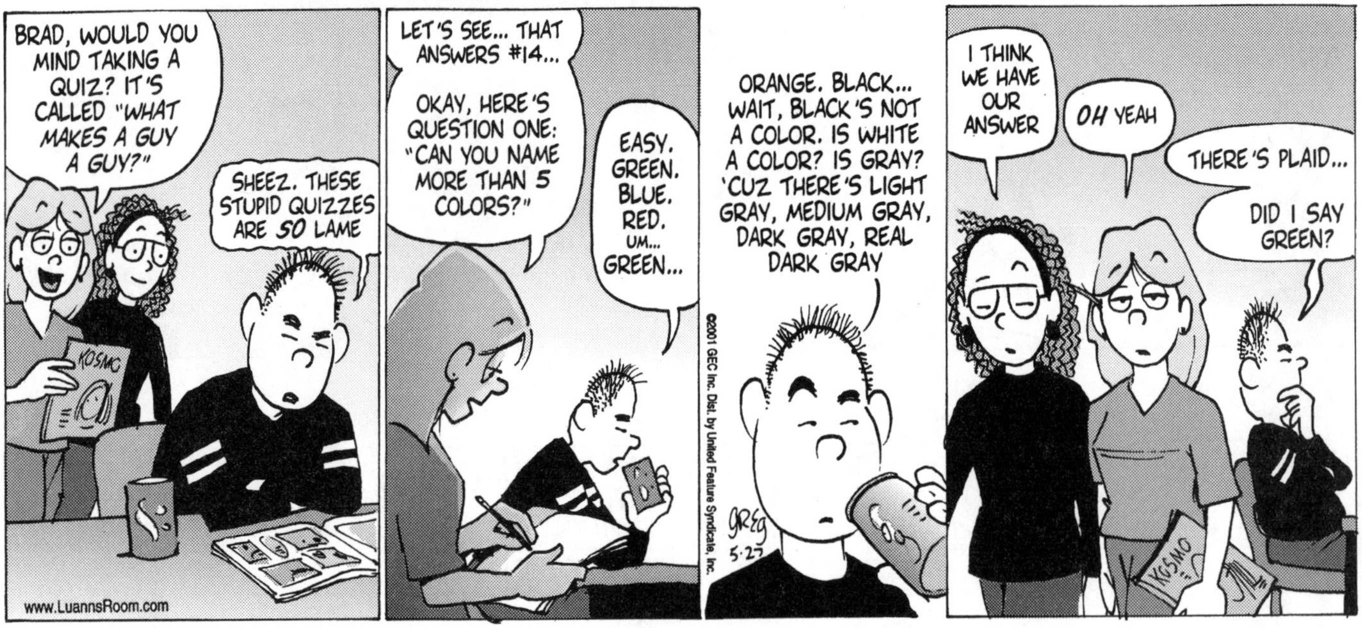

BRAD, WOULD YOU MIND TAKING A QUIZ? IT'S CALLED "*WHAT MAKES A GUY A GUY?*"
KOSMO
SHEEZ. THESE STUPID QUIZZES ARE *SO* LAME
www.LuannsRoom.com
LET'S SEE... THAT ANSWERS #14...
OKAY, HERE'S QUESTION ONE: "CAN YOU NAME MORE THAN 5 COLORS?"
EASY. GREEN. BLUE. RED. UM... GREEN...
©2001 GEC Inc. Dist. by United Feature Syndicate, Inc.
ORANGE. BLACK... WAIT, BLACK'S NOT A COLOR. IS WHITE A COLOR? IS GRAY? 'CUZ THERE'S LIGHT GRAY, MEDIUM GRAY, DARK GRAY, REAL DARK GRAY
GREG 5·27
I THINK WE HAVE OUR ANSWER
OH YEAH
THERE'S PLAID...
DID I SAY GREEN?
KOSMO

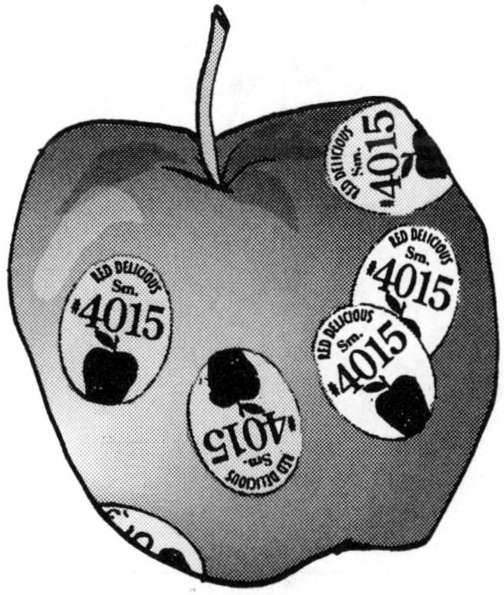
RED DELICIOUS
Sm.
#4015

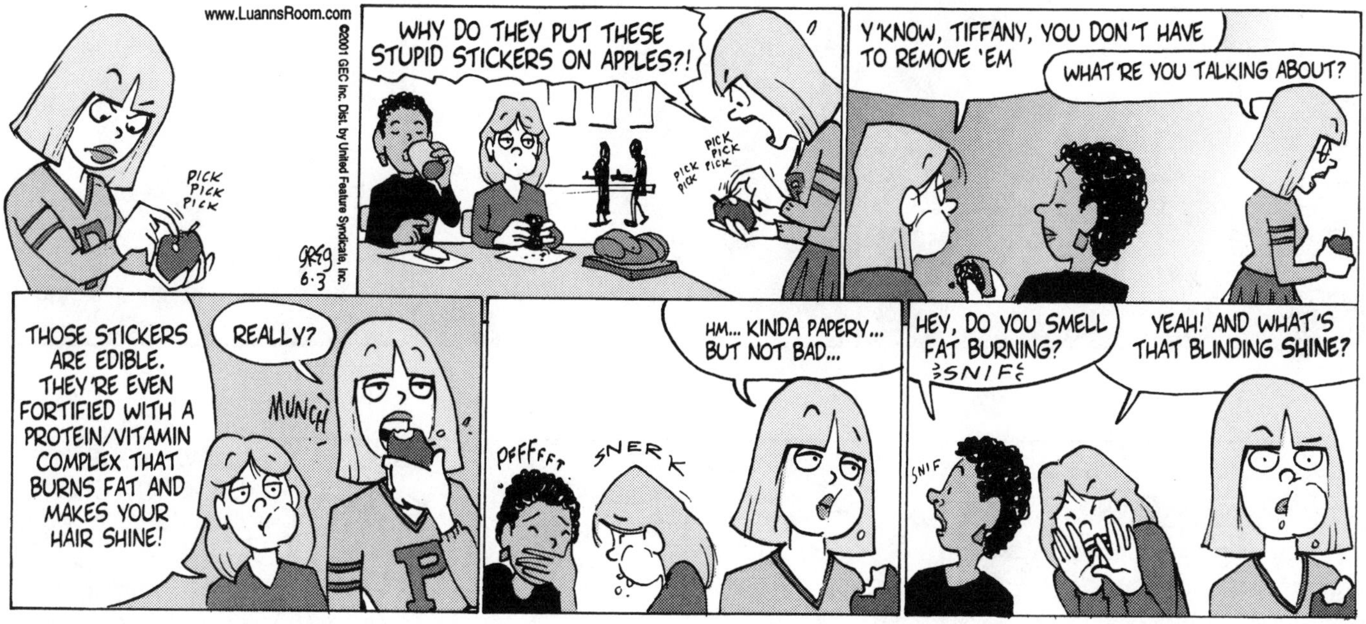
www.LuannsRoom.com
©2001 GEC Inc. Dist. by United Feature Syndicate, Inc.
PICK PICK PICK
WHY DO THEY PUT THESE STUPID STICKERS ON APPLES?!
PICK PICK PICK PICK PICK
Y'KNOW, TIFFANY, YOU DON'T HAVE TO REMOVE 'EM
WHAT'RE YOU TALKING ABOUT?
THOSE STICKERS ARE EDIBLE. THEY'RE EVEN FORTIFIED WITH A PROTEIN/VITAMIN COMPLEX THAT BURNS FAT AND MAKES YOUR HAIR SHINE!
REALLY?
MUNCH
PFFFFFT
SNERK
HM... KINDA PAPERY... BUT NOT BAD...
HEY, DO YOU SMELL FAT BURNING?
SNIF
SNIF
YEAH! AND WHAT'S THAT BLINDING SHINE?

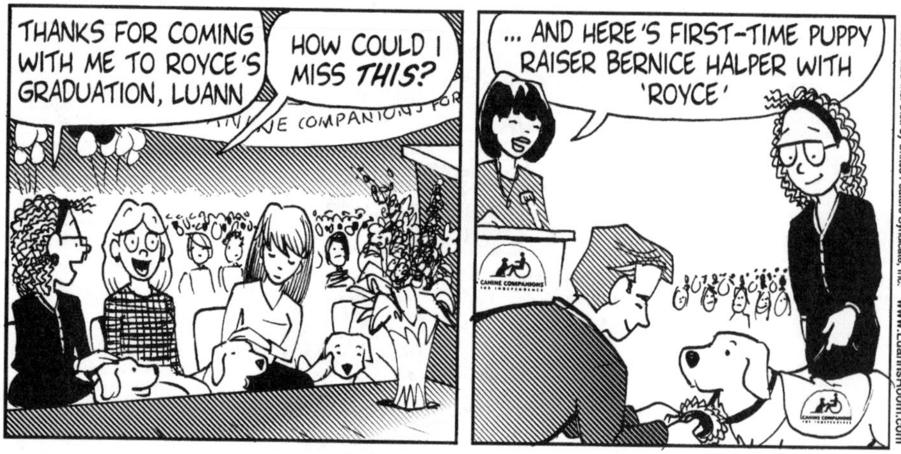
THANKS FOR COMING WITH ME TO ROYCE'S GRADUATION, LUANN
HOW COULD I MISS *THIS?*
CANINE COMPANIONS FOR
... AND HERE'S FIRST-TIME PUPPY RAISER BERNICE HALPER WITH 'ROYCE'
CANINE COMPANIONS FOR INDEPENDENCE
©2001 GEC Inc. Dist. by United Feature Syndicate, Inc. www.LuannsRoom.com
YEAH! GO ROYCE!!
WOO WOO!
GREG 6.25

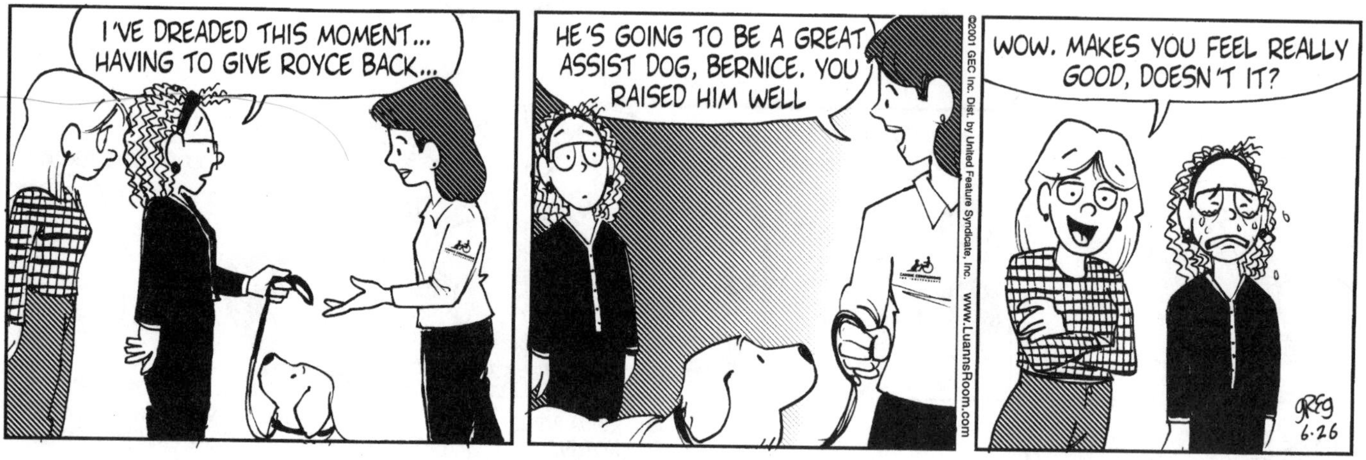
I'VE DREADED THIS MOMENT... HAVING TO GIVE ROYCE BACK...
HE'S GOING TO BE A GREAT ASSIST DOG, BERNICE. YOU RAISED HIM WELL
©2001 GEC Inc. Dist. by United Feature Syndicate, Inc. www.LuannsRoom.com
WOW. MAKES YOU FEEL REALLY GOOD, DOESN'T IT?
GREG 6.26

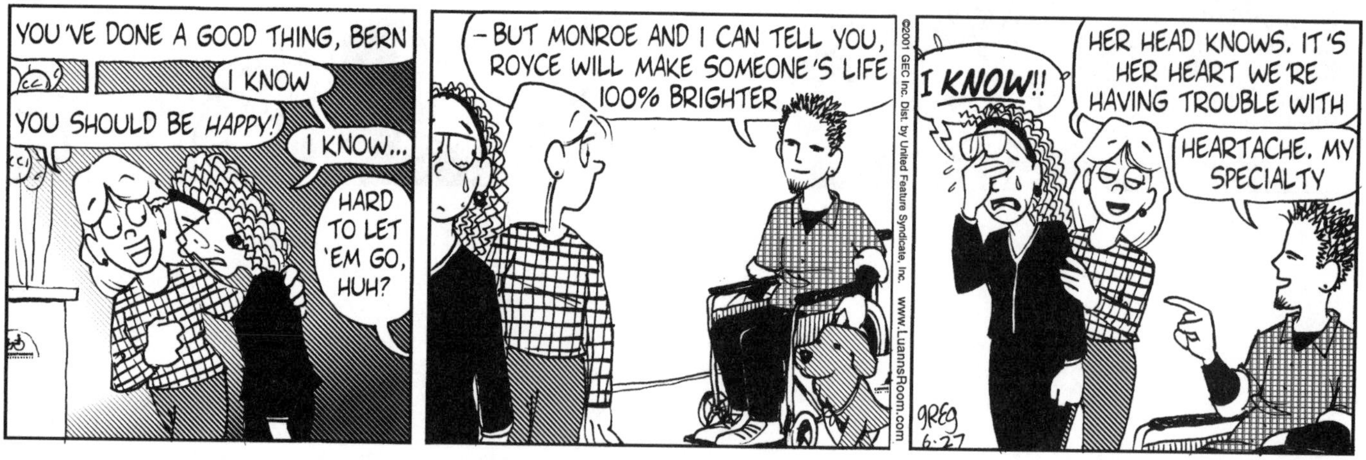
YOU'VE DONE A GOOD THING, BERN
I KNOW
YOU SHOULD BE *HAPPY!*
I KNOW...
HARD TO LET 'EM GO, HUH?
– BUT MONROE AND I CAN TELL YOU, ROYCE WILL MAKE SOMEONE'S LIFE 100% BRIGHTER
©2001 GEC Inc. Dist. by United Feature Syndicate, Inc. www.LuannsRoom.com
I ***KNOW***!!
HER HEAD KNOWS. IT'S HER HEART WE'RE HAVING TROUBLE WITH
HEARTACHE. MY SPECIALTY
GREG 6.27

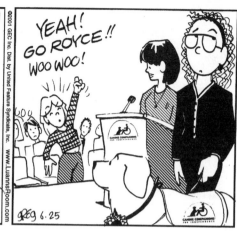

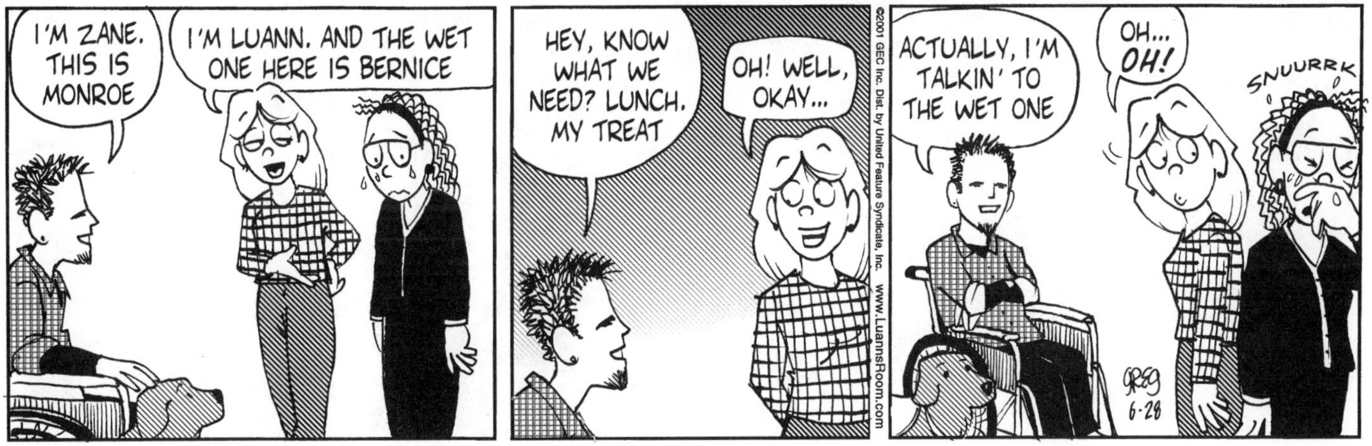
I'M ZANE. THIS IS MONROE
I'M LUANN. AND THE WET ONE HERE IS BERNICE
HEY, KNOW WHAT WE NEED? LUNCH. MY TREAT
OH! WELL, OKAY...
©2001 GEC Inc. Dist. by United Feature Syndicate, Inc. www.LuannsRoom.com
ACTUALLY, I'M TALKIN' TO THE WET ONE
OH... OH!
SNUURRK
GREG 6-28

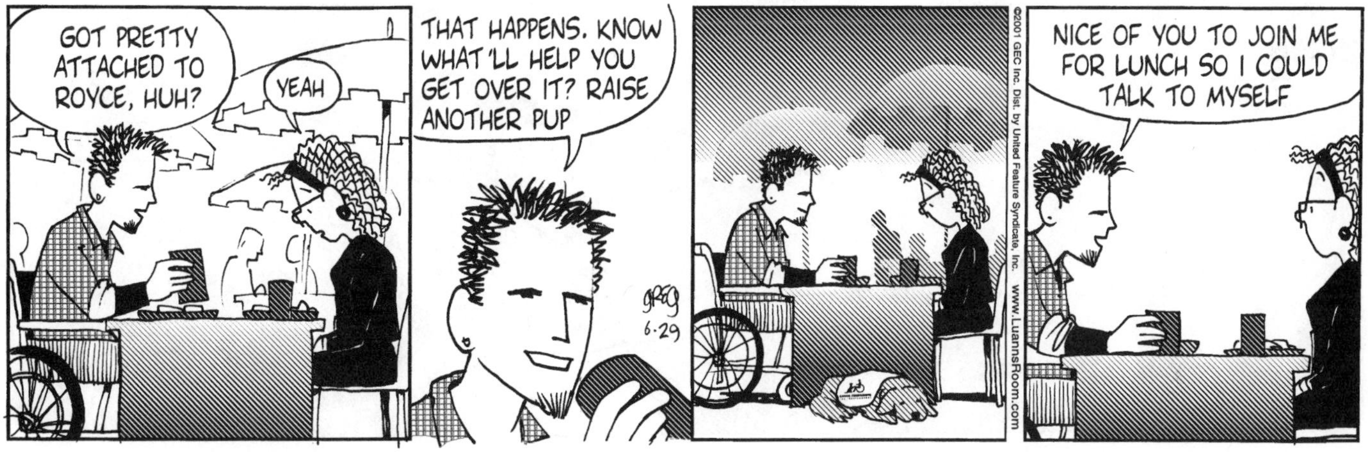
GOT PRETTY ATTACHED TO ROYCE, HUH?
YEAH
THAT HAPPENS. KNOW WHAT'LL HELP YOU GET OVER IT? RAISE ANOTHER PUP
GREG 6-29
©2001 GEC Inc. Dist. by United Feature Syndicate, Inc. www.LuannsRoom.com
NICE OF YOU TO JOIN ME FOR LUNCH SO I COULD TALK TO MYSELF

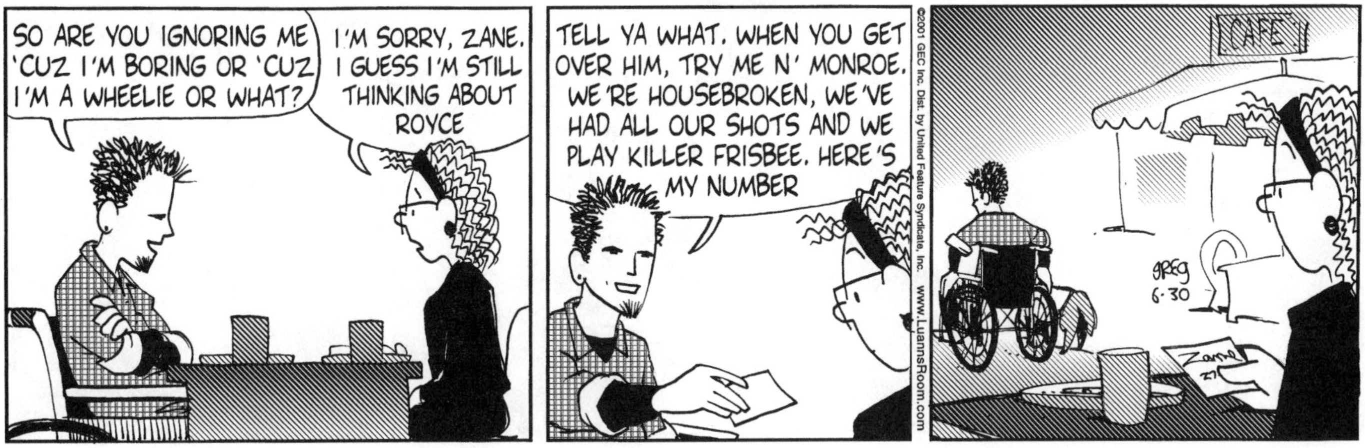
SO ARE YOU IGNORING ME 'CUZ I'M BORING OR 'CUZ I'M A WHEELIE OR WHAT?
I'M SORRY, ZANE. I GUESS I'M STILL THINKING ABOUT ROYCE
TELL YA WHAT. WHEN YOU GET OVER HIM, TRY ME N' MONROE. WE'RE HOUSEBROKEN, WE'VE HAD ALL OUR SHOTS AND WE PLAY KILLER FRISBEE. HERE'S MY NUMBER
©2001 GEC Inc. Dist. by United Feature Syndicate, Inc. www.LuannsRoom.com
CAFE
GREG 6-30

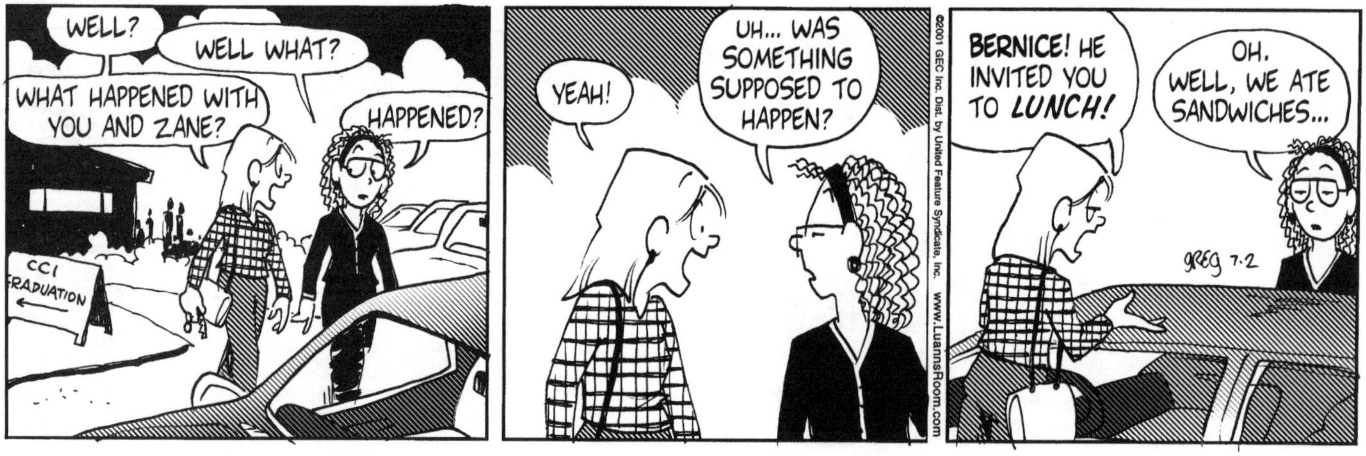
WELL?
WELL WHAT?
WHAT HAPPENED WITH YOU AND ZANE?
HAPPENED?
CCI GRADUATION
YEAH!
UH... WAS SOMETHING SUPPOSED TO HAPPEN?
©2001 GEC Inc. Dist. by United Feature Syndicate, Inc. www.LuannsRoom.com
BERNICE! HE INVITED YOU TO ***LUNCH!***
OH. WELL, WE ATE SANDWICHES...
GREG 7·2

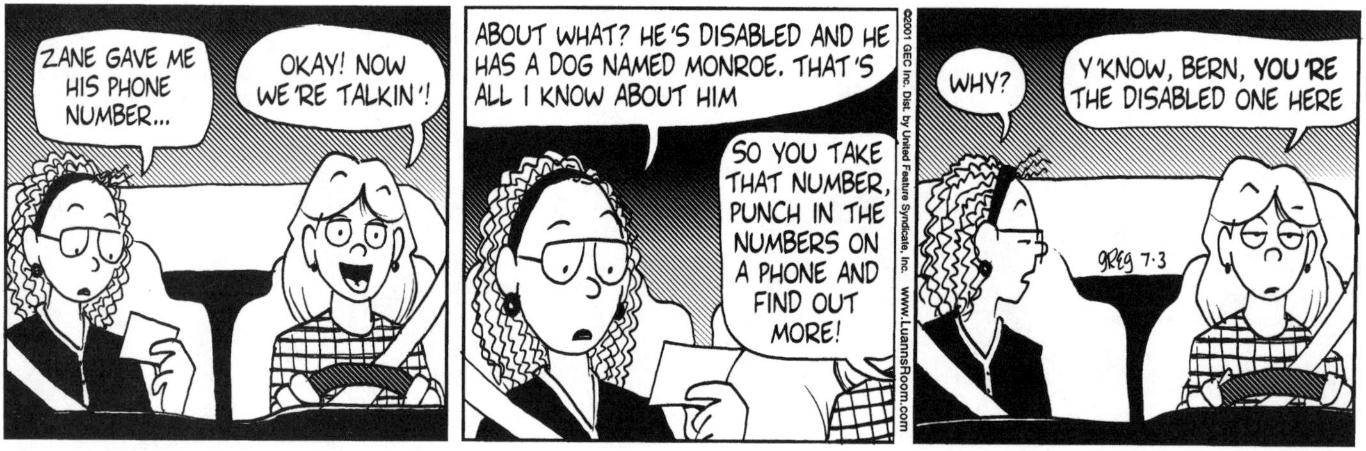
ZANE GAVE ME HIS PHONE NUMBER...
OKAY! NOW WE'RE TALKIN'!
ABOUT WHAT? HE'S DISABLED AND HE HAS A DOG NAMED MONROE. THAT'S ALL I KNOW ABOUT HIM
SO YOU TAKE THAT NUMBER, PUNCH IN THE NUMBERS ON A PHONE AND FIND OUT MORE!
©2001 GEC Inc. Dist. by United Feature Syndicate, Inc. www.LuannsRoom.com
WHY?
Y'KNOW, BERN, **YOU'RE** THE DISABLED ONE HERE
GREG 7·3

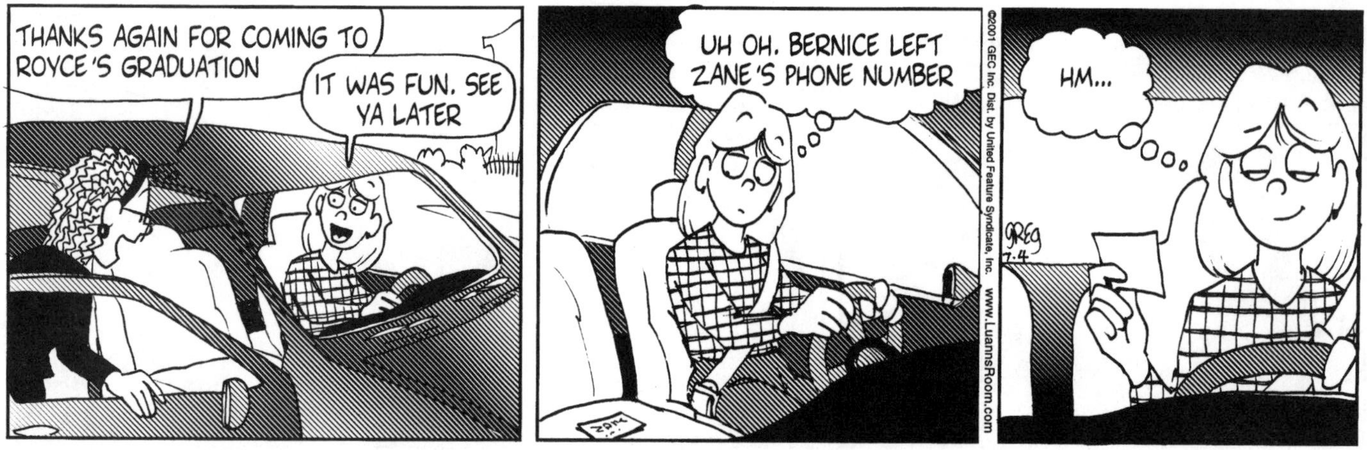
THANKS AGAIN FOR COMING TO ROYCE'S GRADUATION
IT WAS FUN. SEE YA LATER
UH OH. BERNICE LEFT ZANE'S PHONE NUMBER
©2001 GEC Inc. Dist. by United Feature Syndicate, Inc. www.LuannsRoom.com
HM...
GREG 7·4

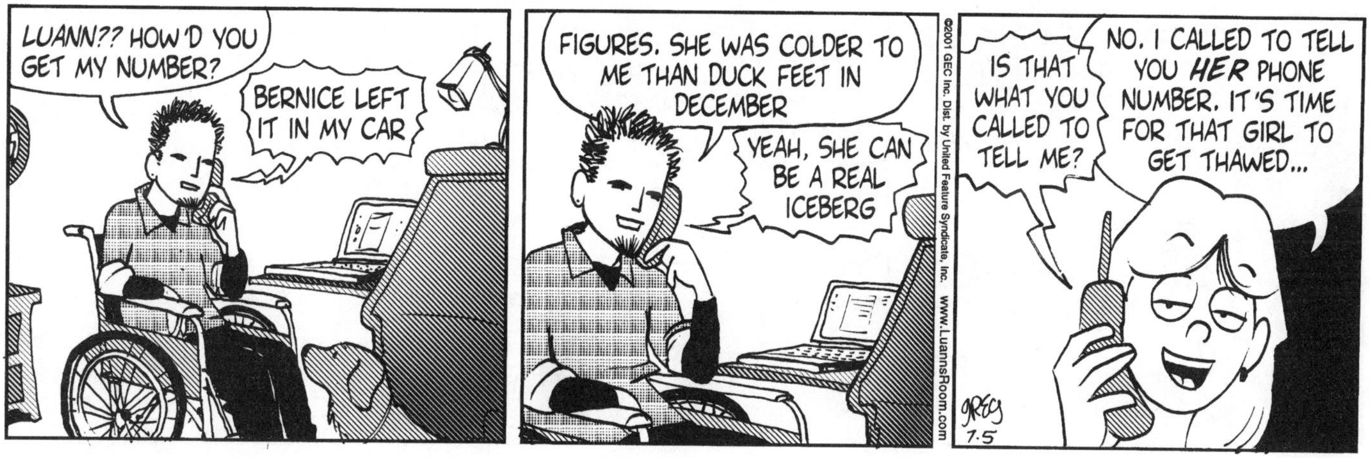
LUANN?? HOW'D YOU GET MY NUMBER?
BERNICE LEFT IT IN MY CAR
FIGURES. SHE WAS COLDER TO ME THAN DUCK FEET IN DECEMBER
YEAH, SHE CAN BE A REAL ICEBERG
©2001 GEC Inc. Dist. by United Feature Syndicate, Inc. www.LuannsRoom.com
IS THAT WHAT YOU CALLED TO TELL ME?
NO. I CALLED TO TELL YOU ***HER*** PHONE NUMBER. IT'S TIME FOR THAT GIRL TO GET THAWED...
GREG 7.5

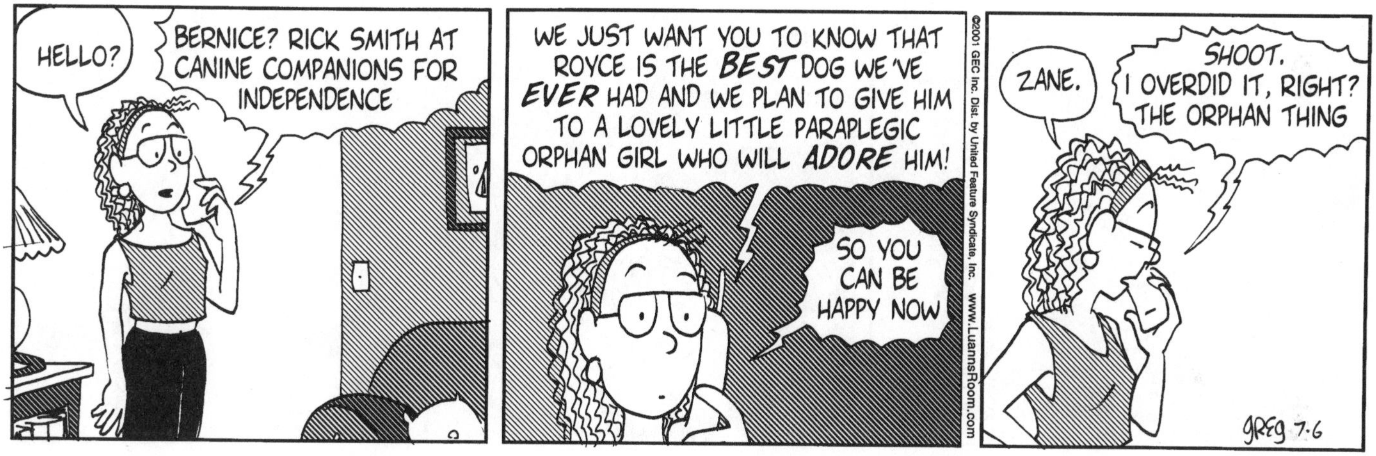
HELLO?
BERNICE? RICK SMITH AT CANINE COMPANIONS FOR INDEPENDENCE
WE JUST WANT YOU TO KNOW THAT ROYCE IS THE ***BEST*** DOG WE'VE ***EVER*** HAD AND WE PLAN TO GIVE HIM TO A LOVELY LITTLE PARAPLEGIC ORPHAN GIRL WHO WILL ***ADORE*** HIM!
SO YOU CAN BE HAPPY NOW
©2001 GEC Inc. Dist. by United Feature Syndicate, Inc. www.LuannsRoom.com
ZANE.
SHOOT. I OVERDID IT, RIGHT? THE ORPHAN THING
GREG 7.6

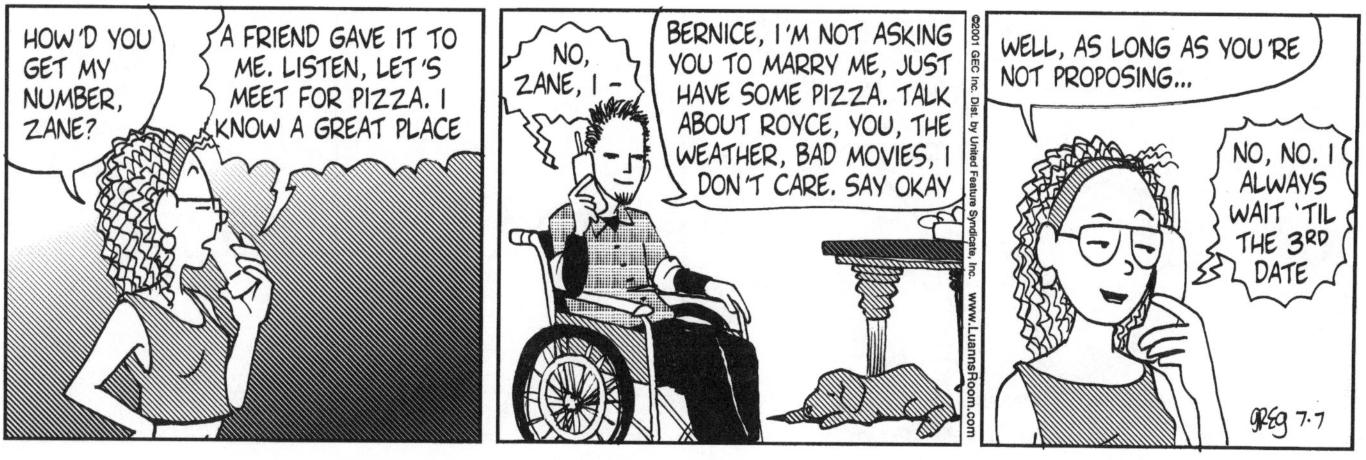
HOW'D YOU GET MY NUMBER, ZANE?
A FRIEND GAVE IT TO ME. LISTEN, LET'S MEET FOR PIZZA. I KNOW A GREAT PLACE
NO, ZANE, I –
BERNICE, I'M NOT ASKING YOU TO MARRY ME, JUST HAVE SOME PIZZA. TALK ABOUT ROYCE, YOU, THE WEATHER, BAD MOVIES, I DON'T CARE. SAY OKAY
©2001 GEC Inc. Dist. by United Feature Syndicate, Inc. www.LuannsRoom.com
WELL, AS LONG AS YOU'RE NOT PROPOSING...
NO, NO. I ALWAYS WAIT 'TIL THE 3RD DATE
GREG 7.7

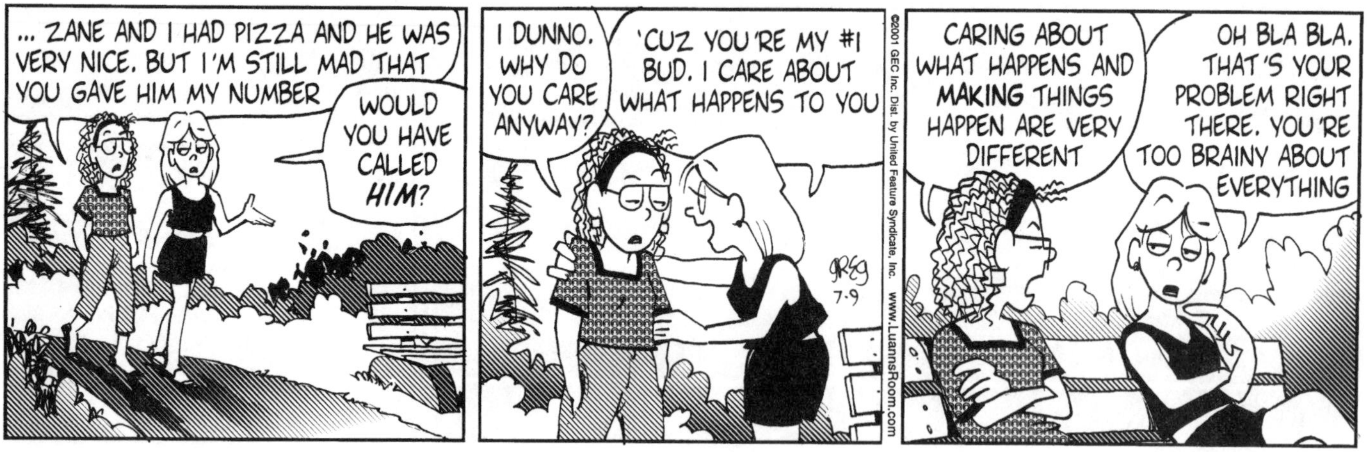
... ZANE AND I HAD PIZZA AND HE WAS VERY NICE. BUT I'M STILL MAD THAT YOU GAVE HIM MY NUMBER
WOULD YOU HAVE CALLED *HIM*?
I DUNNO. WHY DO YOU CARE ANYWAY?
'CUZ YOU'RE MY #1 BUD. I CARE ABOUT WHAT HAPPENS TO YOU
GREG 7-9
©2001 GEC Inc. Dist. by United Feature Syndicate, Inc. www.LuannsRoom.com
CARING ABOUT WHAT HAPPENS AND **MAKING** THINGS HAPPEN ARE VERY DIFFERENT
OH BLA BLA. THAT'S YOUR PROBLEM RIGHT THERE. YOU'RE TOO BRAINY ABOUT EVERYTHING

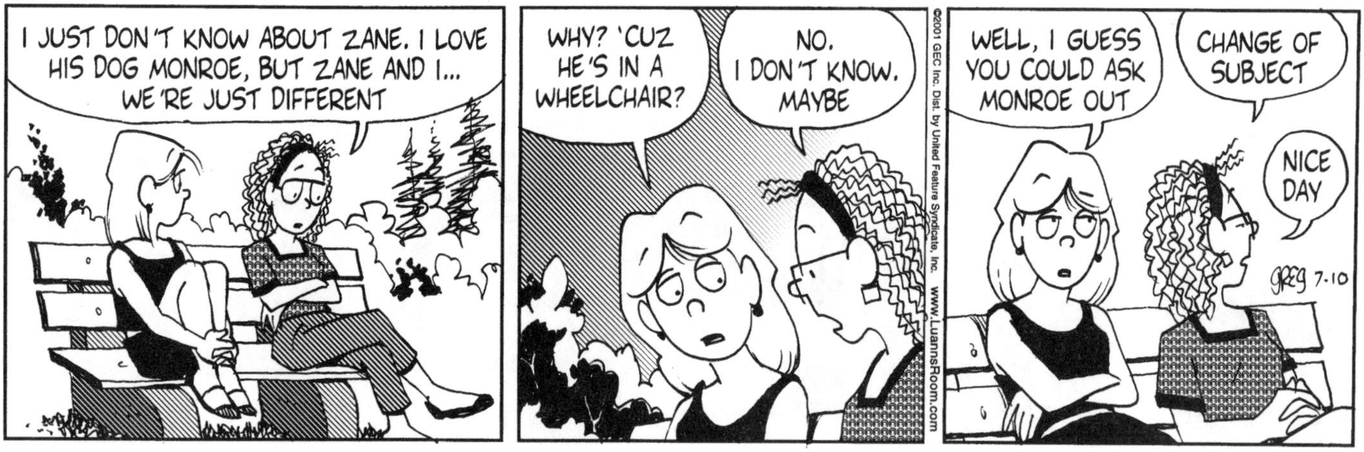
I JUST DON'T KNOW ABOUT ZANE. I LOVE HIS DOG MONROE, BUT ZANE AND I... WE'RE JUST DIFFERENT
WHY? 'CUZ HE'S IN A WHEELCHAIR?
NO. I DON'T KNOW. MAYBE
©2001 GEC Inc. Dist. by United Feature Syndicate, Inc. www.LuannsRoom.com
WELL, I GUESS YOU COULD ASK MONROE OUT
CHANGE OF SUBJECT
NICE DAY
GREG 7-10

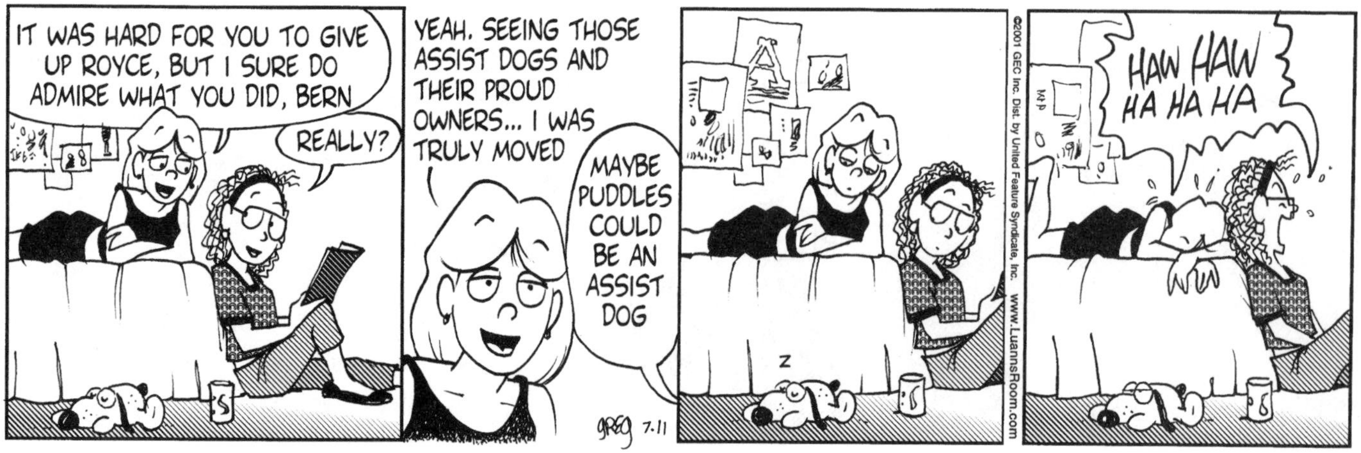
IT WAS HARD FOR YOU TO GIVE UP ROYCE, BUT I SURE DO ADMIRE WHAT YOU DID, BERN
REALLY?
YEAH. SEEING THOSE ASSIST DOGS AND THEIR PROUD OWNERS... I WAS TRULY MOVED
MAYBE PUDDLES COULD BE AN ASSIST DOG
GREG 7-11
Z
©2001 GEC Inc. Dist. by United Feature Syndicate, Inc. www.LuannsRoom.com
HAW HAW HA HA HA

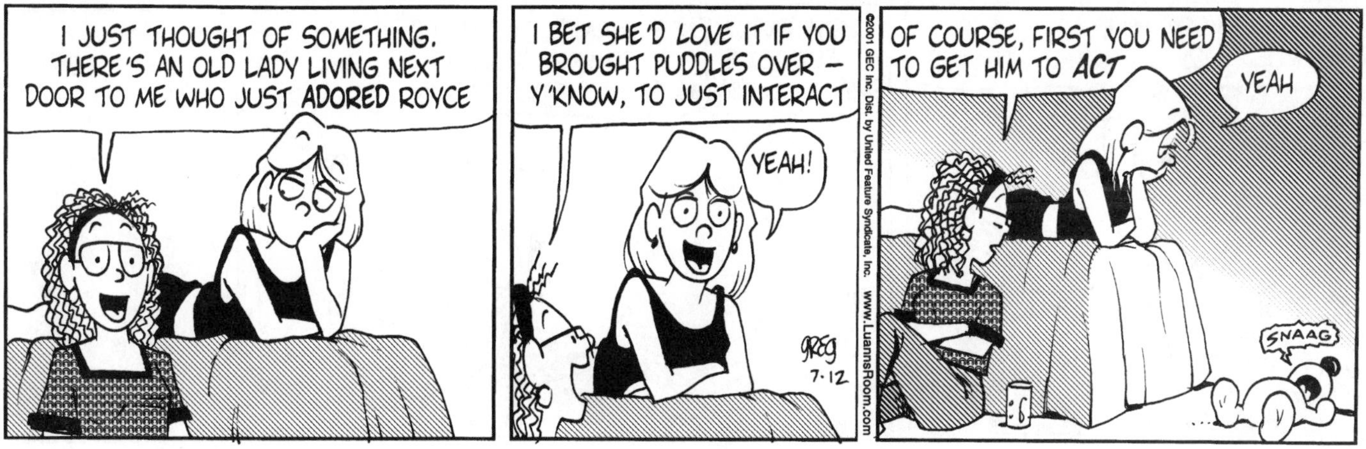
I JUST THOUGHT OF SOMETHING. THERE'S AN OLD LADY LIVING NEXT DOOR TO ME WHO JUST ADORED ROYCE
I BET SHE'D LOVE IT IF YOU BROUGHT PUDDLES OVER — Y'KNOW, TO JUST INTERACT
YEAH!
GREG 7·12
©2001 GEC Inc. Dist. by United Feature Syndicate, Inc. www.LuannsRoom.com
OF COURSE, FIRST YOU NEED TO GET HIM TO ACT
YEAH
SNAAG

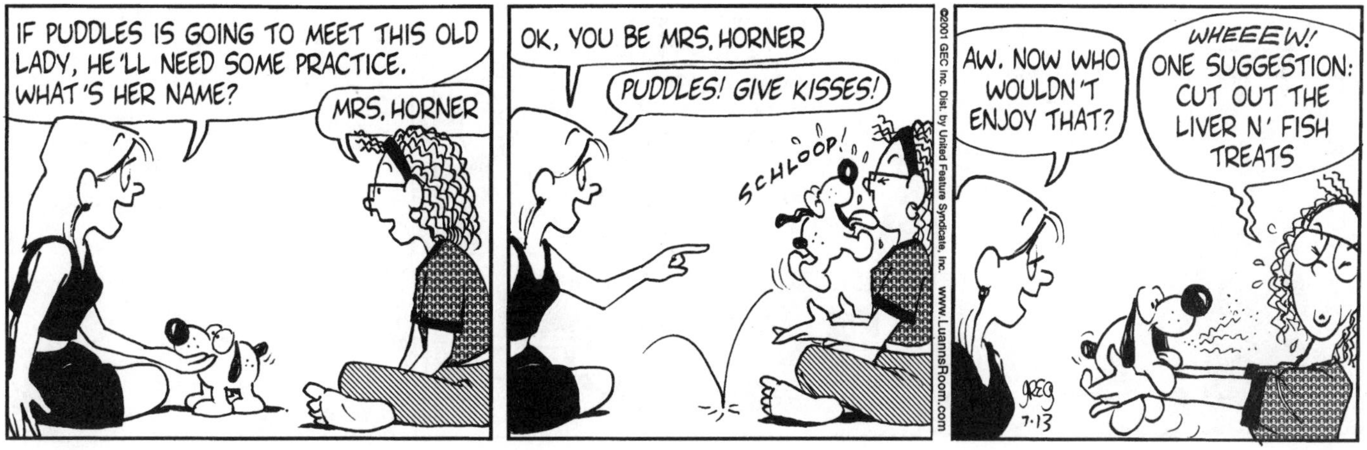
IF PUDDLES IS GOING TO MEET THIS OLD LADY, HE'LL NEED SOME PRACTICE. WHAT'S HER NAME?
MRS. HORNER
OK, YOU BE MRS. HORNER
PUDDLES! GIVE KISSES!
SCHLOOP!
©2001 GEC Inc. Dist. by United Feature Syndicate, Inc. www.LuannsRoom.com
AW. NOW WHO WOULDN'T ENJOY THAT?
WHEEEW! ONE SUGGESTION: CUT OUT THE LIVER N' FISH TREATS
GREG 7·13

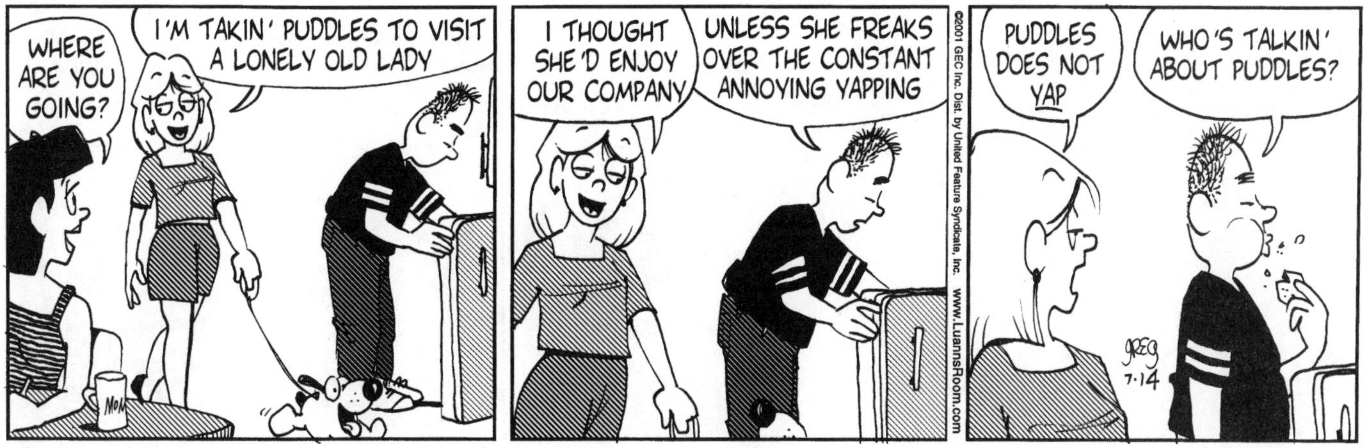
WHERE ARE YOU GOING?
I'M TAKIN' PUDDLES TO VISIT A LONELY OLD LADY
MOM
I THOUGHT SHE'D ENJOY OUR COMPANY
UNLESS SHE FREAKS OVER THE CONSTANT ANNOYING YAPPING
©2001 GEC Inc. Dist. by United Feature Syndicate, Inc. www.LuannsRoom.com
PUDDLES DOES NOT YAP
WHO'S TALKIN' ABOUT PUDDLES?
GREG 7·14

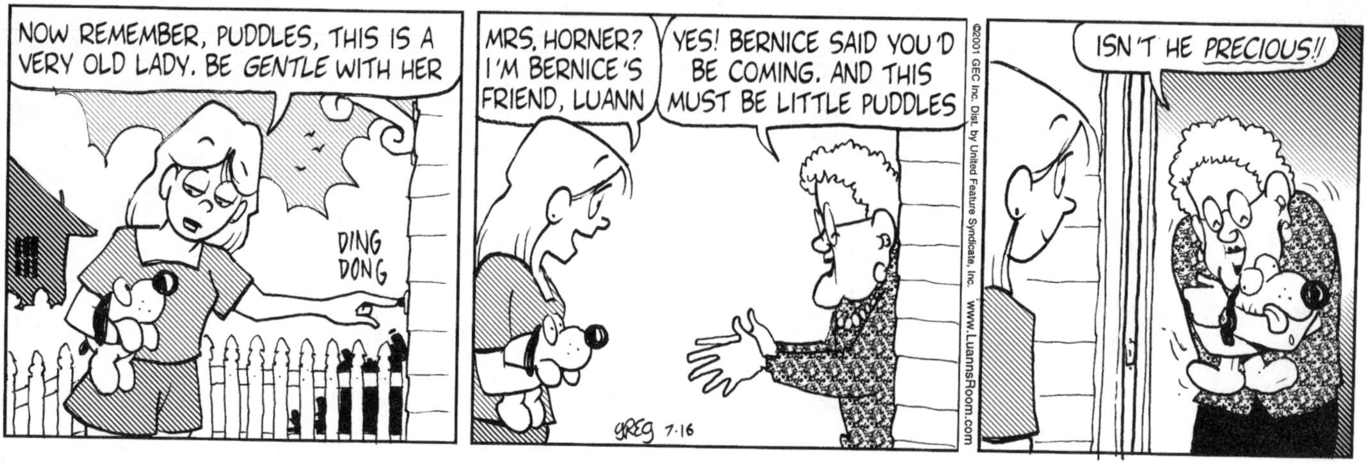
NOW REMEMBER, PUDDLES, THIS IS A VERY OLD LADY. BE *GENTLE* WITH HER
DING DONG
MRS. HORNER? I'M BERNICE'S FRIEND, LUANN
YES! BERNICE SAID YOU'D BE COMING. AND THIS MUST BE LITTLE PUDDLES
©2001 GEC Inc. Dist. by United Feature Syndicate, Inc. www.LuannsRoom.com
ISN'T HE *PRECIOUS!!*

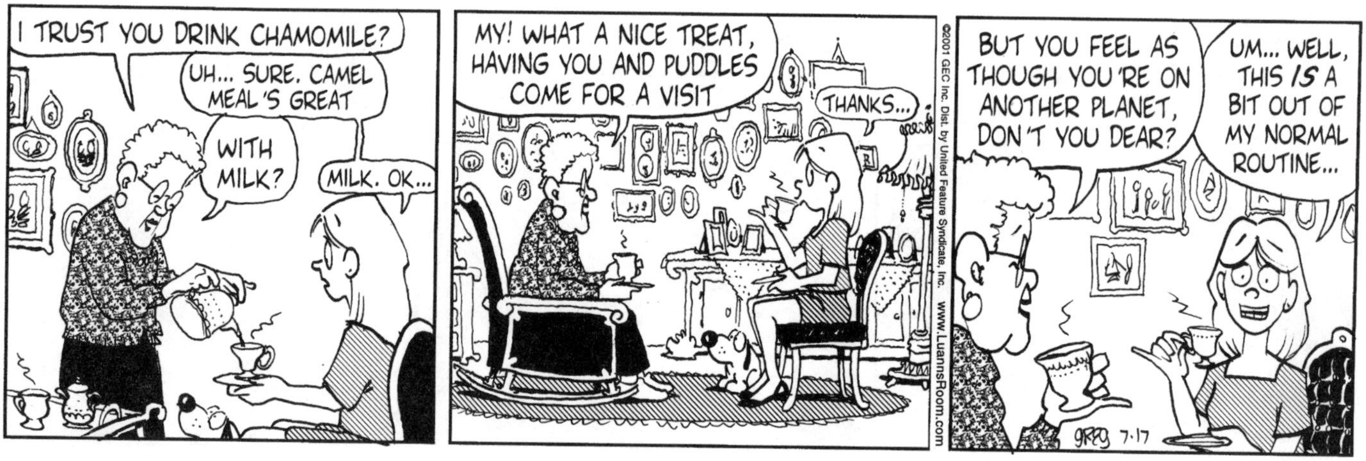
I TRUST YOU DRINK CHAMOMILE?
UH... SURE. CAMEL MEAL'S GREAT
WITH MILK?
MILK. OK...
MY! WHAT A NICE TREAT, HAVING YOU AND PUDDLES COME FOR A VISIT
THANKS...
©2001 GEC Inc. Dist. by United Feature Syndicate, Inc. www.LuannsRoom.com
BUT YOU FEEL AS THOUGH YOU'RE ON ANOTHER PLANET, DON'T YOU DEAR?
UM... WELL, THIS *IS* A BIT OUT OF MY NORMAL ROUTINE...

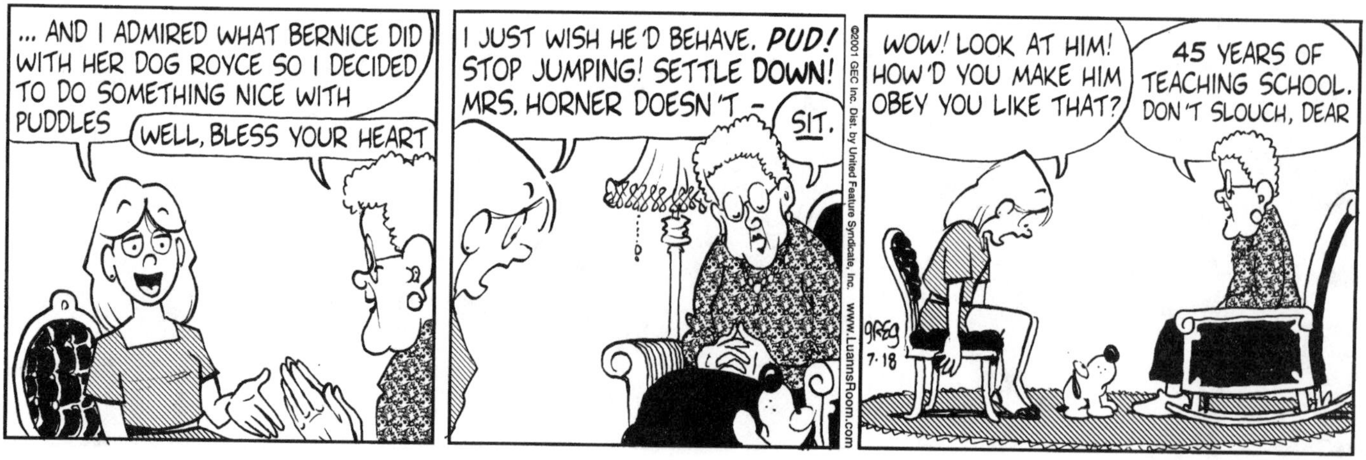
... AND I ADMIRED WHAT BERNICE DID WITH HER DOG ROYCE SO I DECIDED TO DO SOMETHING NICE WITH PUDDLES
WELL, BLESS YOUR HEART
I JUST WISH HE'D BEHAVE. ***PUD!*** STOP JUMPING! SETTLE **DOWN**! MRS. HORNER DOESN'T –
SIT.
©2001 GEC Inc. Dist. by United Feature Syndicate, Inc. www.LuannsRoom.com
WOW! LOOK AT HIM! HOW'D YOU MAKE HIM OBEY YOU LIKE THAT?
45 YEARS OF TEACHING SCHOOL. DON'T SLOUCH, DEAR

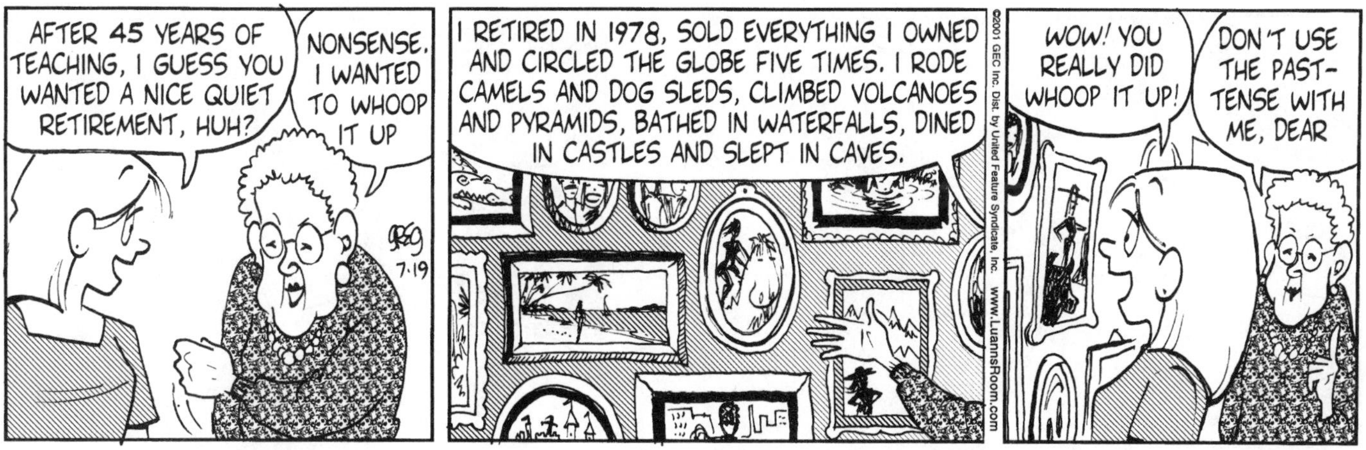
AFTER 45 YEARS OF TEACHING, I GUESS YOU WANTED A NICE QUIET RETIREMENT, HUH?
NONSENSE. I WANTED TO WHOOP IT UP
GREG 7·19
I RETIRED IN 1978, SOLD EVERYTHING I OWNED AND CIRCLED THE GLOBE FIVE TIMES. I RODE CAMELS AND DOG SLEDS, CLIMBED VOLCANOES AND PYRAMIDS, BATHED IN WATERFALLS, DINED IN CASTLES AND SLEPT IN CAVES.
©2001 GEC Inc. Dist. by United Feature Syndicate, Inc. www.LuannsRoom.com
WOW! YOU REALLY DID WHOOP IT UP!
DON'T USE THE PAST-TENSE WITH ME, DEAR

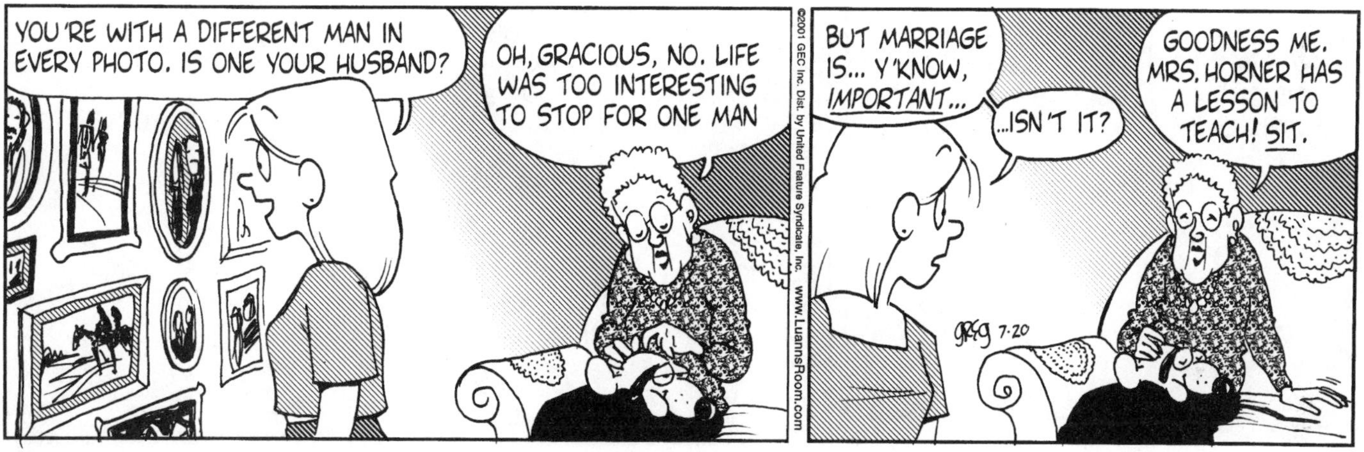
YOU'RE WITH A DIFFERENT MAN IN EVERY PHOTO. IS ONE YOUR HUSBAND?
OH, GRACIOUS, NO. LIFE WAS TOO INTERESTING TO STOP FOR ONE MAN
©2001 GEC Inc. Dist. by United Feature Syndicate, Inc. www.LuannsRoom.com
BUT MARRIAGE IS... Y'KNOW, IMPORTANT...
...ISN'T IT?
GOODNESS ME. MRS. HORNER HAS A LESSON TO TEACH! SIT.
GREG 7·20

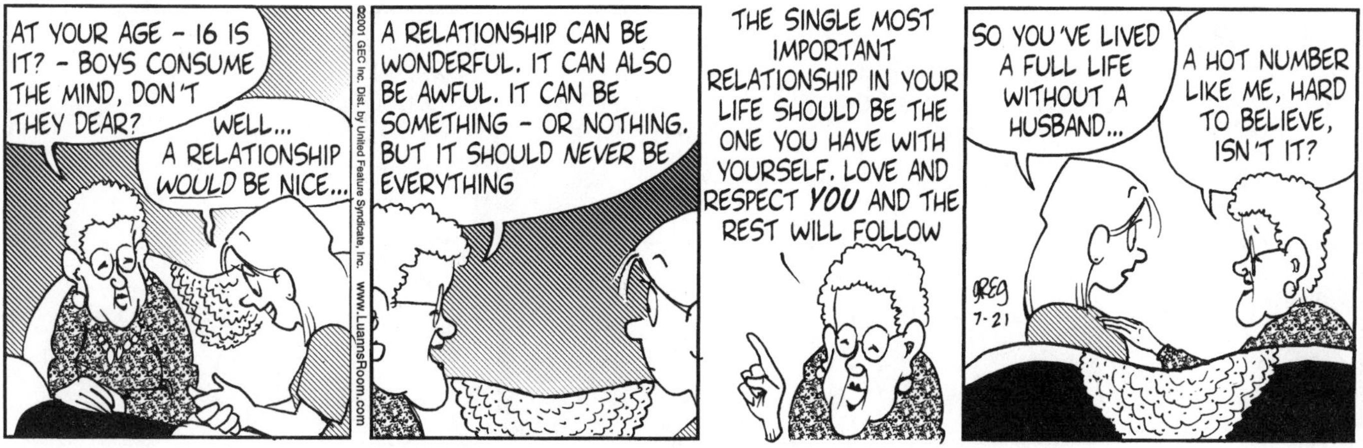
AT YOUR AGE – 16 IS IT? – BOYS CONSUME THE MIND, DON'T THEY DEAR?
WELL... A RELATIONSHIP WOULD BE NICE...
©2001 GEC Inc. Dist. by United Feature Syndicate, Inc. www.LuannsRoom.com
A RELATIONSHIP CAN BE WONDERFUL. IT CAN ALSO BE AWFUL. IT CAN BE SOMETHING – OR NOTHING. BUT IT SHOULD NEVER BE EVERYTHING
THE SINGLE MOST IMPORTANT RELATIONSHIP IN YOUR LIFE SHOULD BE THE ONE YOU HAVE WITH YOURSELF. LOVE AND RESPECT YOU AND THE REST WILL FOLLOW
SO YOU'VE LIVED A FULL LIFE WITHOUT A HUSBAND...
A HOT NUMBER LIKE ME, HARD TO BELIEVE, ISN'T IT?
GREG 7·21

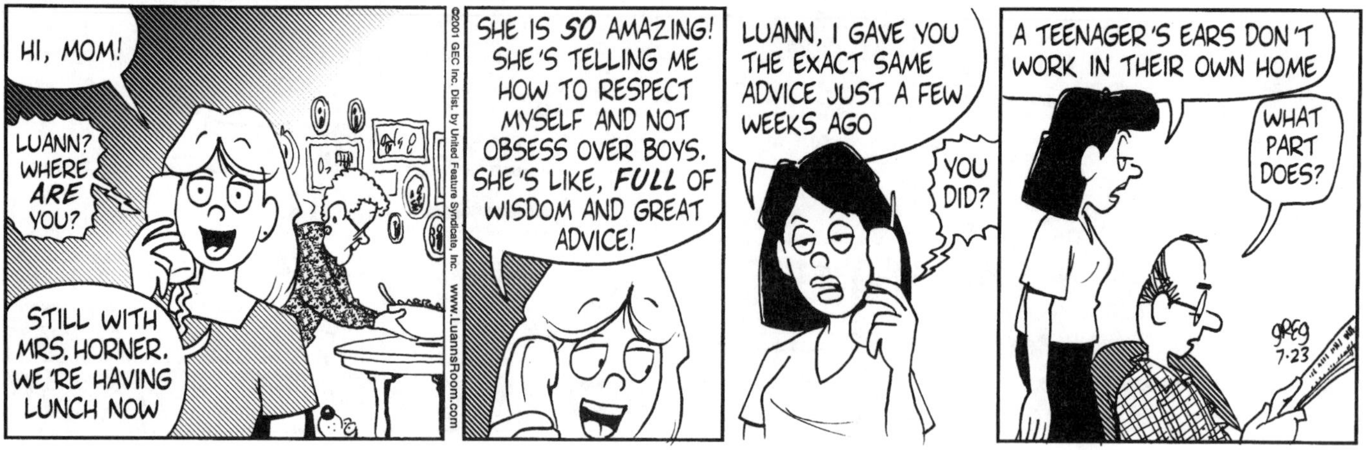
HI, MOM!
LUANN? WHERE ARE YOU?
STILL WITH MRS. HORNER. WE'RE HAVING LUNCH NOW
©2001 GEC Inc. Dist. by United Feature Syndicate, Inc. www.LuannsRoom.com
SHE IS SO AMAZING! SHE'S TELLING ME HOW TO RESPECT MYSELF AND NOT OBSESS OVER BOYS. SHE'S LIKE, FULL OF WISDOM AND GREAT ADVICE!
LUANN, I GAVE YOU THE EXACT SAME ADVICE JUST A FEW WEEKS AGO
YOU DID?
A TEENAGER'S EARS DON'T WORK IN THEIR OWN HOME
WHAT PART DOES?
GREG 7·23

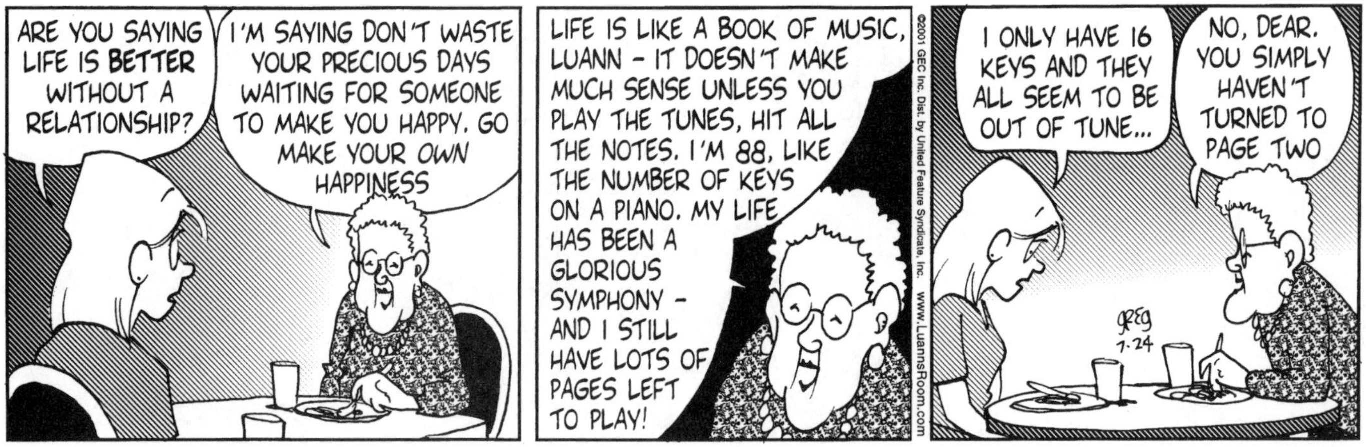
ARE YOU SAYING LIFE IS BETTER WITHOUT A RELATIONSHIP?
I'M SAYING DON'T WASTE YOUR PRECIOUS DAYS WAITING FOR SOMEONE TO MAKE YOU HAPPY. GO MAKE YOUR OWN HAPPINESS
LIFE IS LIKE A BOOK OF MUSIC, LUANN – IT DOESN'T MAKE MUCH SENSE UNLESS YOU PLAY THE TUNES, HIT ALL THE NOTES. I'M 88, LIKE THE NUMBER OF KEYS ON A PIANO. MY LIFE HAS BEEN A GLORIOUS SYMPHONY – AND I STILL HAVE LOTS OF PAGES LEFT TO PLAY!
©2001 GEC Inc. Dist. by United Feature Syndicate, Inc. www.LuannsRoom.com
I ONLY HAVE 16 KEYS AND THEY ALL SEEM TO BE OUT OF TUNE...
NO, DEAR. YOU SIMPLY HAVEN'T TURNED TO PAGE TWO
GREG 7·24

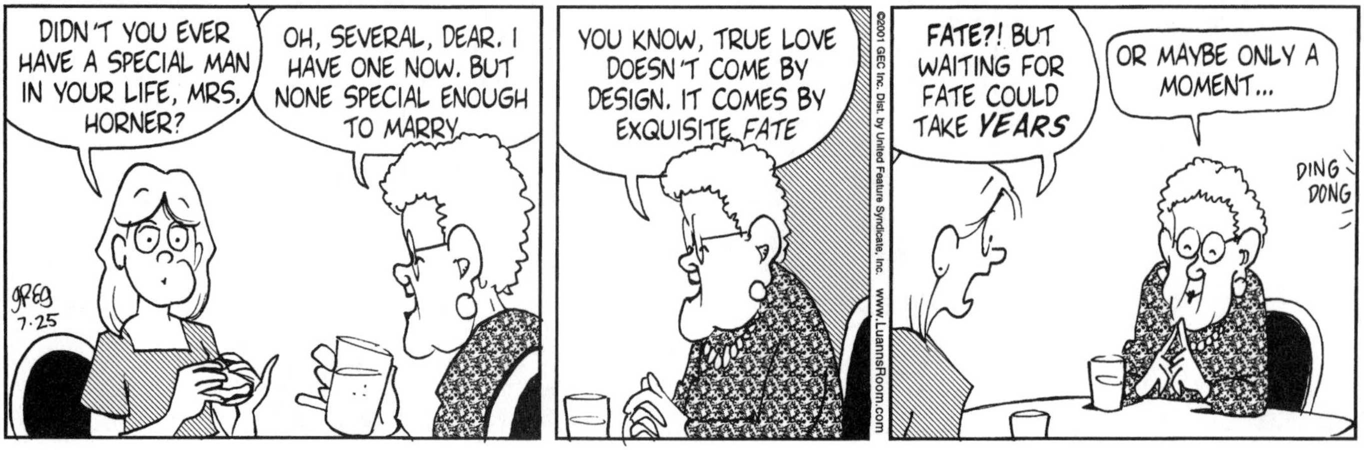
DIDN'T YOU EVER HAVE A SPECIAL MAN IN YOUR LIFE, MRS. HORNER?
OH, SEVERAL, DEAR. I HAVE ONE NOW. BUT NONE SPECIAL ENOUGH TO MARRY
GREG 7·25
YOU KNOW, TRUE LOVE DOESN'T COME BY DESIGN. IT COMES BY EXQUISITE FATE
©2001 GEC Inc. Dist. by United Feature Syndicate, Inc. www.LuannsRoom.com
FATE?! BUT WAITING FOR FATE COULD TAKE YEARS
OR MAYBE ONLY A MOMENT...
DING DONG

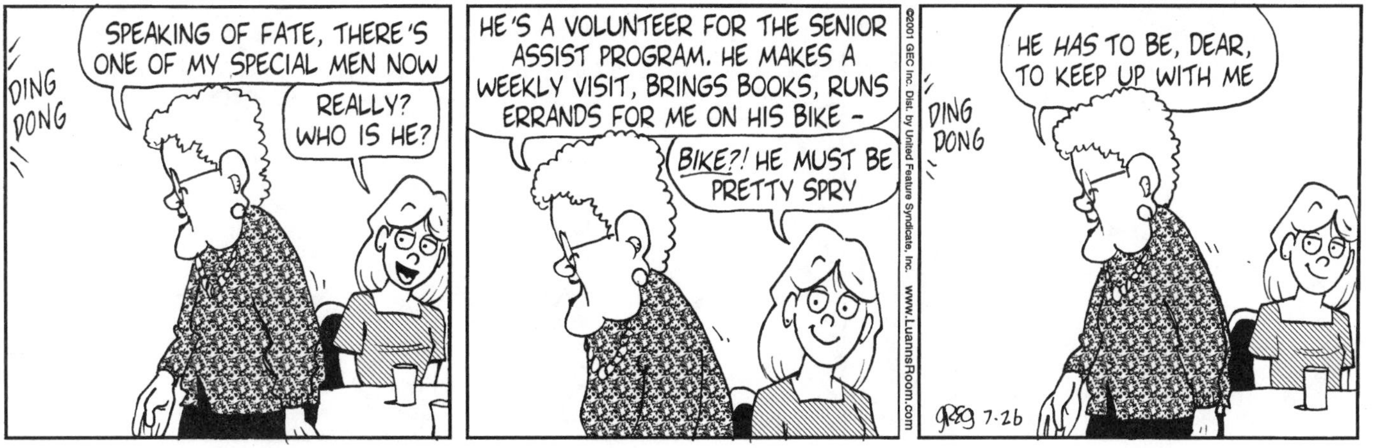
DING DONG
SPEAKING OF FATE, THERE'S ONE OF MY SPECIAL MEN NOW
REALLY? WHO IS HE?
HE'S A VOLUNTEER FOR THE SENIOR ASSIST PROGRAM. HE MAKES A WEEKLY VISIT, BRINGS BOOKS, RUNS ERRANDS FOR ME ON HIS BIKE –
BIKE?! HE MUST BE PRETTY SPRY
©2001 GEC Inc. Dist. by United Feature Syndicate, Inc. www.LuannsRoom.com
DING DONG
HE HAS TO BE, DEAR, TO KEEP UP WITH ME
GREG 7·26

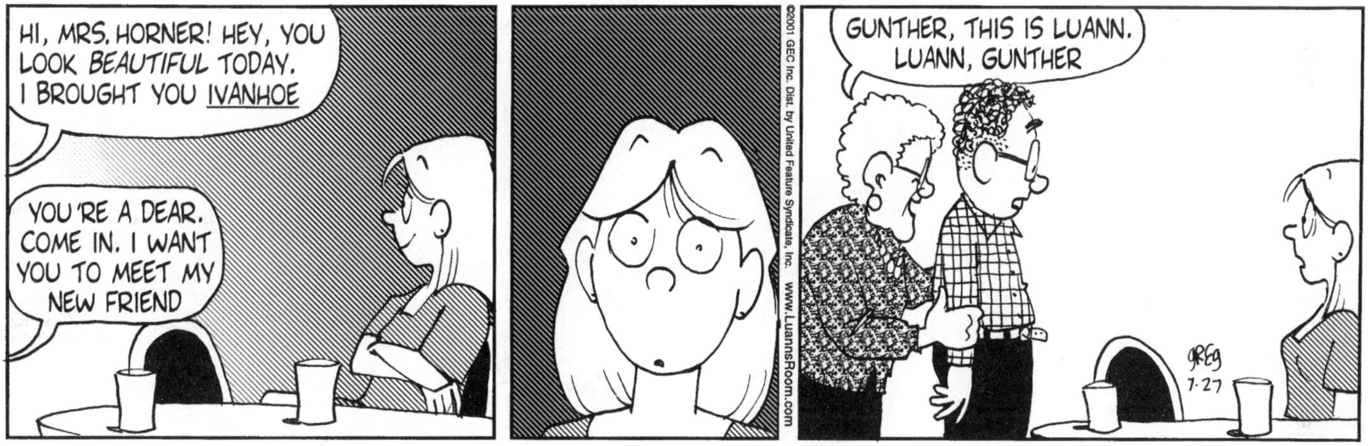
HI, MRS. HORNER! HEY, YOU LOOK BEAUTIFUL TODAY. I BROUGHT YOU IVANHOE
YOU'RE A DEAR. COME IN. I WANT YOU TO MEET MY NEW FRIEND
©2001 GEC Inc. Dist. by United Feature Syndicate, Inc. www.LuannsRoom.com
GUNTHER, THIS IS LUANN. LUANN, GUNTHER
GREG 7·27

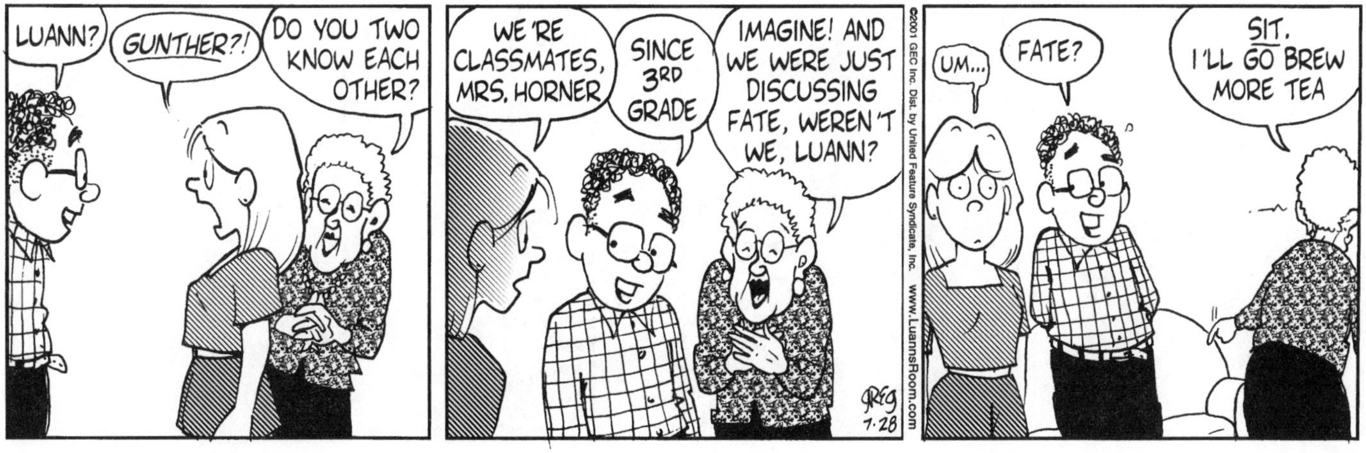
LUANN?
GUNTHER?!
DO YOU TWO KNOW EACH OTHER?
WE'RE CLASSMATES, MRS. HORNER
SINCE 3RD GRADE
IMAGINE! AND WE WERE JUST DISCUSSING FATE, WEREN'T WE, LUANN?
GREG 7·28
©2001 GEC Inc. Dist. by United Feature Syndicate, Inc. www.LuannsRoom.com
UM...
FATE?
SIT. I'LL GO BREW MORE TEA

YOU MAKE THE **BEST** CHAMOMILE, MRS. HORNER
GUNTHER, HOW YOU **DO** FLATTER!
WATCH OUT FOR THIS ONE, DEAR. HE'S BOLDER THAN HE SEEMS
©2001 GEC Inc. Dist. by United Feature Syndicate, Inc. www.LuannsRoom.com
WANT ME TO PUT YOUR MOZART RECORD ON?
SEE WHAT I MEAN? WHY, IF I WERE 72 YEARS YOUNGER, I'D SNAP HIM UP LIKE THAT
SNAP
GREG 7·30

GUNTHER, DEAR, I HAVE A PRESCRIPTION TO BE PICKED UP
NO PROBLEM. I'LL BIKE OVER AND –
I HAVE A CAR OUTSIDE. I'LL DRIVE
IF YOU KIDS WOULD HUMOR ME, I'D LOVE TO SEE YOU BIKE TOGETHER, THE WAY GUYS AND GALS DID WHEN I WAS YOUR AGE
TOGETHER...?
HOW?
©2001 GEC Inc. Dist. by United Feature Syndicate, Inc. www.LuannsRoom.com
GREG 7·31

HUFF PUFF HUFF PUFF
FASTER!
BUMP BUMP
OW OW! OW
OW OW OW
BUMP BUMP BUMP
©2001 GEC Inc. Dist. by United Feature Syndicate, Inc. www.LuannsRoom.com
SLOWER!
GREG 8·1

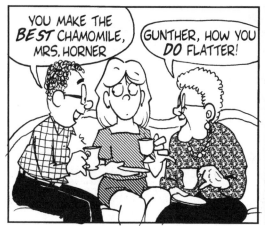

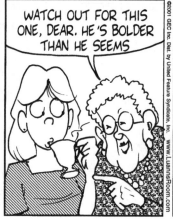

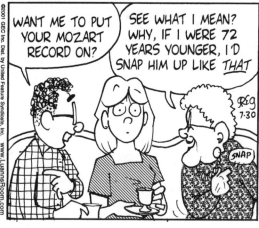

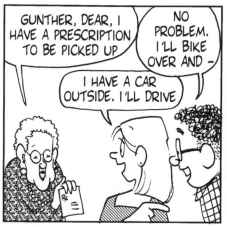

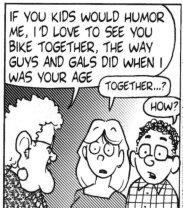

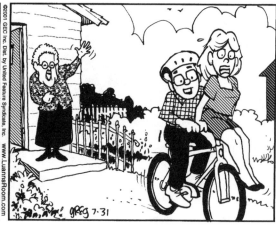

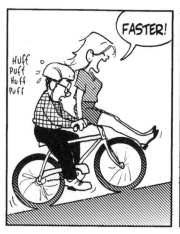

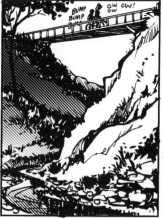

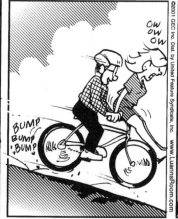

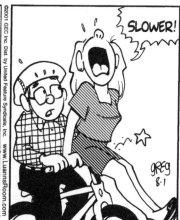

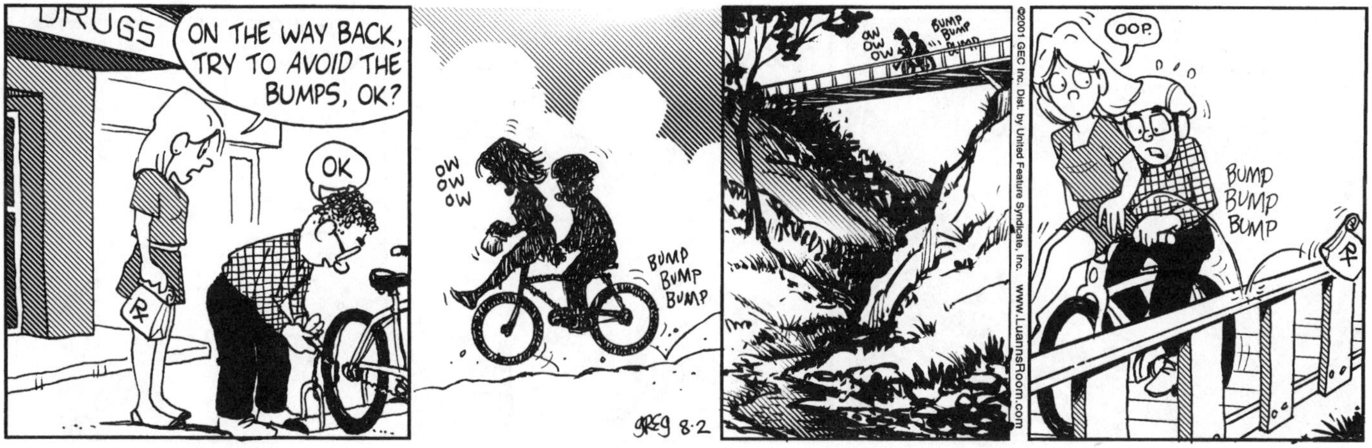
DRUGS
ON THE WAY BACK, TRY TO *AVOID* THE BUMPS, OK?
OK
Rx
OW OW OW
BUMP BUMP BUMP
GREG 8·2
OW OW OW
BUMP BUMP BUMP
©2001 GEC Inc. Dist. by United Feature Syndicate, Inc. www.LuannsRoom.com
OOP.
BUMP BUMP BUMP
Rx

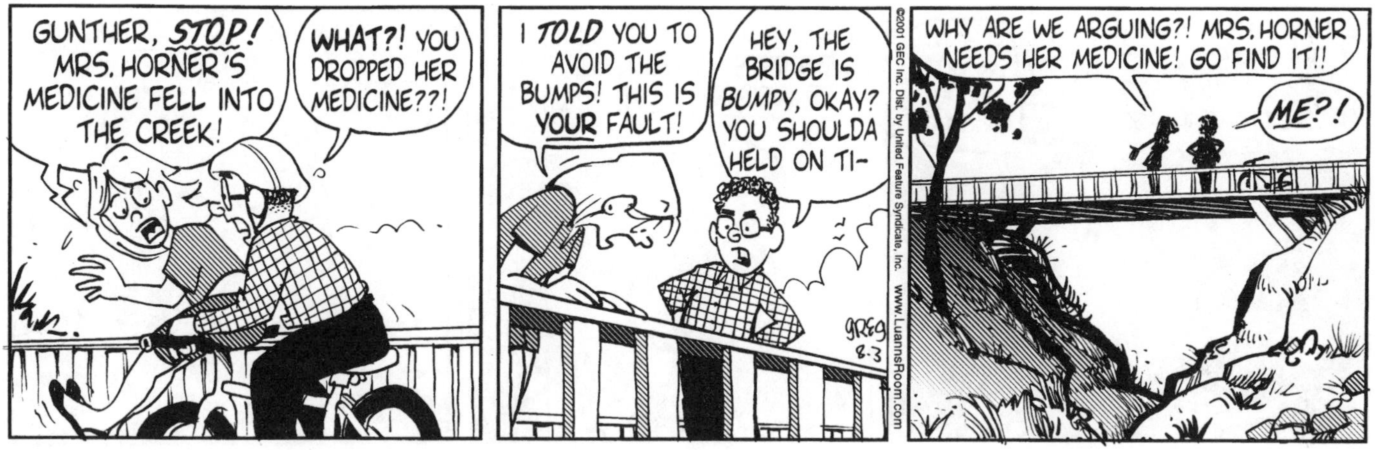
GUNTHER, ***STOP!*** MRS. HORNER'S MEDICINE FELL INTO THE CREEK!
WHAT?! YOU DROPPED HER MEDICINE??!
I ***TOLD*** YOU TO AVOID THE BUMPS! THIS IS **YOUR** FAULT!
HEY, THE BRIDGE IS *BUMPY*, OKAY? YOU SHOULDA HELD ON TI-
GREG 8·3
©2001 GEC Inc. Dist. by United Feature Syndicate, Inc. www.LuannsRoom.com
WHY ARE WE ARGUING?! MRS. HORNER NEEDS HER MEDICINE! GO FIND IT!!
ME?!

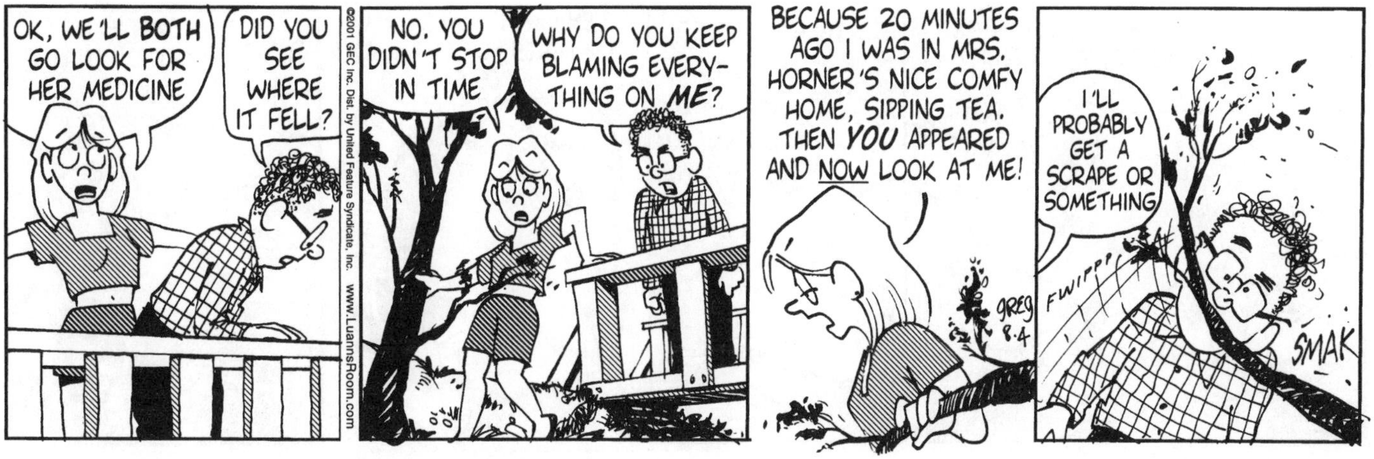
OK, WE'LL **BOTH** GO LOOK FOR HER MEDICINE
DID YOU SEE WHERE IT FELL?
©2001 GEC Inc. Dist. by United Feature Syndicate, Inc. www.LuannsRoom.com
NO. YOU DIDN'T STOP IN TIME
WHY DO YOU KEEP BLAMING EVERYTHING ON ***ME***?
BECAUSE 20 MINUTES AGO I WAS IN MRS. HORNER'S NICE COMFY HOME, SIPPING TEA. THEN ***YOU*** APPEARED AND NOW LOOK AT ME!
GREG 8·4
I'LL PROBABLY GET A SCRAPE OR SOMETHING
FWIPPP
SMAK

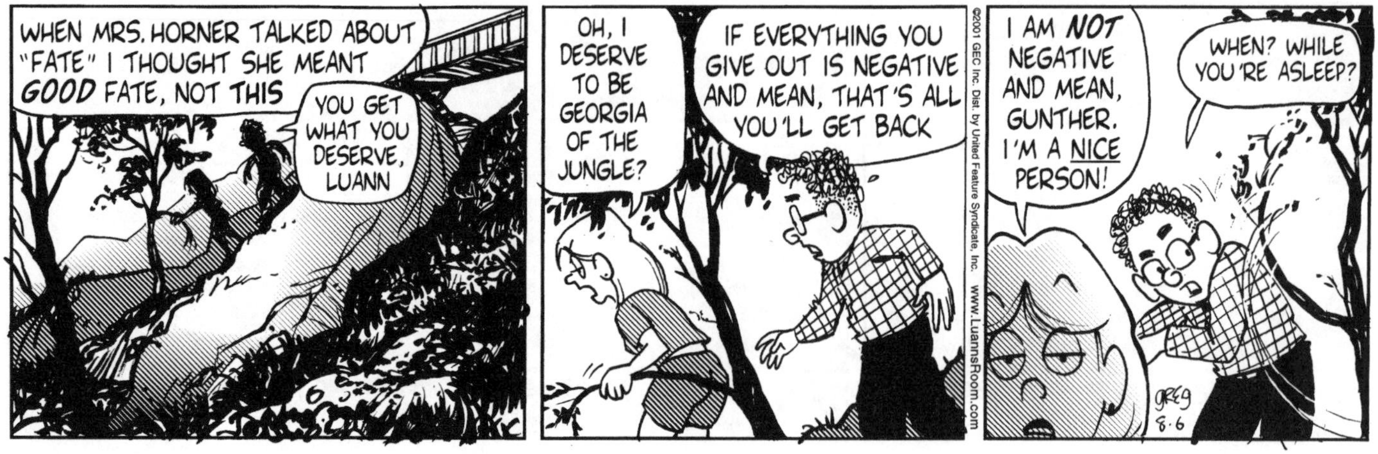
WHEN MRS. HORNER TALKED ABOUT "FATE" I THOUGHT SHE MEANT **GOOD** FATE, NOT **THIS**
YOU GET WHAT YOU DESERVE, LUANN
OH, I DESERVE TO BE GEORGIA OF THE JUNGLE?
IF EVERYTHING YOU GIVE OUT IS NEGATIVE AND MEAN, THAT'S ALL YOU'LL GET BACK
©2001 GEC Inc. Dist. by United Feature Syndicate, Inc.
www.LuannsRoom.com
I AM ***NOT*** NEGATIVE AND MEAN, GUNTHER. I'M A NICE PERSON!
WHEN? WHILE YOU'RE ASLEEP?
GREG 8·6

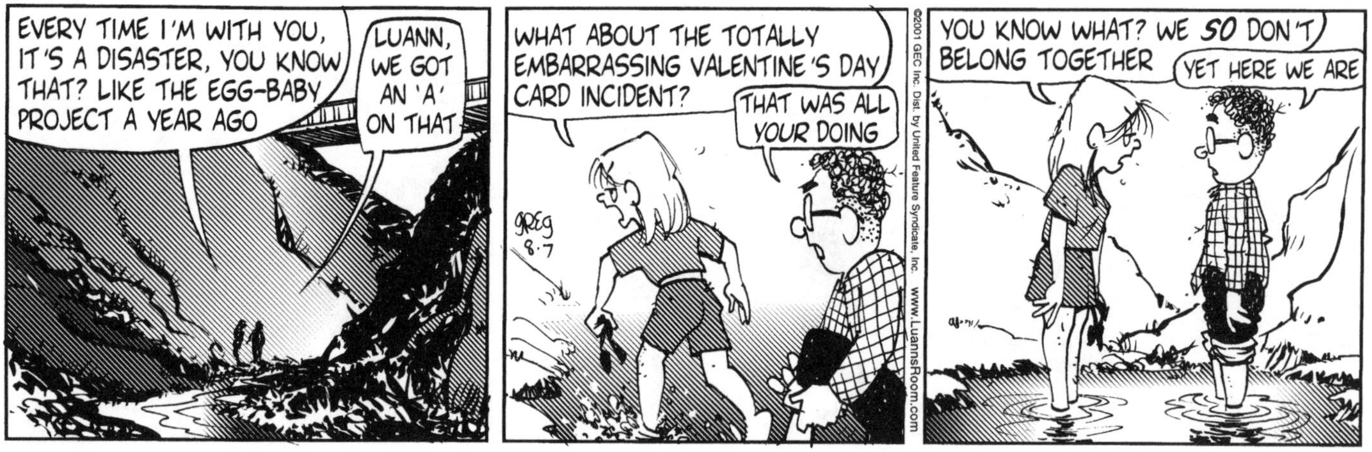
EVERY TIME I'M WITH YOU, IT'S A DISASTER, YOU KNOW THAT? LIKE THE EGG-BABY PROJECT A YEAR AGO
LUANN, WE GOT AN 'A' ON THAT
WHAT ABOUT THE TOTALLY EMBARRASSING VALENTINE'S DAY CARD INCIDENT?
THAT WAS ALL *YOUR* DOING
GREG 8·7
©2001 GEC Inc. Dist. by United Feature Syndicate, Inc.
www.LuannsRoom.com
YOU KNOW WHAT? WE ***SO*** DON'T BELONG TOGETHER
YET HERE WE ARE

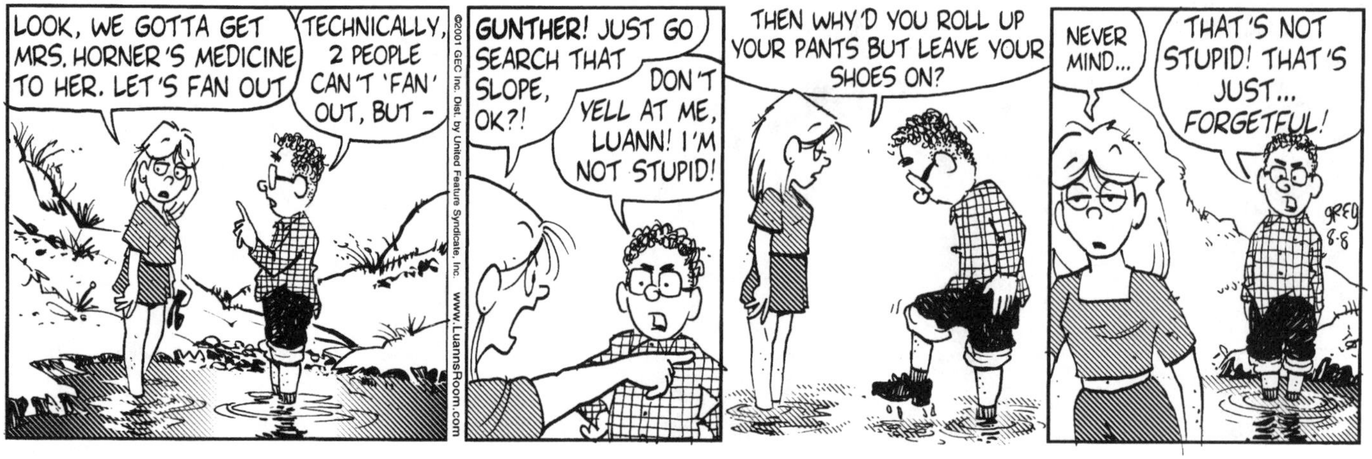
LOOK, WE GOTTA GET MRS. HORNER'S MEDICINE TO HER. LET'S FAN OUT
TECHNICALLY, 2 PEOPLE CAN'T 'FAN' OUT, BUT –
©2001 GEC Inc. Dist. by United Feature Syndicate, Inc.
www.LuannsRoom.com
GUNTHER! JUST GO SEARCH THAT SLOPE, OK?!
DON'T *YELL* AT ME, LUANN! I'M NOT STUPID!
THEN WHY'D YOU ROLL UP YOUR PANTS BUT LEAVE YOUR SHOES ON?
NEVER MIND...
THAT'S NOT STUPID! THAT'S JUST... *FORGETFUL!*
GREG 8·8

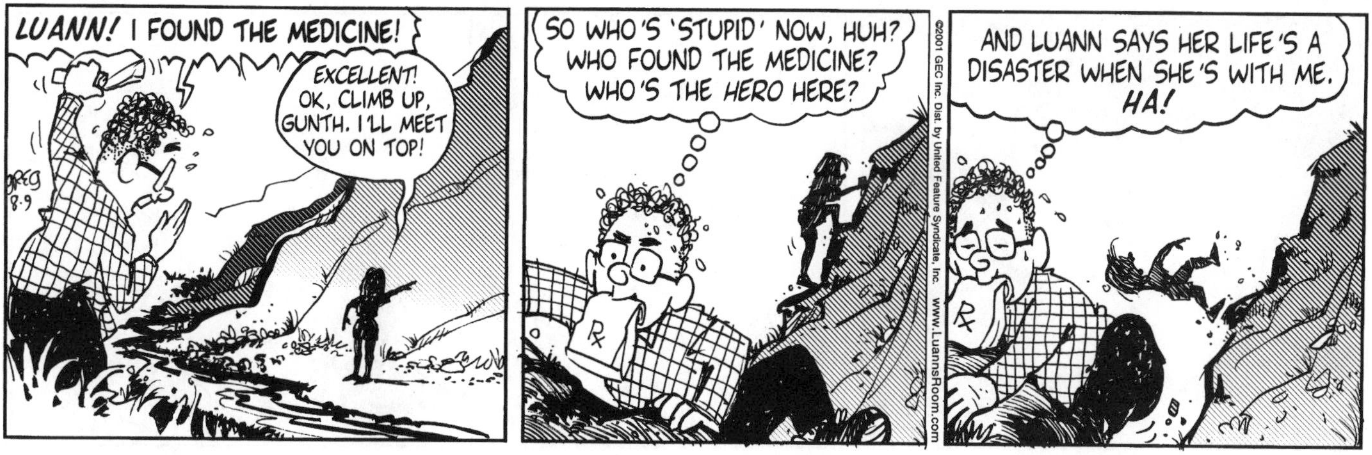
LUANN! I FOUND THE MEDICINE!
EXCELLENT! OK, CLIMB UP, GUNTH. I'LL MEET YOU ON TOP!
GREG 8-9
SO WHO'S 'STUPID' NOW, HUH? WHO FOUND THE MEDICINE? WHO'S THE HERO HERE?
©2001 GEC Inc. Dist. by United Feature Syndicate, Inc. www.LuannsRoom.com
AND LUANN SAYS HER LIFE'S A DISASTER WHEN SHE'S WITH ME. HA!

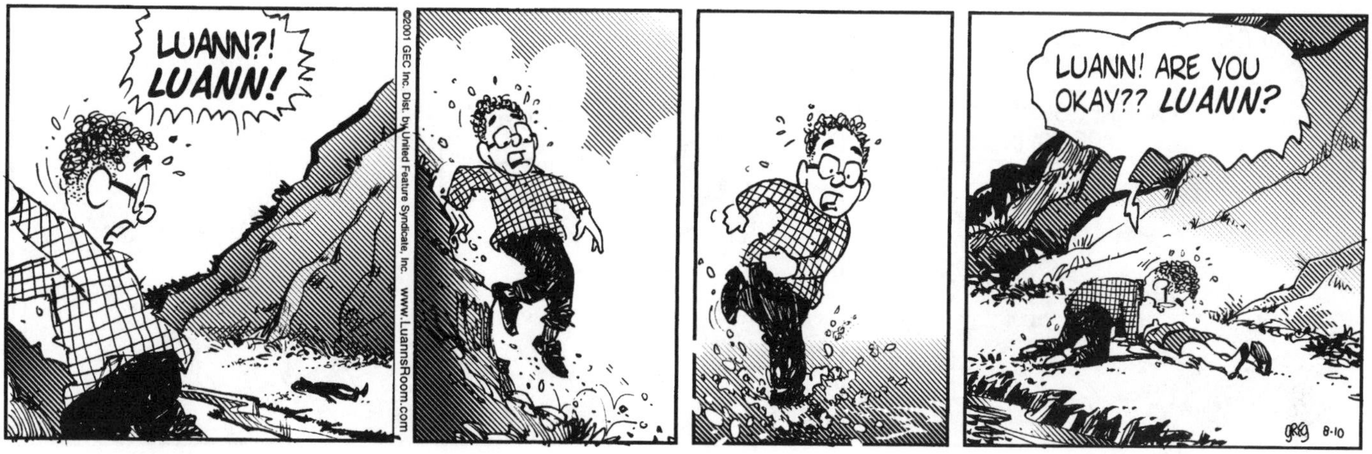
LUANN?! LUANN!
©2001 GEC Inc. Dist. by United Feature Syndicate, Inc. www.LuannsRoom.com
LUANN! ARE YOU OKAY?? LUANN?
GREG 8-10

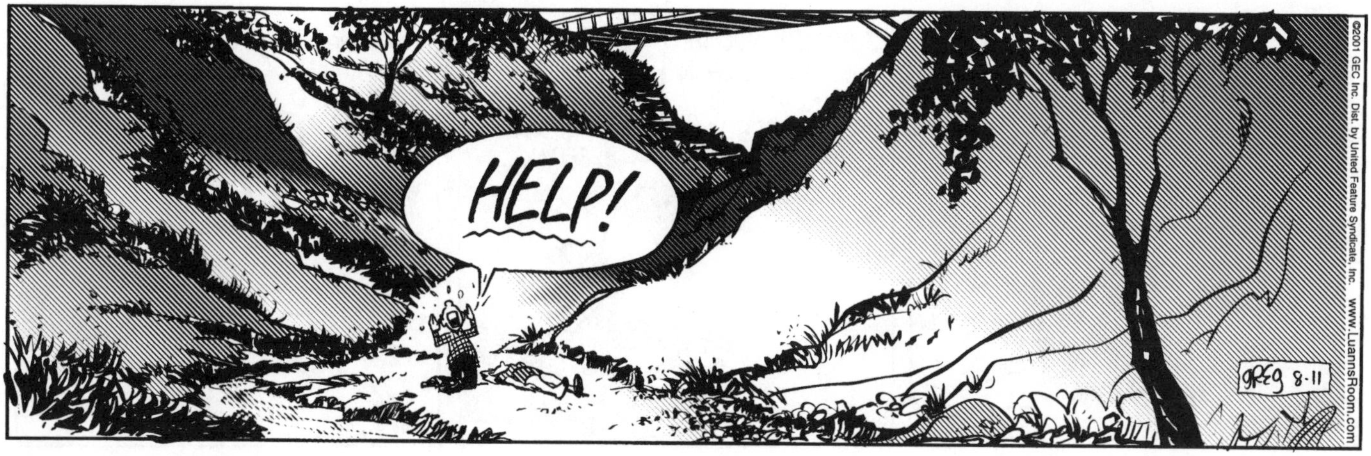
HELP!
GREG 8-11
©2001 GEC Inc. Dist. by United Feature Syndicate, Inc. www.LuannsRoom.com

HELP!
HEEELL~
STOP SCREAMING
©2001 GEC Inc. Dist. by United Feature Syndicate, Inc. www.LuannsRoom.com
YOU'RE GIVING ME A HEADACHE...
GREG 8-13

LUANN! DON'T GET UP! YOU SHOULD REST!!
I'M FINE, GUNTH. NO BONES ARE POKING OUT
BUT... YOUR HAIR'S BLEEDING!
MY HAIR?!
©2001 GEC Inc. Dist. by United Feature Syndicate, Inc. www.LuannsRoom.com
YOUR HEAD - YOU CUT YOUR HEAD!
I'M GONNA REST NOW...
GREG 8-14

HOW BAD IS IT?
JUST A SMALL SCALP LACERATION. BUT THESE TEND TO BLEED PROFUSELY. I HAVE A CLEAN HANKY...
GUNTHER, YOU'RE THE ONLY PERSON I KNOW WHO USES WORDS LIKE LACERATION AND PROFUSELY
I'LL JUST APPLY A LITTLE PRESSURE TO STOP THE BLEEDING...
©2001 GEC Inc. Dist. by United Feature Syndicate, Inc. www.LuannsRoom.com
AND I BET YOU'RE THE ONLY TEENAGE GUY ON EARTH WHO CARRIES A CLEAN HANKY
GREG 8-15

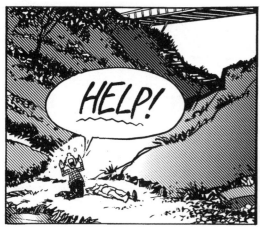

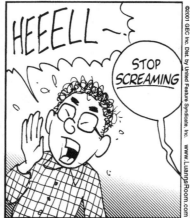

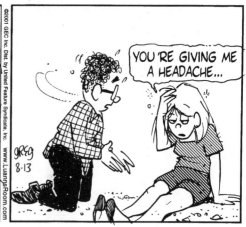

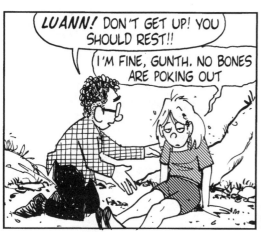

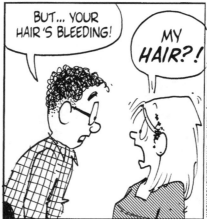

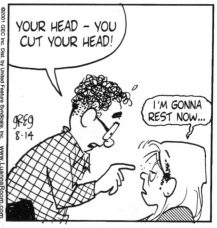

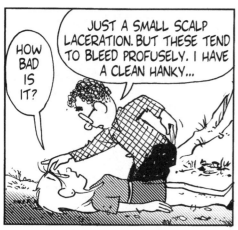

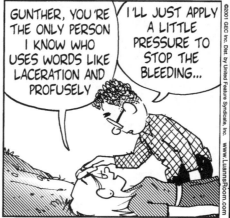

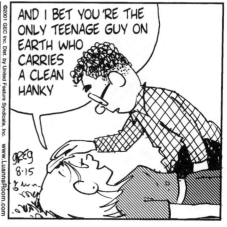

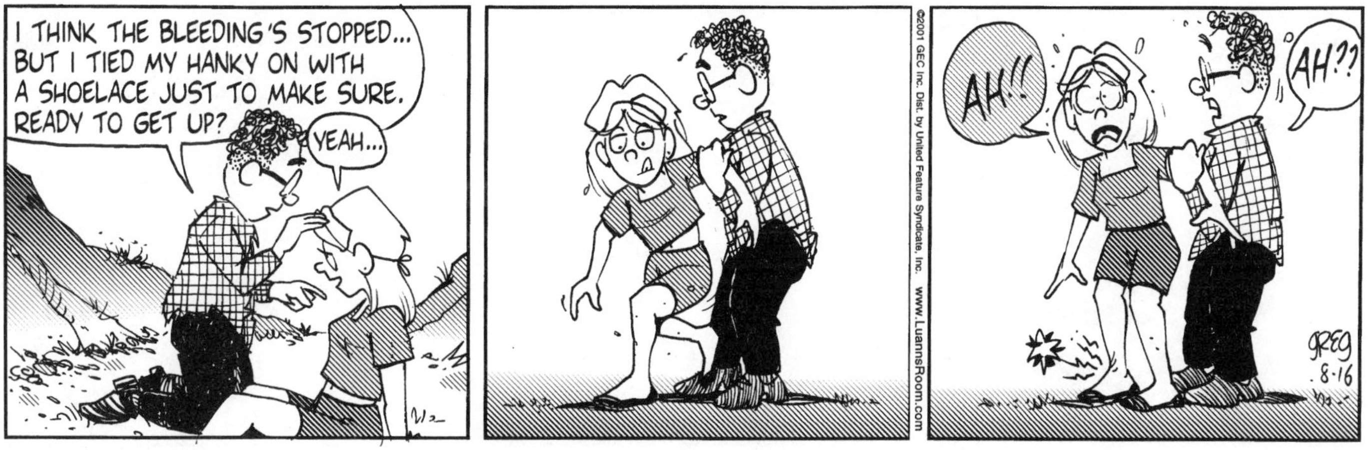
I THINK THE BLEEDING'S STOPPED... BUT I TIED MY HANKY ON WITH A SHOELACE JUST TO MAKE SURE. READY TO GET UP?
YEAH...
©2001 GEC Inc. Dist. by United Feature Syndicate, Inc.
www.LuannsRoom.com
AH!!
AH??
GREG 8·16

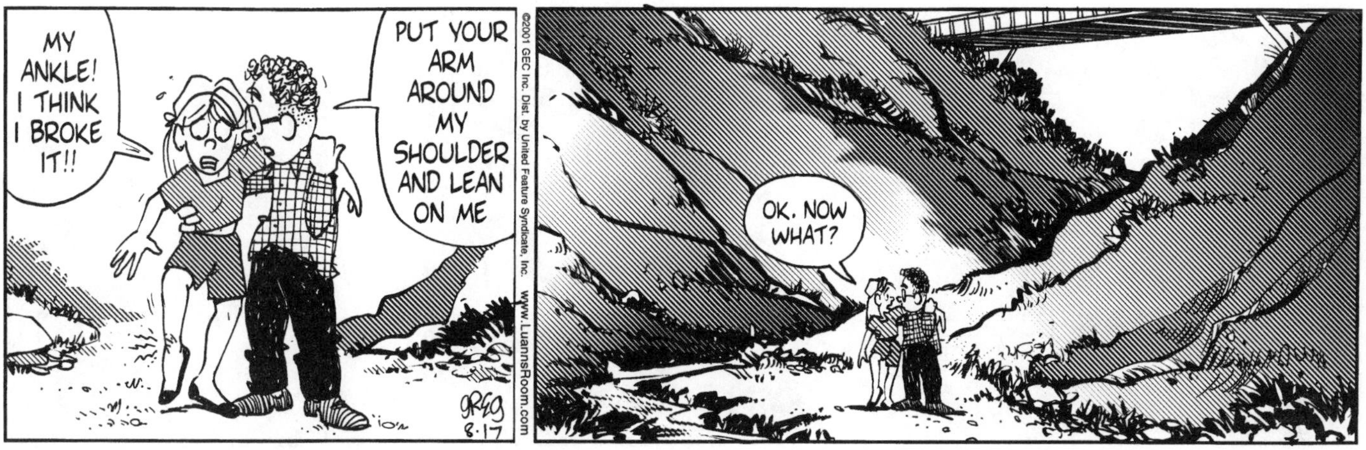
MY ANKLE! I THINK I BROKE IT!!
PUT YOUR ARM AROUND MY SHOULDER AND LEAN ON ME
GREG 8·17
©2001 GEC Inc. Dist. by United Feature Syndicate, Inc.
www.LuannsRoom.com
OK. NOW WHAT?

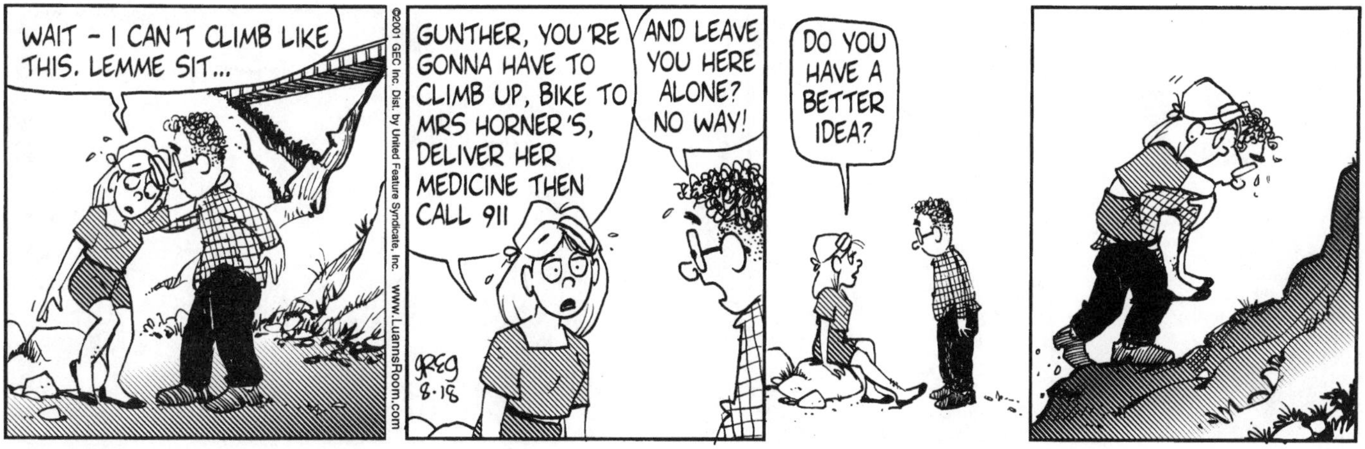
WAIT - I CAN'T CLIMB LIKE THIS. LEMME SIT...
©2001 GEC Inc. Dist. by United Feature Syndicate, Inc.
www.LuannsRoom.com
GUNTHER, YOU'RE GONNA HAVE TO CLIMB UP, BIKE TO MRS HORNER'S, DELIVER HER MEDICINE THEN CALL 911
AND LEAVE YOU HERE ALONE? NO WAY!
GREG 8·18
DO YOU HAVE A BETTER IDEA?

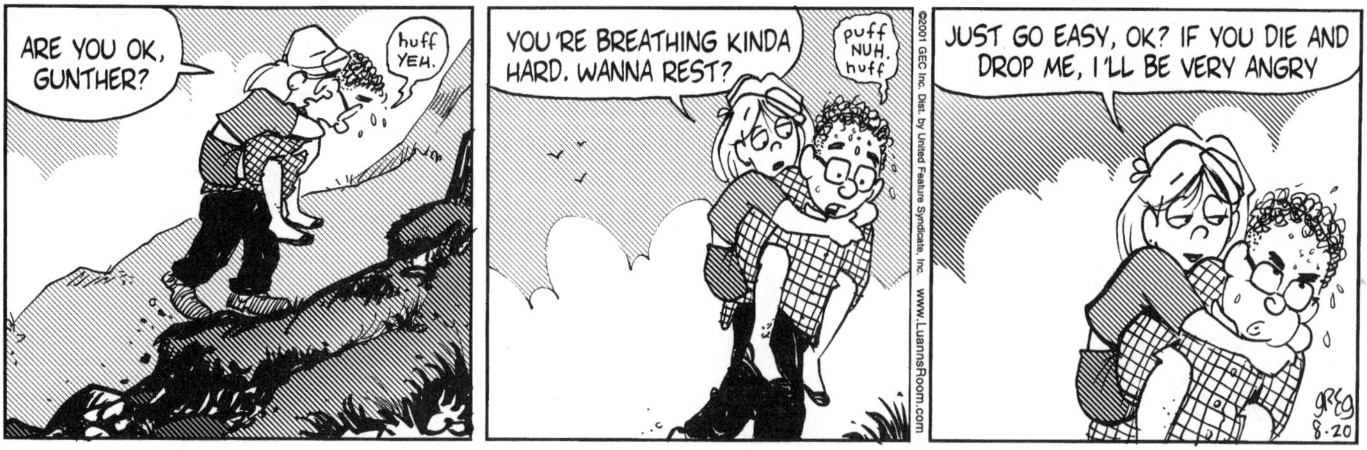
ARE YOU OK, GUNTHER?
huff YEH.
YOU'RE BREATHING KINDA HARD. WANNA REST?
puff NUH. huff
©2001 GEC Inc. Dist. by United Feature Syndicate, Inc. www.LuannsRoom.com
JUST GO EASY, OK? IF YOU DIE AND DROP ME, I'LL BE VERY ANGRY
GREG 8-20

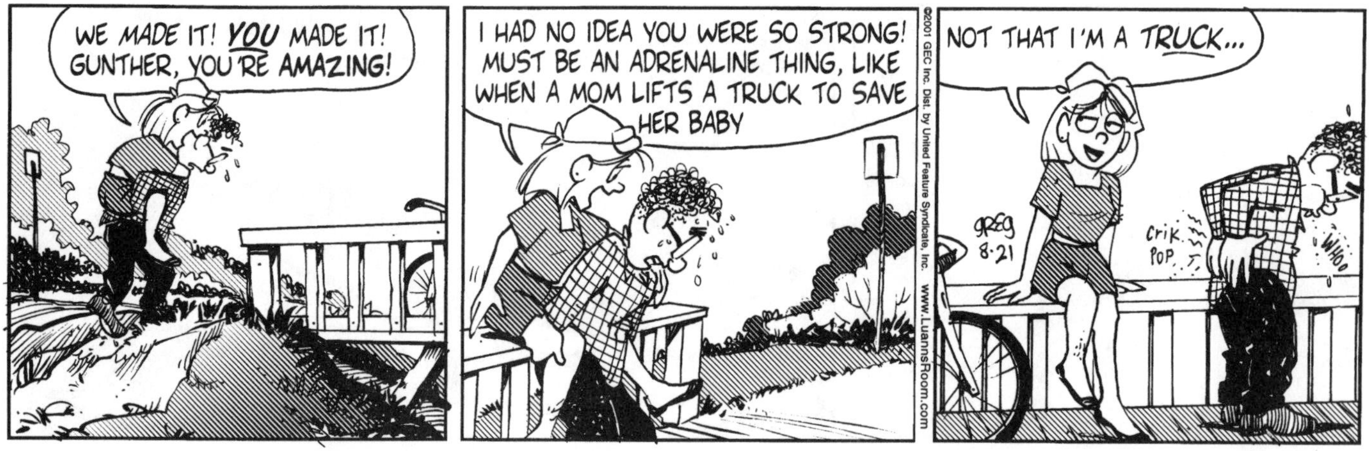
WE MADE IT! YOU MADE IT! GUNTHER, YOU'RE AMAZING!
I HAD NO IDEA YOU WERE SO STRONG! MUST BE AN ADRENALINE THING, LIKE WHEN A MOM LIFTS A TRUCK TO SAVE HER BABY
©2001 GEC Inc. Dist. by United Feature Syndicate, Inc. www.LuannsRoom.com
NOT THAT I'M A TRUCK...
GREG 8-21
CRIK POP
WHOO

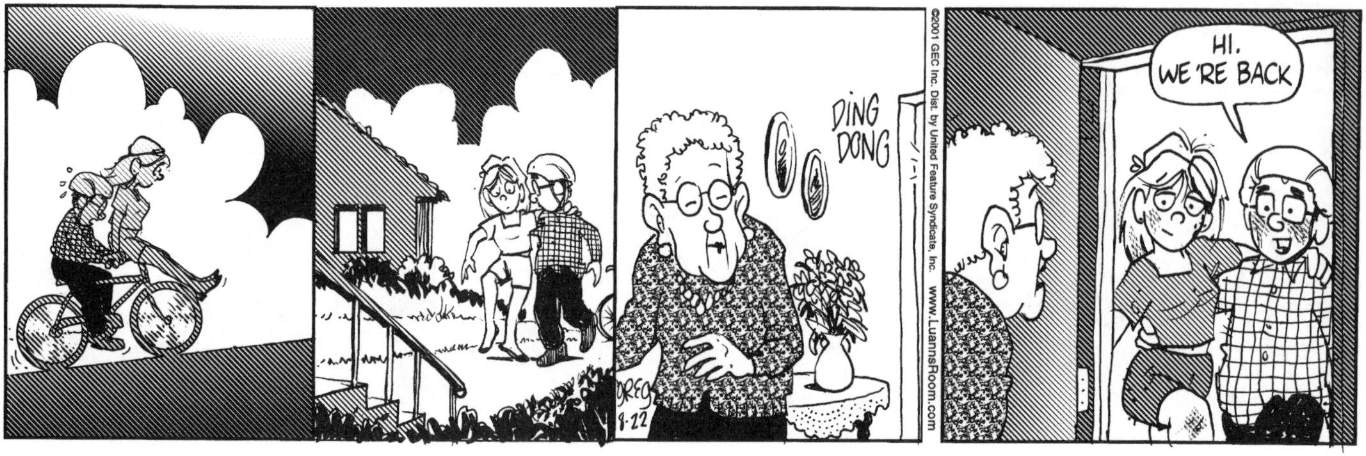
DING DONG
GREG 8-22
©2001 GEC Inc. Dist. by United Feature Syndicate, Inc. www.LuannsRoom.com
HI. WE'RE BACK

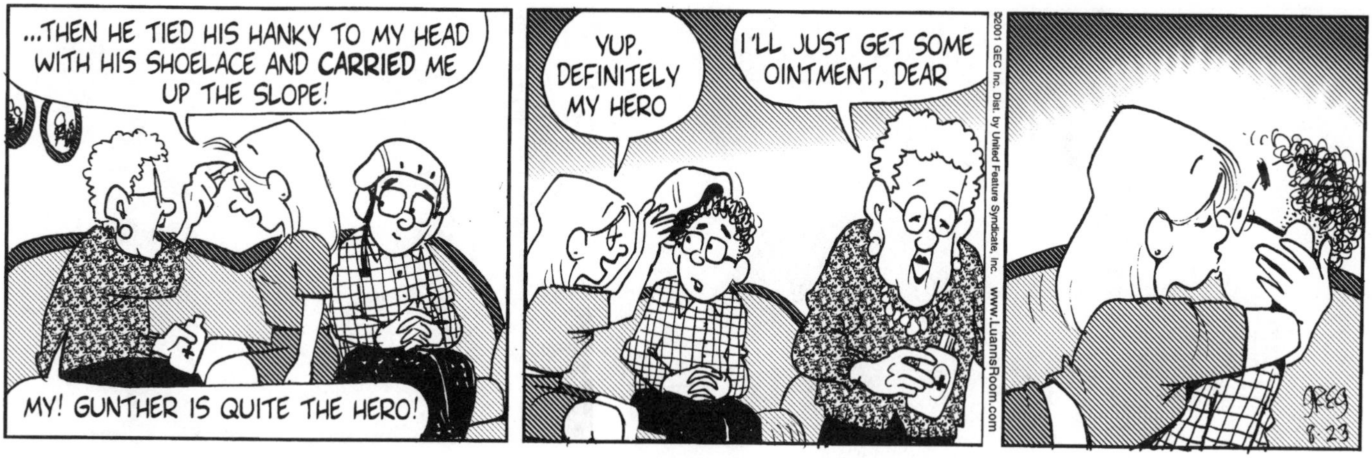
...THEN HE TIED HIS HANKY TO MY HEAD WITH HIS SHOELACE AND CARRIED ME UP THE SLOPE!
MY! GUNTHER IS QUITE THE HERO!
YUP. DEFINITELY MY HERO
I'LL JUST GET SOME OINTMENT, DEAR
©2001 GEC Inc. Dist. by United Feature Syndicate, Inc. www.LuannsRoom.com
GREG 8·23

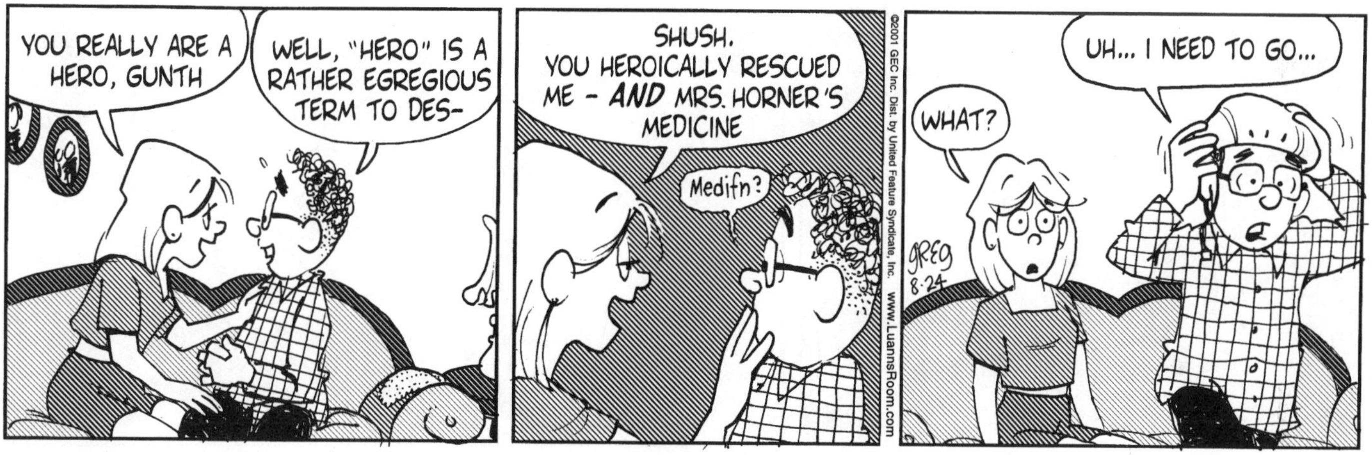
YOU REALLY ARE A HERO, GUNTH
WELL, "HERO" IS A RATHER EGREGIOUS TERM TO DES-
SHUSH. YOU HEROICALLY RESCUED ME – AND MRS. HORNER'S MEDICINE
Medifn?
©2001 GEC Inc. Dist. by United Feature Syndicate, Inc. www.LuannsRoom.com
GREG 8·24
WHAT?
UH... I NEED TO GO...

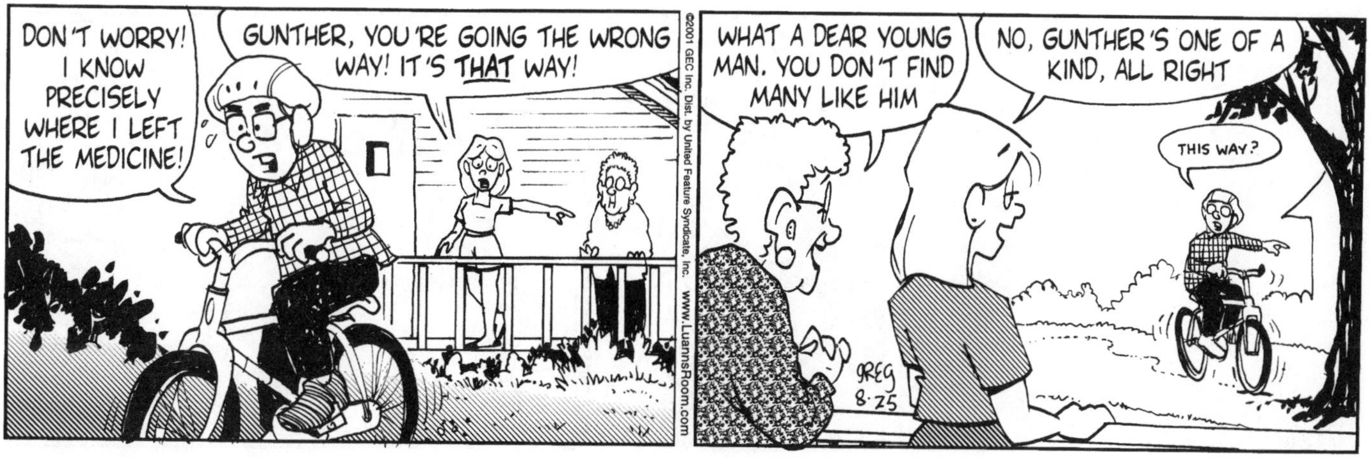
DON'T WORRY! I KNOW PRECISELY WHERE I LEFT THE MEDICINE!
GUNTHER, YOU'RE GOING THE WRONG WAY! IT'S THAT WAY!
©2001 GEC Inc. Dist. by United Feature Syndicate, Inc. www.LuannsRoom.com
WHAT A DEAR YOUNG MAN. YOU DON'T FIND MANY LIKE HIM
NO, GUNTHER'S ONE OF A KIND, ALL RIGHT
THIS WAY?
GREG 8·25

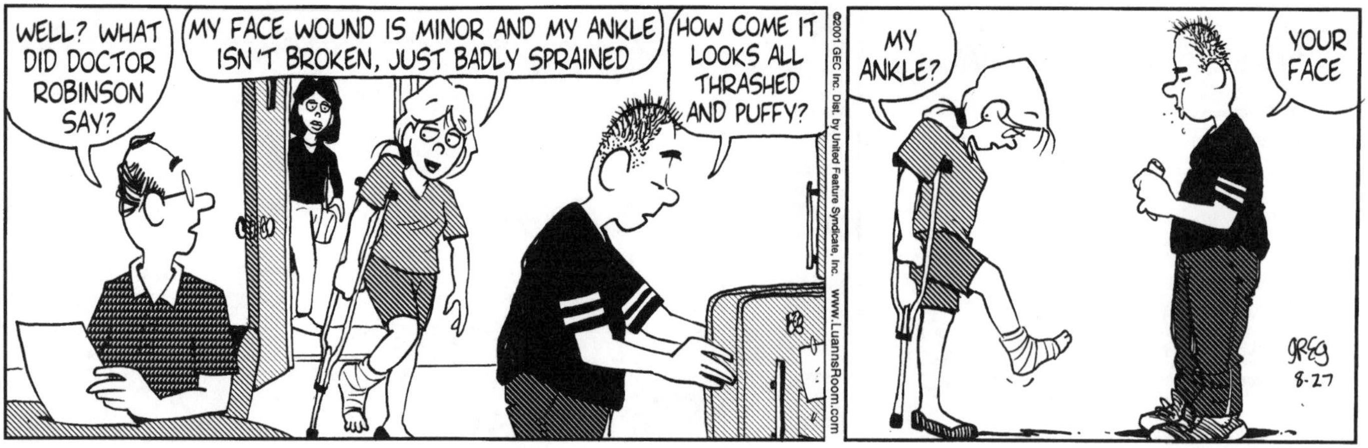
WELL? WHAT DID DOCTOR ROBINSON SAY?
MY FACE WOUND IS MINOR AND MY ANKLE ISN'T BROKEN, JUST BADLY SPRAINED
HOW COME IT LOOKS ALL THRASHED AND PUFFY?
©2001 GEC Inc. Dist. by United Feature Syndicate, Inc. www.LuannsRoom.com
MY ANKLE?
YOUR FACE
GREG 8·27

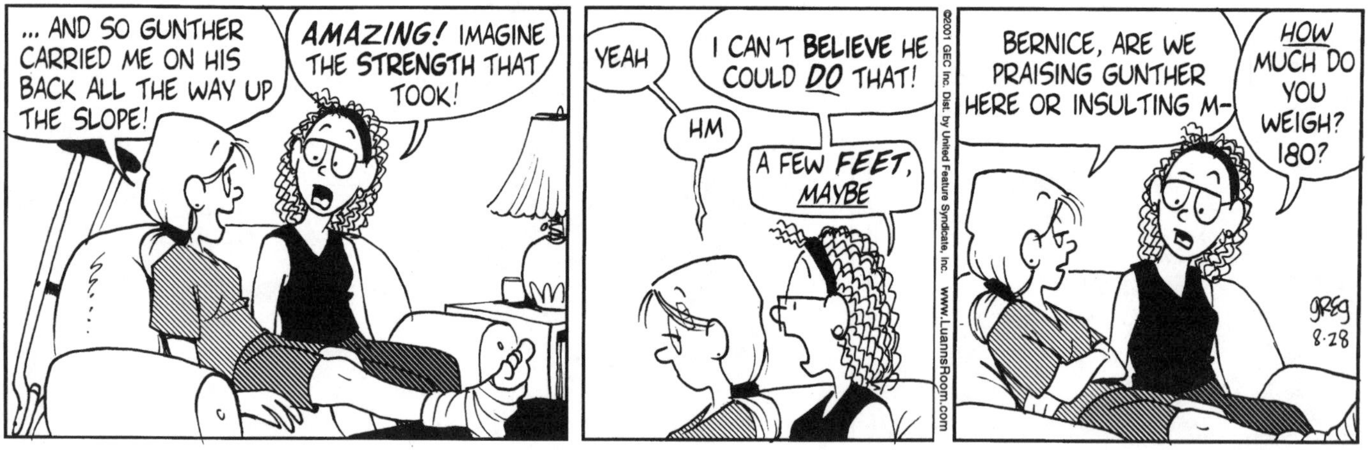
... AND SO GUNTHER CARRIED ME ON HIS BACK ALL THE WAY UP THE SLOPE!
AMAZING! IMAGINE THE STRENGTH THAT TOOK!
YEAH
I CAN'T BELIEVE HE COULD DO THAT!
HM
A FEW FEET, MAYBE
©2001 GEC Inc. Dist. by United Feature Syndicate, Inc. www.LuannsRoom.com
BERNICE, ARE WE PRAISING GUNTHER HERE OR INSULTING M-
HOW MUCH DO YOU WEIGH? 180?
GREG 8·28

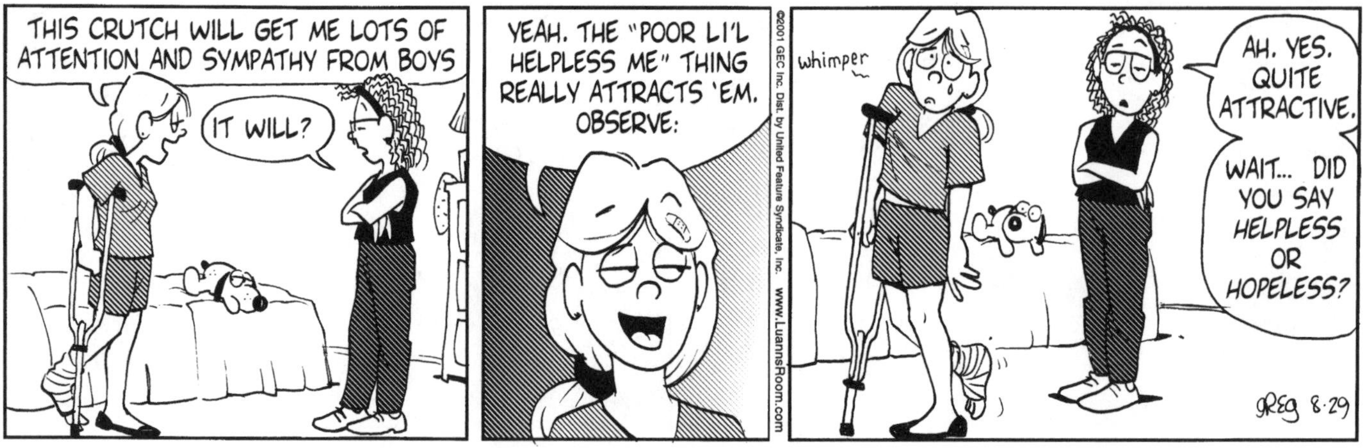
THIS CRUTCH WILL GET ME LOTS OF ATTENTION AND SYMPATHY FROM BOYS
IT WILL?
YEAH. THE "POOR LI'L HELPLESS ME" THING REALLY ATTRACTS 'EM. OBSERVE:
©2001 GEC Inc. Dist. by United Feature Syndicate, Inc. www.LuannsRoom.com
whimper
AH. YES. QUITE ATTRACTIVE.
WAIT... DID YOU SAY HELPLESS OR HOPELESS?
GREG 8·29

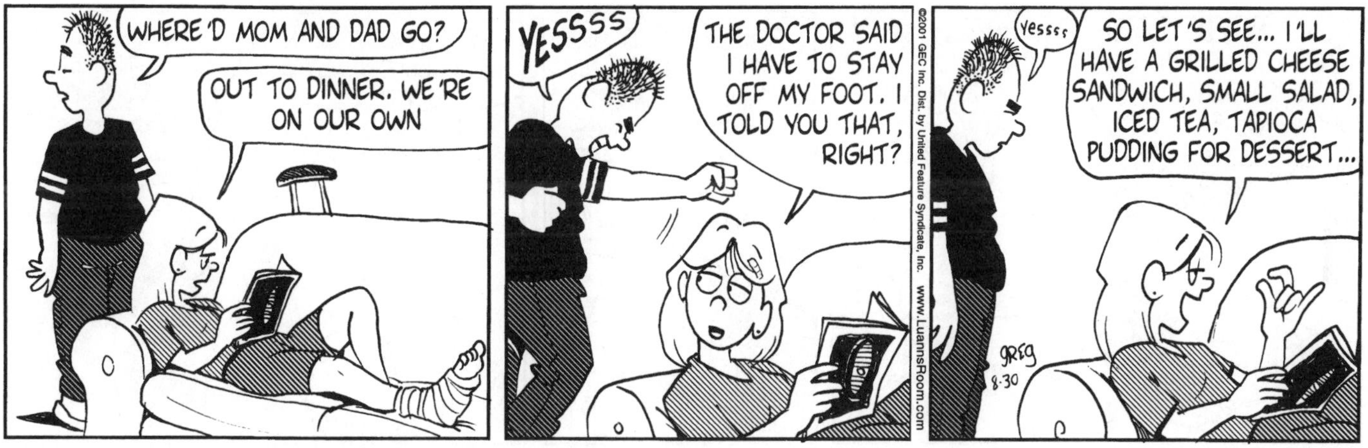
WHERE'D MOM AND DAD GO?
OUT TO DINNER. WE'RE ON OUR OWN
YESSSS
THE DOCTOR SAID I HAVE TO STAY OFF MY FOOT. I TOLD YOU THAT, RIGHT?
©2001 GEC Inc. Dist. by United Feature Syndicate, Inc. www.LuannsRoom.com
Yessss
SO LET'S SEE... I'LL HAVE A GRILLED CHEESE SANDWICH, SMALL SALAD, ICED TEA, TAPIOCA PUDDING FOR DESSERT...
GREG 8·30

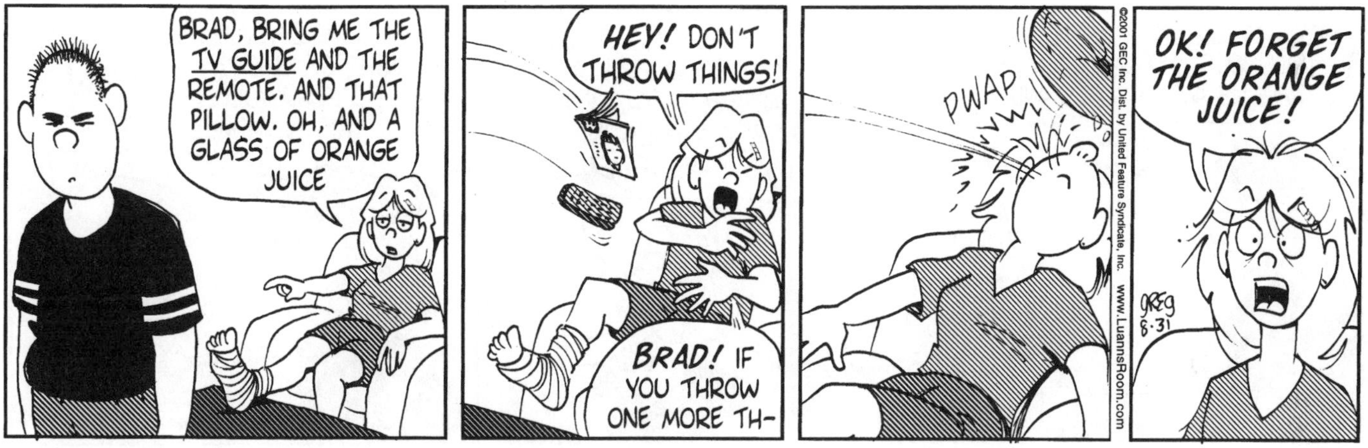
BRAD, BRING ME THE TV GUIDE AND THE REMOTE. AND THAT PILLOW. OH, AND A GLASS OF ORANGE JUICE
HEY! DON'T THROW THINGS!
BRAD! IF YOU THROW ONE MORE TH-
PWAP
©2001 GEC Inc. Dist. by United Feature Syndicate, Inc. www.LuannsRoom.com
OK! FORGET THE ORANGE JUICE!
GREG 8·31

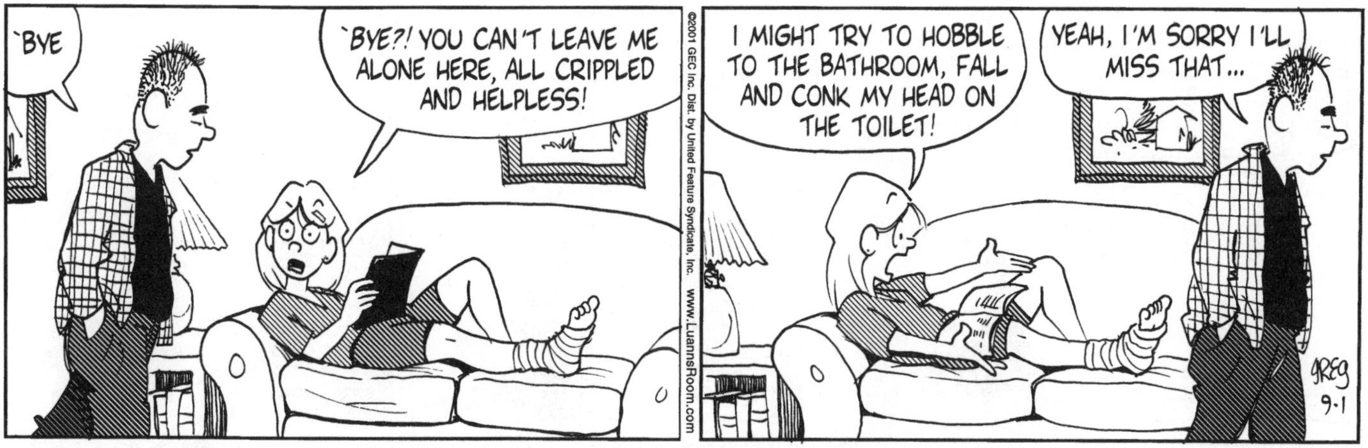
`BYE
`BYE?! YOU CAN'T LEAVE ME ALONE HERE, ALL CRIPPLED AND HELPLESS!
©2001 GEC Inc. Dist. by United Feature Syndicate, Inc. www.LuannsRoom.com
I MIGHT TRY TO HOBBLE TO THE BATHROOM, FALL AND CONK MY HEAD ON THE TOILET!
YEAH, I'M SORRY I'LL MISS THAT...
GREG 9·1

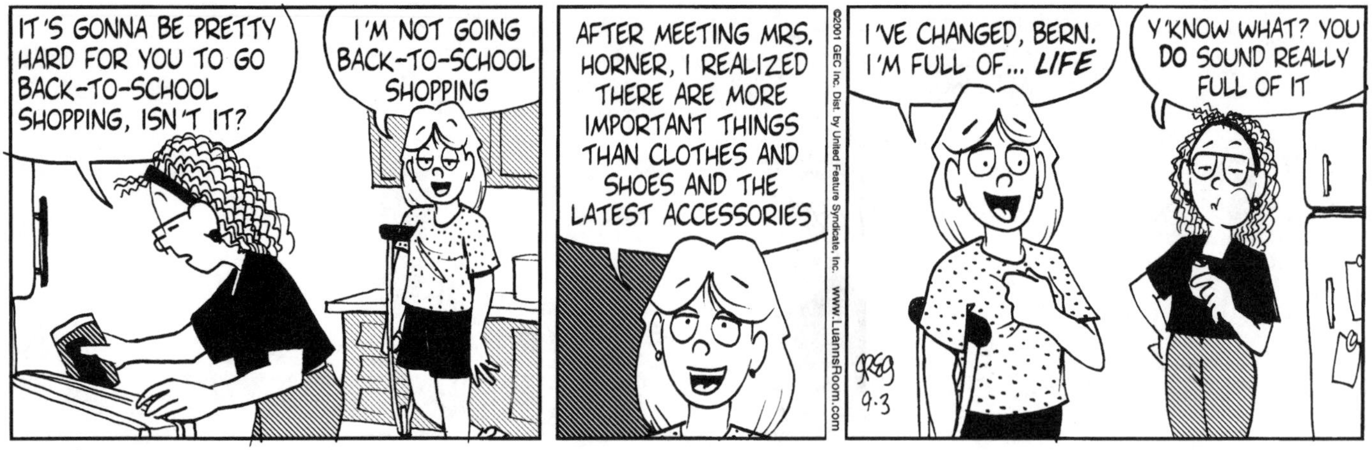
IT'S GONNA BE PRETTY HARD FOR YOU TO GO BACK-TO-SCHOOL SHOPPING, ISN'T IT?
I'M NOT GOING BACK-TO-SCHOOL SHOPPING
AFTER MEETING MRS. HORNER, I REALIZED THERE ARE MORE IMPORTANT THINGS THAN CLOTHES AND SHOES AND THE LATEST ACCESSORIES
©2001 GEC Inc. Dist. by United Feature Syndicate, Inc. www.LuannsRoom.com
I'VE CHANGED, BERN. I'M FULL OF... **LIFE**
Y'KNOW WHAT? YOU **DO** SOUND REALLY FULL OF IT
GREG 9-3

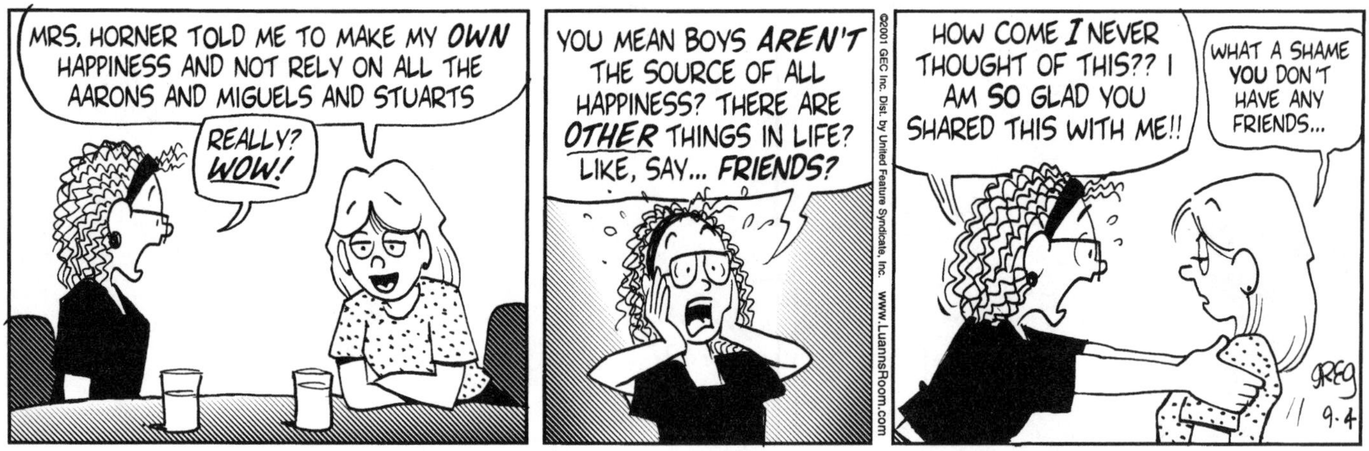
MRS. HORNER TOLD ME TO MAKE MY **OWN** HAPPINESS AND NOT RELY ON ALL THE AARONS AND MIGUELS AND STUARTS
REALLY? **WOW!**
YOU MEAN BOYS **AREN'T** THE SOURCE OF ALL HAPPINESS? THERE ARE **OTHER** THINGS IN LIFE? LIKE, SAY... **FRIENDS?**
©2001 GEC Inc. Dist. by United Feature Syndicate, Inc. www.LuannsRoom.com
HOW COME **I** NEVER THOUGHT OF THIS?? I AM **SO** GLAD YOU SHARED THIS WITH ME!!
WHAT A SHAME **YOU** DON'T HAVE ANY FRIENDS...
GREG 9-4

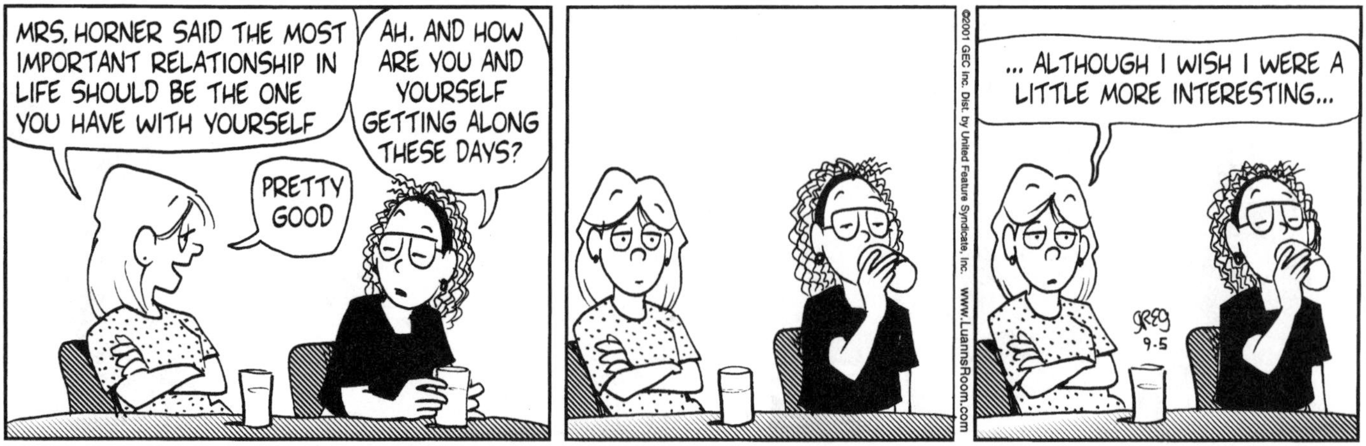
MRS. HORNER SAID THE MOST IMPORTANT RELATIONSHIP IN LIFE SHOULD BE THE ONE YOU HAVE WITH YOURSELF
AH. AND HOW ARE YOU AND YOURSELF GETTING ALONG THESE DAYS?
PRETTY GOOD
©2001 GEC Inc. Dist. by United Feature Syndicate, Inc. www.LuannsRoom.com
... ALTHOUGH I WISH I WERE A LITTLE MORE INTERESTING...
GREG 9-5

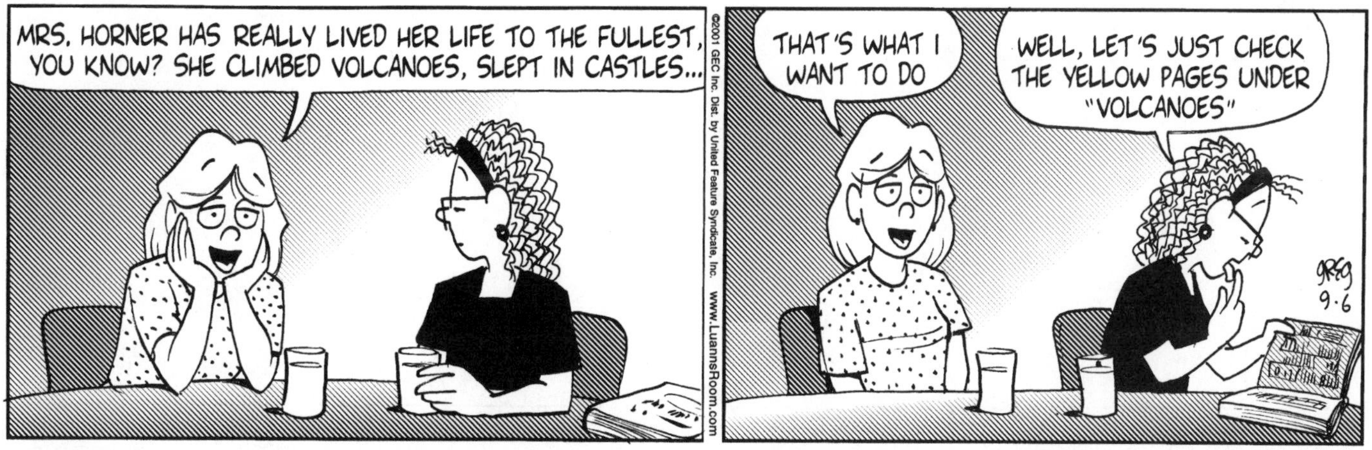
MRS. HORNER HAS REALLY LIVED HER LIFE TO THE FULLEST, YOU KNOW? SHE CLIMBED VOLCANOES, SLEPT IN CASTLES...
©2001 GEC Inc. Dist. by United Feature Syndicate, Inc. www.LuannsRoom.com
THAT'S WHAT I WANT TO DO
WELL, LET'S JUST CHECK THE YELLOW PAGES UNDER "VOLCANOES"
GREG 9·6

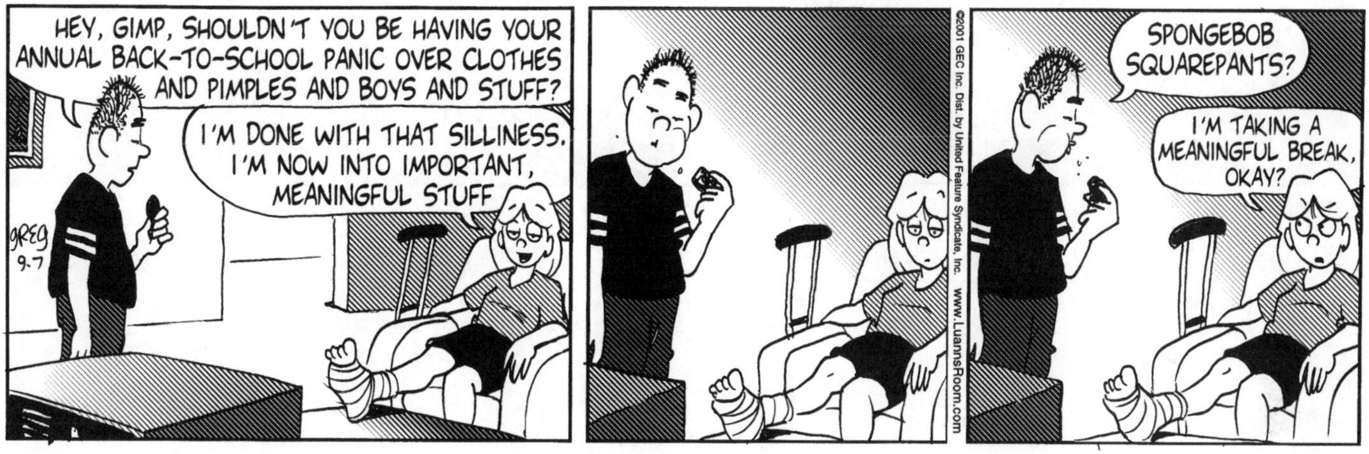
HEY, GIMP, SHOULDN'T YOU BE HAVING YOUR ANNUAL BACK-TO-SCHOOL PANIC OVER CLOTHES AND PIMPLES AND BOYS AND STUFF?
I'M DONE WITH THAT SILLINESS. I'M NOW INTO IMPORTANT, MEANINGFUL STUFF
GREG 9·7
©2001 GEC Inc. Dist. by United Feature Syndicate, Inc. www.LuannsRoom.com
SPONGEBOB SQUAREPANTS?
I'M TAKING A MEANINGFUL BREAK, OKAY?

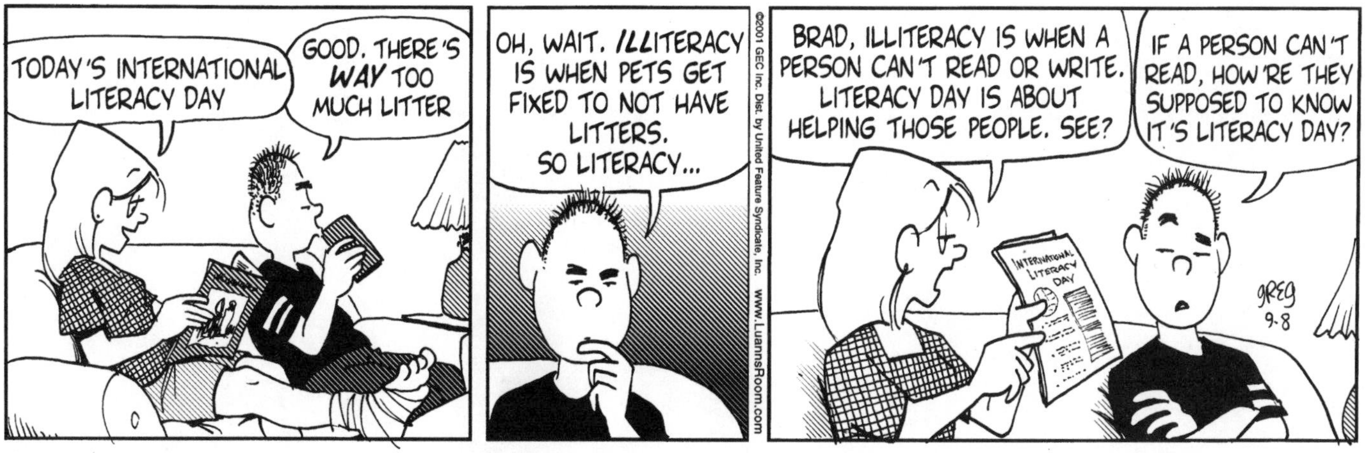
TODAY'S INTERNATIONAL LITERACY DAY
GOOD. THERE'S WAY TOO MUCH LITTER
OH, WAIT. ILLITERACY IS WHEN PETS GET FIXED TO NOT HAVE LITTERS. SO LITERACY...
©2001 GEC Inc. Dist. by United Feature Syndicate, Inc. www.LuannsRoom.com
BRAD, ILLITERACY IS WHEN A PERSON CAN'T READ OR WRITE. LITERACY DAY IS ABOUT HELPING THOSE PEOPLE. SEE?
IF A PERSON CAN'T READ, HOW'RE THEY SUPPOSED TO KNOW IT'S LITERACY DAY?
INTERNATIONAL LITERACY DAY
GREG 9·8

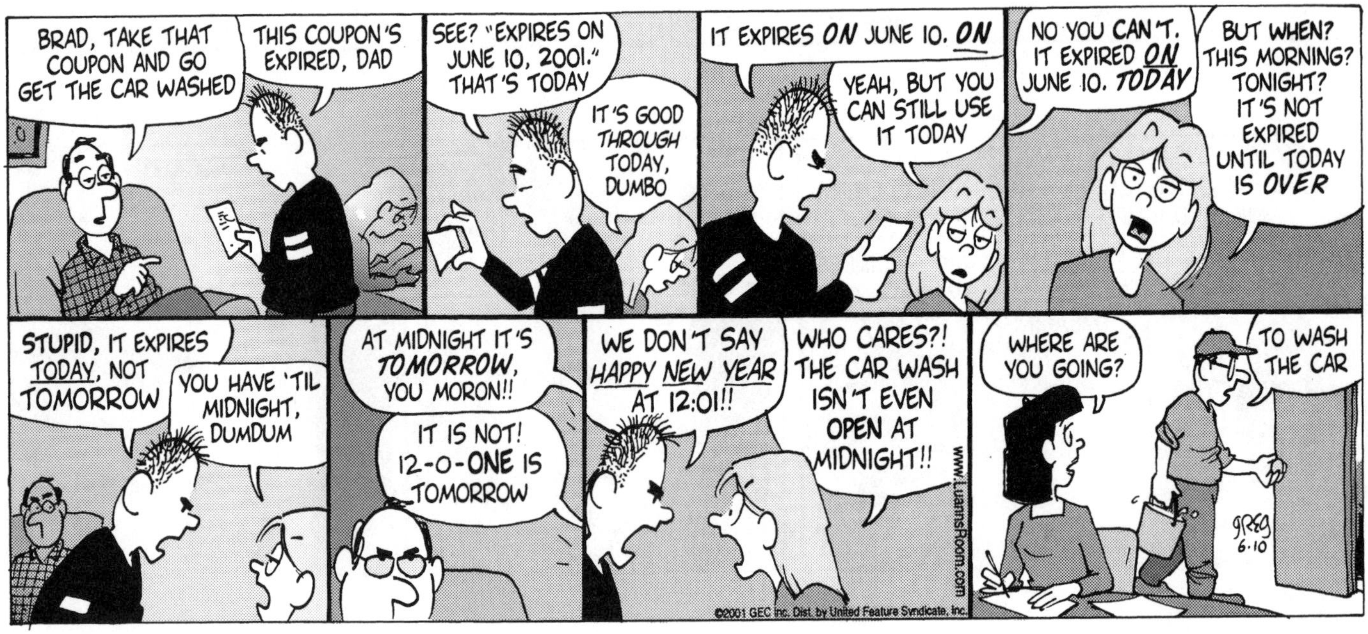
BRAD, TAKE THAT COUPON AND GO GET THE CAR WASHED
THIS COUPON'S EXPIRED, DAD
SEE? "EXPIRES ON JUNE 10, 2001." THAT'S TODAY
IT'S GOOD THROUGH TODAY, DUMBO
IT EXPIRES ON JUNE 10. ON
YEAH, BUT YOU CAN STILL USE IT TODAY
NO YOU CAN'T. IT EXPIRED ON JUNE 10. TODAY
BUT WHEN? THIS MORNING? TONIGHT? IT'S NOT EXPIRED UNTIL TODAY IS OVER
STUPID, IT EXPIRES TODAY, NOT TOMORROW
YOU HAVE 'TIL MIDNIGHT, DUMDUM
AT MIDNIGHT IT'S TOMORROW, YOU MORON!!
IT IS NOT! 12-O-ONE IS TOMORROW
WE DON'T SAY HAPPY NEW YEAR AT 12:01!!
WHO CARES?! THE CAR WASH ISN'T EVEN OPEN AT MIDNIGHT!!
www.LuannsRoom.com
©2001 GEC Inc. Dist. by United Feature Syndicate, Inc.
WHERE ARE YOU GOING?
TO WASH THE CAR
GREG 6.10

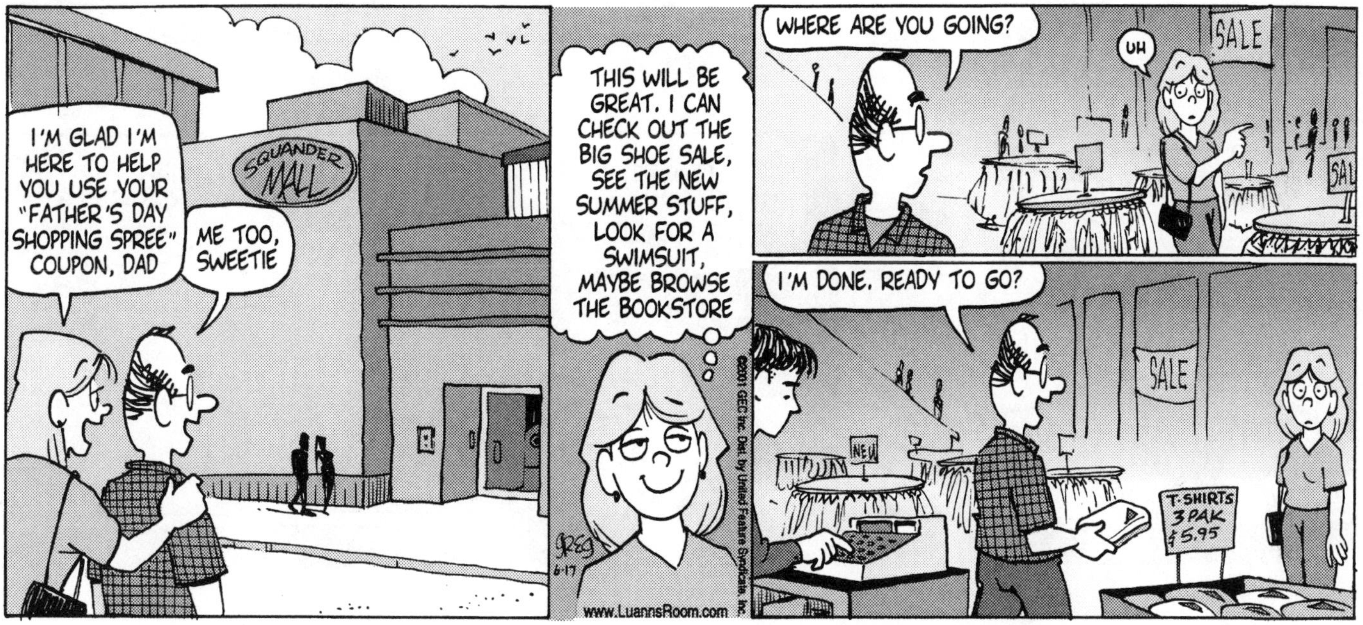
SQUANDER MALL
I'M GLAD I'M HERE TO HELP YOU USE YOUR "FATHER'S DAY SHOPPING SPREE" COUPON, DAD
ME TOO, SWEETIE
THIS WILL BE GREAT. I CAN CHECK OUT THE BIG SHOE SALE, SEE THE NEW SUMMER STUFF, LOOK FOR A SWIMSUIT, MAYBE BROWSE THE BOOKSTORE
©2001 GEC Inc. Dist. by United Feature Syndicate, Inc.
www.LuannsRoom.com
WHERE ARE YOU GOING?
UH
SALE
I'M DONE. READY TO GO?
NEW
SALE
T-SHIRTS 3 PAK $5.95

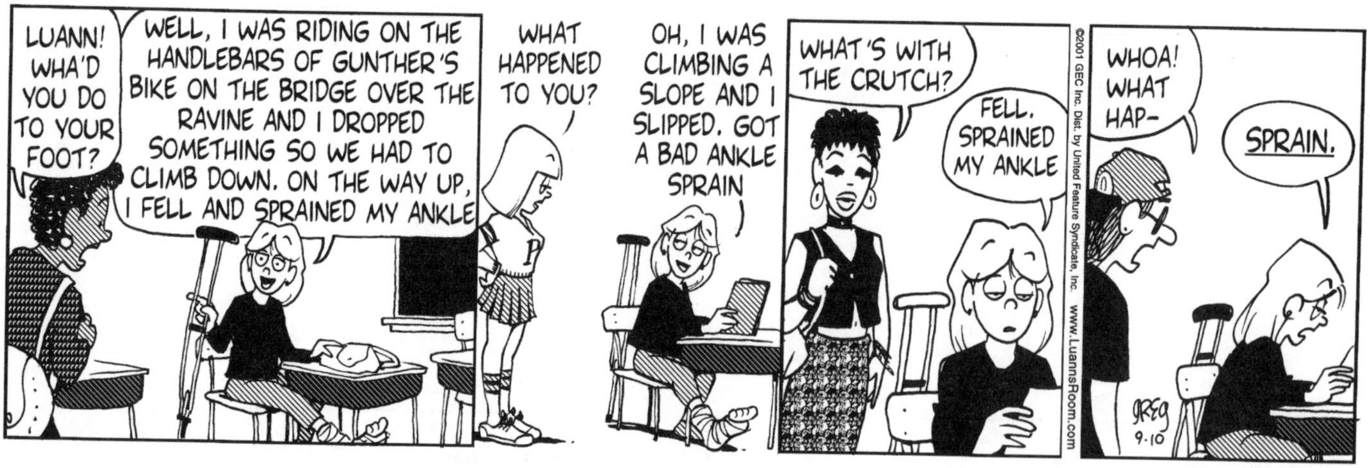
LUANN! WHA'D YOU DO TO YOUR FOOT?
WELL, I WAS RIDING ON THE HANDLEBARS OF GUNTHER'S BIKE ON THE BRIDGE OVER THE RAVINE AND I DROPPED SOMETHING SO WE HAD TO CLIMB DOWN. ON THE WAY UP, I FELL AND SPRAINED MY ANKLE
WHAT HAPPENED TO YOU?
OH, I WAS CLIMBING A SLOPE AND I SLIPPED. GOT A BAD ANKLE SPRAIN
WHAT'S WITH THE CRUTCH?
FELL. SPRAINED MY ANKLE
©2001 GEC Inc. Dist. by United Feature Syndicate, Inc. www.LuannsRoom.com
WHOA! WHAT HAP-
SPRAIN.
GREG 9·10

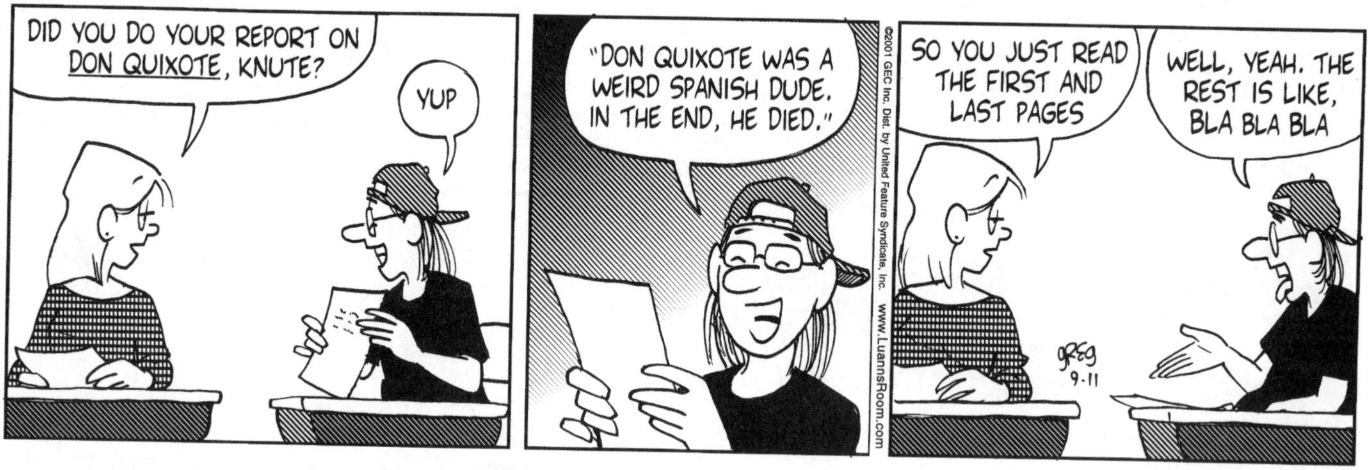
DID YOU DO YOUR REPORT ON DON QUIXOTE, KNUTE?
YUP
"DON QUIXOTE WAS A WEIRD SPANISH DUDE. IN THE END, HE DIED."
©2001 GEC Inc. Dist. by United Feature Syndicate, Inc. www.LuannsRoom.com
SO YOU JUST READ THE FIRST AND LAST PAGES
WELL, YEAH. THE REST IS LIKE, BLA BLA BLA
GREG 9·11

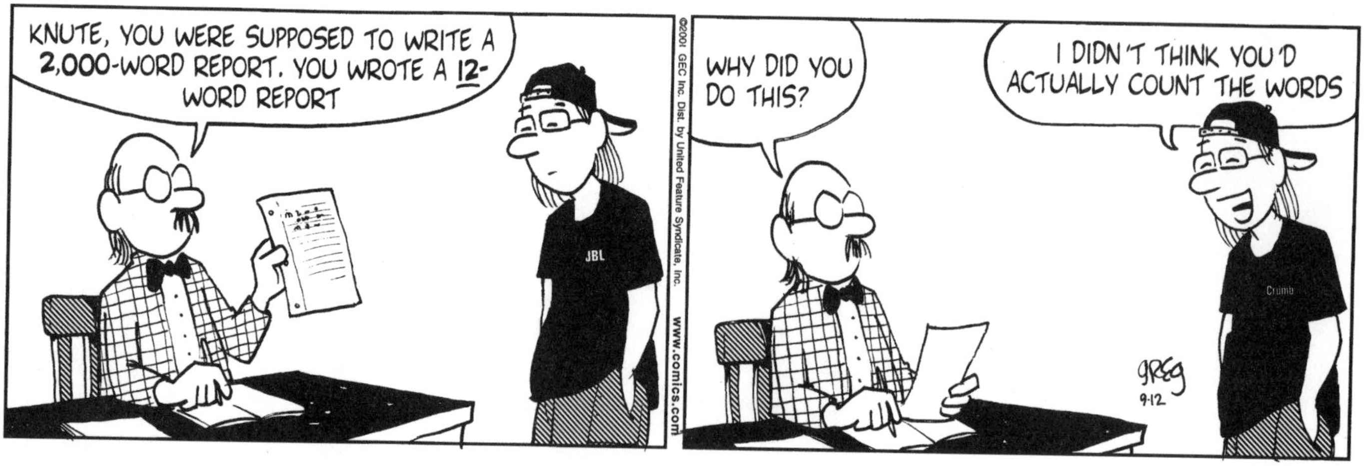
KNUTE, YOU WERE SUPPOSED TO WRITE A 2,000-WORD REPORT. YOU WROTE A 12-WORD REPORT
JBL
©2001 GEC Inc. Dist. by United Feature Syndicate, Inc. www.comics.com
WHY DID YOU DO THIS?
I DIDN'T THINK YOU'D ACTUALLY COUNT THE WORDS
Crumb
GREG 9·12

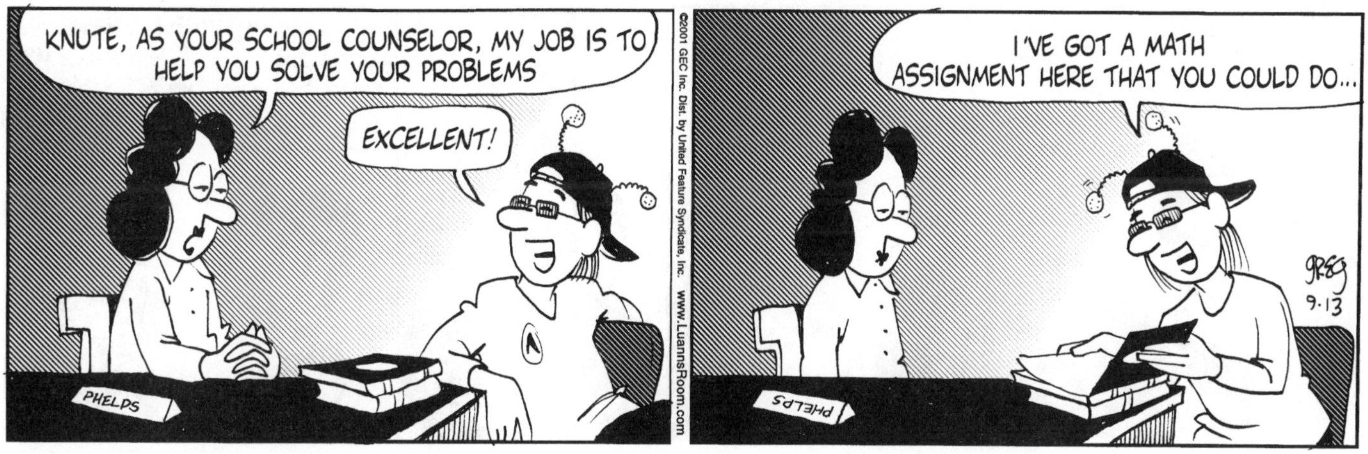
KNUTE, AS YOUR SCHOOL COUNSELOR, MY JOB IS TO HELP YOU SOLVE YOUR PROBLEMS
EXCELLENT!
PHELPS
©2001 GEC Inc. Dist. by United Feature Syndicate, Inc. www.LuannsRoom.com
I'VE GOT A MATH ASSIGNMENT HERE THAT YOU COULD DO...
GREG 9·13
PHELPS

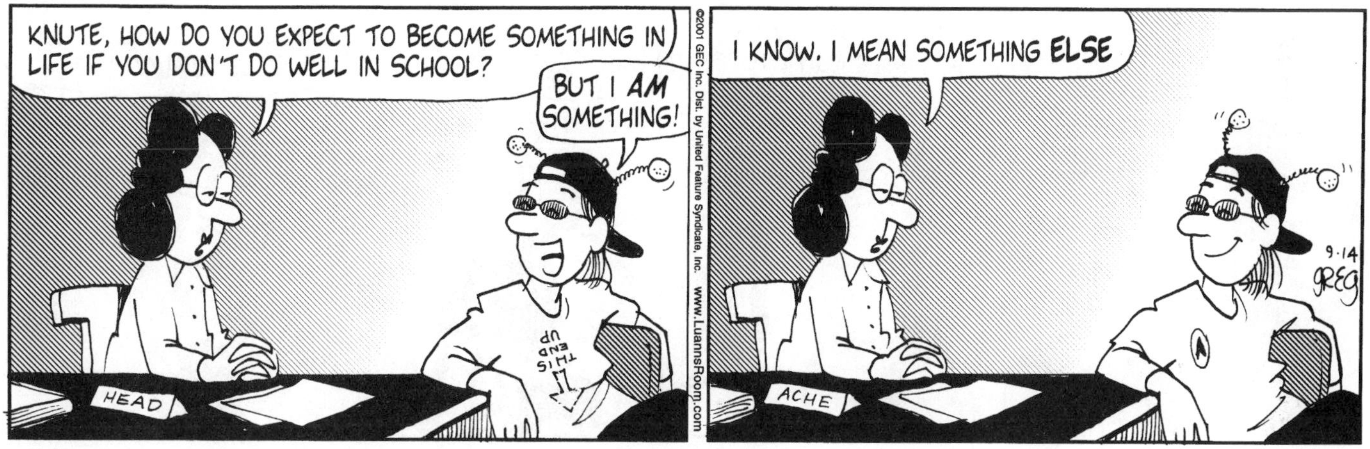
KNUTE, HOW DO YOU EXPECT TO BECOME SOMETHING IN LIFE IF YOU DON'T DO WELL IN SCHOOL?
BUT I **AM** SOMETHING!
THIS END UP
HEAD
©2001 GEC Inc. Dist. by United Feature Syndicate, Inc. www.LuannsRoom.com
I KNOW. I MEAN SOMETHING **ELSE**
9·14 GREG
ACHE

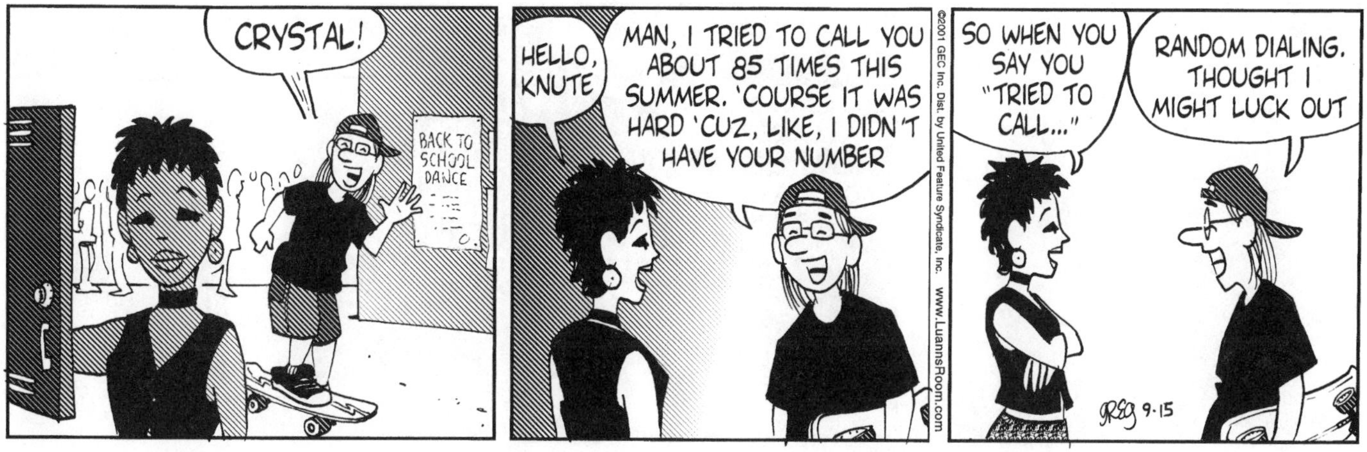
CRYSTAL!
BACK TO SCHOOL DANCE
HELLO, KNUTE
MAN, I TRIED TO CALL YOU ABOUT 85 TIMES THIS SUMMER. 'COURSE IT WAS HARD 'CUZ, LIKE, I DIDN'T HAVE YOUR NUMBER
©2001 GEC Inc. Dist. by United Feature Syndicate, Inc. www.LuannsRoom.com
SO WHEN YOU SAY YOU "TRIED TO CALL..."
RANDOM DIALING. THOUGHT I MIGHT LUCK OUT
GREG 9·15

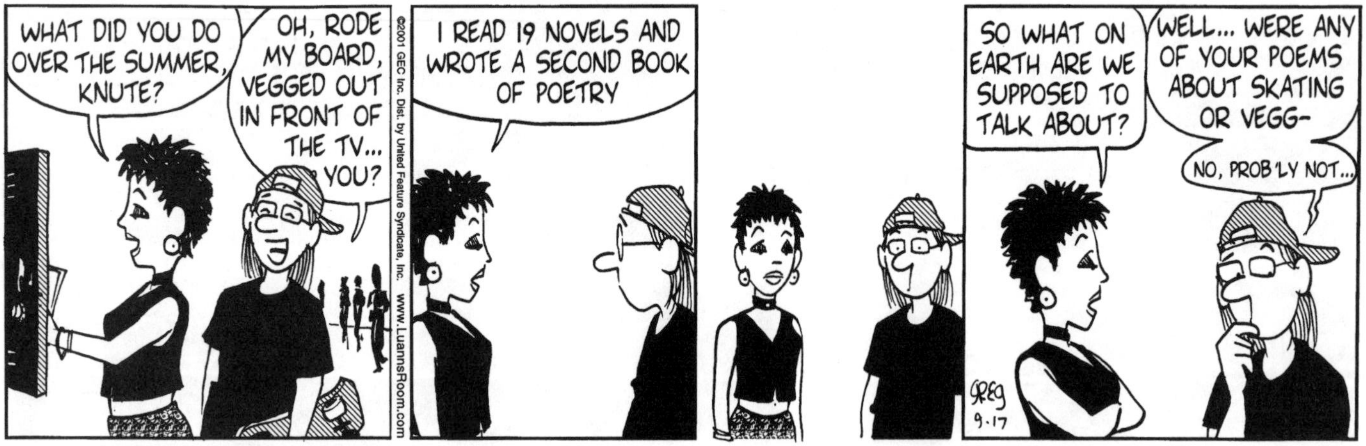
WHAT DID YOU DO OVER THE SUMMER, KNUTE?
OH, RODE MY BOARD, VEGGED OUT IN FRONT OF THE TV... YOU?
©2001 GEC Inc. Dist. by United Feature Syndicate, Inc. www.LuannsRoom.com
I READ 19 NOVELS AND WROTE A SECOND BOOK OF POETRY
SO WHAT ON EARTH ARE WE SUPPOSED TO TALK ABOUT?
WELL... WERE ANY OF YOUR POEMS ABOUT SKATING OR VEGG-
NO, PROB'LY NOT...
GREG 9.17

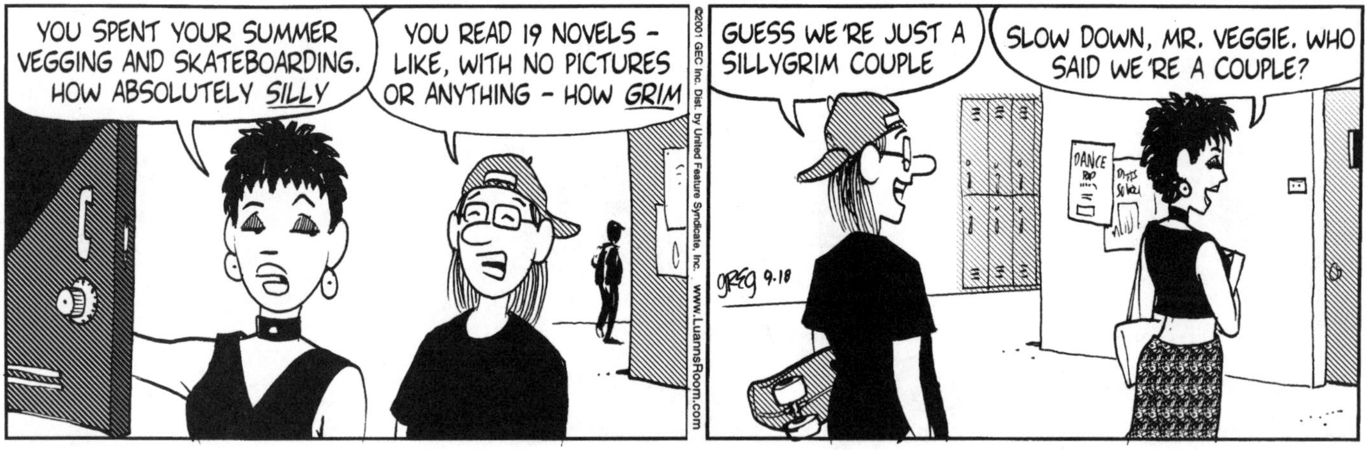
YOU SPENT YOUR SUMMER VEGGING AND SKATEBOARDING. HOW ABSOLUTELY SILLY
YOU READ 19 NOVELS - LIKE, WITH NO PICTURES OR ANYTHING - HOW GRIM
©2001 GEC Inc. Dist. by United Feature Syndicate, Inc. www.LuannsRoom.com
GUESS WE'RE JUST A SILLYGRIM COUPLE
SLOW DOWN, MR. VEGGIE. WHO SAID WE'RE A COUPLE?
DANCE
GREG 9.18

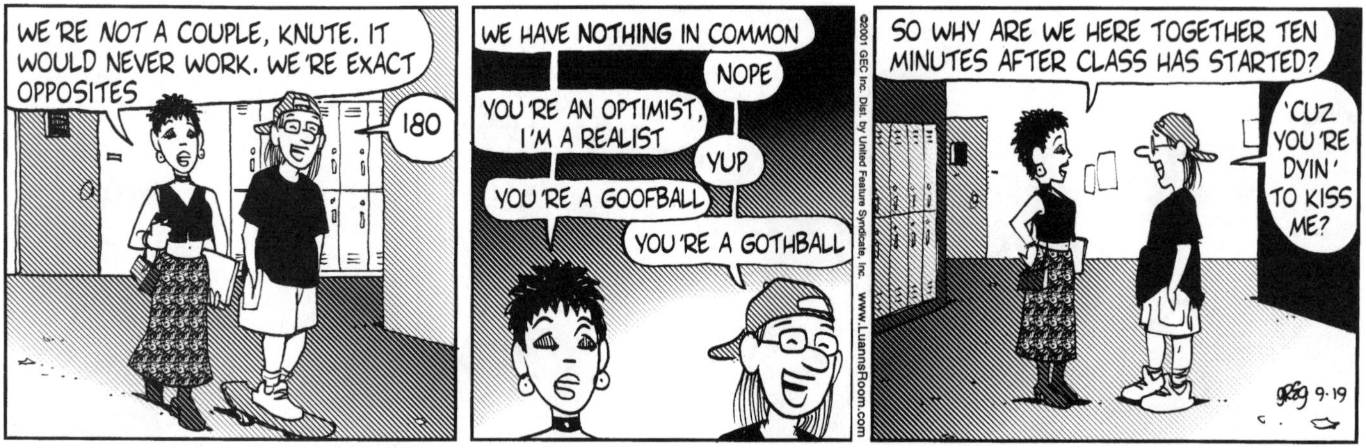
WE'RE NOT A COUPLE, KNUTE. IT WOULD NEVER WORK. WE'RE EXACT OPPOSITES
180
WE HAVE NOTHING IN COMMON
NOPE
YOU'RE AN OPTIMIST, I'M A REALIST
YUP
YOU'RE A GOOFBALL
YOU'RE A GOTHBALL
©2001 GEC Inc. Dist. by United Feature Syndicate, Inc. www.LuannsRoom.com
SO WHY ARE WE HERE TOGETHER TEN MINUTES AFTER CLASS HAS STARTED?
'CUZ YOU'RE DYIN' TO KISS ME?
GREG 9.19

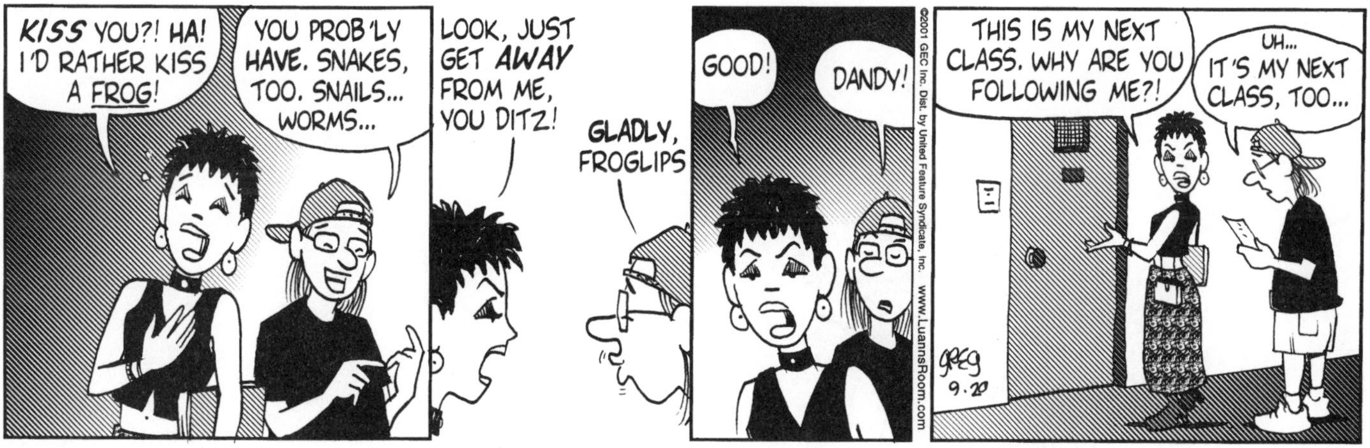
KISS YOU?! HA! I'D RATHER KISS A FROG!
YOU PROB'LY HAVE. SNAKES, TOO. SNAILS... WORMS...
LOOK, JUST GET AWAY FROM ME, YOU DITZ!
GLADLY, FROGLIPS
GOOD!
DANDY!
©2001 GEC Inc. Dist. by United Feature Syndicate, Inc. www.LuannsRoom.com
THIS IS MY NEXT CLASS. WHY ARE YOU FOLLOWING ME?!
UH... IT'S MY NEXT CLASS, TOO...
GREG 9.20

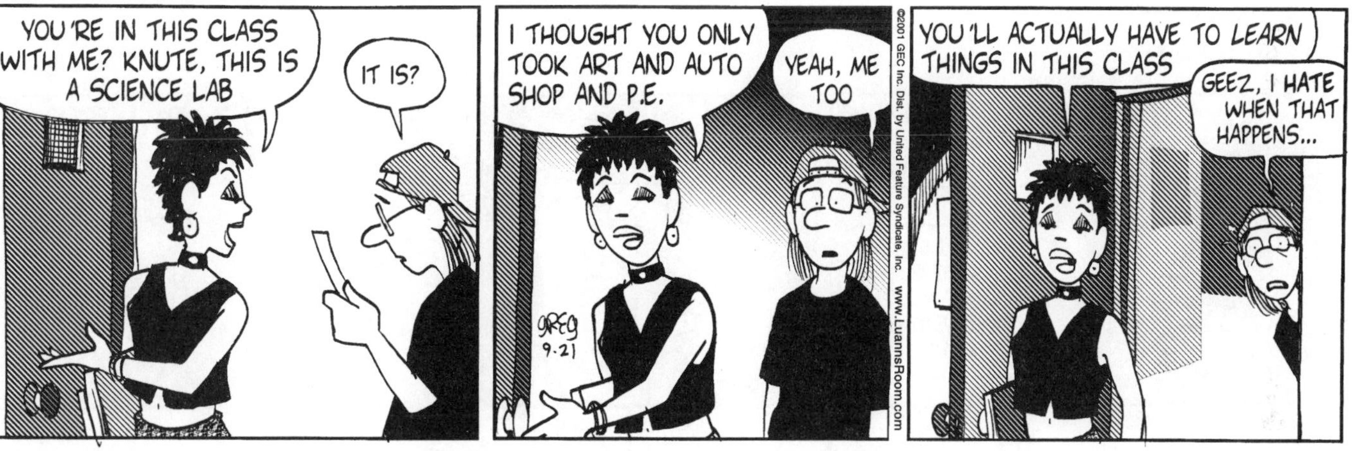
YOU'RE IN THIS CLASS WITH ME? KNUTE, THIS IS A SCIENCE LAB
IT IS?
I THOUGHT YOU ONLY TOOK ART AND AUTO SHOP AND P.E.
YEAH, ME TOO
GREG 9.21
©2001 GEC Inc. Dist. by United Feature Syndicate, Inc. www.LuannsRoom.com
YOU'LL ACTUALLY HAVE TO LEARN THINGS IN THIS CLASS
GEEZ, I HATE WHEN THAT HAPPENS...

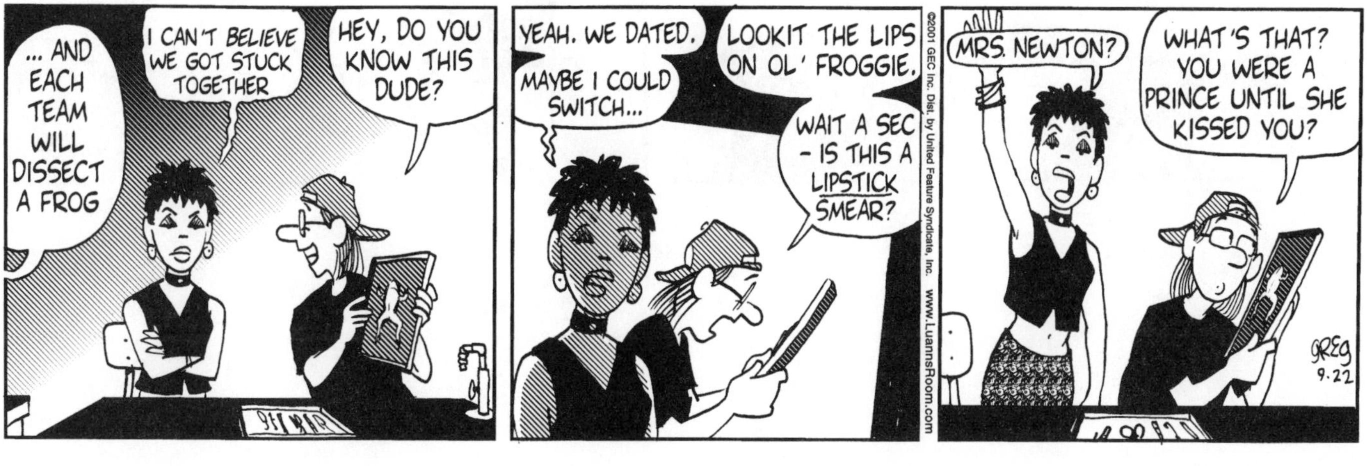
... AND EACH TEAM WILL DISSECT A FROG
I CAN'T BELIEVE WE GOT STUCK TOGETHER
HEY, DO YOU KNOW THIS DUDE?
YEAH. WE DATED.
MAYBE I COULD SWITCH...
LOOKIT THE LIPS ON OL' FROGGIE.
WAIT A SEC - IS THIS A LIPSTICK SMEAR?
©2001 GEC Inc. Dist. by United Feature Syndicate, Inc. www.LuannsRoom.com
MRS. NEWTON?
WHAT'S THAT? YOU WERE A PRINCE UNTIL SHE KISSED YOU?
GREG 9.22

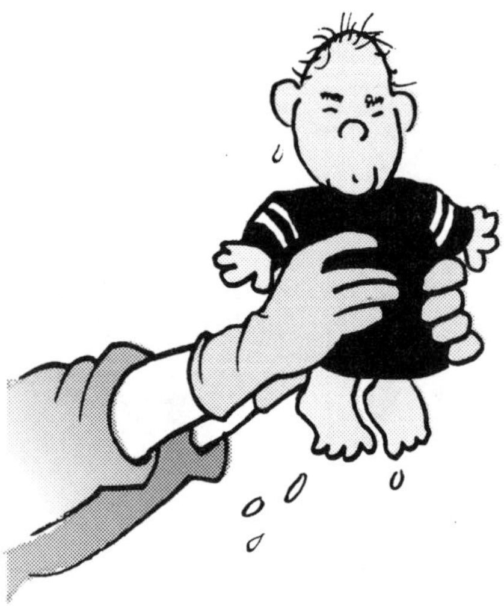

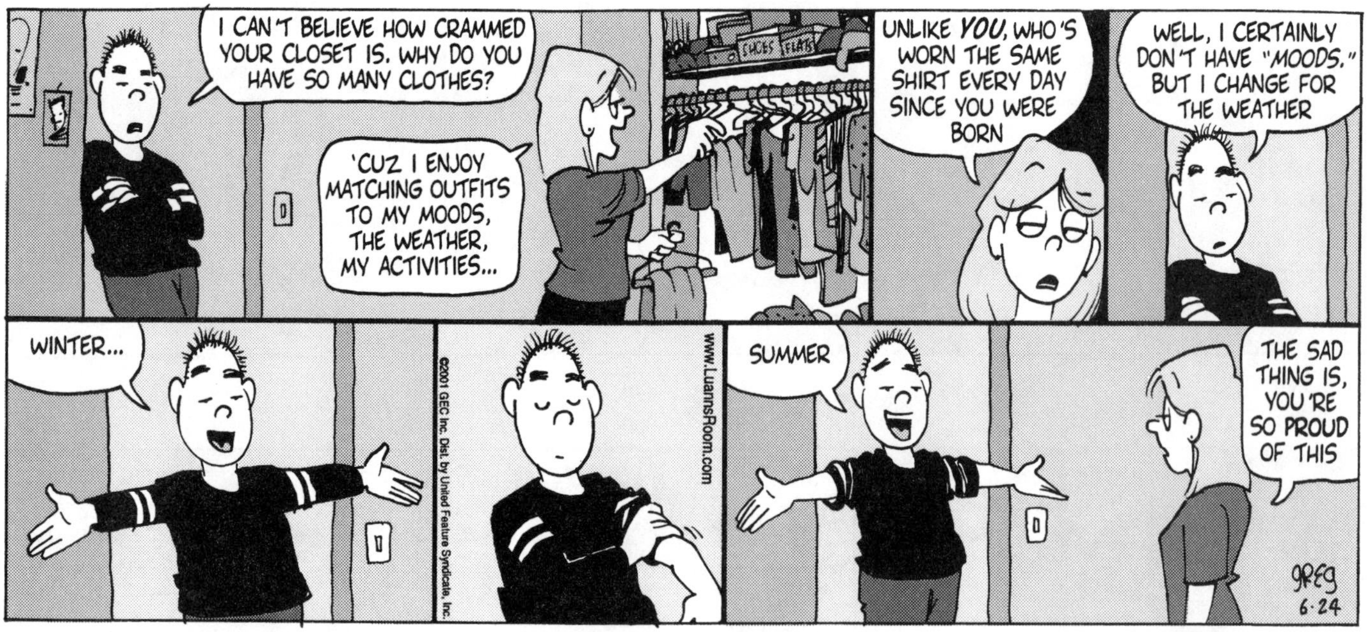

I CAN'T BELIEVE HOW CRAMMED YOUR CLOSET IS. WHY DO YOU HAVE SO MANY CLOTHES?
'CUZ I ENJOY MATCHING OUTFITS TO MY MOODS, THE WEATHER, MY ACTIVITIES...
SHOES
FLATS
UNLIKE *YOU*, WHO'S WORN THE SAME SHIRT EVERY DAY SINCE YOU WERE BORN
WELL, I CERTAINLY DON'T HAVE "*MOODS*," BUT I CHANGE FOR THE WEATHER
WINTER...
©2001 GEC Inc. Dist. by United Feature Syndicate, Inc.
www.LuannsRoom.com
SUMMER
THE SAD THING IS, YOU'RE SO **PROUD** OF THIS
GREG
6·24

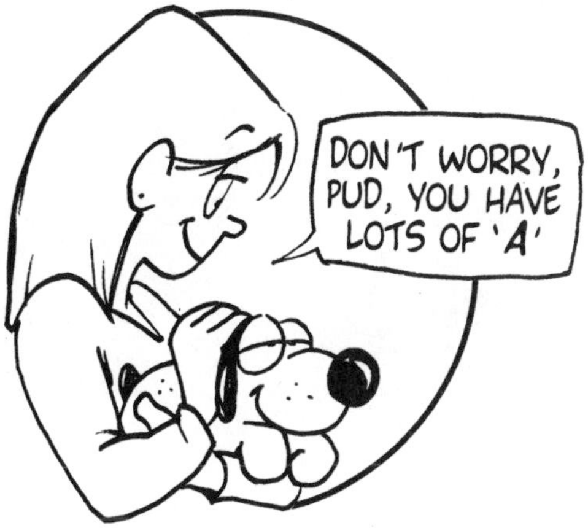
DON'T WORRY, PUD, YOU HAVE LOTS OF 'A'

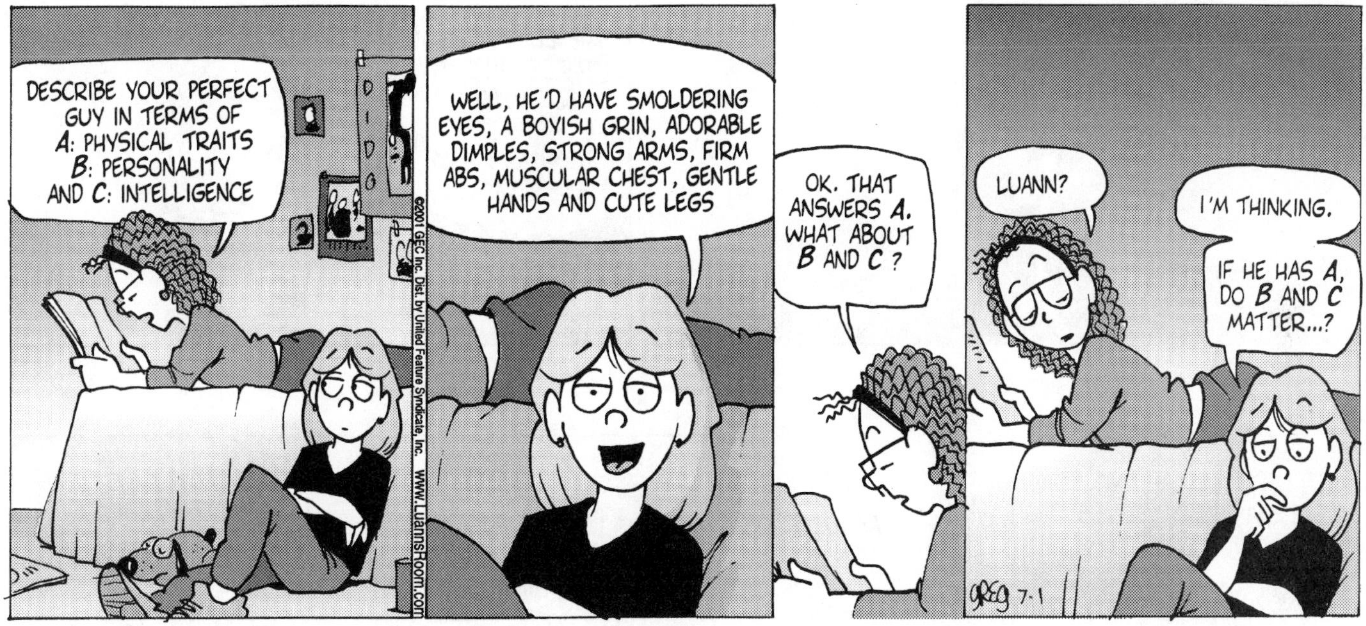
DESCRIBE YOUR PERFECT GUY IN TERMS OF A: PHYSICAL TRAITS B: PERSONALITY AND C: INTELLIGENCE
DIDO
©2001 GEC Inc. Dist. by United Feature Syndicate, Inc. www.LuannsRoom.com
WELL, HE'D HAVE SMOLDERING EYES, A BOYISH GRIN, ADORABLE DIMPLES, STRONG ARMS, FIRM ABS, MUSCULAR CHEST, GENTLE HANDS AND CUTE LEGS
OK. THAT ANSWERS A. WHAT ABOUT B AND C ?
LUANN?
I'M THINKING.
IF HE HAS A, DO B AND C MATTER...?
GREG 7-1

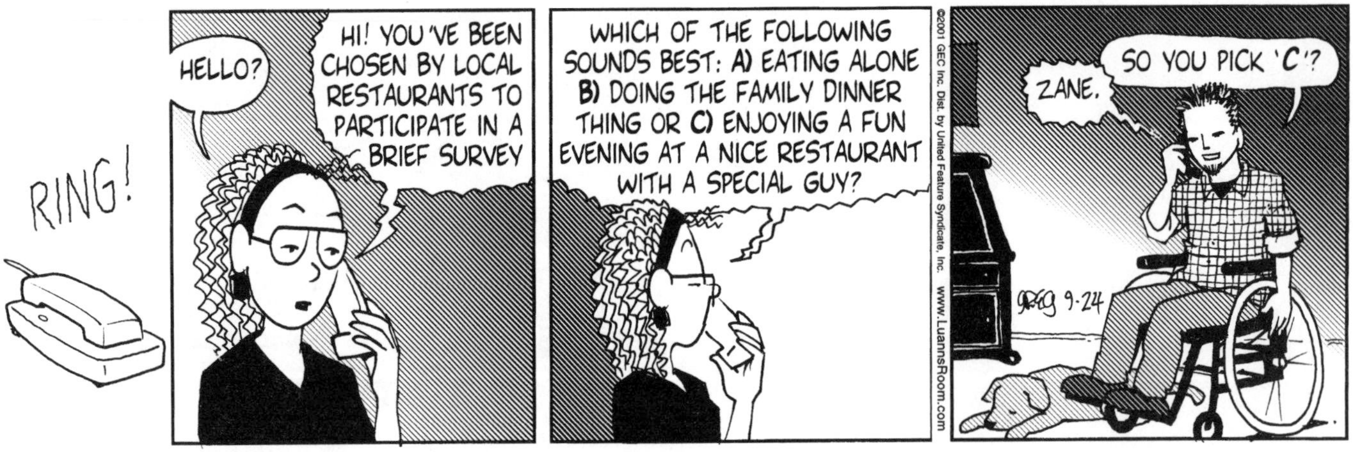
RING!
HELLO?
HI! YOU'VE BEEN CHOSEN BY LOCAL RESTAURANTS TO PARTICIPATE IN A BRIEF SURVEY
WHICH OF THE FOLLOWING SOUNDS BEST: A) EATING ALONE B) DOING THE FAMILY DINNER THING OR C) ENJOYING A FUN EVENING AT A NICE RESTAURANT WITH A SPECIAL GUY?
©2001 GEC Inc. Dist. by United Feature Syndicate, Inc. www.LuannsRoom.com
ZANE.
SO YOU PICK 'C'?
GREG 9·24

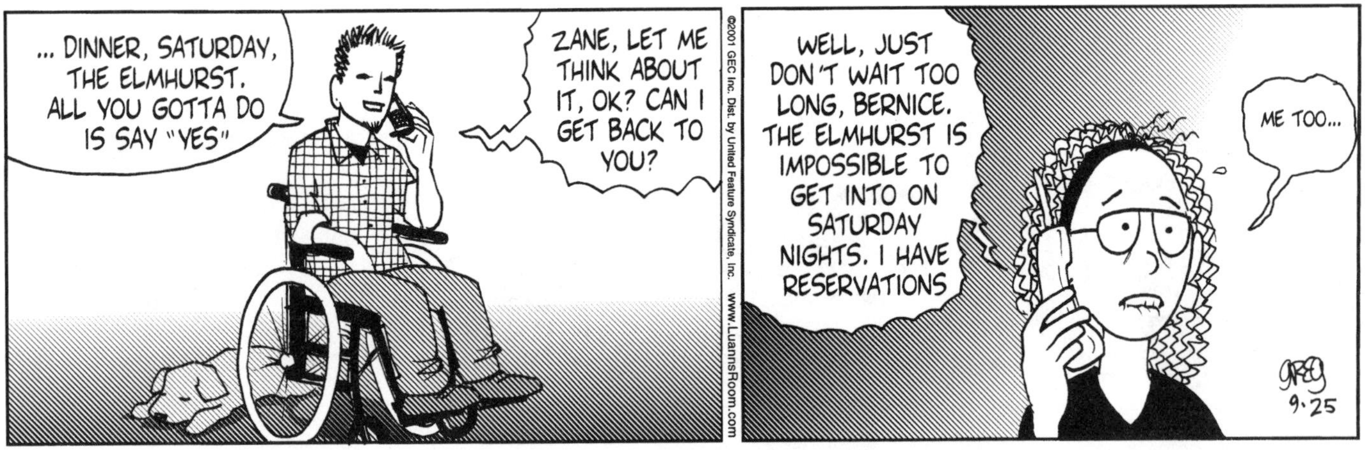
... DINNER, SATURDAY, THE ELMHURST. ALL YOU GOTTA DO IS SAY "YES"
ZANE, LET ME THINK ABOUT IT, OK? CAN I GET BACK TO YOU?
©2001 GEC Inc. Dist. by United Feature Syndicate, Inc. www.LuannsRoom.com
WELL, JUST DON'T WAIT TOO LONG, BERNICE. THE ELMHURST IS IMPOSSIBLE TO GET INTO ON SATURDAY NIGHTS. I HAVE RESERVATIONS
ME TOO...
GREG 9·25

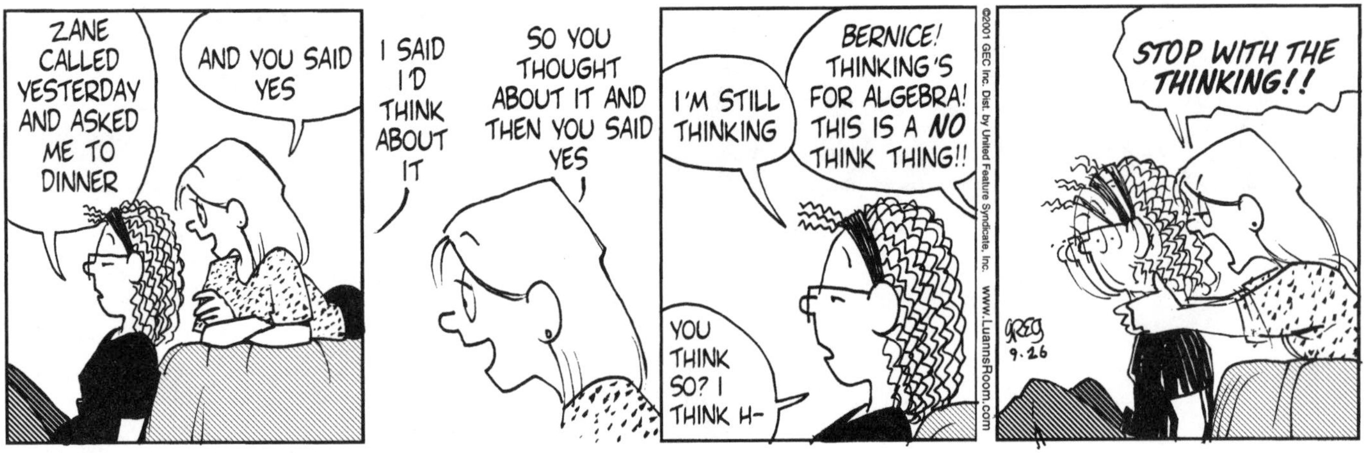
ZANE CALLED YESTERDAY AND ASKED ME TO DINNER
AND YOU SAID YES
I SAID I'D THINK ABOUT IT
SO YOU THOUGHT ABOUT IT AND THEN YOU SAID YES
I'M STILL THINKING
BERNICE! THINKING'S FOR ALGEBRA! THIS IS A NO THINK THING!!
YOU THINK SO? I THINK H-
©2001 GEC Inc. Dist. by United Feature Syndicate, Inc. www.LuannsRoom.com
STOP WITH THE THINKING!!
GREG 9·26

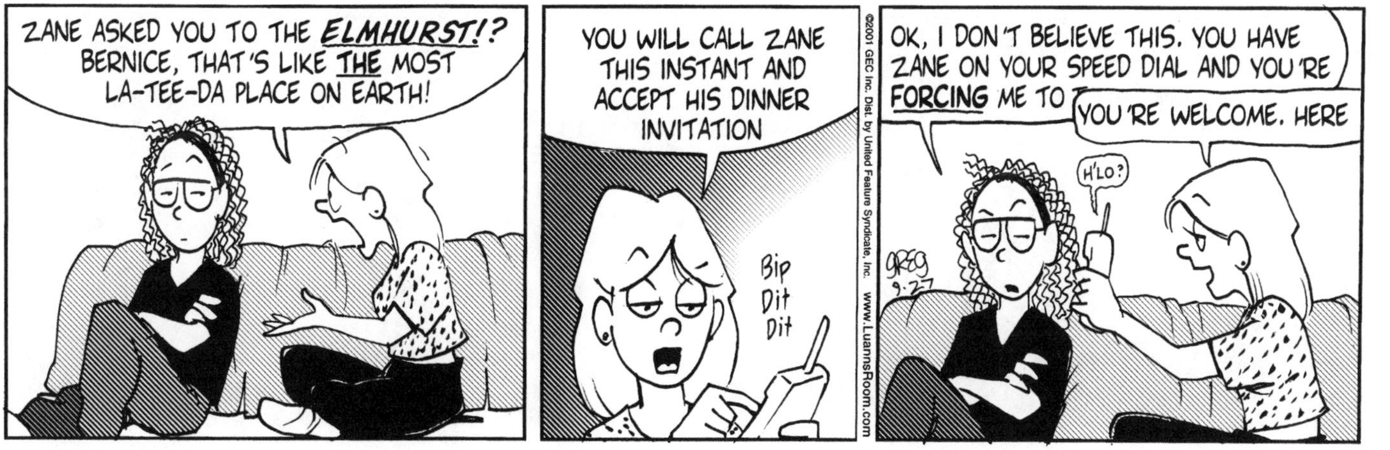
ZANE ASKED YOU TO THE ELMHURST!? BERNICE, THAT'S LIKE THE MOST LA-TEE-DA PLACE ON EARTH!
YOU WILL CALL ZANE THIS INSTANT AND ACCEPT HIS DINNER INVITATION
Bip Dit Dit
©2001 GEC Inc. Dist. by United Feature Syndicate, Inc. www.LuannsRoom.com
OK, I DON'T BELIEVE THIS. YOU HAVE ZANE ON YOUR SPEED DIAL AND YOU'RE FORCING ME TO
YOU'RE WELCOME. HERE
H'LO?
GREG 9.27

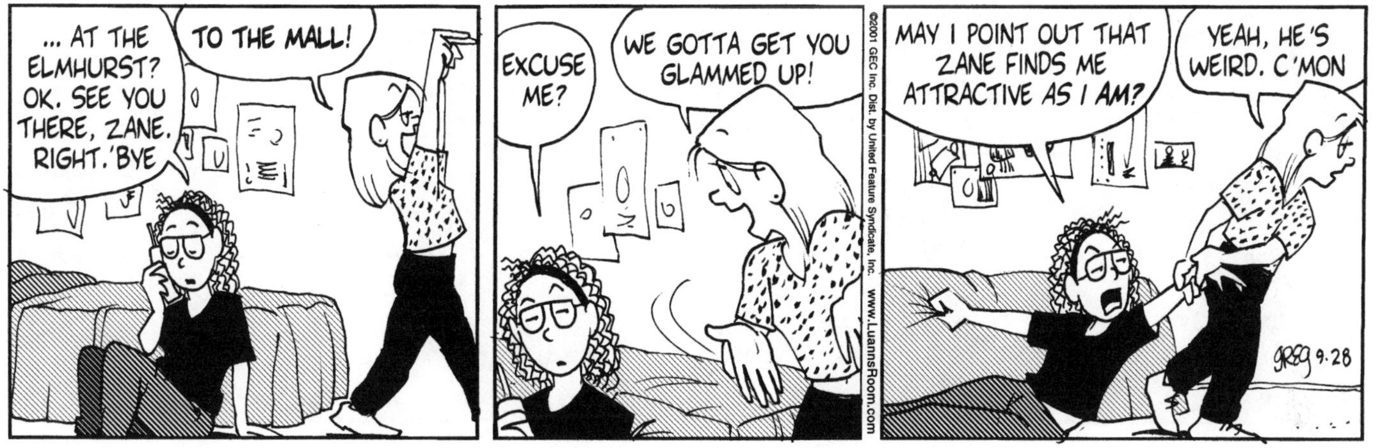
... AT THE ELMHURST? OK. SEE YOU THERE, ZANE. RIGHT. 'BYE
TO THE MALL!
EXCUSE ME?
WE GOTTA GET YOU GLAMMED UP!
©2001 GEC Inc. Dist. by United Feature Syndicate, Inc. www.LuannsRoom.com
MAY I POINT OUT THAT ZANE FINDS ME ATTRACTIVE AS I AM?
YEAH, HE'S WEIRD. C'MON
GREG 9.28

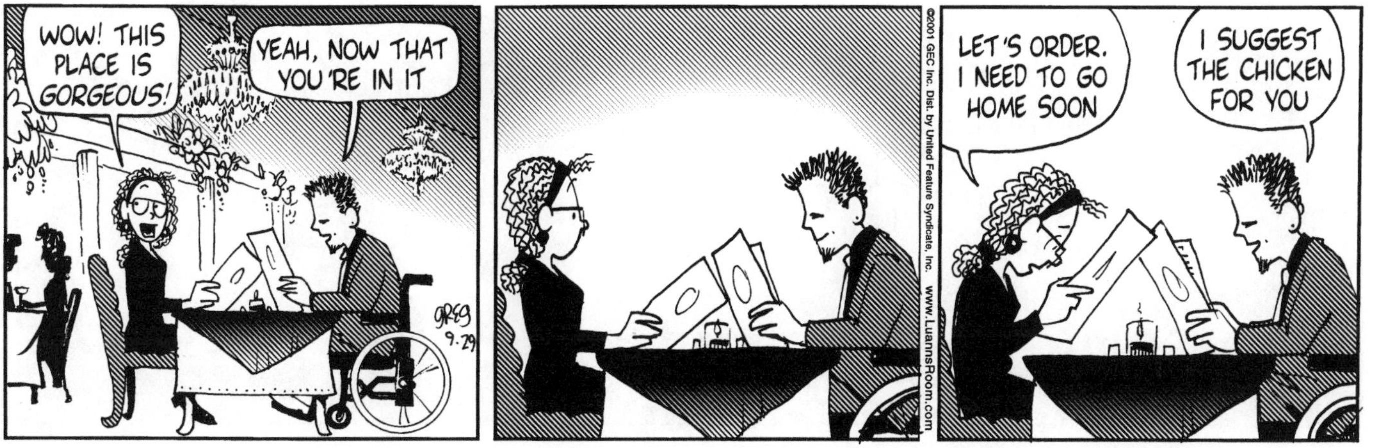
WOW! THIS PLACE IS GORGEOUS!
YEAH, NOW THAT YOU'RE IN IT
GREG 9.29
©2001 GEC Inc. Dist. by United Feature Syndicate, Inc. www.LuannsRoom.com
LET'S ORDER. I NEED TO GO HOME SOON
I SUGGEST THE CHICKEN FOR YOU

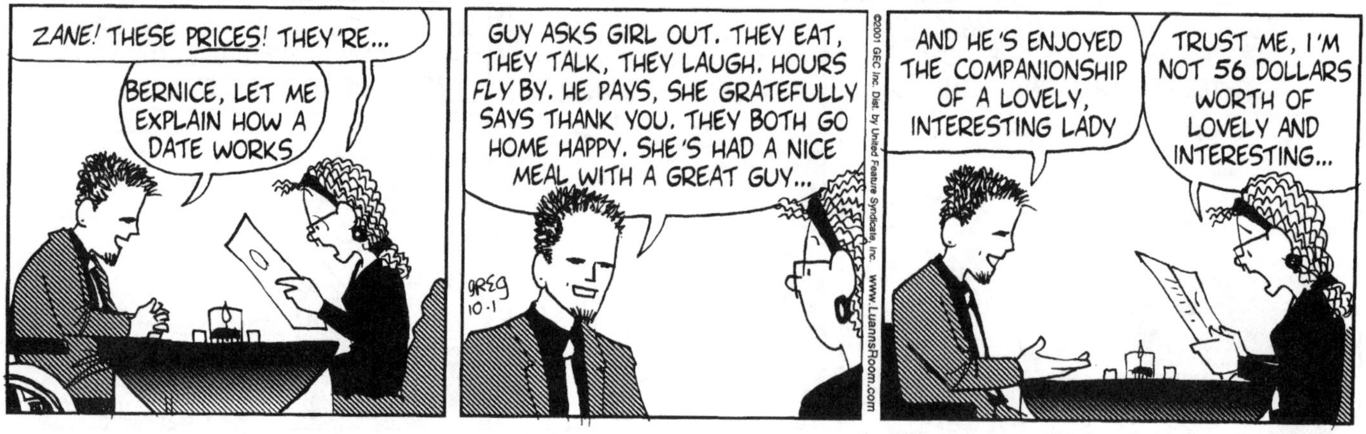
ZANE! THESE PRICES! THEY'RE...
BERNICE, LET ME EXPLAIN HOW A DATE WORKS
GUY ASKS GIRL OUT. THEY EAT, THEY TALK, THEY LAUGH. HOURS FLY BY. HE PAYS, SHE GRATEFULLY SAYS THANK YOU. THEY BOTH GO HOME HAPPY. SHE'S HAD A NICE MEAL WITH A GREAT GUY...
GREG 10·1
©2001 GEC Inc. Dist. by United Feature Syndicate, Inc. www.LuannsRoom.com
AND HE'S ENJOYED THE COMPANIONSHIP OF A LOVELY, INTERESTING LADY
TRUST ME, I'M NOT 56 DOLLARS WORTH OF LOVELY AND INTERESTING...

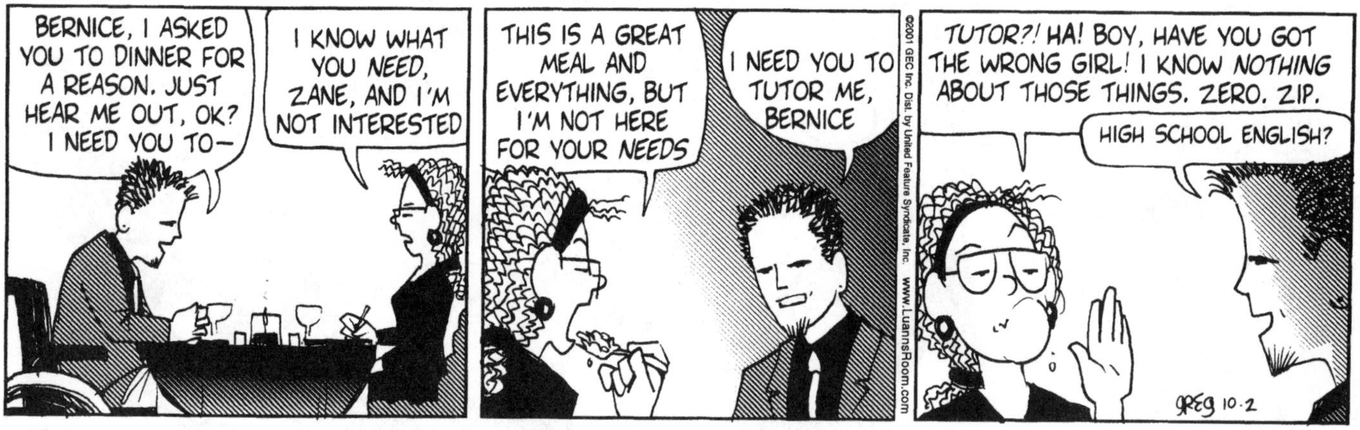
BERNICE, I ASKED YOU TO DINNER FOR A REASON. JUST HEAR ME OUT, OK? I NEED YOU TO–
I KNOW WHAT YOU NEED, ZANE, AND I'M NOT INTERESTED
THIS IS A GREAT MEAL AND EVERYTHING, BUT I'M NOT HERE FOR YOUR NEEDS
I NEED YOU TO TUTOR ME, BERNICE
©2001 GEC Inc. Dist. by United Feature Syndicate, Inc. www.LuannsRoom.com
TUTOR?! HA! BOY, HAVE YOU GOT THE WRONG GIRL! I KNOW NOTHING ABOUT THOSE THINGS. ZERO. ZIP.
HIGH SCHOOL ENGLISH?
GREG 10·2

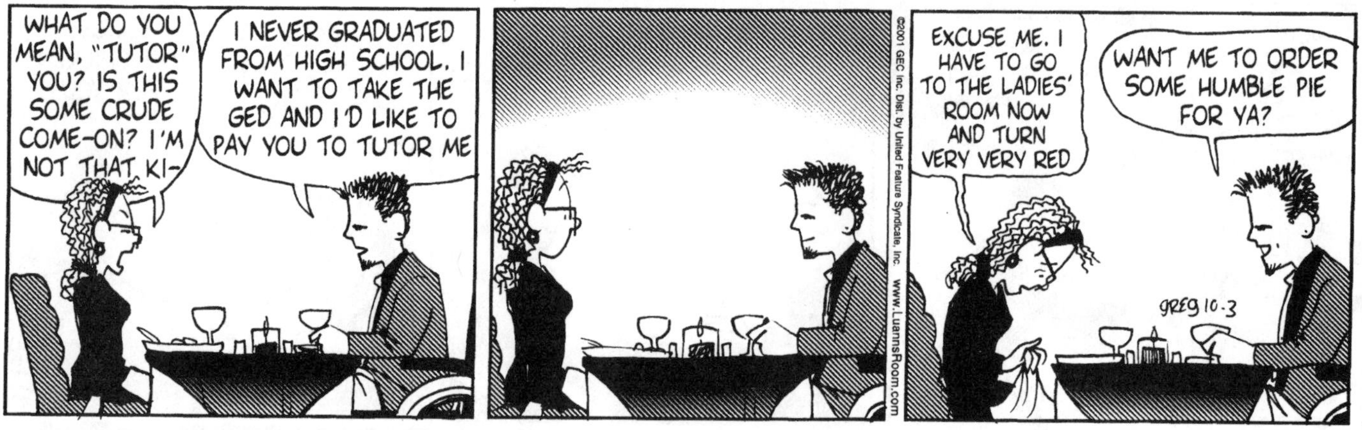
WHAT DO YOU MEAN, "TUTOR" YOU? IS THIS SOME CRUDE COME-ON? I'M NOT THAT KI–
I NEVER GRADUATED FROM HIGH SCHOOL. I WANT TO TAKE THE GED AND I'D LIKE TO PAY YOU TO TUTOR ME
©2001 GEC Inc. Dist. by United Feature Syndicate, Inc. www.LuannsRoom.com
EXCUSE ME. I HAVE TO GO TO THE LADIES' ROOM NOW AND TURN VERY VERY RED
WANT ME TO ORDER SOME HUMBLE PIE FOR YA?
GREG 10·3

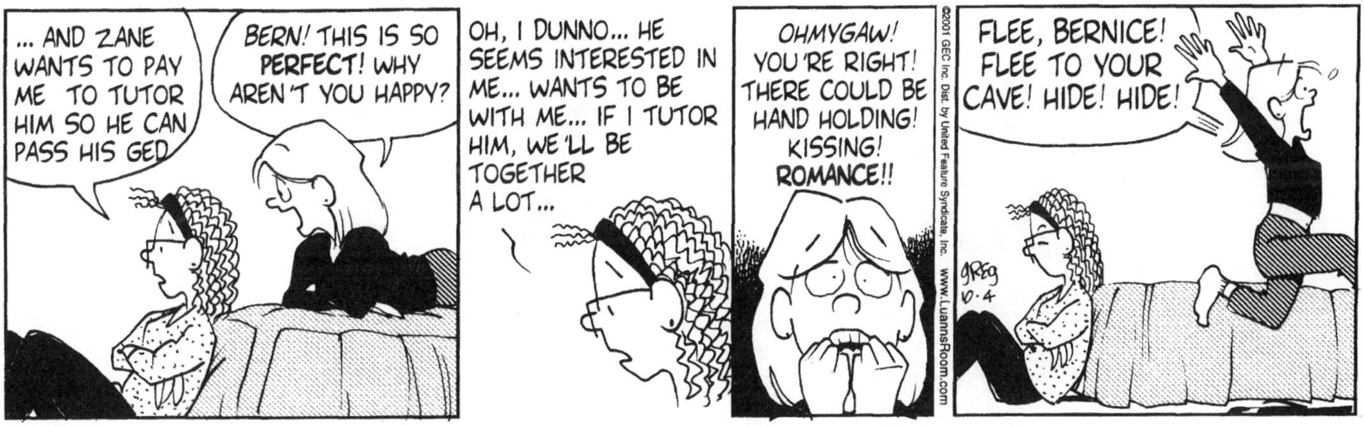
... AND ZANE WANTS TO PAY ME TO TUTOR HIM SO HE CAN PASS HIS GED
BERN! THIS IS SO **PERFECT**! WHY AREN'T YOU HAPPY?
OH, I DUNNO... HE SEEMS INTERESTED IN ME... WANTS TO BE WITH ME... IF I TUTOR HIM, WE'LL BE TOGETHER A LOT...
OHMYGAW! YOU'RE RIGHT! THERE COULD BE HAND HOLDING! KISSING! **ROMANCE**!!
©2001 GEC Inc. Dist. by United Feature Syndicate, Inc. www.LuannsRoom.com
FLEE, BERNICE! FLEE TO YOUR CAVE! HIDE! HIDE!
GREG 10·4

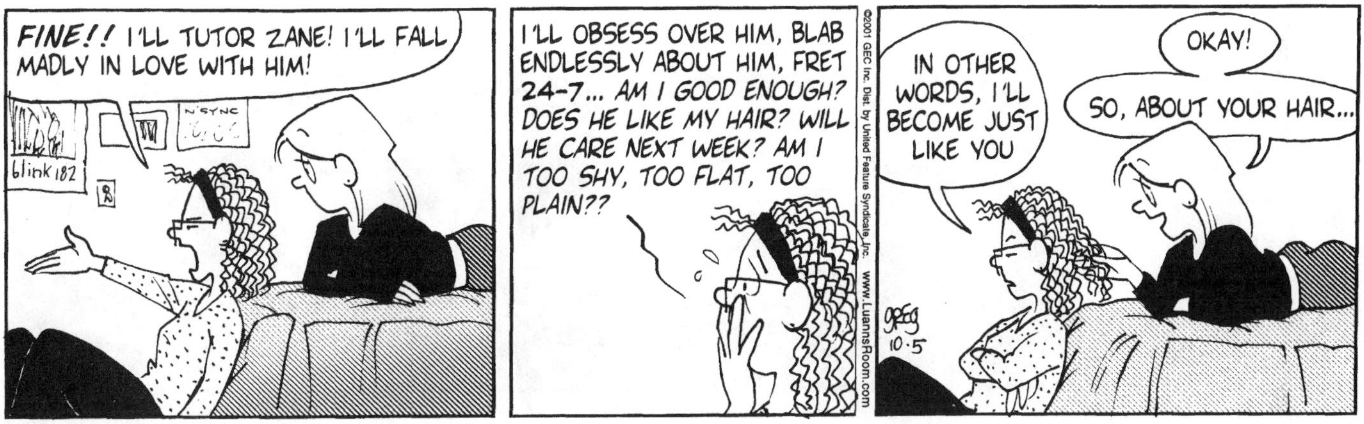
FINE!! I'LL TUTOR ZANE! I'LL FALL MADLY IN LOVE WITH HIM!
blink 182
N'SYNC
I'LL OBSESS OVER HIM, BLAB ENDLESSLY ABOUT HIM, FRET **24-7**... *AM I GOOD ENOUGH? DOES HE LIKE MY HAIR? WILL HE CARE NEXT WEEK? AM I TOO SHY, TOO FLAT, TOO PLAIN??*
©2001 GEC Inc. Dist. by United Feature Syndicate, Inc. www.LuannsRoom.com
GREG 10·5
IN OTHER WORDS, I'LL BECOME JUST LIKE YOU
OKAY!
SO, ABOUT YOUR HAIR...

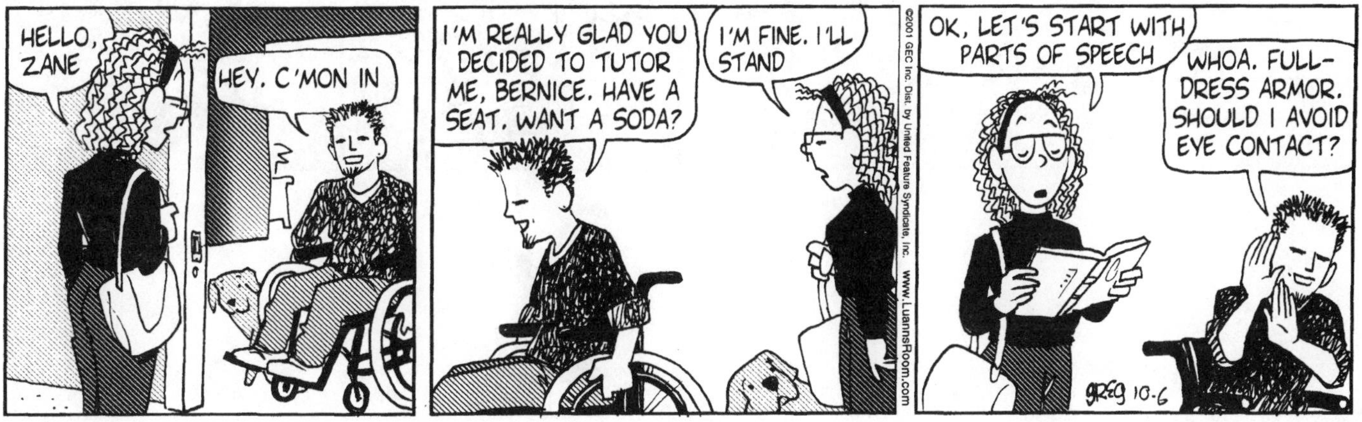
HELLO, ZANE
HEY. C'MON IN
I'M REALLY GLAD YOU DECIDED TO TUTOR ME, BERNICE. HAVE A SEAT. WANT A SODA?
I'M FINE. I'LL STAND
©2001 GEC Inc. Dist. by United Feature Syndicate, Inc. www.LuannsRoom.com
OK, LET'S START WITH PARTS OF SPEECH
WHOA. FULL-DRESS ARMOR. SHOULD I AVOID EYE CONTACT?
GREG 10-6

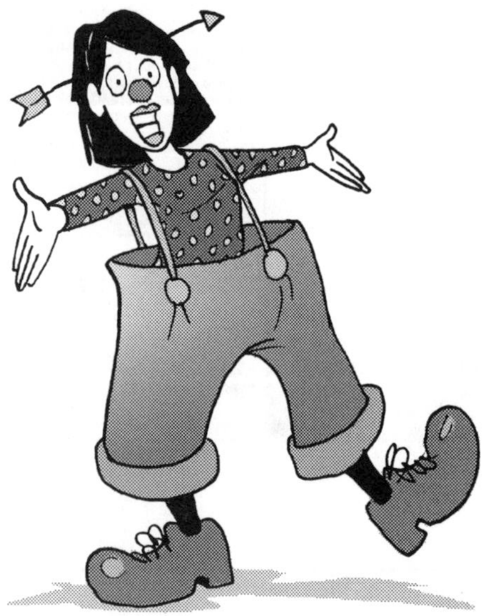

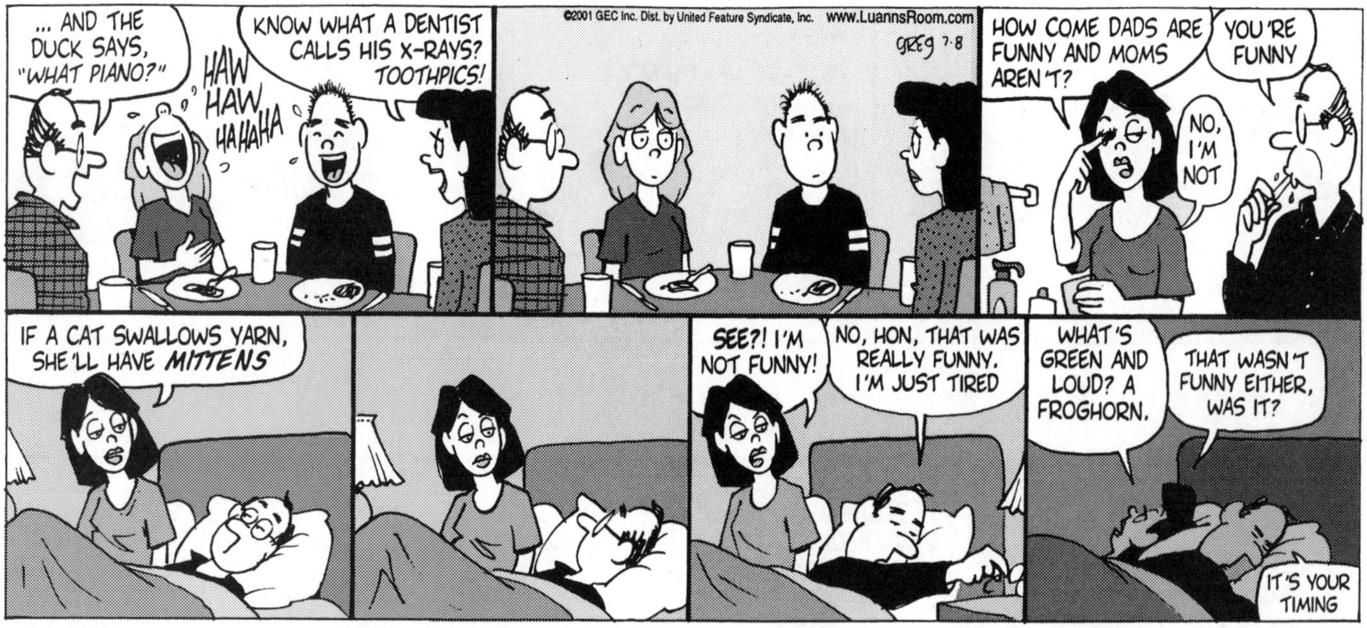

... AND THE DUCK SAYS, "WHAT PIANO?"
HAW HAW HAHAHA
KNOW WHAT A DENTIST CALLS HIS X-RAYS? TOOTHPICS!
©2001 GEC Inc. Dist. by United Feature Syndicate, Inc. www.LuannsRoom.com
GREG 7-8
HOW COME DADS ARE FUNNY AND MOMS AREN'T?
YOU'RE FUNNY
NO, I'M NOT
IF A CAT SWALLOWS YARN, SHE'LL HAVE MITTENS
SEE?! I'M NOT FUNNY!
NO, HON, THAT WAS REALLY FUNNY. I'M JUST TIRED
WHAT'S GREEN AND LOUD? A FROGHORN.
THAT WASN'T FUNNY EITHER, WAS IT?
IT'S YOUR TIMING

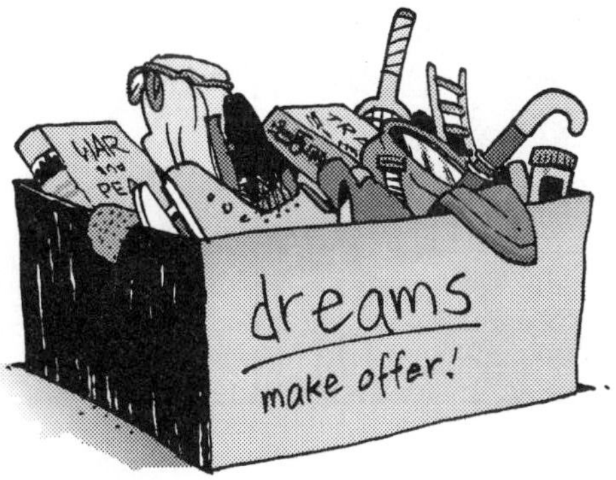
dreams
make offer!

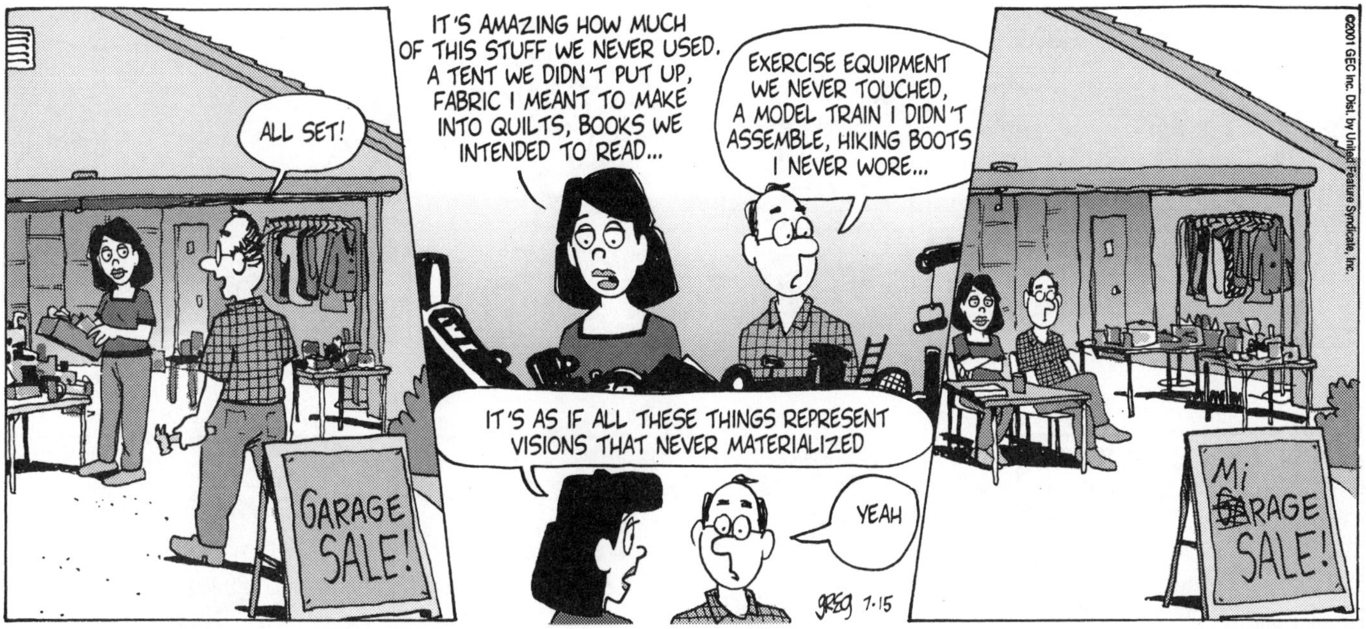
ALL SET!
GARAGE SALE!
IT'S AMAZING HOW MUCH OF THIS STUFF WE NEVER USED. A TENT WE DIDN'T PUT UP, FABRIC I MEANT TO MAKE INTO QUILTS, BOOKS WE INTENDED TO READ...
EXERCISE EQUIPMENT WE NEVER TOUCHED, A MODEL TRAIN I DIDN'T ASSEMBLE, HIKING BOOTS I NEVER WORE...
IT'S AS IF ALL THESE THINGS REPRESENT VISIONS THAT NEVER MATERIALIZED
YEAH
GREG 7-15
Mi
~~GA~~RAGE SALE!
©2001 GEC Inc. Dist. by United Feature Syndicate, Inc.

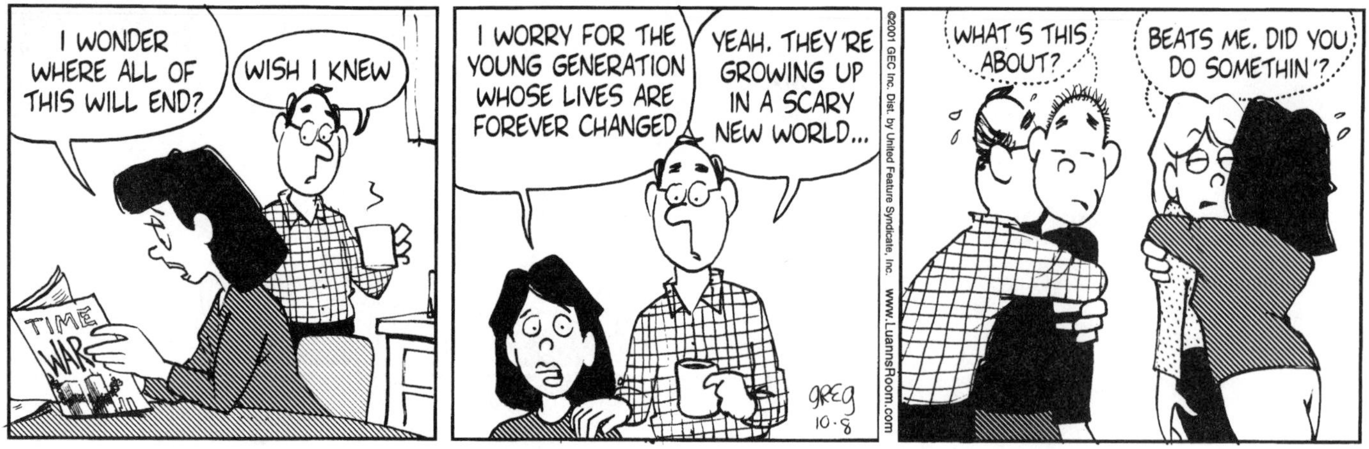
I WONDER WHERE ALL OF THIS WILL END?
WISH I KNEW
TIME
WAR
I WORRY FOR THE YOUNG GENERATION WHOSE LIVES ARE FOREVER CHANGED
YEAH. THEY'RE GROWING UP IN A SCARY NEW WORLD...
GREG 10·8
©2001 GEC Inc. Dist. by United Feature Syndicate, Inc. www.LuannsRoom.com
WHAT'S THIS ABOUT?
BEATS ME. DID YOU DO SOMETHIN'?

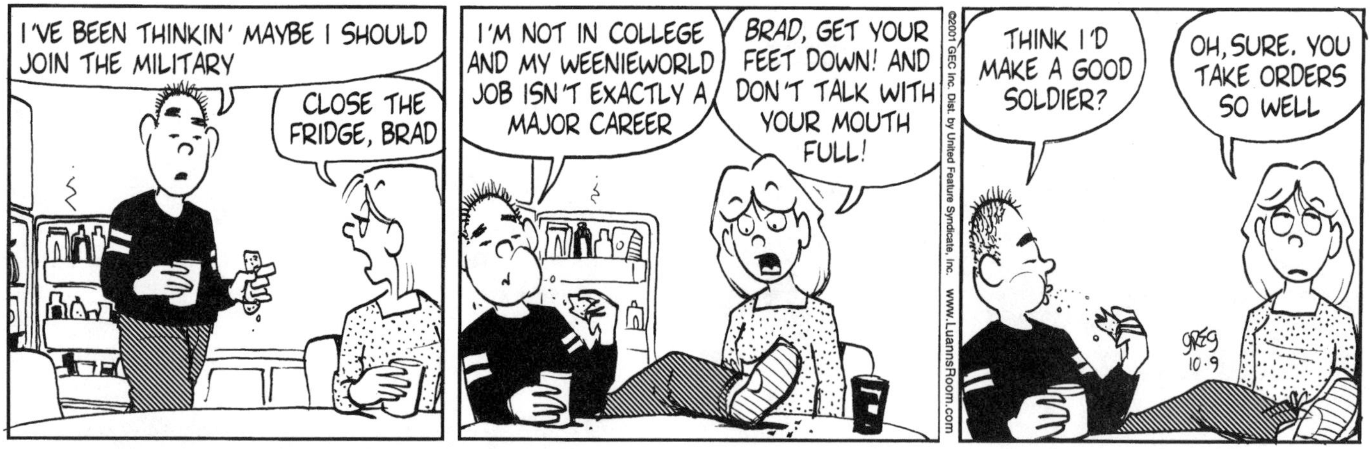
I'VE BEEN THINKIN' MAYBE I SHOULD JOIN THE MILITARY
CLOSE THE FRIDGE, BRAD
I'M NOT IN COLLEGE AND MY WEENIEWORLD JOB ISN'T EXACTLY A MAJOR CAREER
BRAD, GET YOUR FEET DOWN! AND DON'T TALK WITH YOUR MOUTH FULL!
©2001 GEC Inc. Dist. by United Feature Syndicate, Inc. www.LuannsRoom.com
THINK I'D MAKE A GOOD SOLDIER?
OH, SURE. YOU TAKE ORDERS SO WELL
GREG 10·9

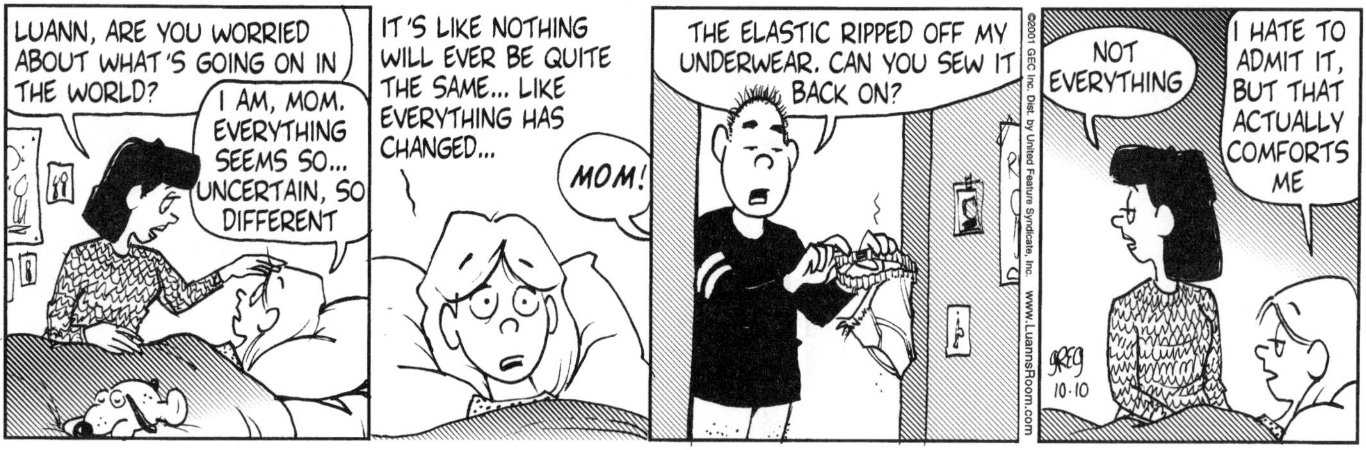
LUANN, ARE YOU WORRIED ABOUT WHAT'S GOING ON IN THE WORLD?
I AM, MOM. EVERYTHING SEEMS SO... UNCERTAIN, SO DIFFERENT
IT'S LIKE NOTHING WILL EVER BE QUITE THE SAME... LIKE EVERYTHING HAS CHANGED...
MOM!
THE ELASTIC RIPPED OFF MY UNDERWEAR. CAN YOU SEW IT BACK ON?
©2001 GEC Inc. Dist. by United Feature Syndicate, Inc. www.LuannsRoom.com
NOT EVERYTHING
I HATE TO ADMIT IT, BUT THAT ACTUALLY COMFORTS ME
GREG 10·10

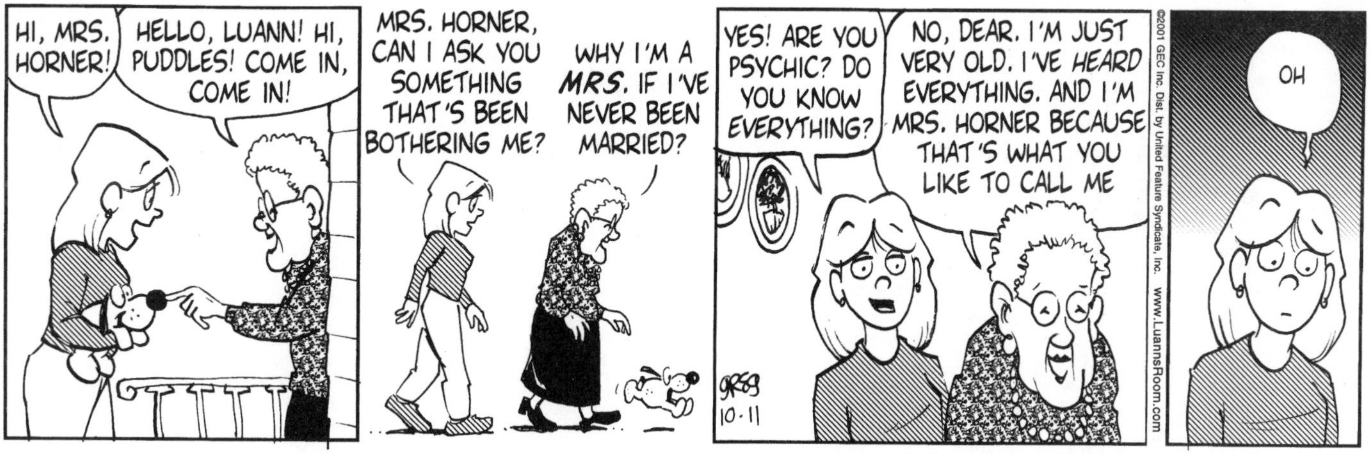
HI, MRS. HORNER!
HELLO, LUANN! HI, PUDDLES! COME IN, COME IN!
MRS. HORNER, CAN I ASK YOU SOMETHING THAT'S BEEN BOTHERING ME?
WHY I'M A *MRS.* IF I'VE NEVER BEEN MARRIED?
GREG 10-11
YES! ARE YOU PSYCHIC? DO YOU KNOW EVERYTHING?
NO, DEAR. I'M JUST VERY OLD. I'VE *HEARD* EVERYTHING. AND I'M MRS. HORNER BECAUSE THAT'S WHAT YOU LIKE TO CALL ME
©2001 GEC Inc. Dist. by United Feature Syndicate, Inc. www.LuannsRoom.com
OH

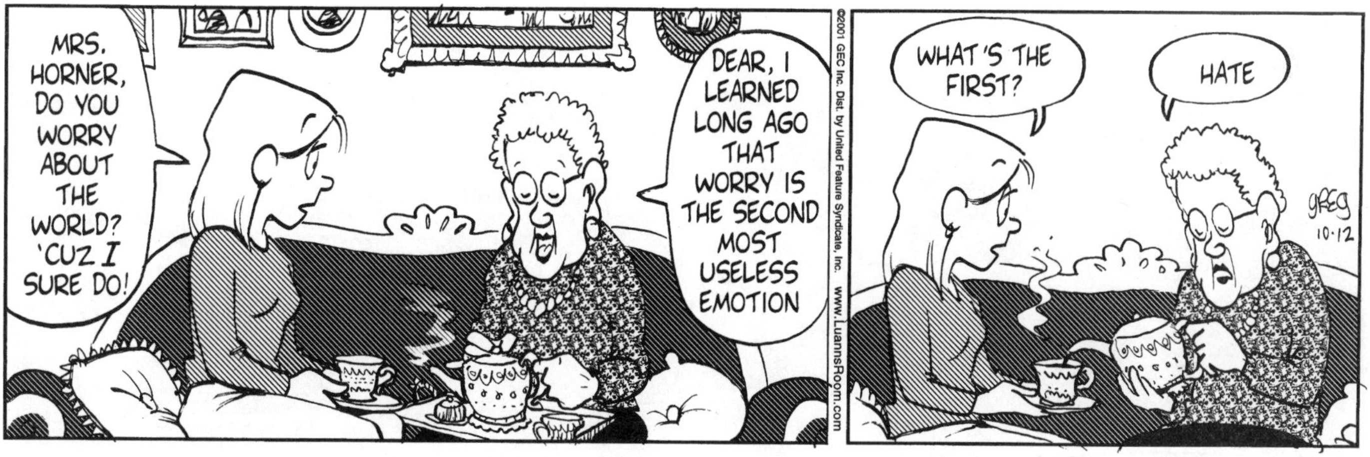
MRS. HORNER, DO YOU WORRY ABOUT THE WORLD? 'CUZ *I* SURE DO!
DEAR, I LEARNED LONG AGO THAT WORRY IS THE SECOND MOST USELESS EMOTION
©2001 GEC Inc. Dist. by United Feature Syndicate, Inc. www.LuannsRoom.com
WHAT'S THE FIRST?
HATE
GREG 10-12

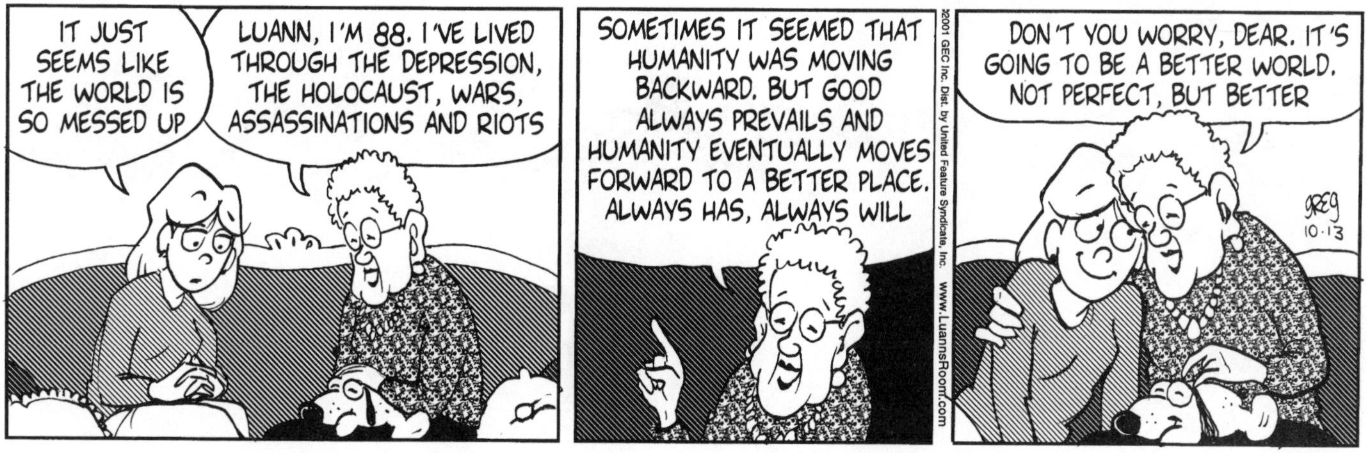
IT JUST SEEMS LIKE THE WORLD IS SO MESSED UP
LUANN, I'M 88. I'VE LIVED THROUGH THE DEPRESSION, THE HOLOCAUST, WARS, ASSASSINATIONS AND RIOTS
SOMETIMES IT SEEMED THAT HUMANITY WAS MOVING BACKWARD. BUT GOOD ALWAYS PREVAILS AND HUMANITY EVENTUALLY MOVES FORWARD TO A BETTER PLACE. ALWAYS HAS, ALWAYS WILL
©2001 GEC Inc. Dist. by United Feature Syndicate, Inc. www.LuannsRoom.com
DON'T YOU WORRY, DEAR. IT'S GOING TO BE A BETTER WORLD. NOT PERFECT, BUT BETTER
GREG 10-13

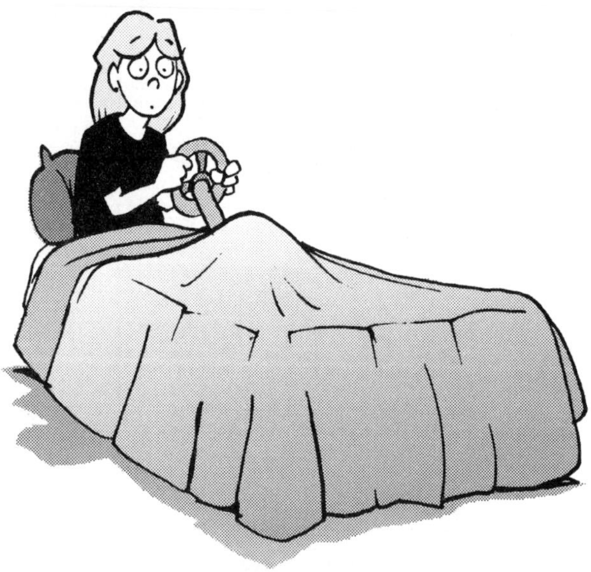

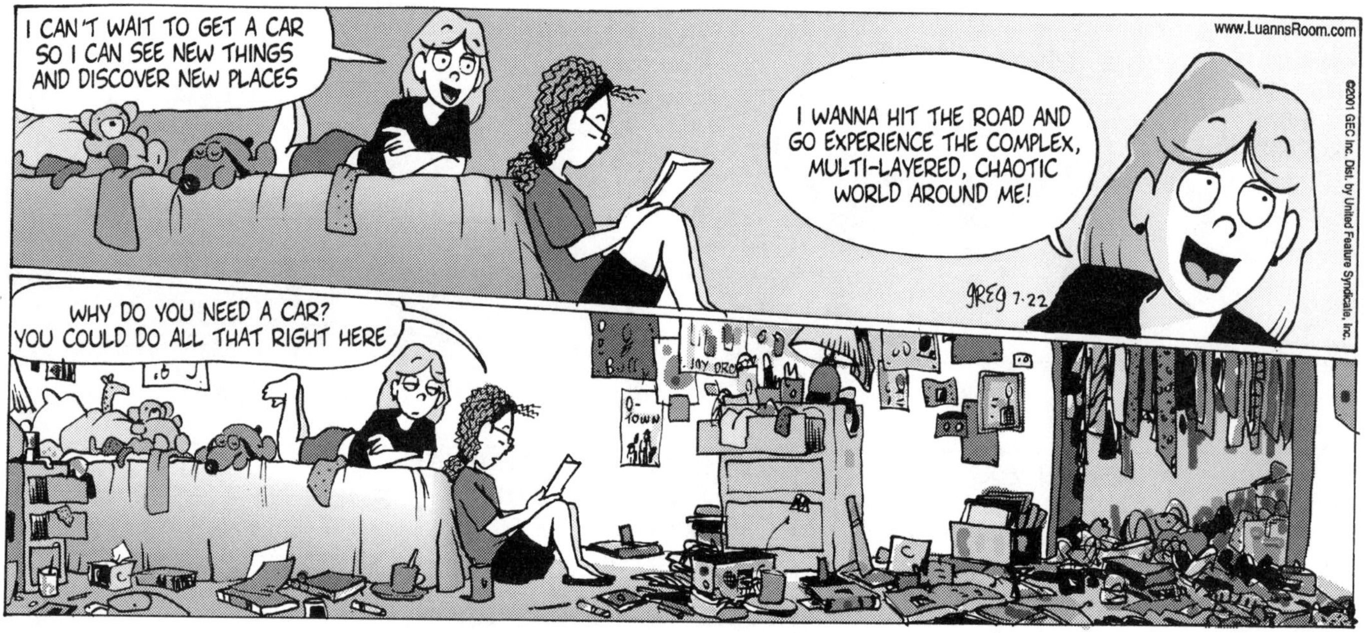
I CAN'T WAIT TO GET A CAR SO I CAN SEE NEW THINGS AND DISCOVER NEW PLACES
www.LuannsRoom.com
I WANNA HIT THE ROAD AND GO EXPERIENCE THE COMPLEX, MULTI-LAYERED, CHAOTIC WORLD AROUND ME!
©2001 GEC Inc. Dist. by United Feature Syndicate, Inc.
GREG 7·22
WHY DO YOU NEED A CAR? YOU COULD DO ALL THAT RIGHT HERE

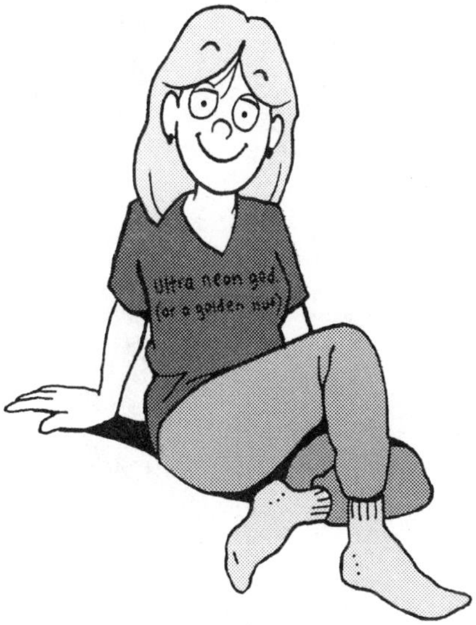
ultra neon god
(or a golden nut)

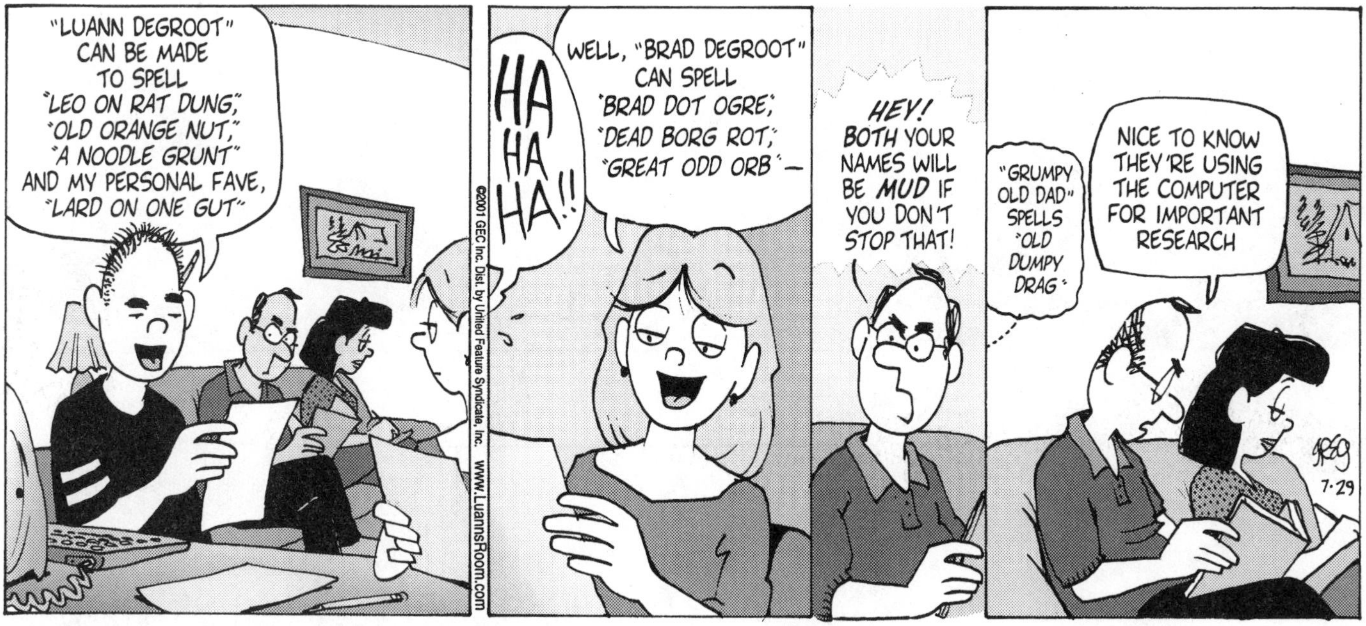
"LUANN DEGROOT" CAN BE MADE TO SPELL "LEO ON RAT DUNG," "OLD ORANGE NUT," "A NOODLE GRUNT" AND MY PERSONAL FAVE, "LARD ON ONE GUT"
HA HA HA!!
WELL, "BRAD DEGROOT" CAN SPELL "BRAD DOT OGRE," "DEAD BORG ROT," "GREAT ODD ORB" —
©2001 GEC Inc. Dist. by United Feature Syndicate, Inc. www.LuannsRoom.com
HEY! BOTH YOUR NAMES WILL BE MUD IF YOU DON'T STOP THAT!
"GRUMPY OLD DAD" SPELLS "OLD DUMPY DRAG"
NICE TO KNOW THEY'RE USING THE COMPUTER FOR IMPORTANT RESEARCH
GREG
7·29

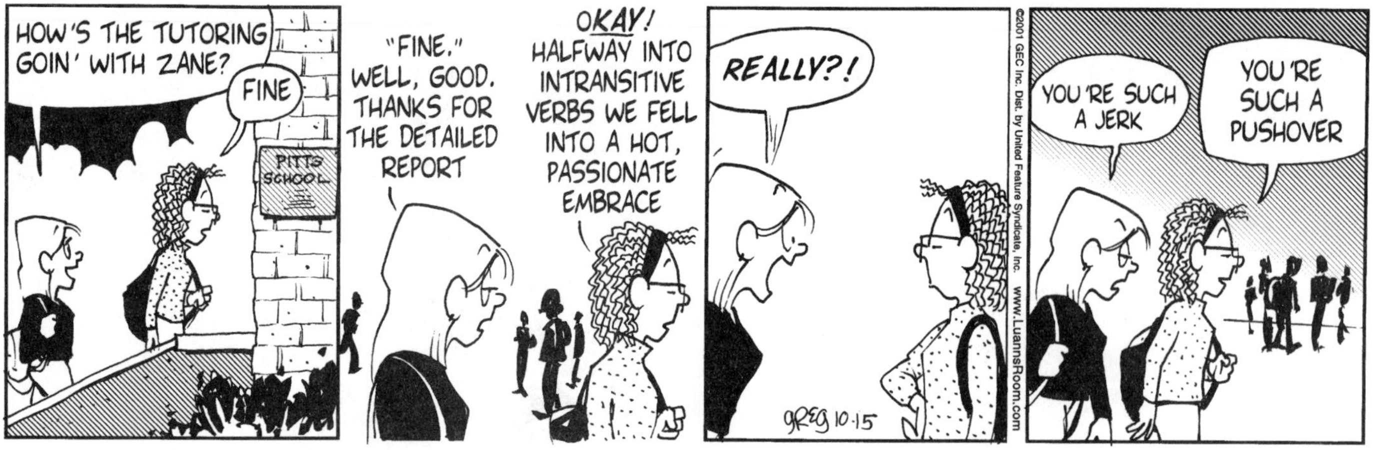
HOW'S THE TUTORING GOIN' WITH ZANE?
FINE
PITTS SCHOOL
"FINE." WELL, GOOD. THANKS FOR THE DETAILED REPORT
OKAY! HALFWAY INTO INTRANSITIVE VERBS WE FELL INTO A HOT, PASSIONATE EMBRACE
REALLY?!
GREG 10·15
©2001 GEC Inc. Dist. by United Feature Syndicate, Inc. www.LuannsRoom.com
YOU'RE SUCH A JERK
YOU'RE SUCH A PUSHOVER

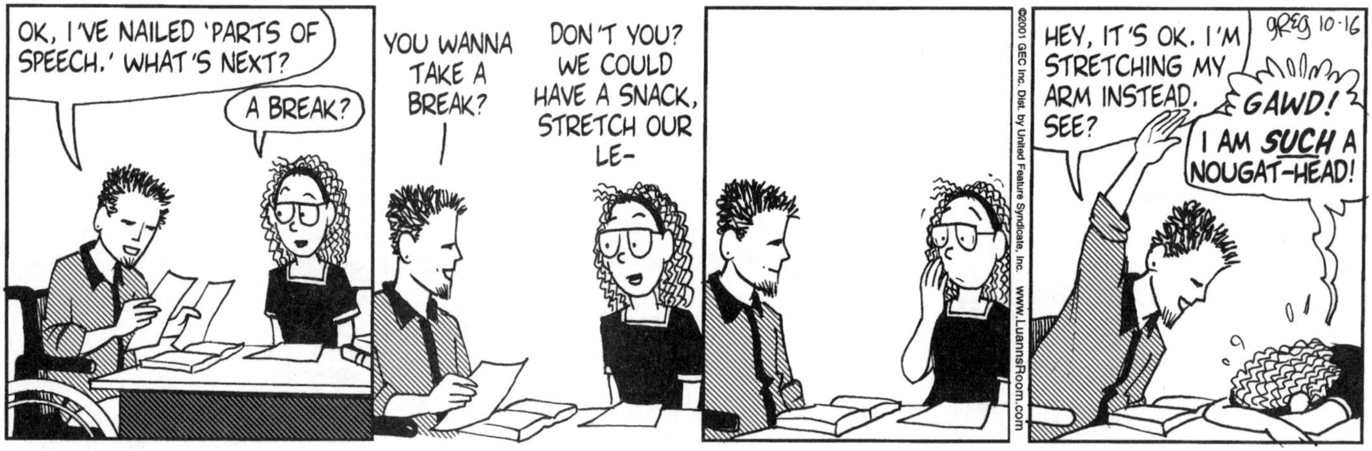
OK, I'VE NAILED 'PARTS OF SPEECH.' WHAT'S NEXT?
A BREAK?
YOU WANNA TAKE A BREAK?
DON'T YOU? WE COULD HAVE A SNACK, STRETCH OUR LE-
©2001 GEC Inc. Dist. by United Feature Syndicate, Inc. www.LuannsRoom.com
HEY, IT'S OK. I'M STRETCHING MY ARM INSTEAD. SEE?
GREG 10·16
GAWD! I AM SUCH A NOUGAT-HEAD!

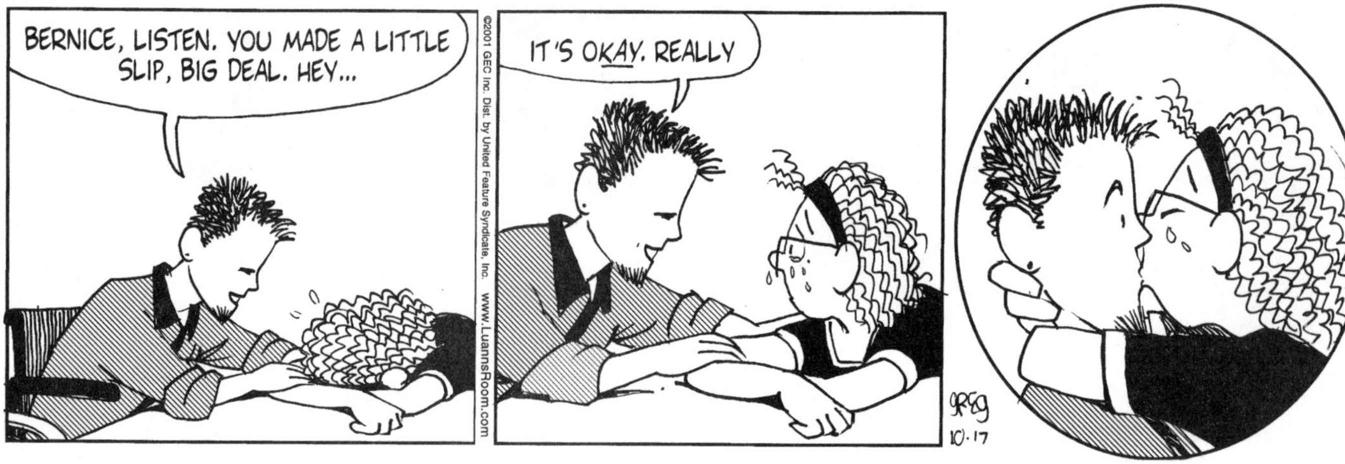
BERNICE, LISTEN. YOU MADE A LITTLE SLIP, BIG DEAL. HEY...
©2001 GEC Inc. Dist. by United Feature Syndicate, Inc. www.LuannsRoom.com
IT'S OKAY. REALLY
GREG 10·17

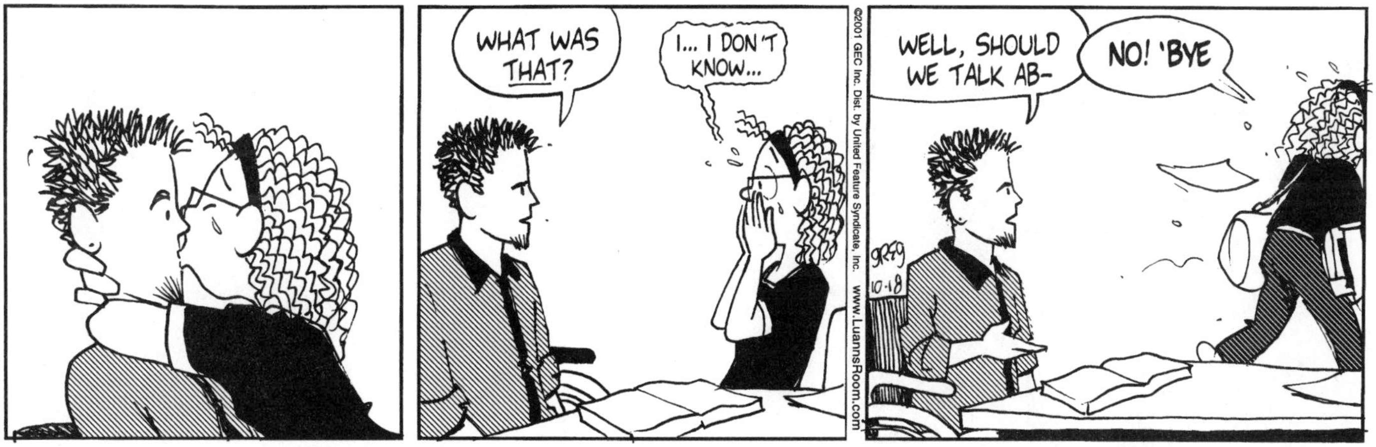
WHAT WAS THAT?
I... I DON'T KNOW...
©2001 GEC Inc. Dist. by United Feature Syndicate, Inc. www.LuannsRoom.com
WELL, SHOULD WE TALK AB-
NO! 'BYE
GREG 10-18

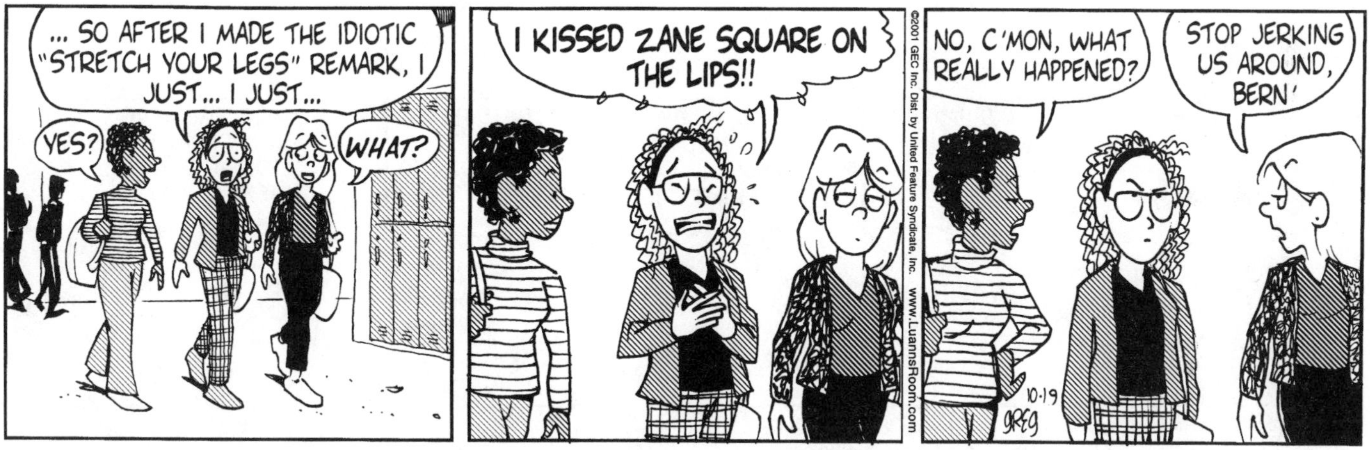
... SO AFTER I MADE THE IDIOTIC "STRETCH YOUR LEGS" REMARK, I JUST... I JUST...
YES?
WHAT?
I KISSED ZANE SQUARE ON THE LIPS!!
©2001 GEC Inc. Dist. by United Feature Syndicate, Inc. www.LuannsRoom.com
NO, C'MON, WHAT REALLY HAPPENED?
STOP JERKING US AROUND, BERN'
10-19 GREG

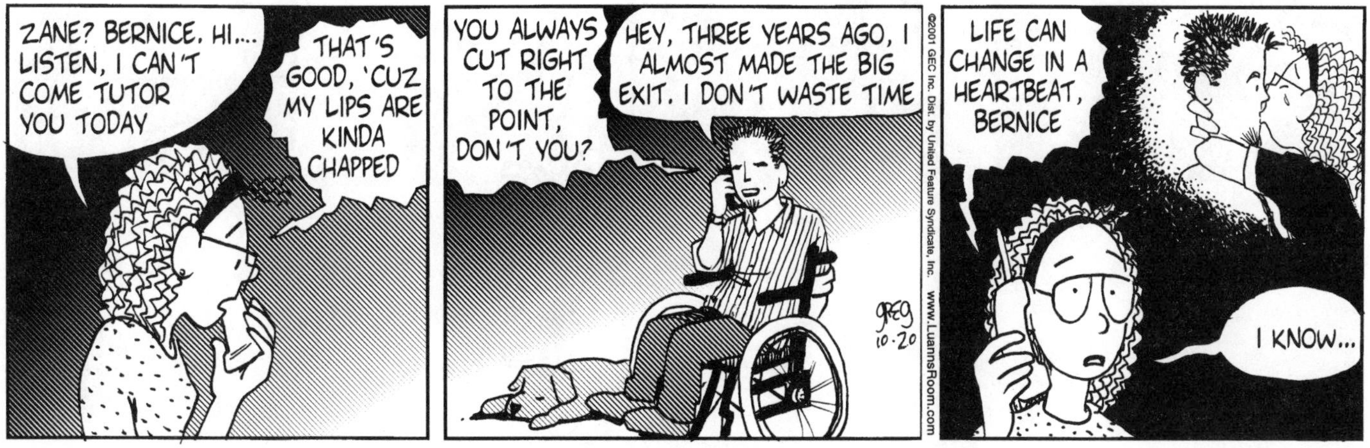
ZANE? BERNICE. HI.... LISTEN, I CAN'T COME TUTOR YOU TODAY
THAT'S GOOD, 'CUZ MY LIPS ARE KINDA CHAPPED
YOU ALWAYS CUT RIGHT TO THE POINT, DON'T YOU?
HEY, THREE YEARS AGO, I ALMOST MADE THE BIG EXIT. I DON'T WASTE TIME
GREG 10-20
©2001 GEC Inc. Dist. by United Feature Syndicate, Inc. www.LuannsRoom.com
LIFE CAN CHANGE IN A HEARTBEAT, BERNICE
I KNOW...

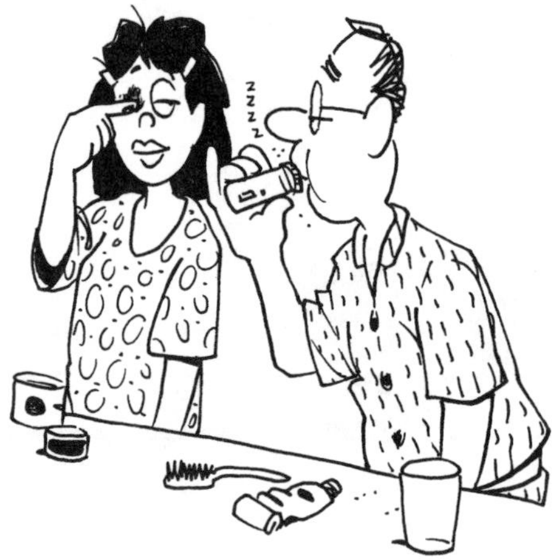

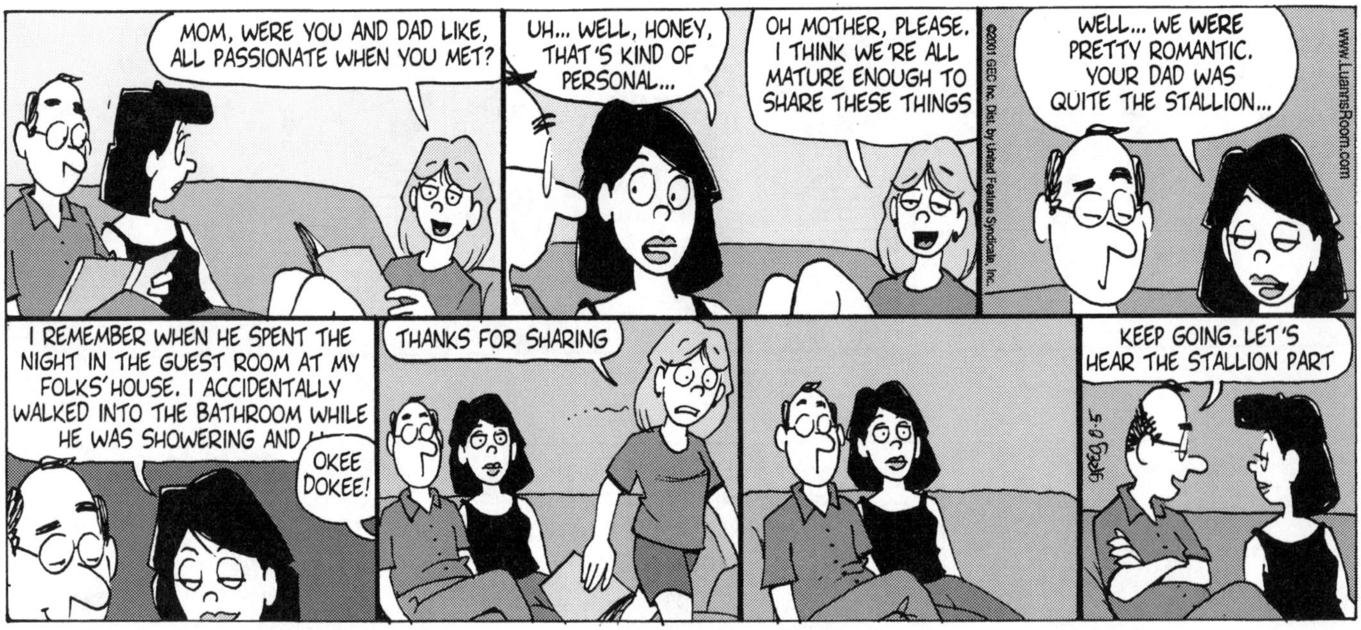

MOM, WERE YOU AND DAD LIKE, ALL PASSIONATE WHEN YOU MET?
UH... WELL, HONEY, THAT'S KIND OF PERSONAL...
OH MOTHER, PLEASE. I THINK WE'RE ALL MATURE ENOUGH TO SHARE THESE THINGS
©2001 GEC Inc. Dist. by United Feature Syndicate, Inc.
WELL... WE WERE PRETTY ROMANTIC. YOUR DAD WAS QUITE THE STALLION...
www.LuannsRoom.com
I REMEMBER WHEN HE SPENT THE NIGHT IN THE GUEST ROOM AT MY FOLKS' HOUSE. I ACCIDENTALLY WALKED INTO THE BATHROOM WHILE HE WAS SHOWERING AND
OKEE DOKEE!
THANKS FOR SHARING
greg 8-5
KEEP GOING. LET'S HEAR THE STALLION PART

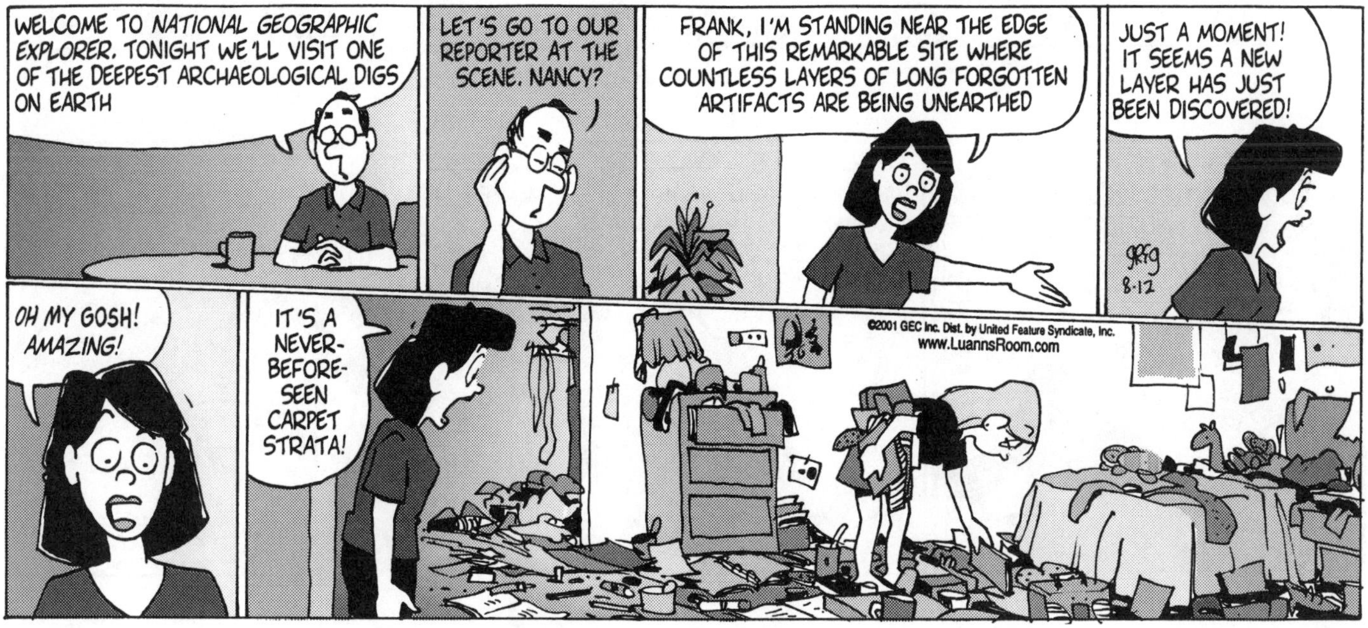
WELCOME TO NATIONAL GEOGRAPHIC EXPLORER. TONIGHT WE'LL VISIT ONE OF THE DEEPEST ARCHAEOLOGICAL DIGS ON EARTH
LET'S GO TO OUR REPORTER AT THE SCENE. NANCY?
FRANK, I'M STANDING NEAR THE EDGE OF THIS REMARKABLE SITE WHERE COUNTLESS LAYERS OF LONG FORGOTTEN ARTIFACTS ARE BEING UNEARTHED
JUST A MOMENT! IT SEEMS A NEW LAYER HAS JUST BEEN DISCOVERED!
GREG
8-12
OH MY GOSH! AMAZING!
IT'S A NEVER-BEFORE-SEEN CARPET STRATA!
©2001 GEC Inc. Dist. by United Feature Syndicate, Inc.
www.LuannsRoom.com

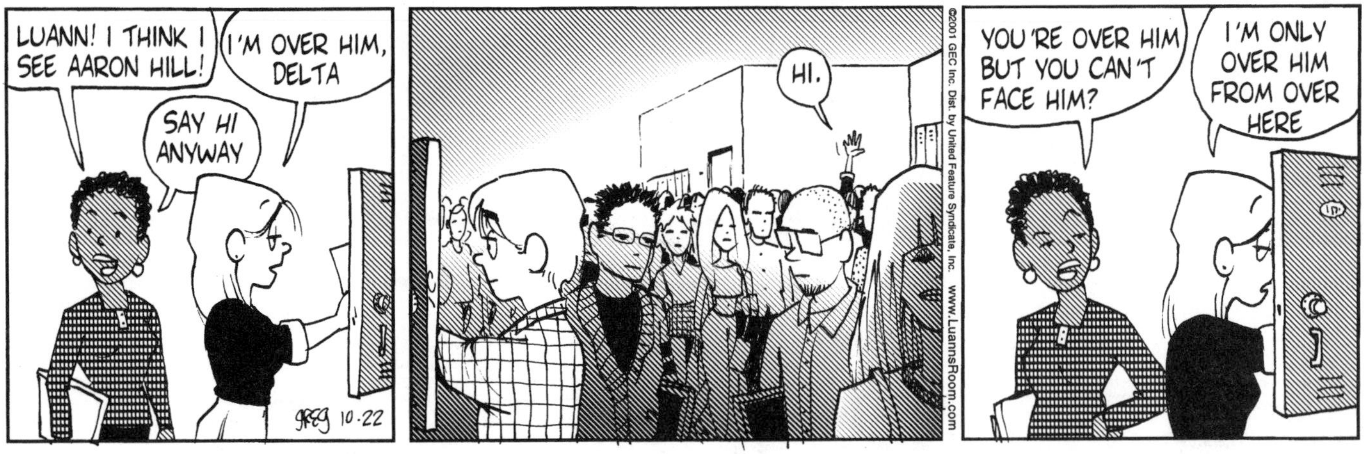
LUANN! I THINK I SEE AARON HILL!
I'M OVER HIM, DELTA
SAY HI ANYWAY
GREG 10·22
HI.
©2001 GEC Inc. Dist. by United Feature Syndicate, Inc. www.LuannsRoom.com
YOU'RE OVER HIM BUT YOU CAN'T FACE HIM?
I'M ONLY OVER HIM FROM OVER HERE

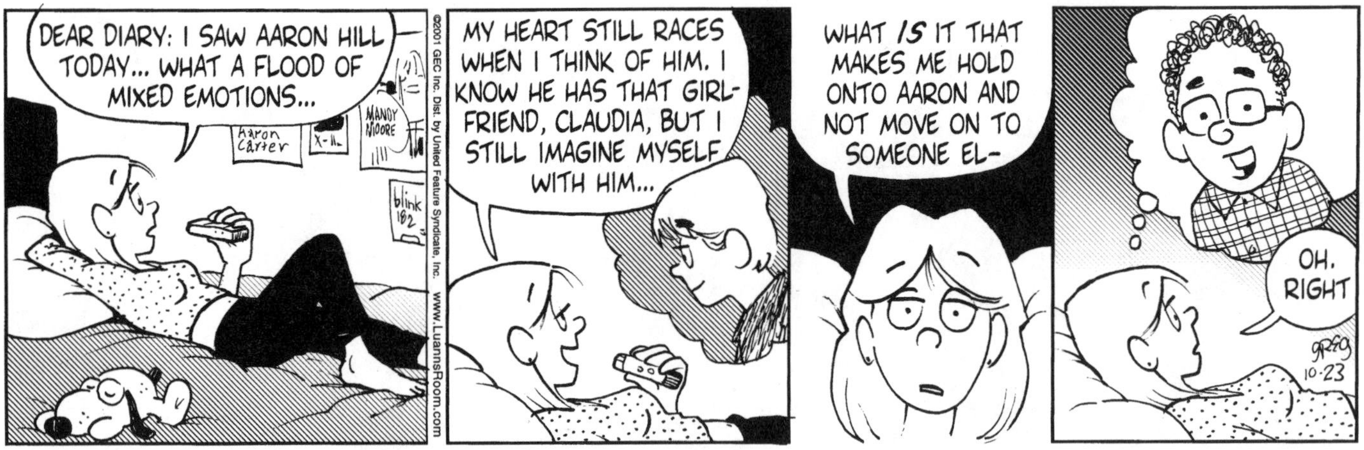
DEAR DIARY: I SAW AARON HILL TODAY... WHAT A FLOOD OF MIXED EMOTIONS...
Aaron Carter
MANDY MOORE
blink 182
©2001 GEC Inc. Dist. by United Feature Syndicate, Inc. www.LuannsRoom.com
MY HEART STILL RACES WHEN I THINK OF HIM. I KNOW HE HAS THAT GIRLFRIEND, CLAUDIA, BUT I STILL IMAGINE MYSELF WITH HIM...
WHAT *IS* IT THAT MAKES ME HOLD ONTO AARON AND NOT MOVE ON TO SOMEONE EL-
OH. RIGHT
GREG 10·23

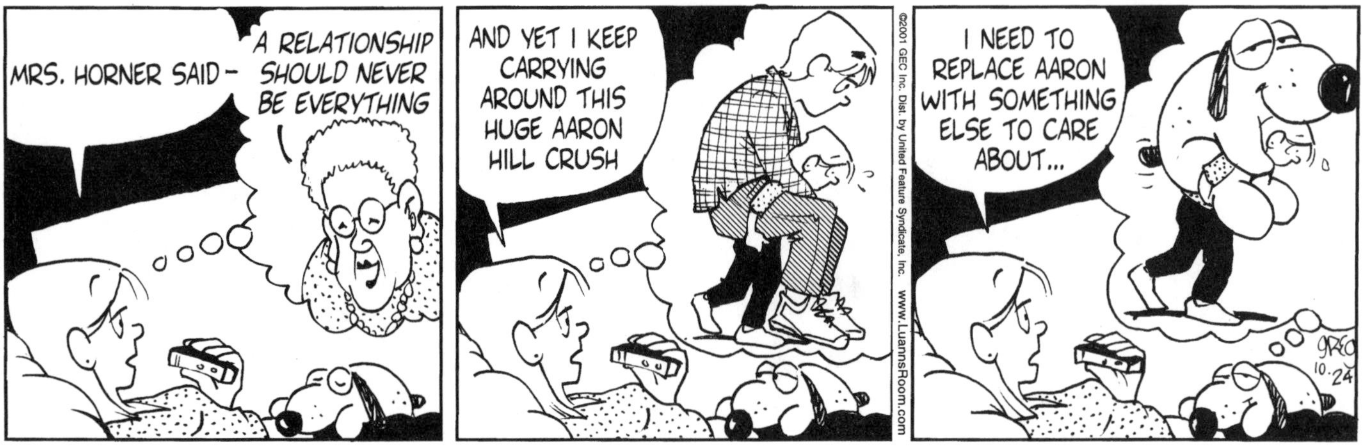
MRS. HORNER SAID –
A RELATIONSHIP SHOULD NEVER BE EVERYTHING
AND YET I KEEP CARRYING AROUND THIS HUGE AARON HILL CRUSH
©2001 GEC Inc. Dist. by United Feature Syndicate, Inc. www.LuannsRoom.com
I NEED TO REPLACE AARON WITH SOMETHING ELSE TO CARE ABOUT...
GREG 10·24

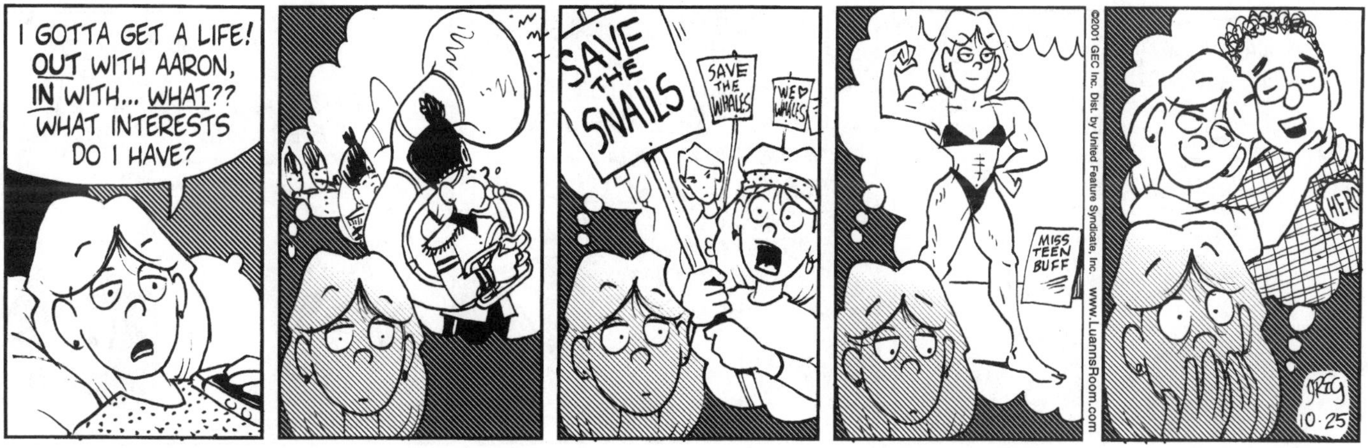
I GOTTA GET A LIFE! OUT WITH AARON, IN WITH... WHAT?? WHAT INTERESTS DO I HAVE?
SAVE THE SNAILS
SAVE THE WHALES
MISS TEEN BUFF
©2001 GEC Inc. Dist. by United Feature Syndicate, Inc. www.LuannsRoom.com
HERO
GREG 10·25

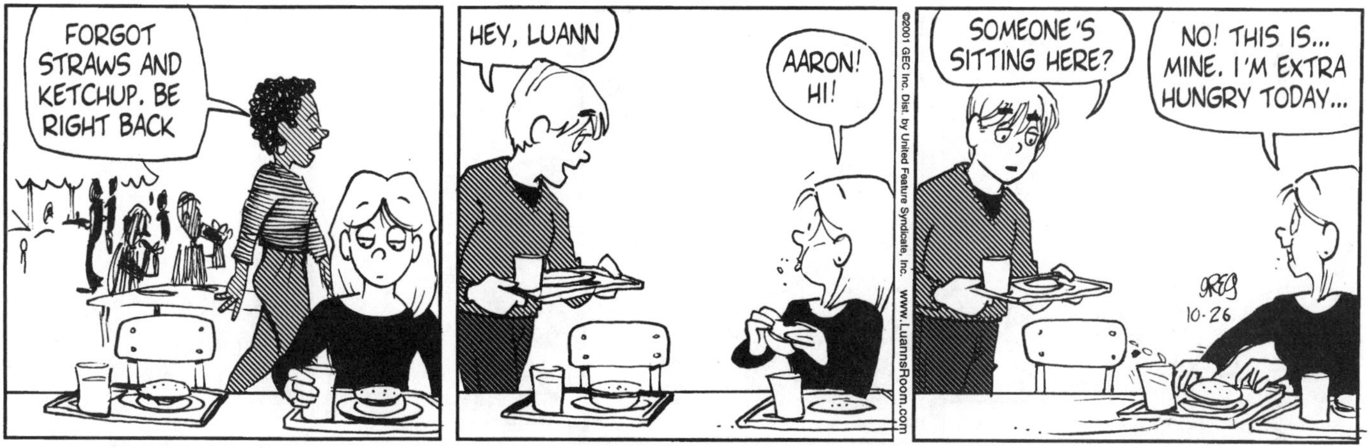
FORGOT STRAWS AND KETCHUP. BE RIGHT BACK
©2001 GEC Inc. Dist. by United Feature Syndicate, Inc. www.LuannsRoom.com
HEY, LUANN
AARON! HI!
SOMEONE'S SITTING HERE?
NO! THIS IS... MINE. I'M EXTRA HUNGRY TODAY...
GREG 10·26

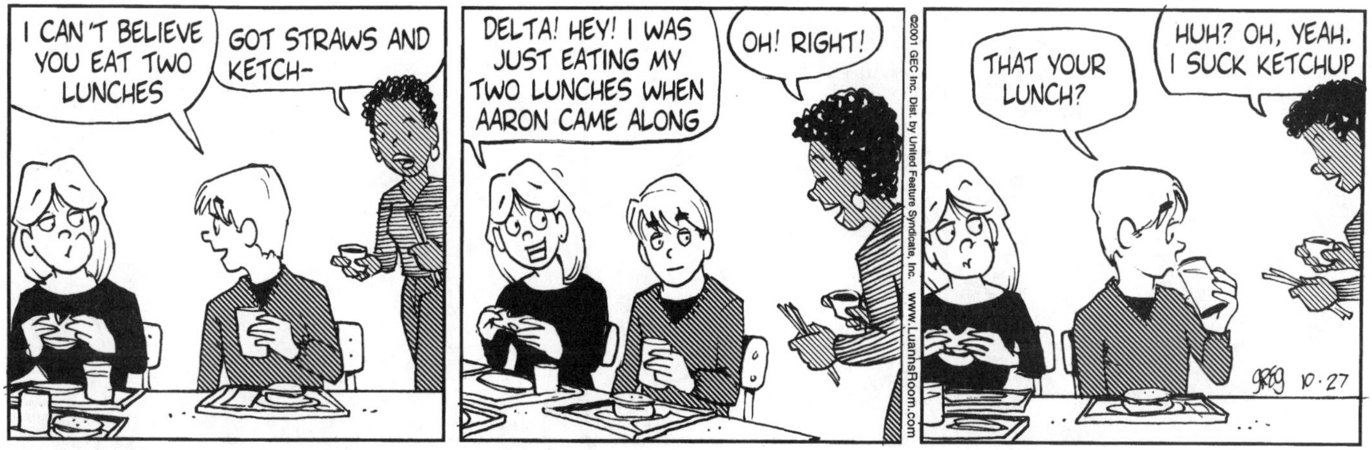
I CAN'T BELIEVE YOU EAT TWO LUNCHES
GOT STRAWS AND KETCH-
DELTA! HEY! I WAS JUST EATING MY TWO LUNCHES WHEN AARON CAME ALONG
OH! RIGHT!
©2001 GEC Inc. Dist. by United Feature Syndicate, Inc. www.LuannsRoom.com
THAT YOUR LUNCH?
HUH? OH, YEAH. I SUCK KETCHUP
GREG 10·27

HOW WAS YOUR SUMMER, AARON?

PRETTY BUSY. I HELPED MY DAD PUT A NEW ROOF ON THE HOUSE

FULL OF HIS GIRLFRIEND, I'M SURE

IT WAS HARD WORK BECAUSE WE HAD TO TAKE OFF ALL THE OLD SHINGLES AND THEN PUT DOWN BIG SHEETS OF PLYWOOD ALL OV

HE AND CLAUDIA PROBABLY MADE WEDDING PLANS OR SOMETHING. AS IF I WANNA HEAR ABOUT THAT

SO HOW WAS YOUR SUMMER?

WONDER IF HE KNOWS I'M NOT EVEN LISTENING?

GREG 10-29

AARON! C'MERE! I WANT YOU TO BE THE FIRST TO SEE MY CUTE NEW CHEER OUTFIT!

BUT, TIFFANY, MY TRAY —

LUANN CAN TAKE CARE OF IT. C'MON!

GREG 10-30

LOOK AT TIFF... WHAT A FLIRT! AND AARON LAPS IT UP!

I THOUGHT HE HAD A GIRLFRIEND

HE DOES! BUT CLAUDIA LIVES FAR AWAY, SO, HECK, WHY NOT MESS AROUND?

ACTUALLY, IT LOOKS PRETTY INNOCENT

OOPS. INNOCENCE LOST...

DO YOU HAVE A BRICK ON YOU?

GREG 10-31

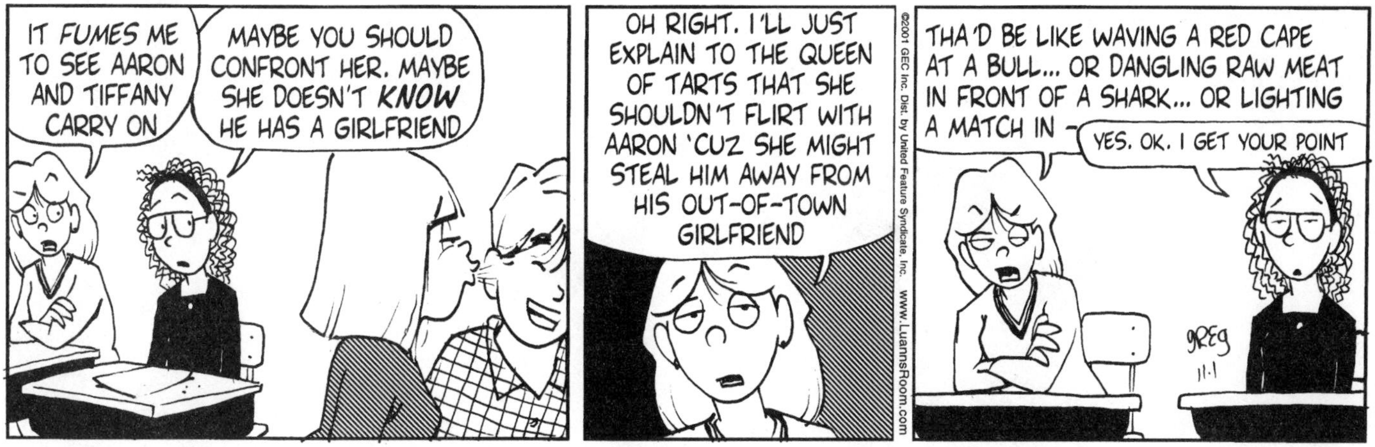
IT *FUMES* ME TO SEE AARON AND TIFFANY CARRY ON
MAYBE YOU SHOULD CONFRONT HER. MAYBE SHE DOESN'T ***KNOW*** HE HAS A GIRLFRIEND
OH RIGHT. I'LL JUST EXPLAIN TO THE QUEEN OF TARTS THAT SHE SHOULDN'T FLIRT WITH AARON 'CUZ SHE MIGHT STEAL HIM AWAY FROM HIS OUT-OF-TOWN GIRLFRIEND
©2001 GEC Inc. Dist. by United Feature Syndicate, Inc. www.LuannsRoom.com
THA'D BE LIKE WAVING A RED CAPE AT A BULL... OR DANGLING RAW MEAT IN FRONT OF A SHARK... OR LIGHTING A MATCH IN -
YES. OK. I GET YOUR POINT
GREG 11·1

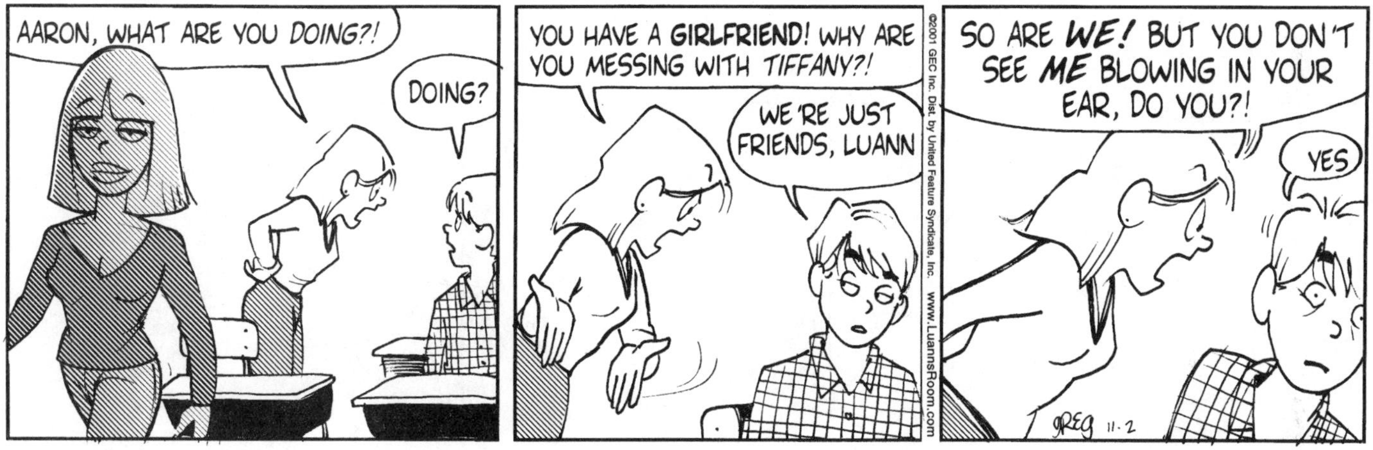
AARON, WHAT ARE YOU *DOING?!*
DOING?
YOU HAVE A **GIRLFRIEND**! WHY ARE YOU MESSING WITH *TIFFANY?!*
WE'RE JUST FRIENDS, LUANN
©2001 GEC Inc. Dist. by United Feature Syndicate, Inc. www.LuannsRoom.com
SO ARE ***WE!*** BUT YOU DON'T SEE ***ME*** BLOWING IN YOUR EAR, DO YOU?!
YES
GREG 11·2

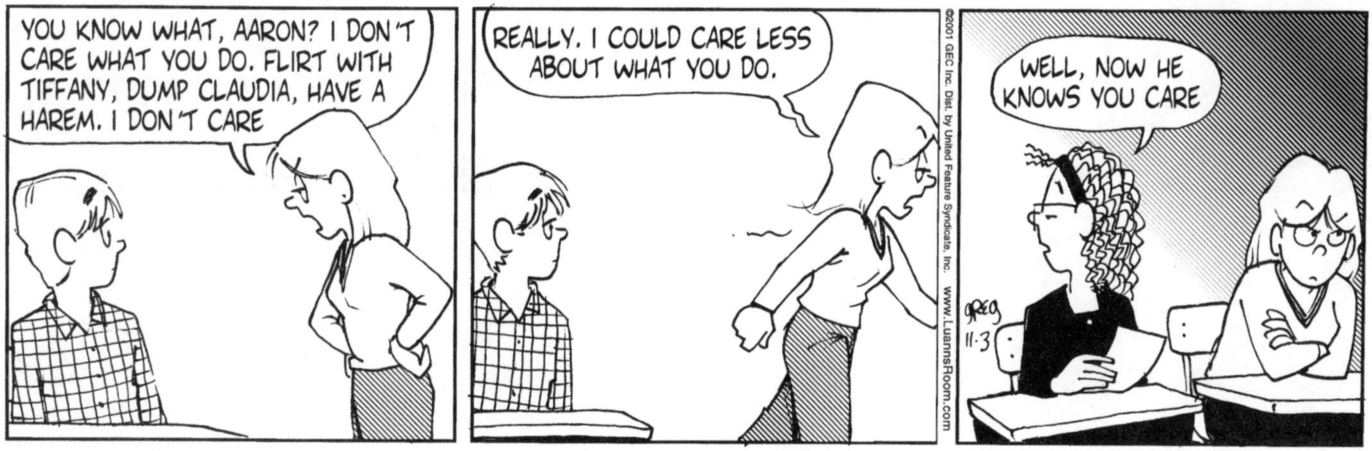
YOU KNOW WHAT, AARON? I DON'T CARE WHAT YOU DO. FLIRT WITH TIFFANY, DUMP CLAUDIA, HAVE A HAREM. I DON'T CARE
REALLY. I COULD CARE LESS ABOUT WHAT YOU DO.
©2001 GEC Inc. Dist. by United Feature Syndicate, Inc. www.LuannsRoom.com
WELL, NOW HE KNOWS YOU CARE
GREG 11·3

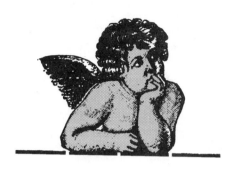

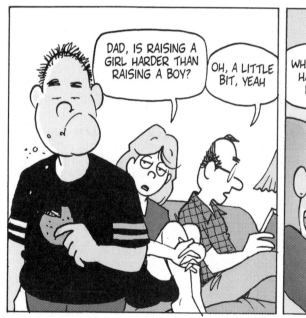

DAD, IS RAISING A GIRL HARDER THAN RAISING A BOY?
OH, A LITTLE BIT, YEAH
WHAT'S THE HARDEST PART?
WELL, LET'S SEE...
©2001 GEC Inc. Dist. by United Feature Syndicate, Inc.
PROBABLY THAT PART BETWEEN "IT'S A GIRL" AND "WHO GIVES THIS BRIDE?"
www.LuannsRoom.com
GREG 8·19

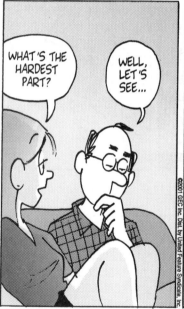

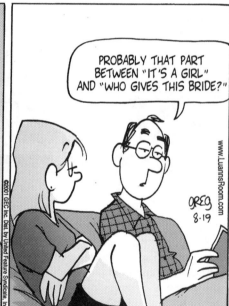

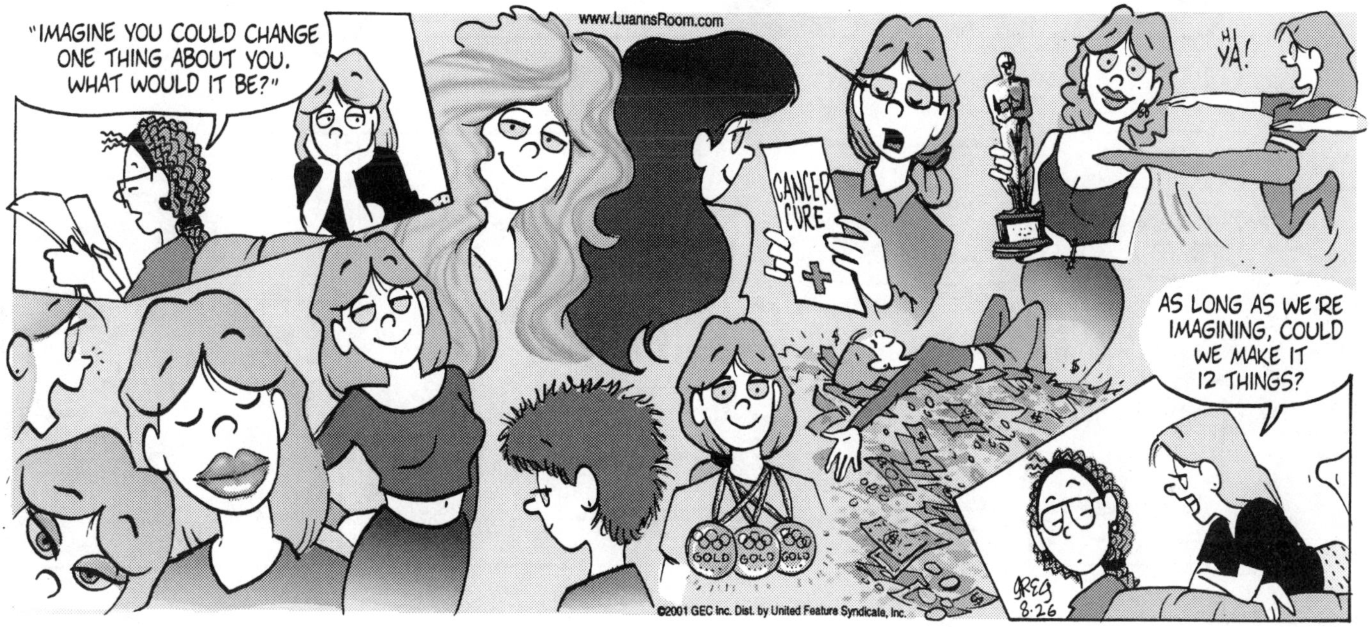

www.LuannsRoom.com
"IMAGINE YOU COULD CHANGE ONE THING ABOUT YOU. WHAT WOULD IT BE?"
CANCER CURE
HI YA!
GOLD
GOLD
GOLD
AS LONG AS WE'RE IMAGINING, COULD WE MAKE IT 12 THINGS?
GREG 8·26
©2001 GEC Inc. Dist. by United Feature Syndicate, Inc.

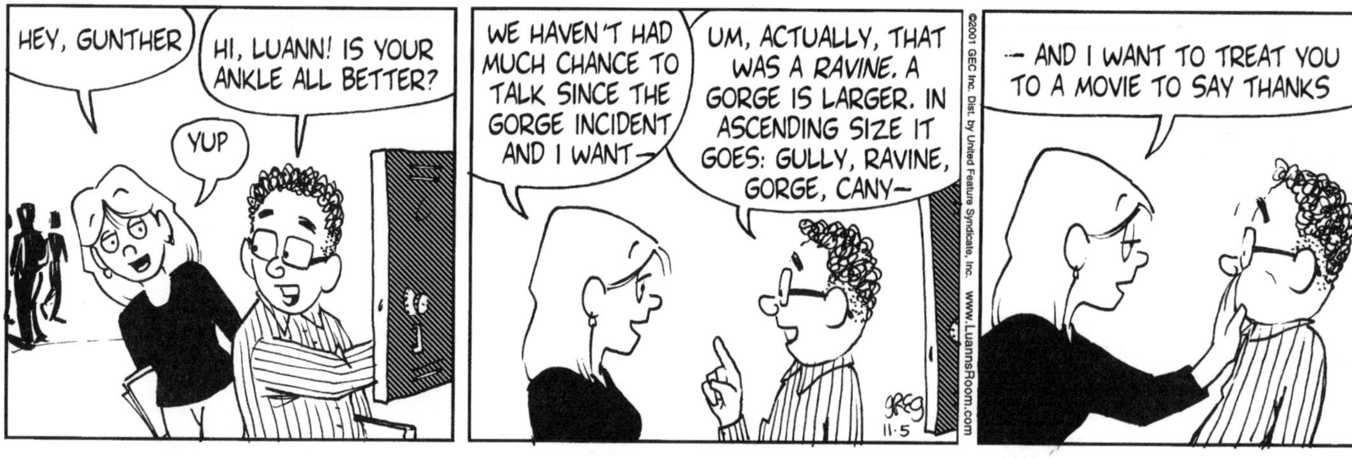
HEY, GUNTHER
HI, LUANN! IS YOUR ANKLE ALL BETTER?
YUP
WE HAVEN'T HAD MUCH CHANCE TO TALK SINCE THE GORGE INCIDENT AND I WANT—
UM, ACTUALLY, THAT WAS A *RAVINE*. A GORGE IS LARGER. IN ASCENDING SIZE IT GOES: GULLY, RAVINE, GORGE, CANY—
GREG 11.5
©2001 GEC Inc. Dist. by United Feature Syndicate, Inc.
www.LuannsRoom.com
— AND I WANT TO TREAT YOU TO A MOVIE TO SAY THANKS

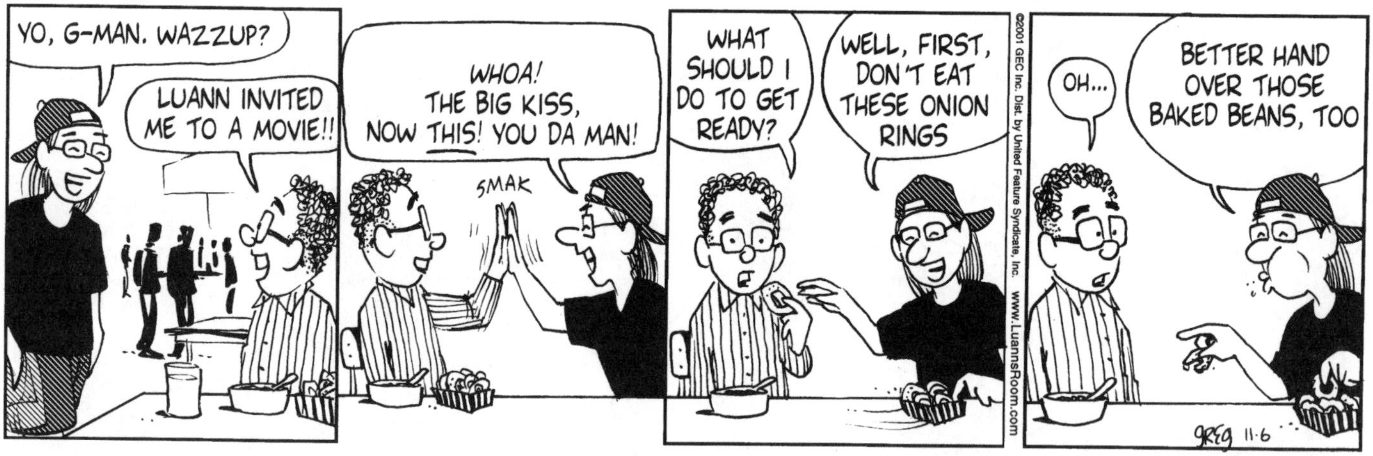
YO, G-MAN. WAZZUP?
LUANN INVITED ME TO A MOVIE!!
WHOA! THE BIG KISS, NOW THIS! YOU DA MAN!
SMAK
WHAT SHOULD I DO TO GET READY?
WELL, FIRST, DON'T EAT THESE ONION RINGS
©2001 GEC Inc. Dist. by United Feature Syndicate, Inc.
www.LuannsRoom.com
OH...
BETTER HAND OVER THOSE BAKED BEANS, TOO
GREG 11.6

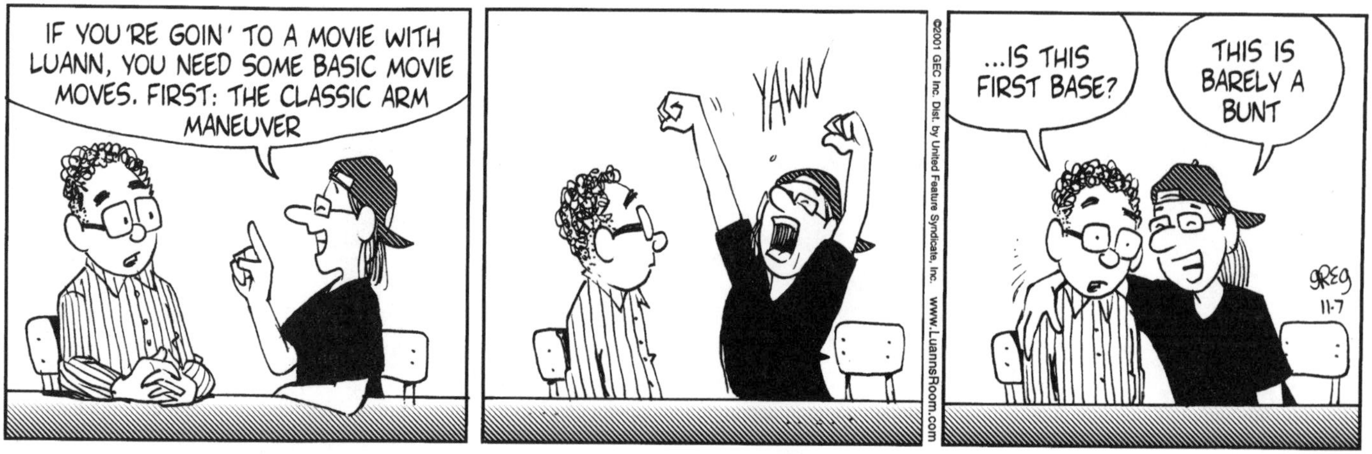
IF YOU'RE GOIN' TO A MOVIE WITH LUANN, YOU NEED SOME BASIC MOVIE MOVES. FIRST: THE CLASSIC ARM MANEUVER
YAWN
©2001 GEC Inc. Dist. by United Feature Syndicate, Inc.
www.LuannsRoom.com
...IS THIS FIRST BASE?
THIS IS BARELY A BUNT
GREG 11.7

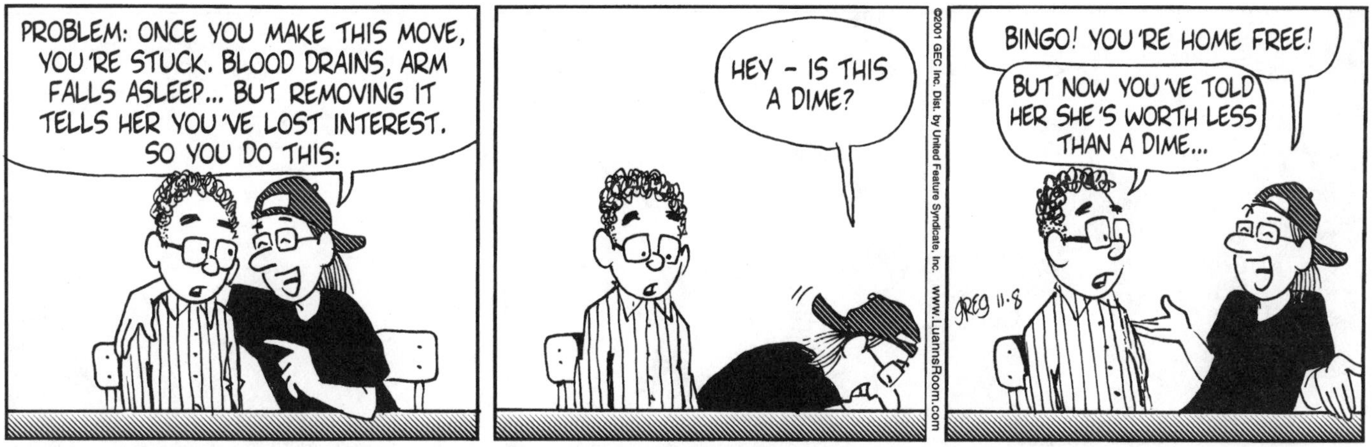
PROBLEM: ONCE YOU MAKE THIS MOVE, YOU'RE STUCK. BLOOD DRAINS, ARM FALLS ASLEEP... BUT REMOVING IT TELLS HER YOU'VE LOST INTEREST. SO YOU DO THIS:
HEY – IS THIS A DIME?
©2001 GEC Inc. Dist. by United Feature Syndicate, Inc. www.LuannsRoom.com
GREG 11·8
BINGO! YOU'RE HOME FREE!
BUT NOW YOU'VE TOLD HER SHE'S WORTH LESS THAN A DIME...

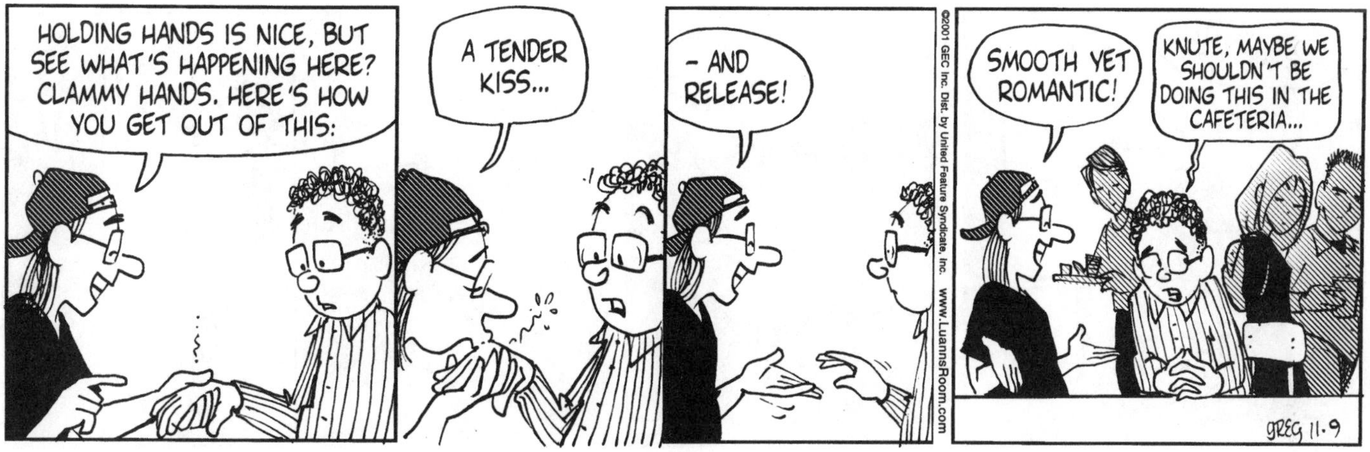
HOLDING HANDS IS NICE, BUT SEE WHAT'S HAPPENING HERE? CLAMMY HANDS. HERE'S HOW YOU GET OUT OF THIS:
A TENDER KISS...
– AND RELEASE!
©2001 GEC Inc. Dist. by United Feature Syndicate, Inc. www.LuannsRoom.com
SMOOTH YET ROMANTIC!
KNUTE, MAYBE WE SHOULDN'T BE DOING THIS IN THE CAFETERIA...
GREG 11·9

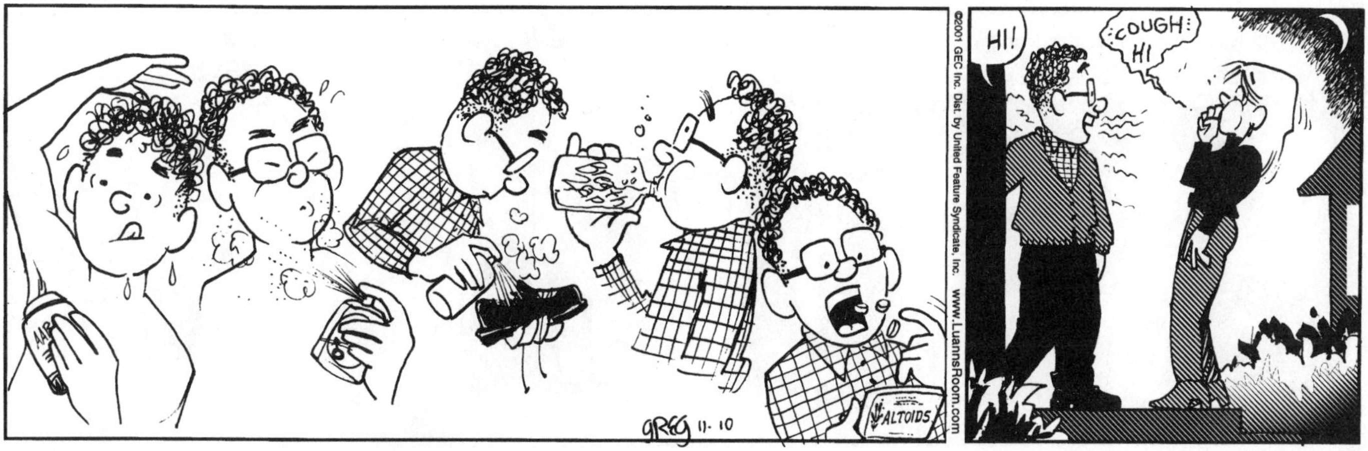
AIR
ALTOIDS
GREG 11·10
©2001 GEC Inc. Dist. by United Feature Syndicate, Inc. www.LuannsRoom.com
HI!
COUGH HI

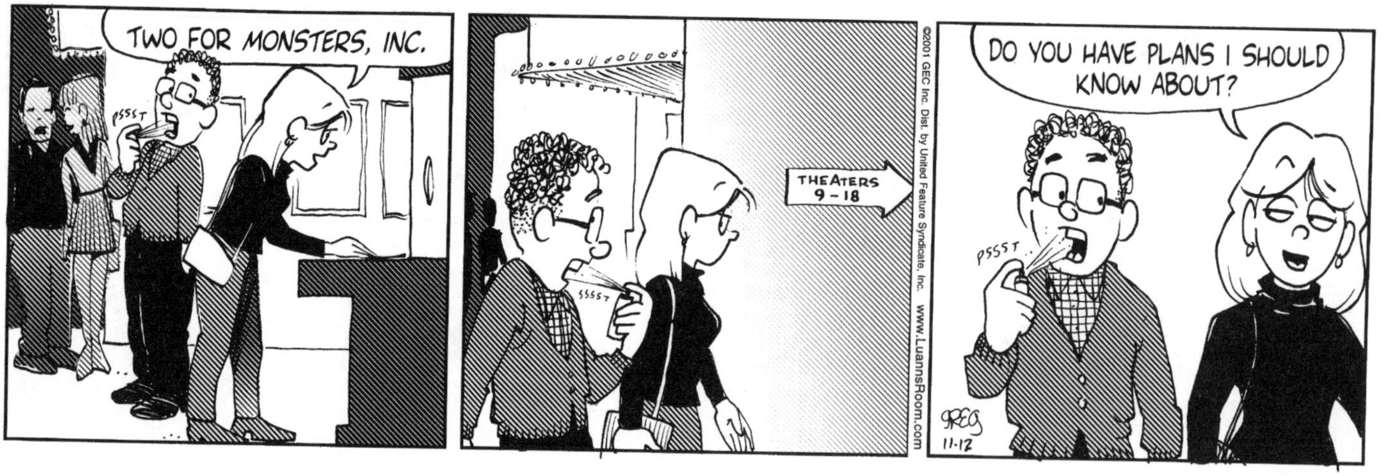
TWO FOR MONSTERS, INC.
PSSST
SSSST
THEATERS 9 – 18
©2001 GEC Inc. Dist. by United Feature Syndicate, Inc. www.LuannsRoom.com
DO YOU HAVE PLANS I SHOULD KNOW ABOUT?
PSSST...
GREG 11-12

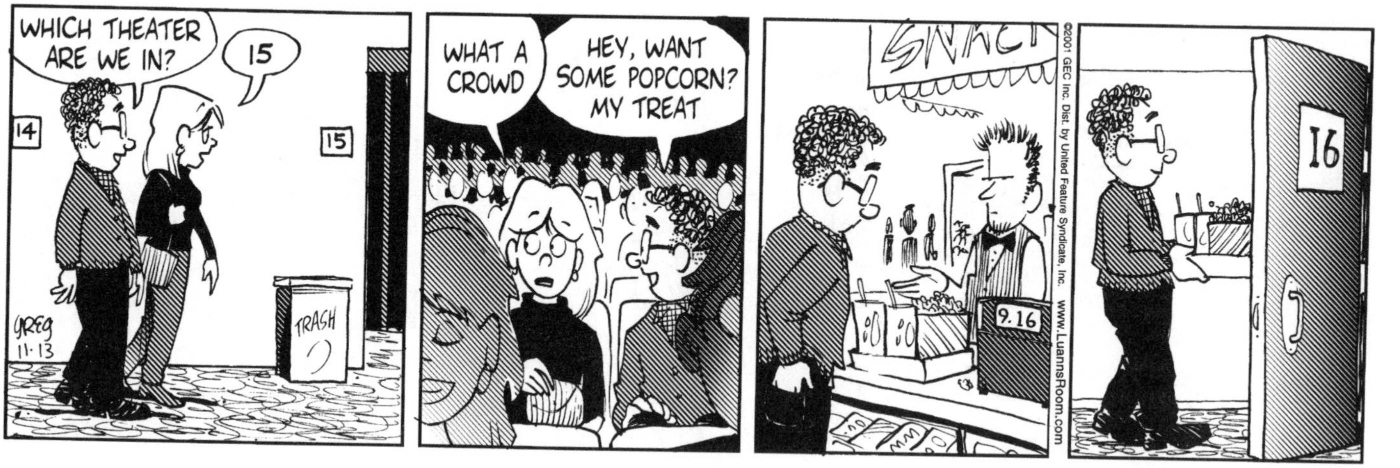
WHICH THEATER ARE WE IN?
15
14
15
TRASH
GREG 11-13
WHAT A CROWD
HEY, WANT SOME POPCORN? MY TREAT
9.16
©2001 GEC Inc. Dist. by United Feature Syndicate, Inc. www.LuannsRoom.com
16

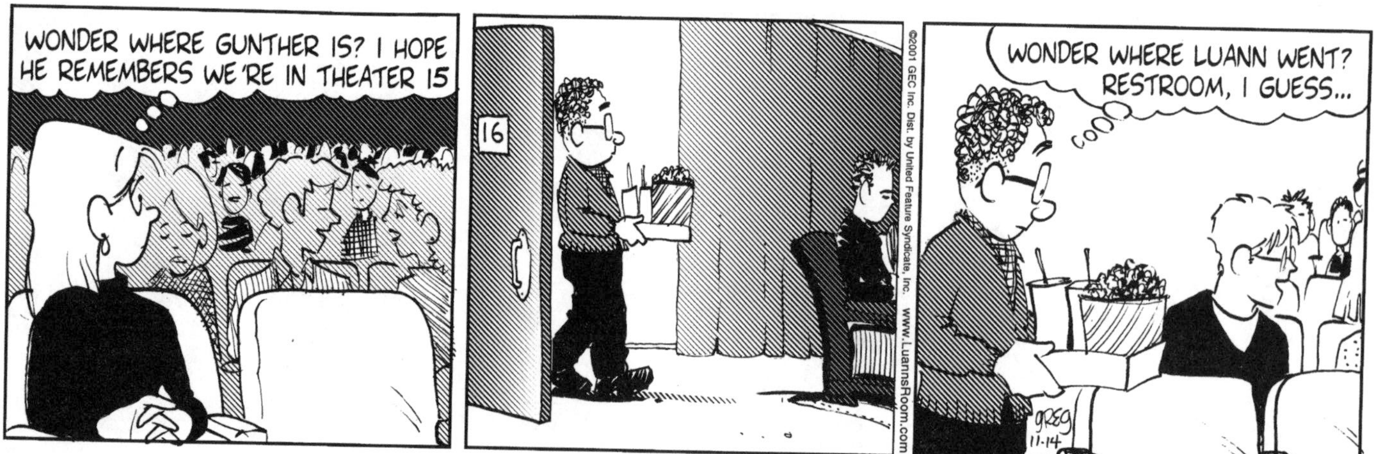
WONDER WHERE GUNTHER IS? I HOPE HE REMEMBERS WE'RE IN THEATER 15
16
©2001 GEC Inc. Dist. by United Feature Syndicate, Inc. www.LuannsRoom.com
WONDER WHERE LUANN WENT? RESTROOM, I GUESS...
GREG 11-14

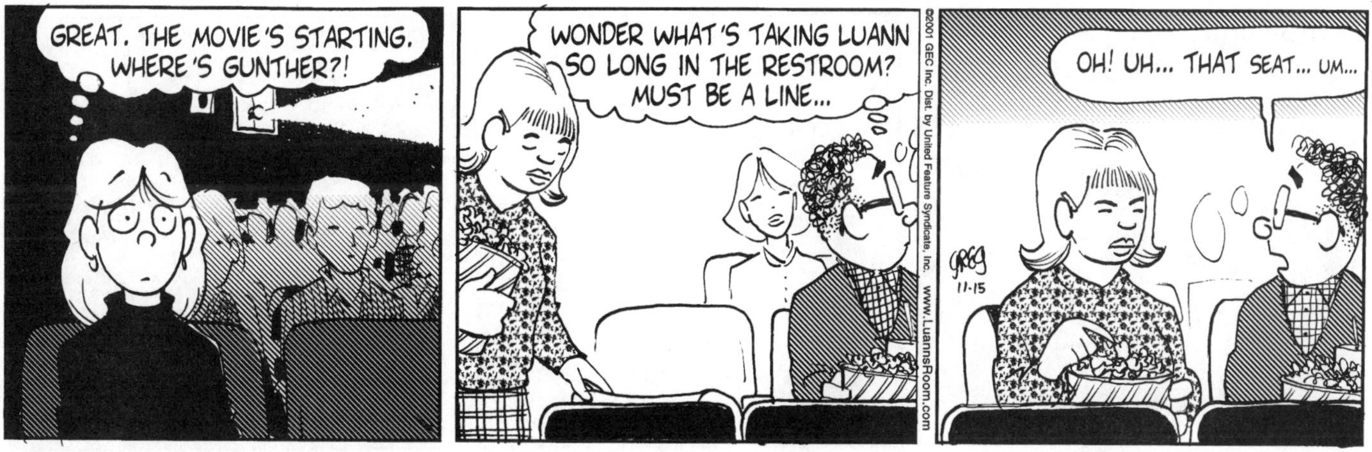
GREAT. THE MOVIE'S STARTING. WHERE'S GUNTHER?!
WONDER WHAT'S TAKING LUANN SO LONG IN THE RESTROOM? MUST BE A LINE...
©2001 GEC Inc. Dist. by United Feature Syndicate, Inc. www.LuannsRoom.com
OH! UH... THAT SEAT... UM...
GREG 11-15

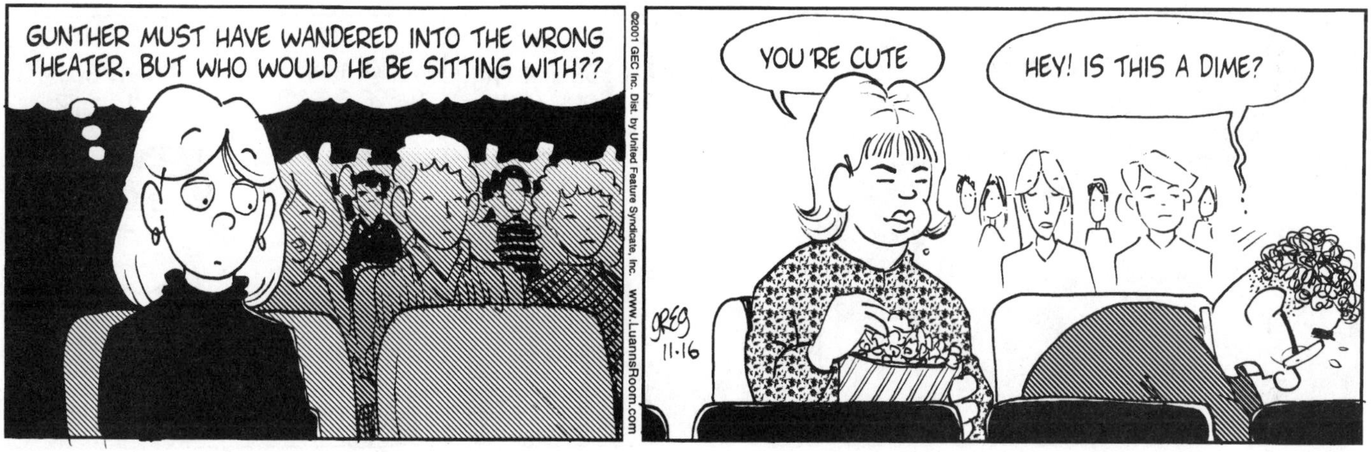
GUNTHER MUST HAVE WANDERED INTO THE WRONG THEATER. BUT WHO WOULD HE BE SITTING WITH??
©2001 GEC Inc. Dist. by United Feature Syndicate, Inc. www.LuannsRoom.com
YOU'RE CUTE
HEY! IS THIS A DIME?
GREG 11-16

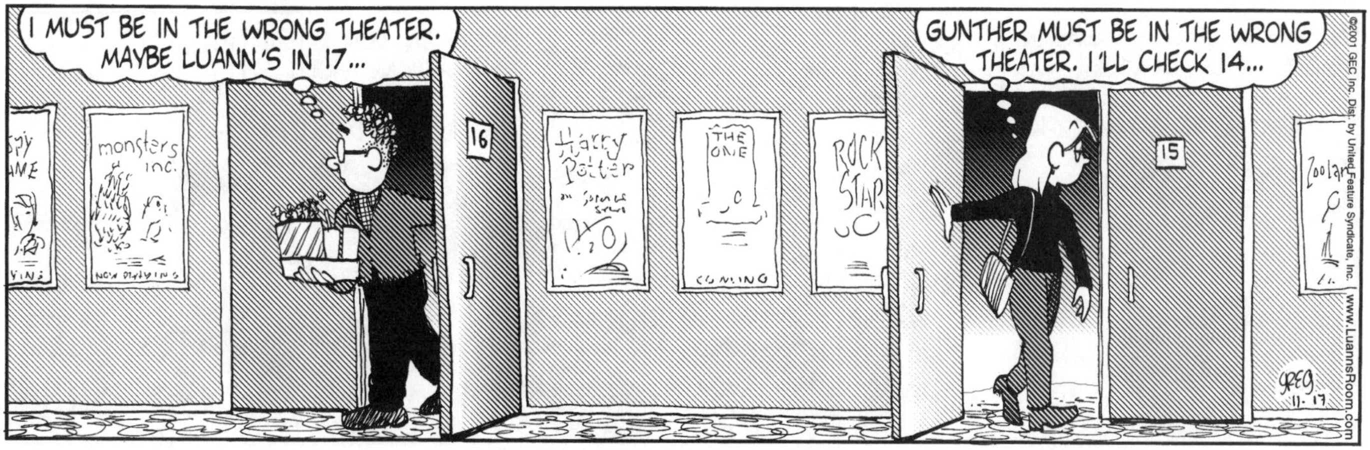
I MUST BE IN THE WRONG THEATER. MAYBE LUANN'S IN 17...
GUNTHER MUST BE IN THE WRONG THEATER. I'LL CHECK 14...
monsters inc.
16
Harry Potter
THE ONE
ROCK STAR
15
©2001 GEC Inc. Dist. by United Feature Syndicate, Inc. www.LuannsRoom.com
GREG 11-17

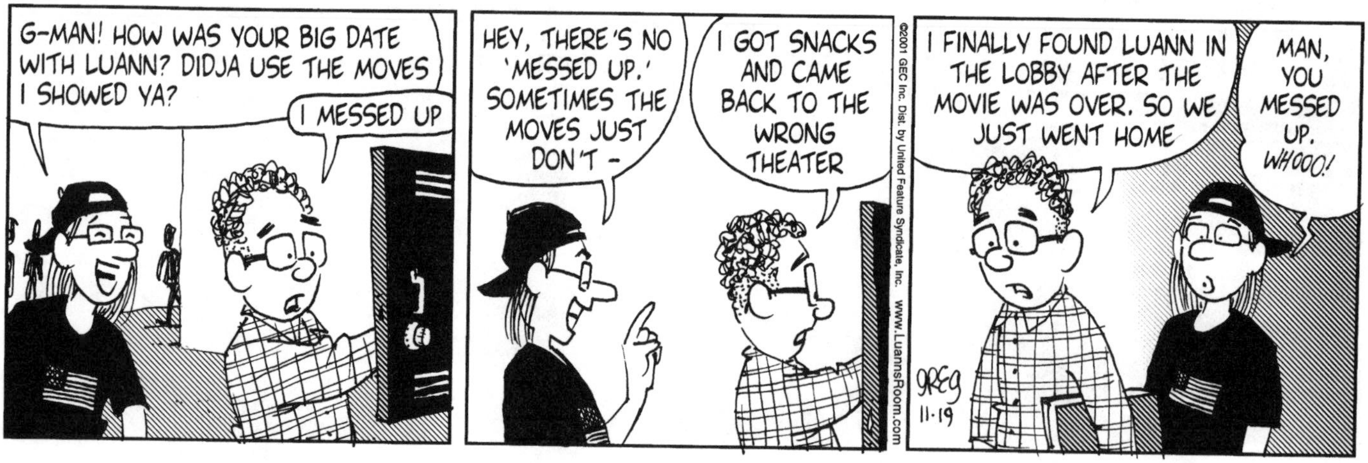
G-MAN! HOW WAS YOUR BIG DATE WITH LUANN? DIDJA USE THE MOVES I SHOWED YA?
I MESSED UP
HEY, THERE'S NO 'MESSED UP.' SOMETIMES THE MOVES JUST DON'T –
I GOT SNACKS AND CAME BACK TO THE WRONG THEATER
©2001 GEC Inc. Dist. by United Feature Syndicate, Inc. www.LuannsRoom.com
I FINALLY FOUND LUANN IN THE LOBBY AFTER THE MOVIE WAS OVER. SO WE JUST WENT HOME
MAN, YOU MESSED UP. WHOOO!
GREG 11·19

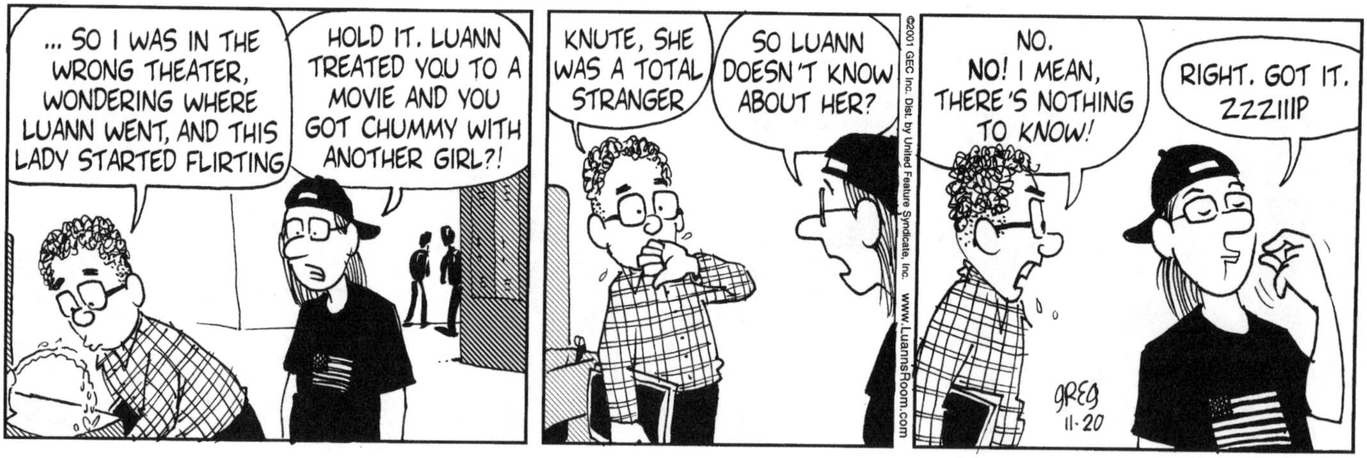
... SO I WAS IN THE WRONG THEATER, WONDERING WHERE LUANN WENT, AND THIS LADY STARTED FLIRTING
HOLD IT. LUANN TREATED YOU TO A MOVIE AND YOU GOT CHUMMY WITH ANOTHER GIRL?!
KNUTE, SHE WAS A TOTAL STRANGER
SO LUANN DOESN'T KNOW ABOUT HER?
©2001 GEC Inc. Dist. by United Feature Syndicate, Inc. www.LuannsRoom.com
NO. NO! I MEAN, THERE'S NOTHING TO KNOW!
RIGHT. GOT IT. ZZZIIIP
GREG 11·20

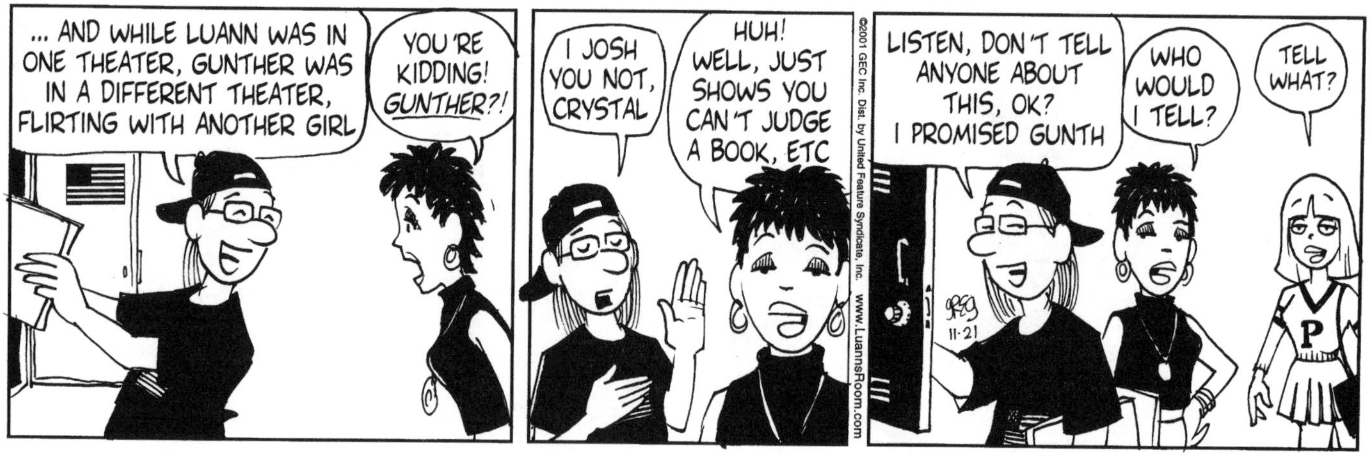
... AND WHILE LUANN WAS IN ONE THEATER, GUNTHER WAS IN A DIFFERENT THEATER, FLIRTING WITH ANOTHER GIRL
YOU'RE KIDDING! GUNTHER?!
I JOSH YOU NOT, CRYSTAL
HUH! WELL, JUST SHOWS YOU CAN'T JUDGE A BOOK, ETC
©2001 GEC Inc. Dist. by United Feature Syndicate, Inc. www.LuannsRoom.com
LISTEN, DON'T TELL ANYONE ABOUT THIS, OK? I PROMISED GUNTH
WHO WOULD I TELL?
TELL WHAT?
GREG 11·21

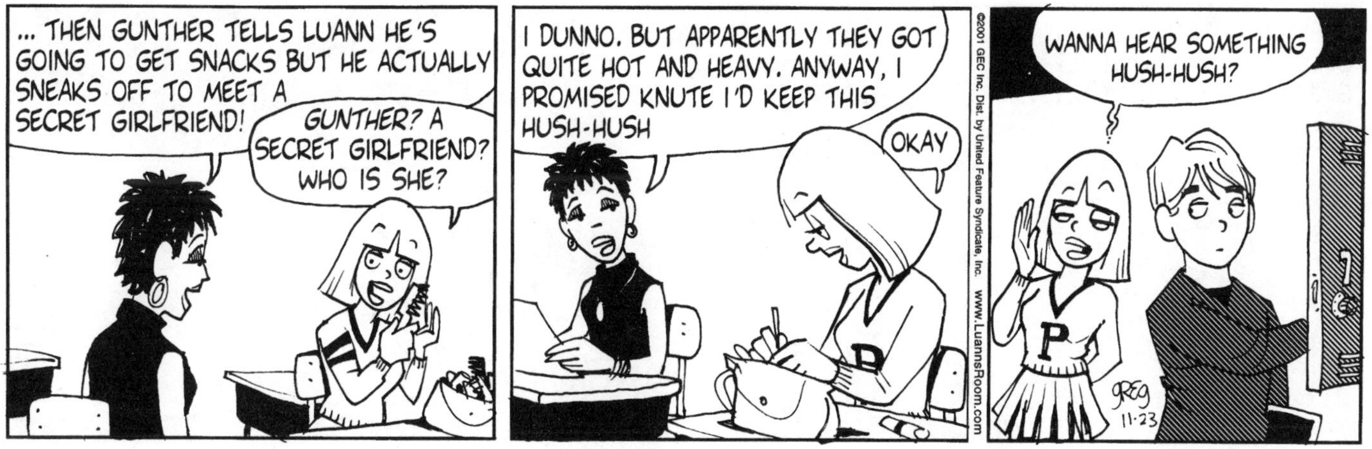
... THEN GUNTHER TELLS LUANN HE'S GOING TO GET SNACKS BUT HE ACTUALLY SNEAKS OFF TO MEET A SECRET GIRLFRIEND!
GUNTHER? A SECRET GIRLFRIEND? WHO IS SHE?
I DUNNO. BUT APPARENTLY THEY GOT QUITE HOT AND HEAVY. ANYWAY, I PROMISED KNUTE I'D KEEP THIS HUSH-HUSH
OKAY
©2001 GEC Inc. Dist. by United Feature Syndicate, Inc. www.LuannsRoom.com
WANNA HEAR SOMETHING HUSH-HUSH?
GREG 11·23

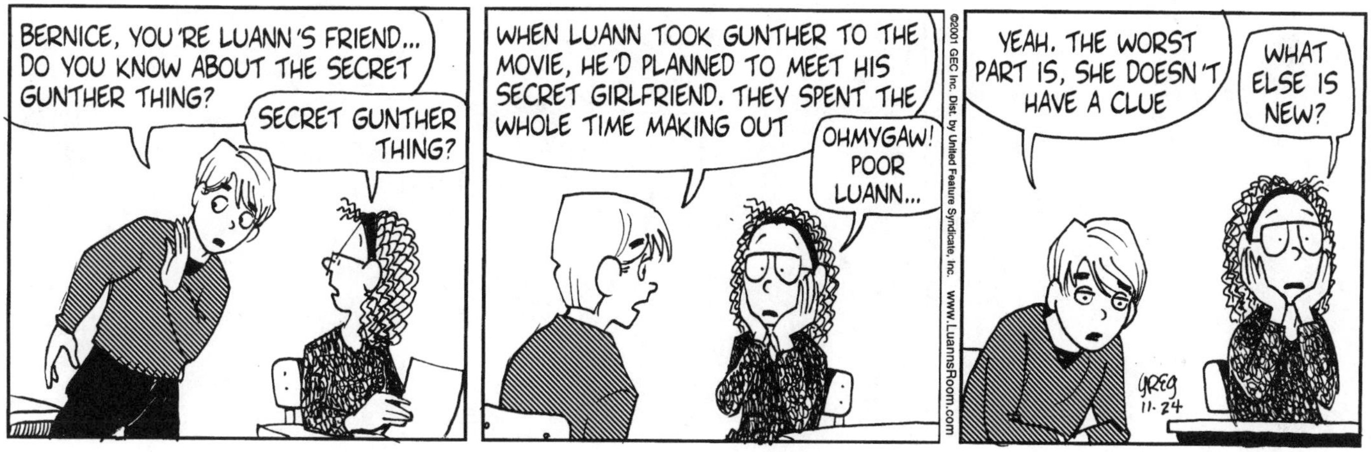
BERNICE, YOU'RE LUANN'S FRIEND... DO YOU KNOW ABOUT THE SECRET GUNTHER THING?
SECRET GUNTHER THING?
WHEN LUANN TOOK GUNTHER TO THE MOVIE, HE'D PLANNED TO MEET HIS SECRET GIRLFRIEND. THEY SPENT THE WHOLE TIME MAKING OUT
OHMYGAW! POOR LUANN...
©2001 GEC Inc. Dist. by United Feature Syndicate, Inc. www.LuannsRoom.com
YEAH. THE WORST PART IS, SHE DOESN'T HAVE A CLUE
WHAT ELSE IS NEW?
GREG 11·24

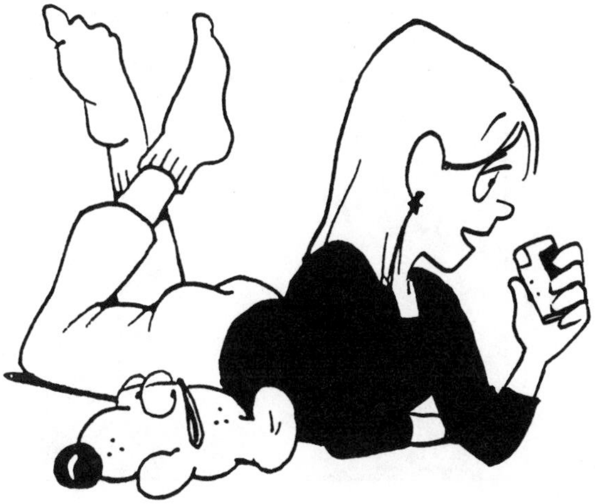

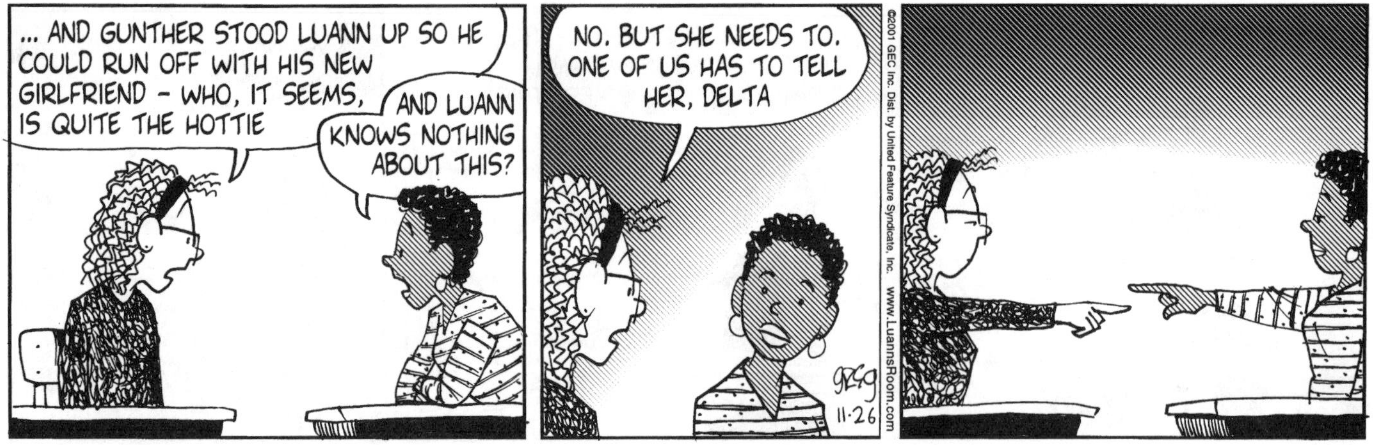
... AND GUNTHER STOOD LUANN UP SO HE COULD RUN OFF WITH HIS NEW GIRLFRIEND - WHO, IT SEEMS, IS QUITE THE HOTTIE
AND LUANN KNOWS NOTHING ABOUT THIS?
NO. BUT SHE NEEDS TO. ONE OF US HAS TO TELL HER, DELTA
©2001 GEC Inc. Dist. by United Feature Syndicate, Inc. www.LuannsRoom.com
GREG 11·26

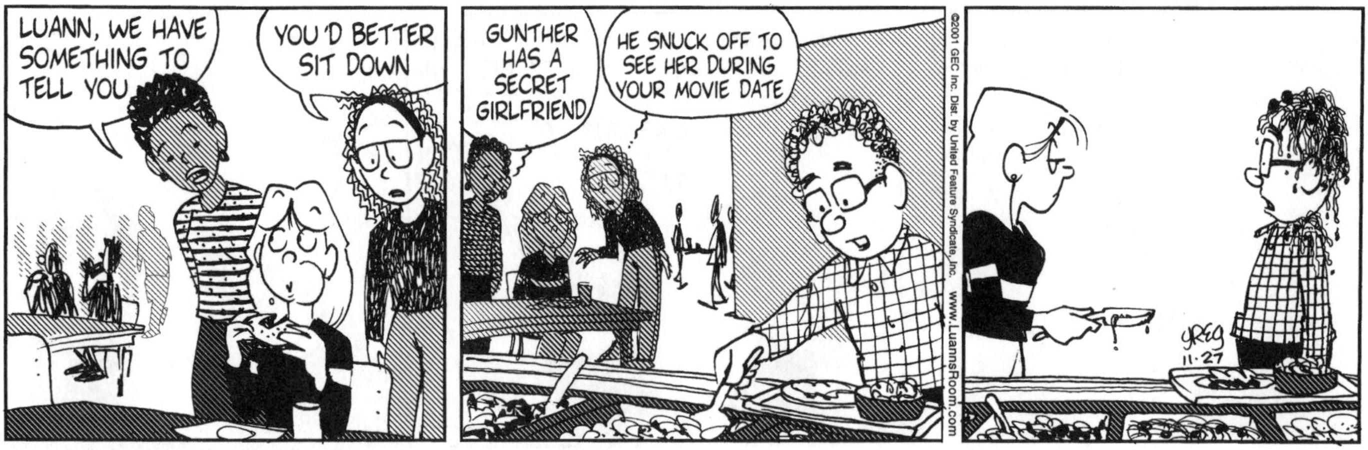
LUANN, WE HAVE SOMETHING TO TELL YOU
YOU'D BETTER SIT DOWN
GUNTHER HAS A SECRET GIRLFRIEND
HE SNUCK OFF TO SEE HER DURING YOUR MOVIE DATE
©2001 GEC Inc. Dist. by United Feature Syndicate, Inc. www.LuannsRoom.com
GREG 11·27

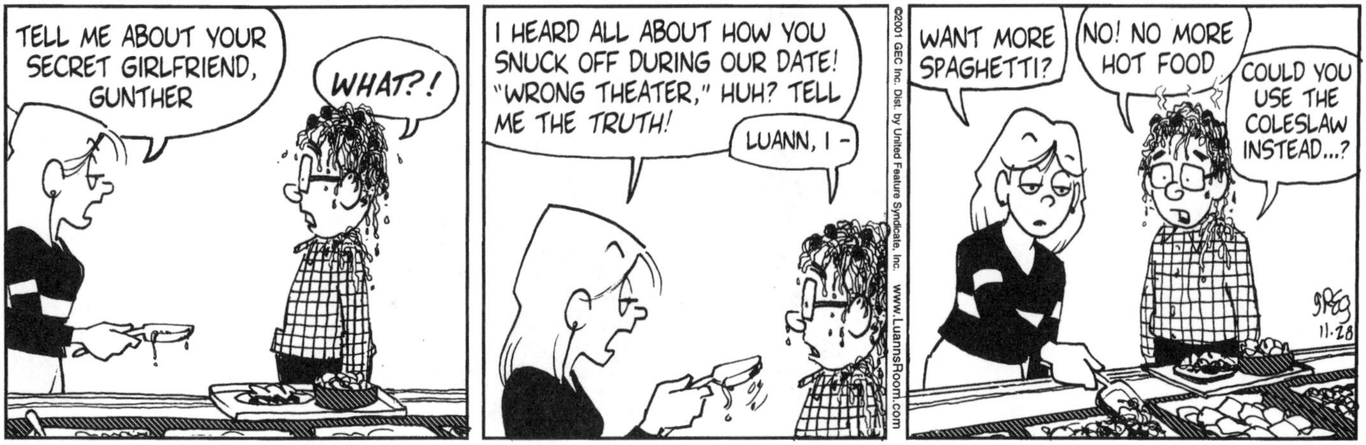
TELL ME ABOUT YOUR SECRET GIRLFRIEND, GUNTHER
WHAT?!
I HEARD ALL ABOUT HOW YOU SNUCK OFF DURING OUR DATE! "WRONG THEATER," HUH? TELL ME THE TRUTH!
LUANN, I -
WANT MORE SPAGHETTI?
NO! NO MORE HOT FOOD
COULD YOU USE THE COLESLAW INSTEAD...?
©2001 GEC Inc. Dist. by United Feature Syndicate, Inc. www.LuannsRoom.com
GREG 11·28

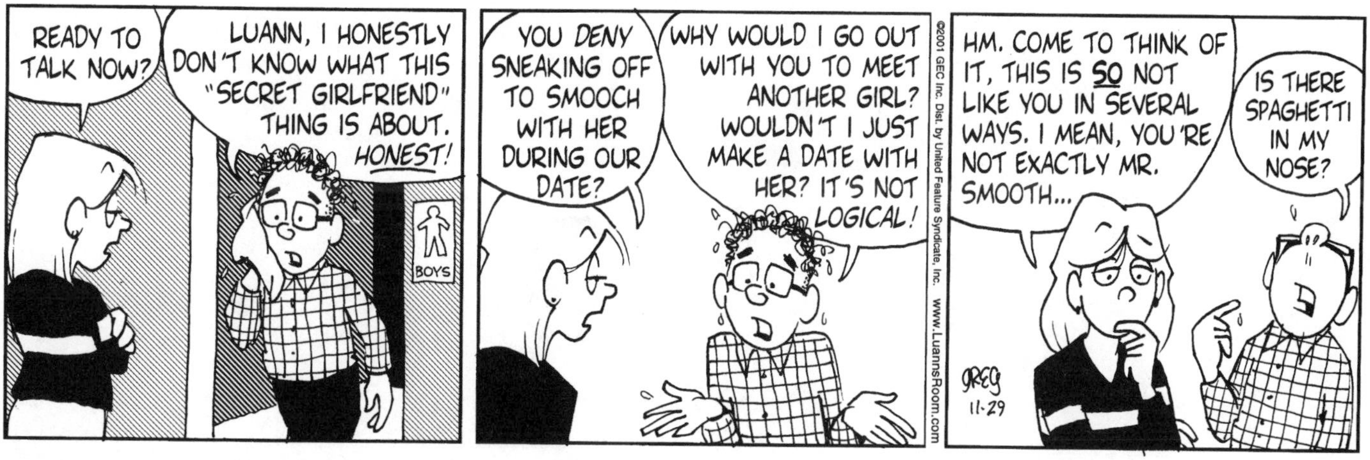
READY TO TALK NOW?
LUANN, I HONESTLY DON'T KNOW WHAT THIS "SECRET GIRLFRIEND" THING IS ABOUT. *HONEST!*
BOYS
YOU *DENY* SNEAKING OFF TO SMOOCH WITH HER DURING OUR DATE?
WHY WOULD I GO OUT WITH YOU TO MEET ANOTHER GIRL? WOULDN'T I JUST MAKE A DATE WITH HER? IT'S NOT *LOGICAL!*
©2001 GEC Inc. Dist. by United Feature Syndicate, Inc.
www.LuannsRoom.com
HM. COME TO THINK OF IT, THIS IS **SO** NOT LIKE YOU IN SEVERAL WAYS. I MEAN, YOU'RE NOT EXACTLY MR. SMOOTH...
IS THERE SPAGHETTI IN MY NOSE?
GREG 11-29

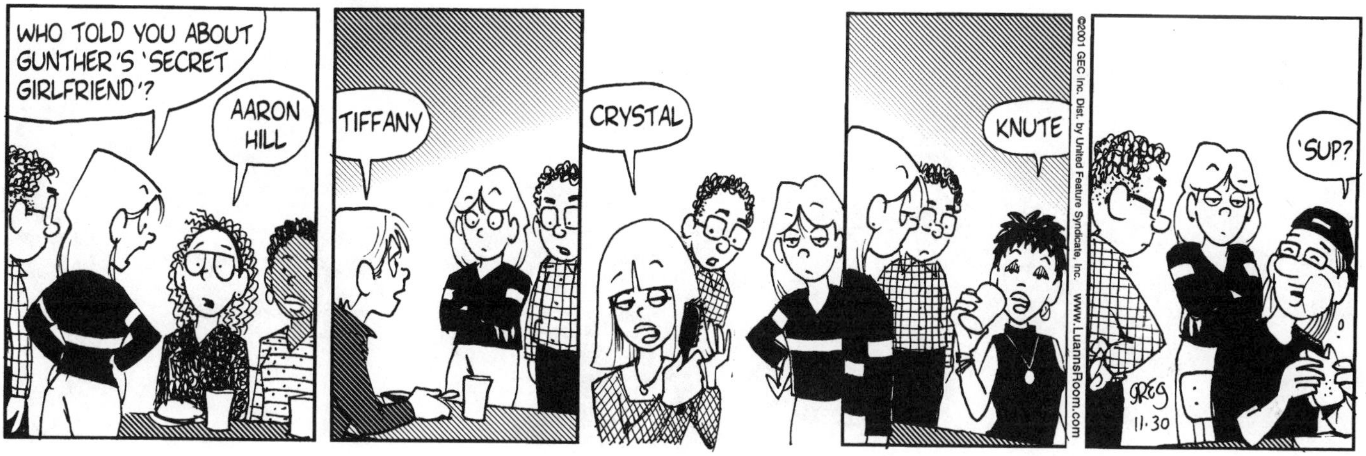
WHO TOLD YOU ABOUT GUNTHER'S 'SECRET GIRLFRIEND'?
AARON HILL
TIFFANY
CRYSTAL
KNUTE
©2001 GEC Inc. Dist. by United Feature Syndicate, Inc.
www.LuannsRoom.com
'SUP?
GREG 11-30

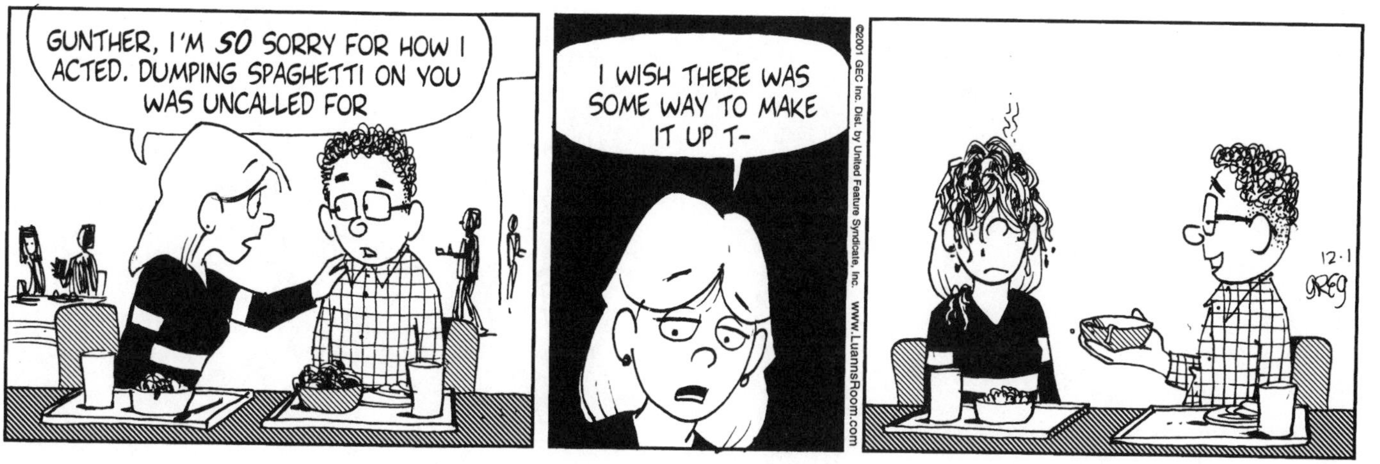
GUNTHER, I'M *SO* SORRY FOR HOW I ACTED. DUMPING SPAGHETTI ON YOU WAS UNCALLED FOR
I WISH THERE WAS SOME WAY TO MAKE IT UP T-
©2001 GEC Inc. Dist. by United Feature Syndicate, Inc.
www.LuannsRoom.com
12-1 GREG

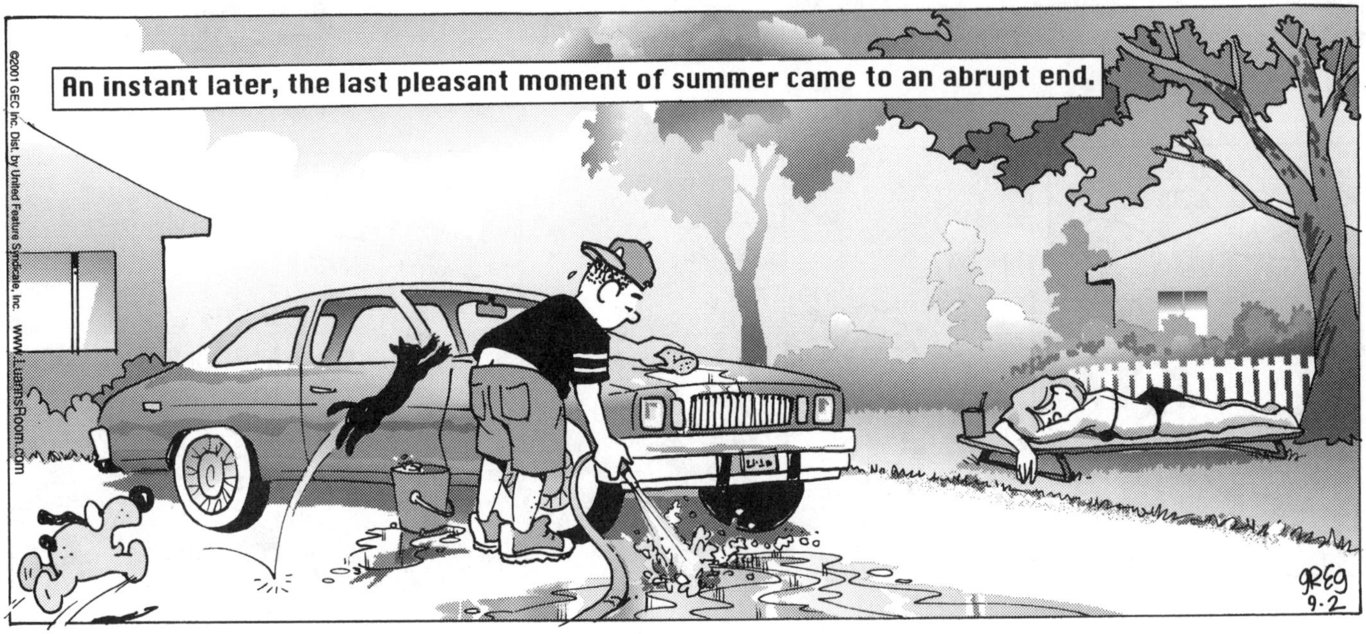
An instant later, the last pleasant moment of summer came to an abrupt end.
©2001 GEC Inc. Dist. by United Feature Syndicate, Inc. www.LuannsRoom.com
GREG 9·2

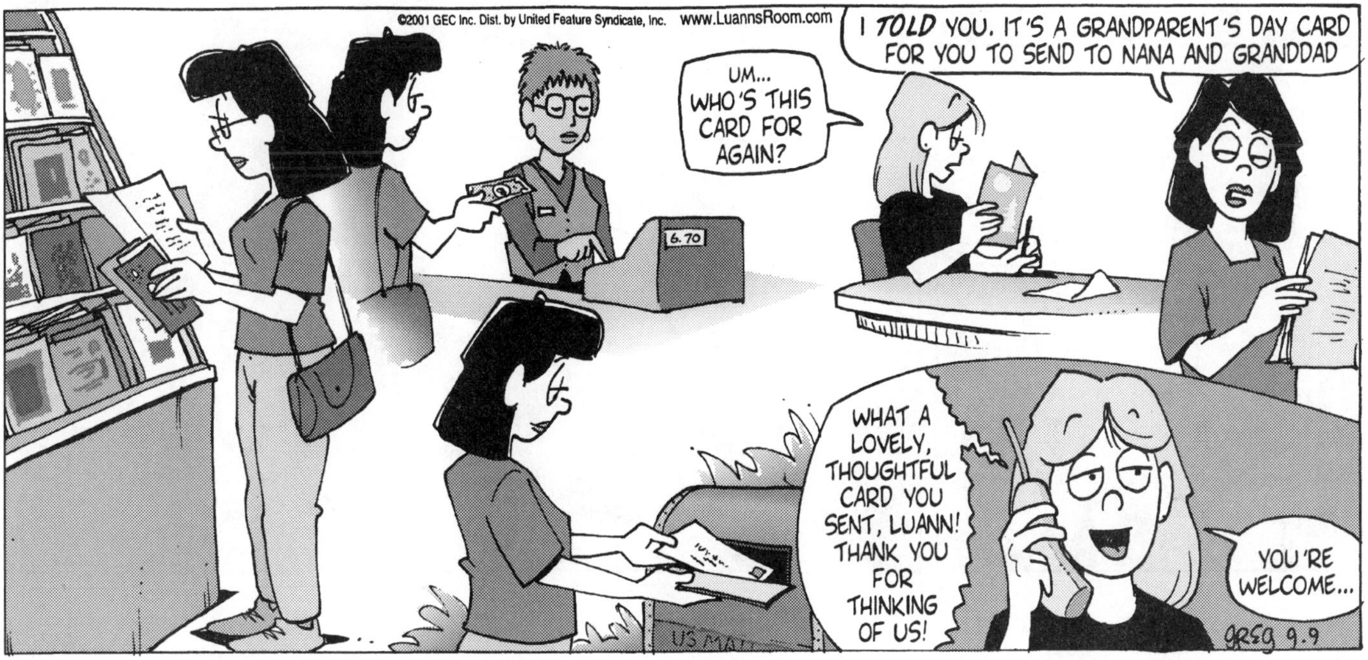
©2001 GEC Inc. Dist. by United Feature Syndicate, Inc. www.LuannsRoom.com
6.70
UM... WHO'S THIS CARD FOR AGAIN?
I *TOLD* YOU. IT'S A GRANDPARENT'S DAY CARD FOR YOU TO SEND TO NANA AND GRANDDAD
WHAT A LOVELY, THOUGHTFUL CARD YOU SENT, LUANN! THANK YOU FOR THINKING OF US!
YOU'RE WELCOME...
GREG 9.9

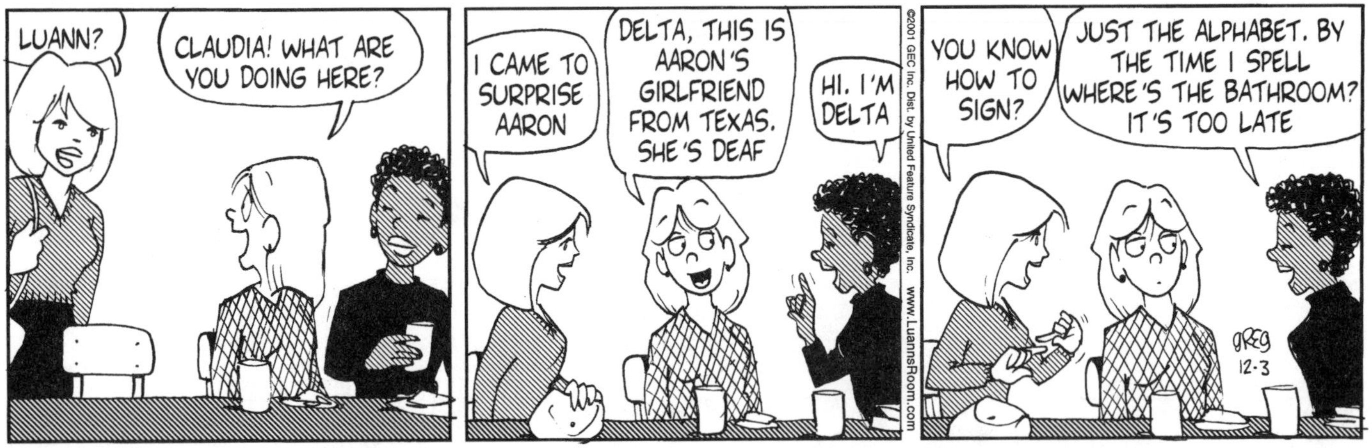
LUANN?
CLAUDIA! WHAT ARE YOU DOING HERE?
I CAME TO SURPRISE AARON
DELTA, THIS IS AARON'S GIRLFRIEND FROM TEXAS. SHE'S DEAF
HI. I'M DELTA
©2001 GEC Inc. Dist. by United Feature Syndicate, Inc. www.LuannsRoom.com
YOU KNOW HOW TO SIGN?
JUST THE ALPHABET. BY THE TIME I SPELL WHERE'S THE BATHROOM? IT'S TOO LATE
GREG 12-3

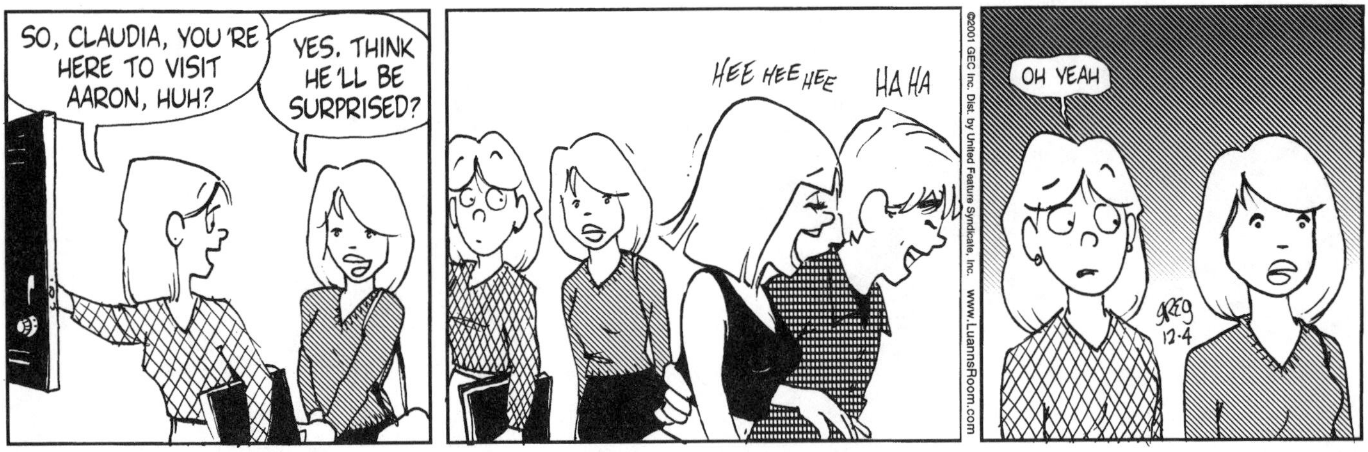
SO, CLAUDIA, YOU'RE HERE TO VISIT AARON, HUH?
YES. THINK HE'LL BE SURPRISED?
HEE HEE HEE
HA HA
©2001 GEC Inc. Dist. by United Feature Syndicate, Inc. www.LuannsRoom.com
OH YEAH
GREG 12-4

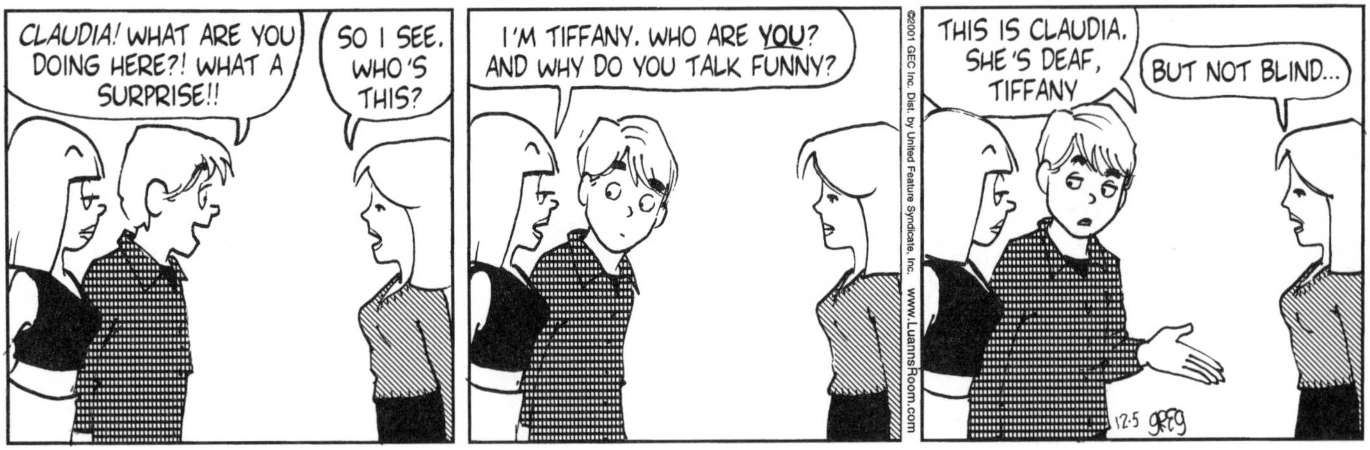
CLAUDIA! WHAT ARE YOU DOING HERE?! WHAT A SURPRISE!!
SO I SEE. WHO'S THIS?
I'M TIFFANY. WHO ARE YOU? AND WHY DO YOU TALK FUNNY?
©2001 GEC Inc. Dist. by United Feature Syndicate, Inc. www.LuannsRoom.com
THIS IS CLAUDIA. SHE'S DEAF, TIFFANY
BUT NOT BLIND...
12-5 GREG

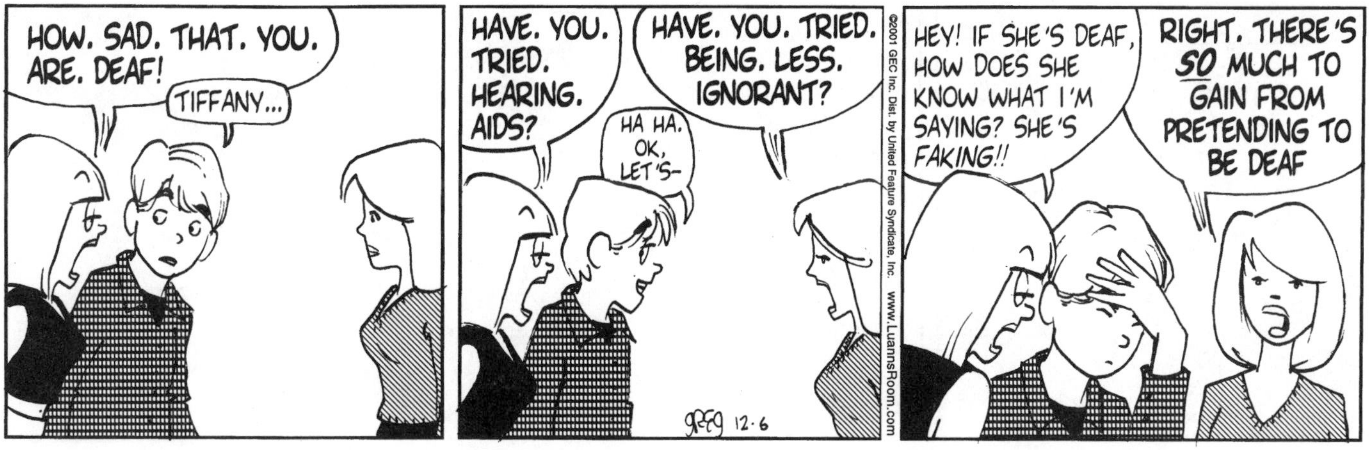
HOW. SAD. THAT. YOU. ARE. DEAF!
TIFFANY...
HAVE. YOU. TRIED. HEARING. AIDS?
HA HA. OK, LET'S-
HAVE. YOU. TRIED. BEING. LESS. IGNORANT?
GREG 12·6
©2001 GEC Inc. Dist. by United Feature Syndicate, Inc. www.LuannsRoom.com
HEY! IF SHE'S DEAF, HOW DOES SHE KNOW WHAT I'M SAYING? SHE'S FAKING!!
RIGHT. THERE'S SO MUCH TO GAIN FROM PRETENDING TO BE DEAF

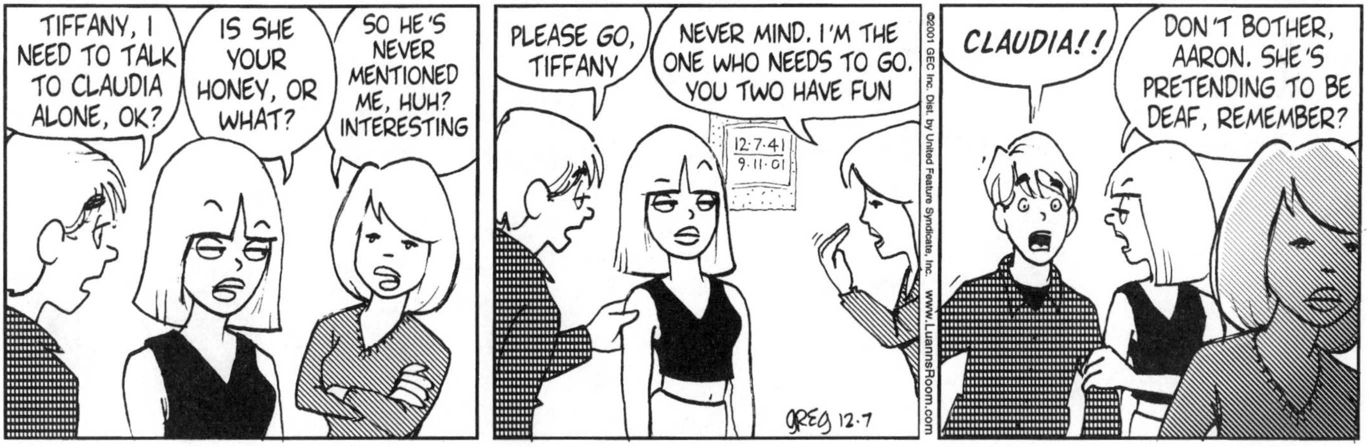
TIFFANY, I NEED TO TALK TO CLAUDIA ALONE, OK?
IS SHE YOUR HONEY, OR WHAT?
SO HE'S NEVER MENTIONED ME, HUH? INTERESTING
PLEASE GO, TIFFANY
NEVER MIND. I'M THE ONE WHO NEEDS TO GO. YOU TWO HAVE FUN
12·7·41
9·11·01
GREG 12·7
©2001 GEC Inc. Dist. by United Feature Syndicate, Inc. www.LuannsRoom.com
CLAUDIA!!
DON'T BOTHER, AARON. SHE'S PRETENDING TO BE DEAF, REMEMBER?

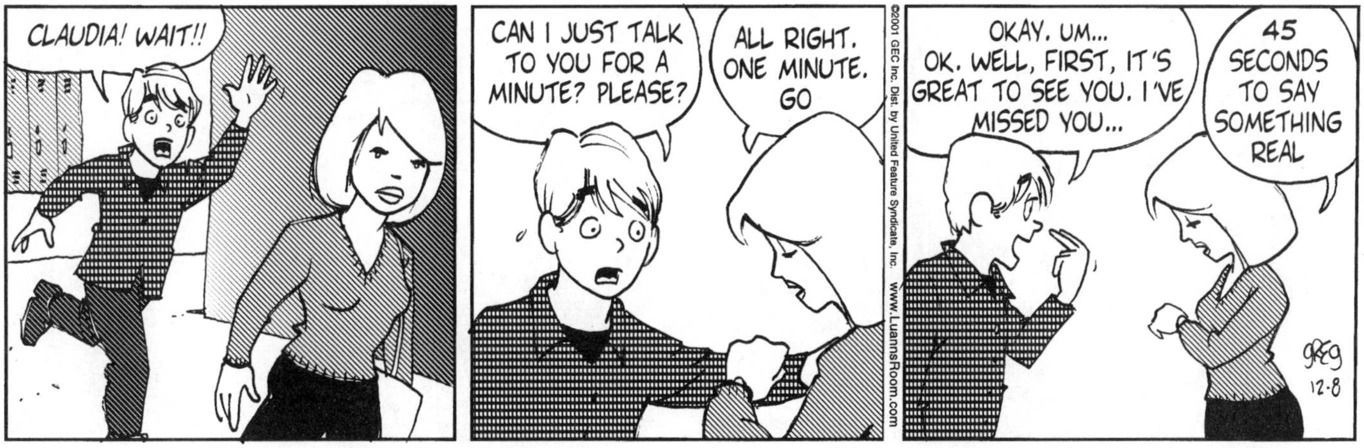
CLAUDIA! WAIT!!
CAN I JUST TALK TO YOU FOR A MINUTE? PLEASE?
ALL RIGHT. ONE MINUTE. GO
©2001 GEC Inc. Dist. by United Feature Syndicate, Inc. www.LuannsRoom.com
OKAY. UM... OK. WELL, FIRST, IT'S GREAT TO SEE YOU. I'VE MISSED YOU...
45 SECONDS TO SAY SOMETHING REAL
GREG 12·8

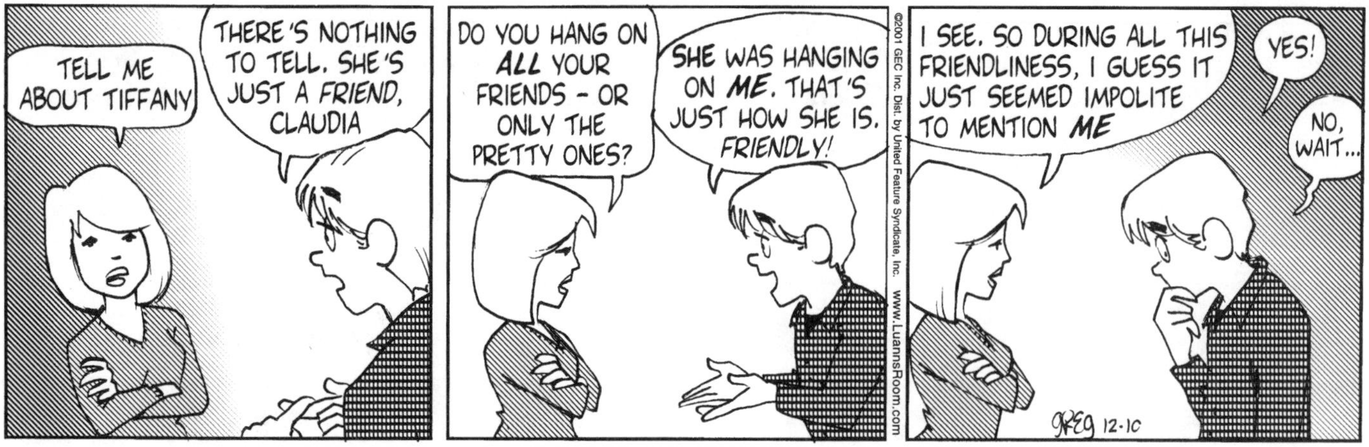
TELL ME ABOUT TIFFANY
THERE'S NOTHING TO TELL. SHE'S JUST A *FRIEND*, CLAUDIA
DO YOU HANG ON **ALL** YOUR FRIENDS - OR ONLY THE PRETTY ONES?
SHE WAS HANGING ON **ME**. THAT'S JUST HOW SHE IS. *FRIENDLY!*
©2001 GEC Inc. Dist. by United Feature Syndicate, Inc. www.LuannsRoom.com
I SEE. SO DURING ALL THIS FRIENDLINESS, I GUESS IT JUST SEEMED IMPOLITE TO MENTION **ME**
YES!
NO, WAIT...
GREG 12-10

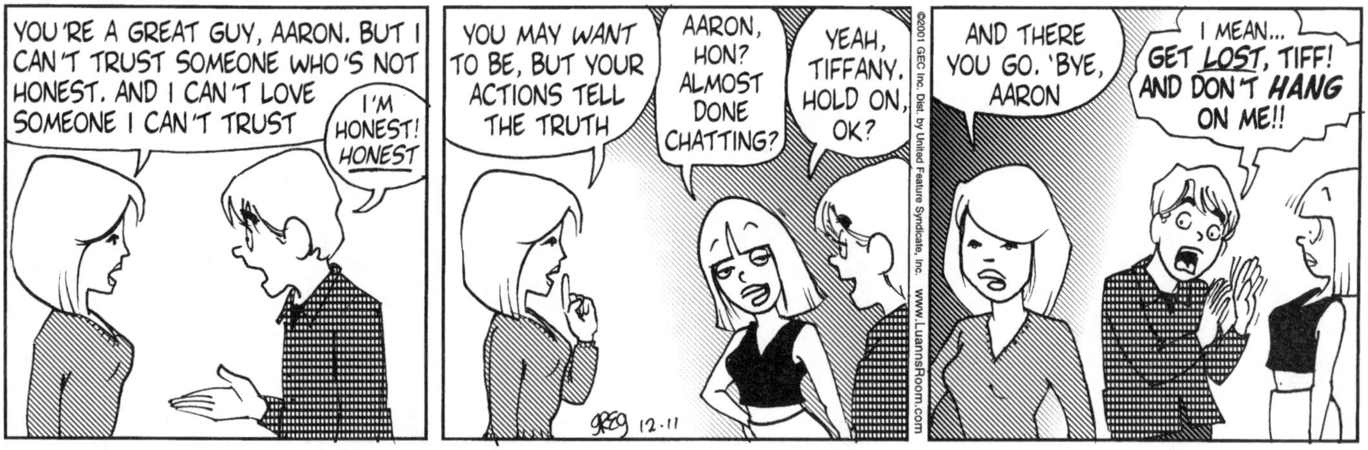
YOU'RE A GREAT GUY, AARON. BUT I CAN'T TRUST SOMEONE WHO'S NOT HONEST. AND I CAN'T LOVE SOMEONE I CAN'T TRUST
I'M HONEST! HONEST
YOU MAY *WANT* TO BE, BUT YOUR ACTIONS TELL THE TRUTH
AARON, HON? ALMOST DONE CHATTING?
YEAH, TIFFANY. HOLD ON, OK?
GREG 12-11
©2001 GEC Inc. Dist. by United Feature Syndicate, Inc. www.LuannsRoom.com
AND THERE YOU GO. 'BYE, AARON
I MEAN... **GET LOST, TIFF! AND DON'T *HANG* ON ME!!**

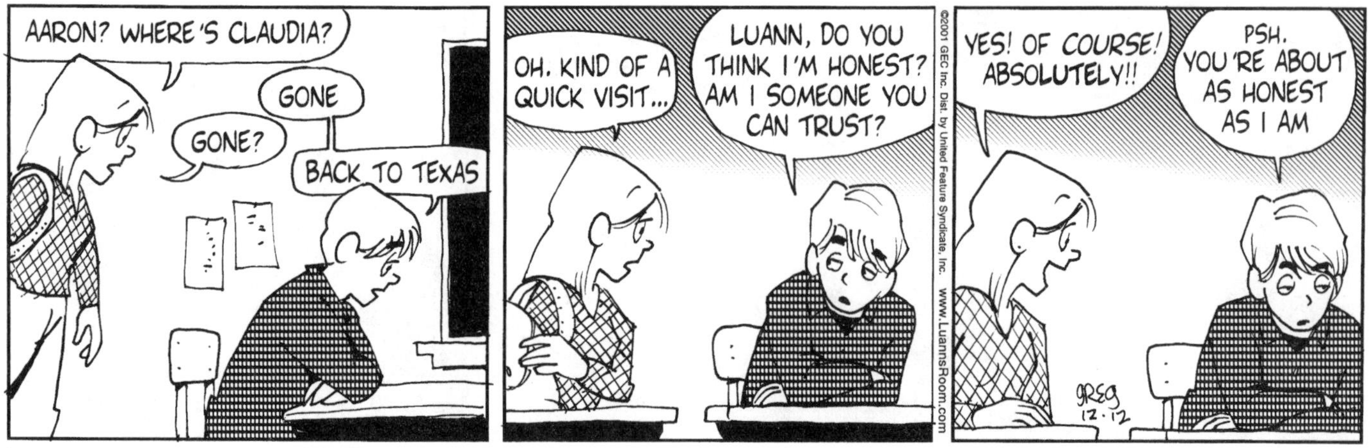
AARON? WHERE'S CLAUDIA?
GONE
GONE?
BACK TO TEXAS
OH. KIND OF A QUICK VISIT...
LUANN, DO YOU THINK I'M HONEST? AM I SOMEONE YOU CAN TRUST?
©2001 GEC Inc. Dist. by United Feature Syndicate, Inc. www.LuannsRoom.com
YES! OF *COURSE!* **ABSOLUTELY!!**
PSH. YOU'RE ABOUT AS HONEST AS I AM
GREG 12-12

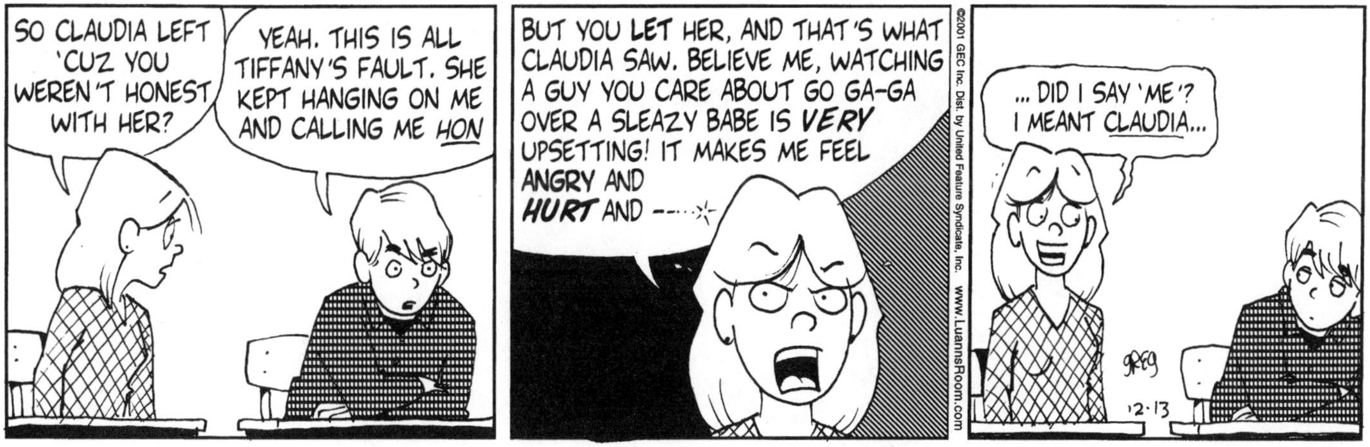
SO CLAUDIA LEFT 'CUZ YOU WEREN'T HONEST WITH HER?
YEAH. THIS IS ALL TIFFANY'S FAULT. SHE KEPT HANGING ON ME AND CALLING ME HON
BUT YOU LET HER, AND THAT'S WHAT CLAUDIA SAW. BELIEVE ME, WATCHING A GUY YOU CARE ABOUT GO GA-GA OVER A SLEAZY BABE IS VERY UPSETTING! IT MAKES ME FEEL ANGRY AND HURT AND ---
©2001 GEC Inc. Dist. by United Feature Syndicate, Inc. www.LuannsRoom.com
... DID I SAY 'ME'? I MEANT CLAUDIA...
GREG
12·13

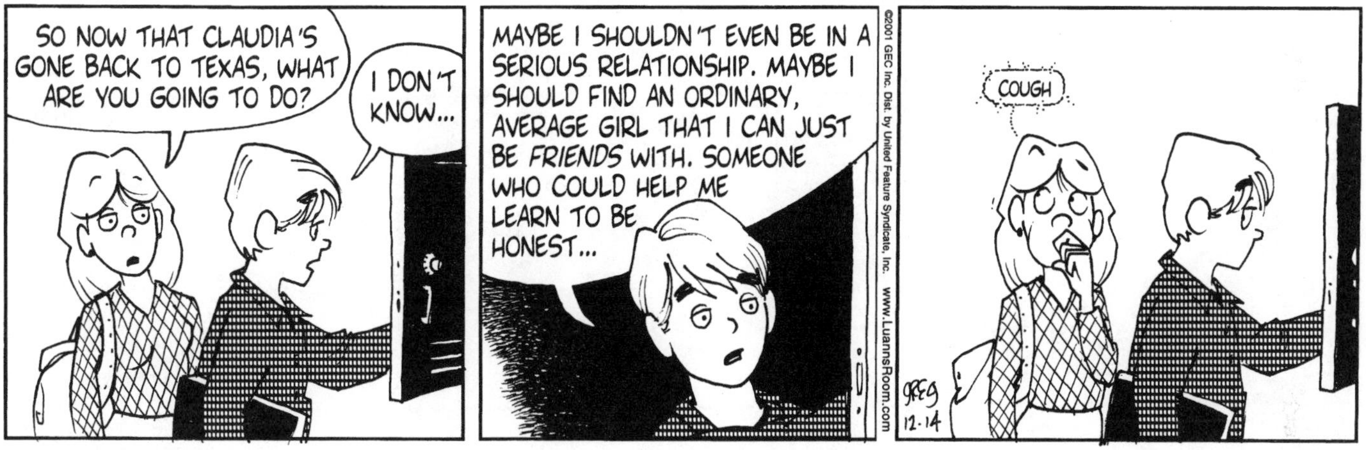
SO NOW THAT CLAUDIA'S GONE BACK TO TEXAS, WHAT ARE YOU GOING TO DO?
I DON'T KNOW...
MAYBE I SHOULDN'T EVEN BE IN A SERIOUS RELATIONSHIP. MAYBE I SHOULD FIND AN ORDINARY, AVERAGE GIRL THAT I CAN JUST BE FRIENDS WITH. SOMEONE WHO COULD HELP ME LEARN TO BE HONEST...
©2001 GEC Inc. Dist. by United Feature Syndicate, Inc. www.LuannsRoom.com
GREG
12·14
COUGH

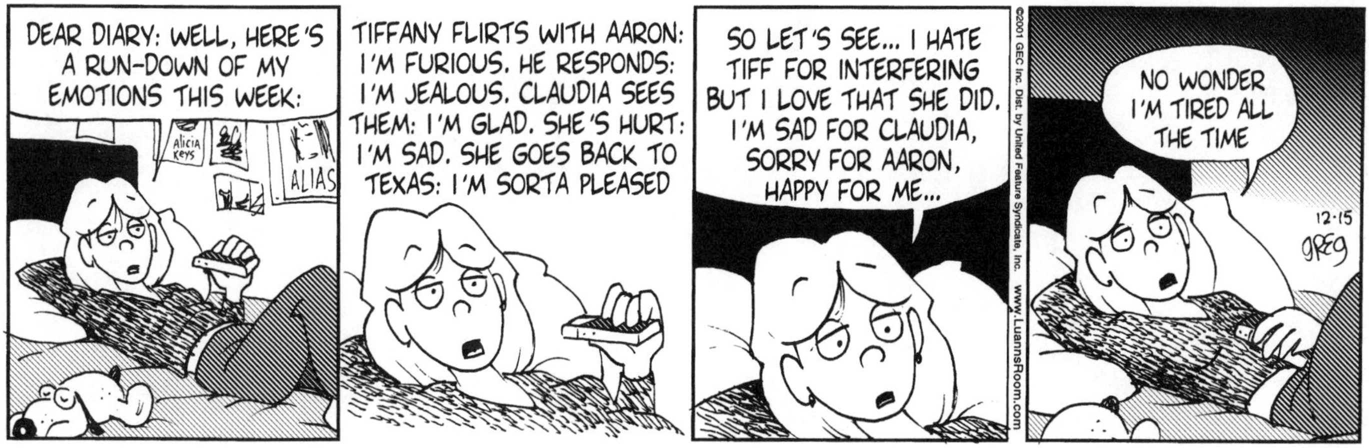
DEAR DIARY: WELL, HERE'S A RUN-DOWN OF MY EMOTIONS THIS WEEK:
Alicia Keys
ALIAS
TIFFANY FLIRTS WITH AARON: I'M FURIOUS. HE RESPONDS: I'M JEALOUS. CLAUDIA SEES THEM: I'M GLAD. SHE'S HURT: I'M SAD. SHE GOES BACK TO TEXAS: I'M SORTA PLEASED
SO LET'S SEE... I HATE TIFF FOR INTERFERING BUT I LOVE THAT SHE DID. I'M SAD FOR CLAUDIA, SORRY FOR AARON, HAPPY FOR ME...
©2001 GEC Inc. Dist. by United Feature Syndicate, Inc. www.LuannsRoom.com
NO WONDER I'M TIRED ALL THE TIME
12·15
GREG

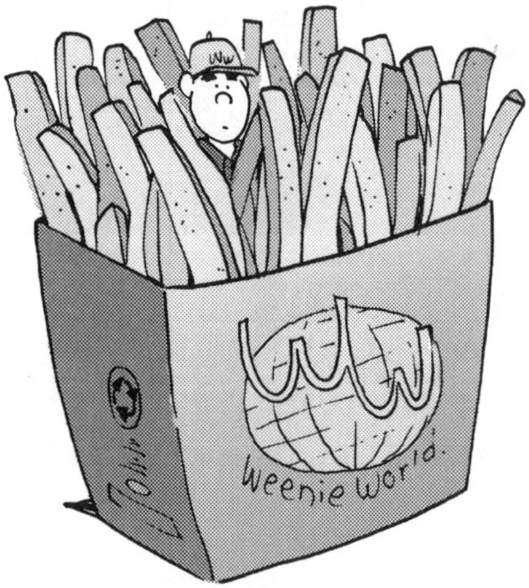
Weenie World.

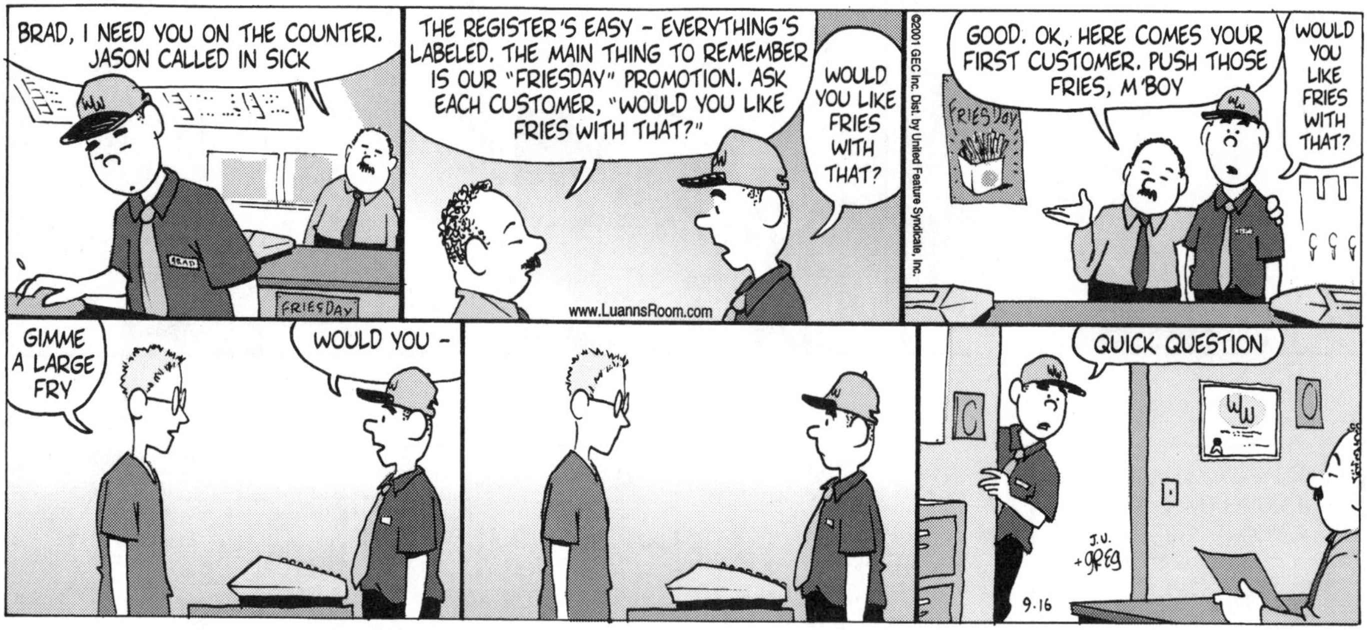
BRAD, I NEED YOU ON THE COUNTER. JASON CALLED IN SICK
BRAD
FRIESDAY
THE REGISTER'S EASY - EVERYTHING'S LABELED. THE MAIN THING TO REMEMBER IS OUR "FRIESDAY" PROMOTION. ASK EACH CUSTOMER, "WOULD YOU LIKE FRIES WITH THAT?"
WOULD YOU LIKE FRIES WITH THAT?
www.LuannsRoom.com
©2001 GEC Inc. Dist. by United Feature Syndicate, Inc.
GOOD. OK, HERE COMES YOUR FIRST CUSTOMER. PUSH THOSE FRIES, M'BOY
FRIESDAY
WOULD YOU LIKE FRIES WITH THAT?
GIMME A LARGE FRY
WOULD YOU -
QUICK QUESTION
J.V. + Greg
9.16

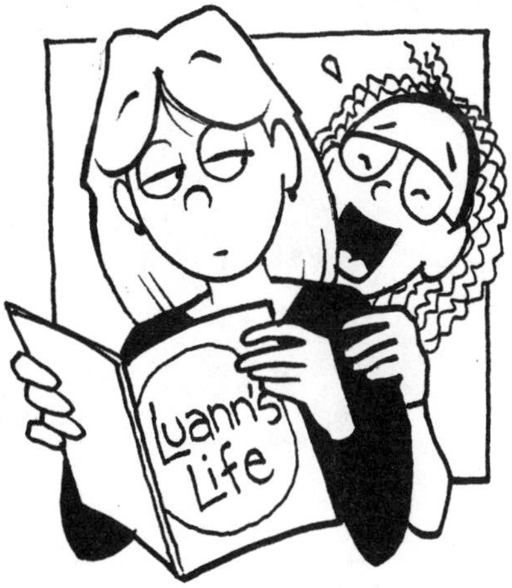
Luann's Life

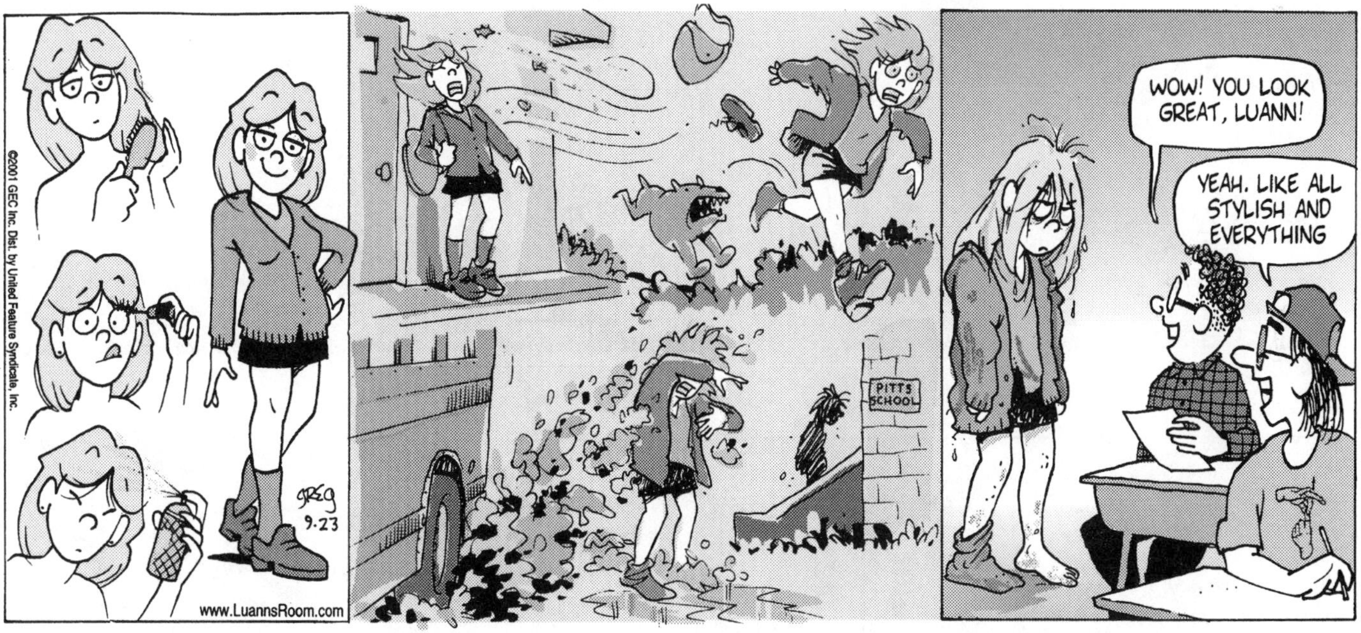
©2001 GEC Inc. Dist. by United Feature Syndicate, Inc.
GREG 9-23
www.LuannsRoom.com
PITTS SCHOOL
WOW! YOU LOOK GREAT, LUANN!
YEAH. LIKE ALL STYLISH AND EVERYTHING

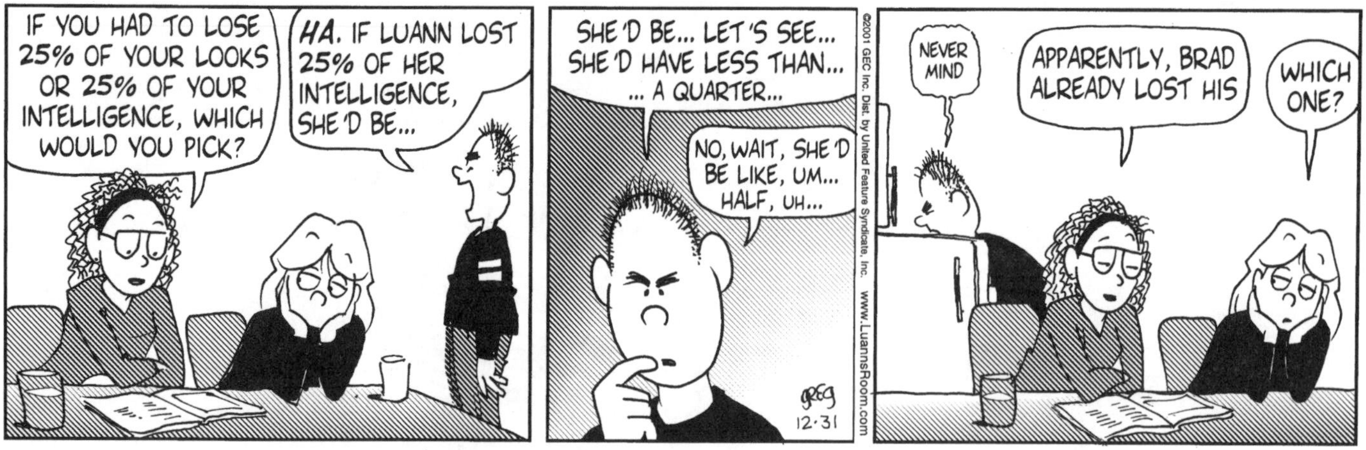

IF YOU HAD TO LOSE 25% OF YOUR LOOKS OR 25% OF YOUR INTELLIGENCE, WHICH WOULD YOU PICK?
HA. IF LUANN LOST 25% OF HER INTELLIGENCE, SHE'D BE...
SHE'D BE... LET'S SEE... SHE'D HAVE LESS THAN... ... A QUARTER...
NO, WAIT, SHE'D BE LIKE, UM... HALF, UH...
GREG 12·31
©2001 GEC Inc. Dist. by United Feature Syndicate, Inc. www.LuannsRoom.com
NEVER MIND
APPARENTLY, BRAD ALREADY LOST HIS
WHICH ONE?

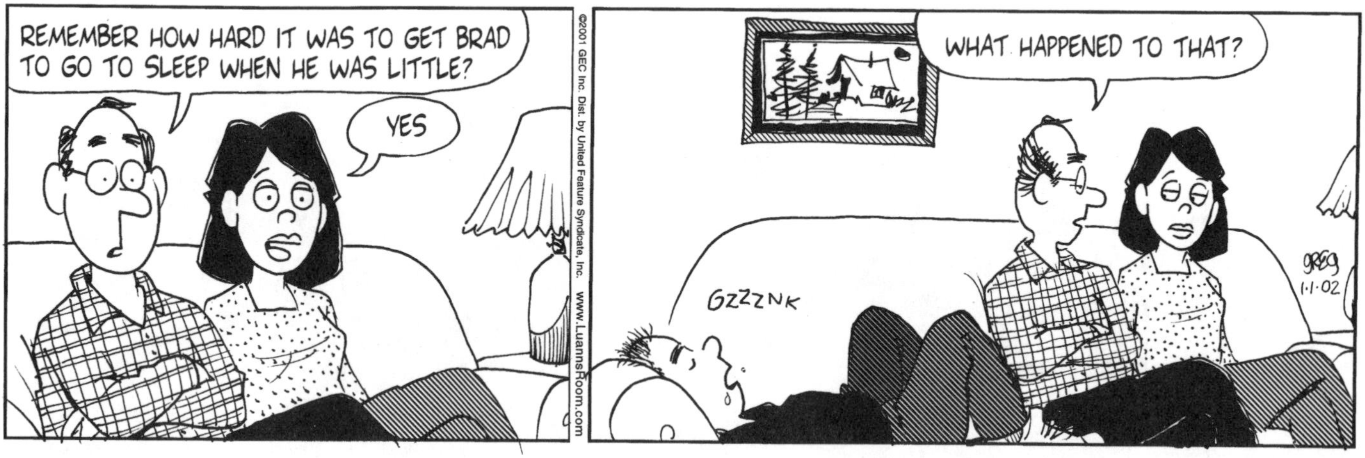

REMEMBER HOW HARD IT WAS TO GET BRAD TO GO TO SLEEP WHEN HE WAS LITTLE?
YES
©2001 GEC Inc. Dist. by United Feature Syndicate, Inc. www.LuannsRoom.com
WHAT HAPPENED TO THAT?
GZZZNK
GREG 1·1·02

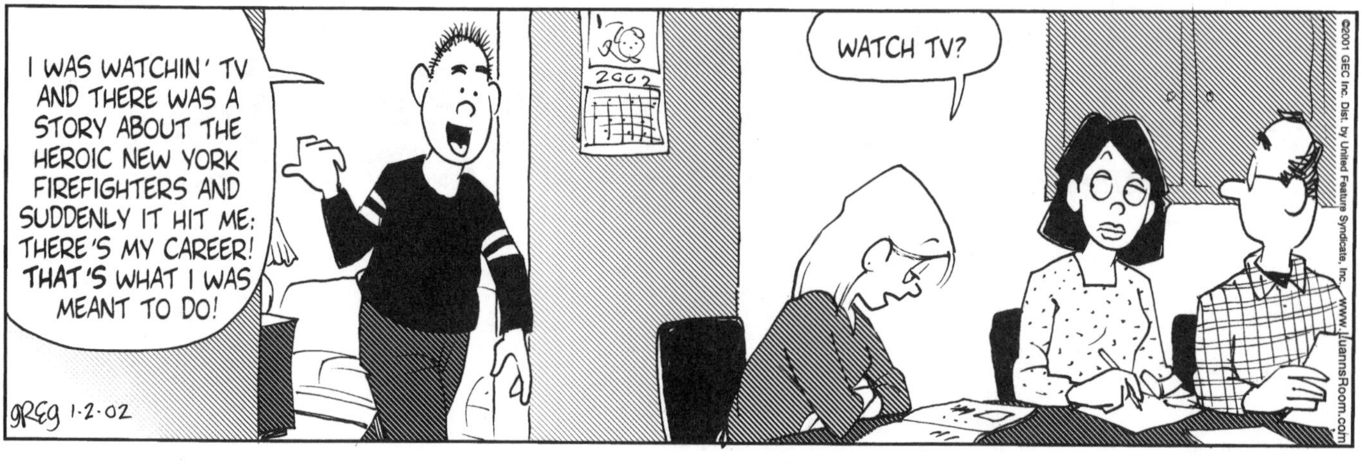

I WAS WATCHIN' TV AND THERE WAS A STORY ABOUT THE HEROIC NEW YORK FIREFIGHTERS AND SUDDENLY IT HIT ME: THERE'S MY CAREER! THAT'S WHAT I WAS MEANT TO DO!
2002
WATCH TV?
GREG 1·2·02
©2001 GEC Inc. Dist. by United Feature Syndicate, Inc. www.LuannsRoom.com

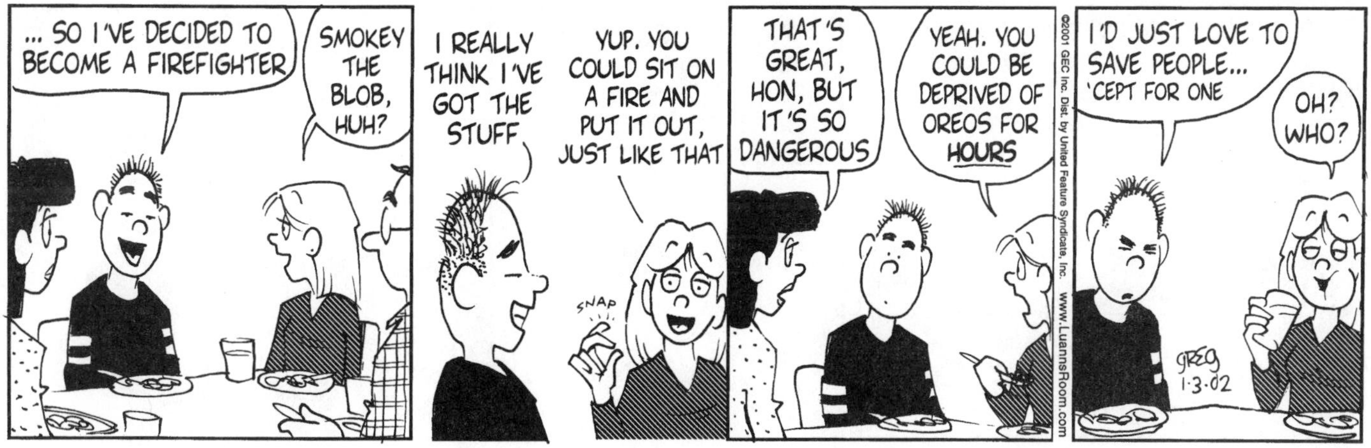
... SO I'VE DECIDED TO BECOME A FIREFIGHTER
SMOKEY THE BLOB, HUH?
I REALLY THINK I'VE GOT THE STUFF
YUP. YOU COULD SIT ON A FIRE AND PUT IT OUT, JUST LIKE THAT
SNAP
THAT'S GREAT, HON, BUT IT'S SO DANGEROUS
YEAH. YOU COULD BE DEPRIVED OF OREOS FOR HOURS
©2001 GEC Inc. Dist. by United Feature Syndicate, Inc. www.LuannsRoom.com
I'D JUST LOVE TO SAVE PEOPLE... 'CEPT FOR ONE
OH? WHO?
GREG 1·3·02

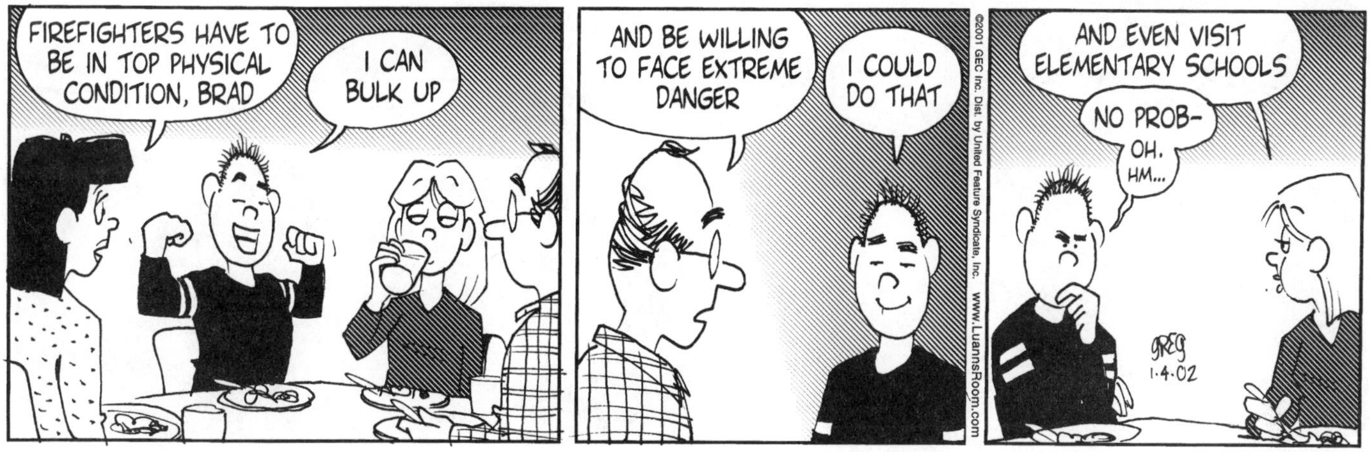
FIREFIGHTERS HAVE TO BE IN TOP PHYSICAL CONDITION, BRAD
I CAN BULK UP
AND BE WILLING TO FACE EXTREME DANGER
I COULD DO THAT
©2001 GEC Inc. Dist. by United Feature Syndicate, Inc. www.LuannsRoom.com
AND EVEN VISIT ELEMENTARY SCHOOLS
NO PROB– OH. HM...
GREG 1·4·02

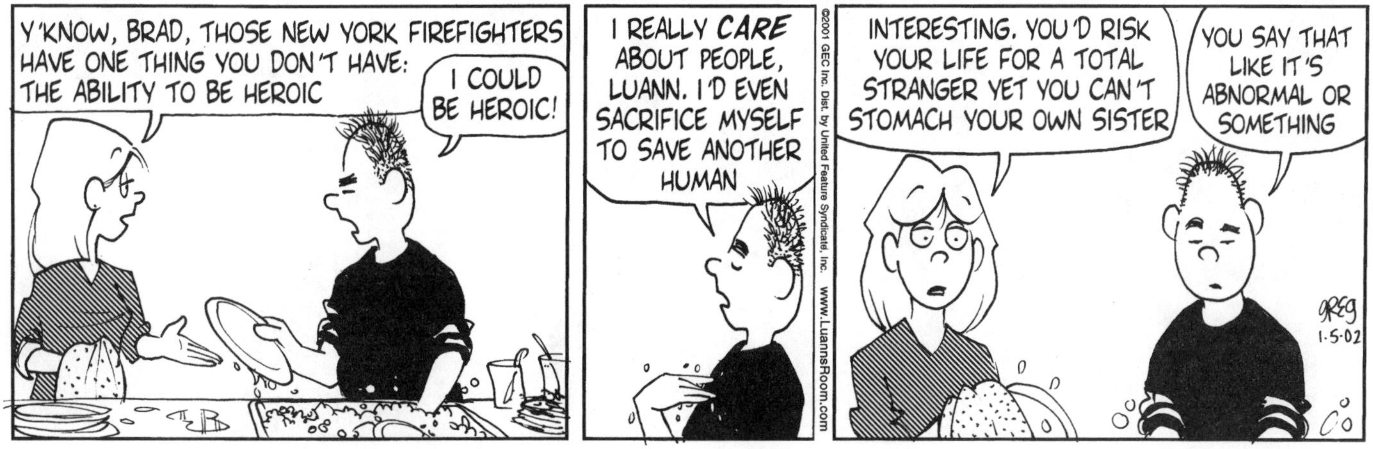
Y'KNOW, BRAD, THOSE NEW YORK FIREFIGHTERS HAVE ONE THING YOU DON'T HAVE: THE ABILITY TO BE HEROIC
I COULD BE HEROIC!
©2001 GEC Inc. Dist. by United Feature Syndicate, Inc. www.LuannsRoom.com
I REALLY CARE ABOUT PEOPLE, LUANN. I'D EVEN SACRIFICE MYSELF TO SAVE ANOTHER HUMAN
INTERESTING. YOU'D RISK YOUR LIFE FOR A TOTAL STRANGER YET YOU CAN'T STOMACH YOUR OWN SISTER
YOU SAY THAT LIKE IT'S ABNORMAL OR SOMETHING
GREG 1·5·02

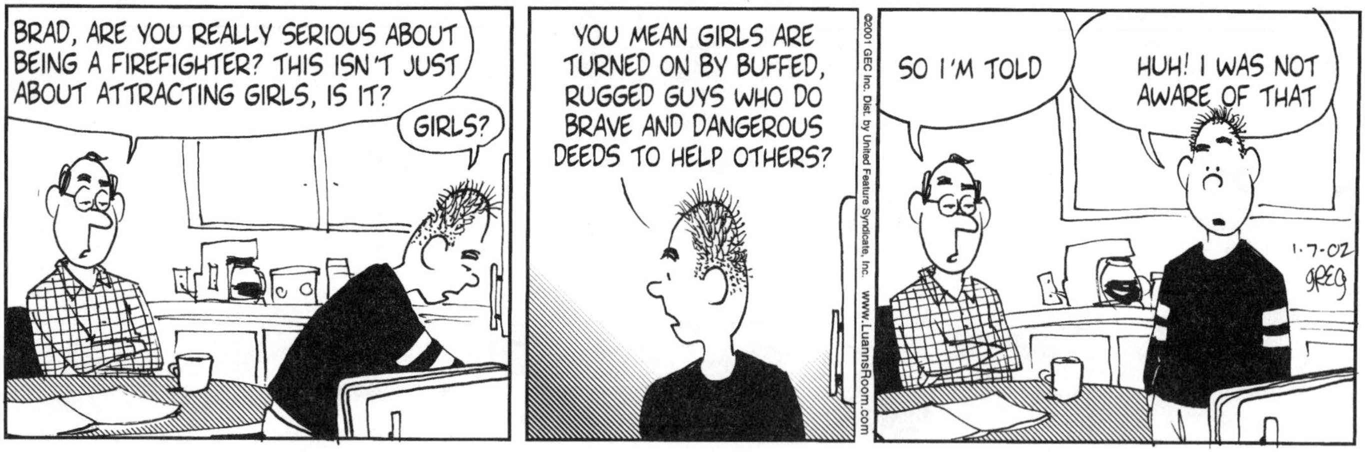
BRAD, ARE YOU REALLY SERIOUS ABOUT BEING A FIREFIGHTER? THIS ISN'T JUST ABOUT ATTRACTING GIRLS, IS IT?
GIRLS?
YOU MEAN GIRLS ARE TURNED ON BY BUFFED, RUGGED GUYS WHO DO BRAVE AND DANGEROUS DEEDS TO HELP OTHERS?
©2001 GEC Inc. Dist. by United Feature Syndicate, Inc. www.LuannsRoom.com
SO I'M TOLD
HUH! I WAS NOT AWARE OF THAT
1-7-02
GREG

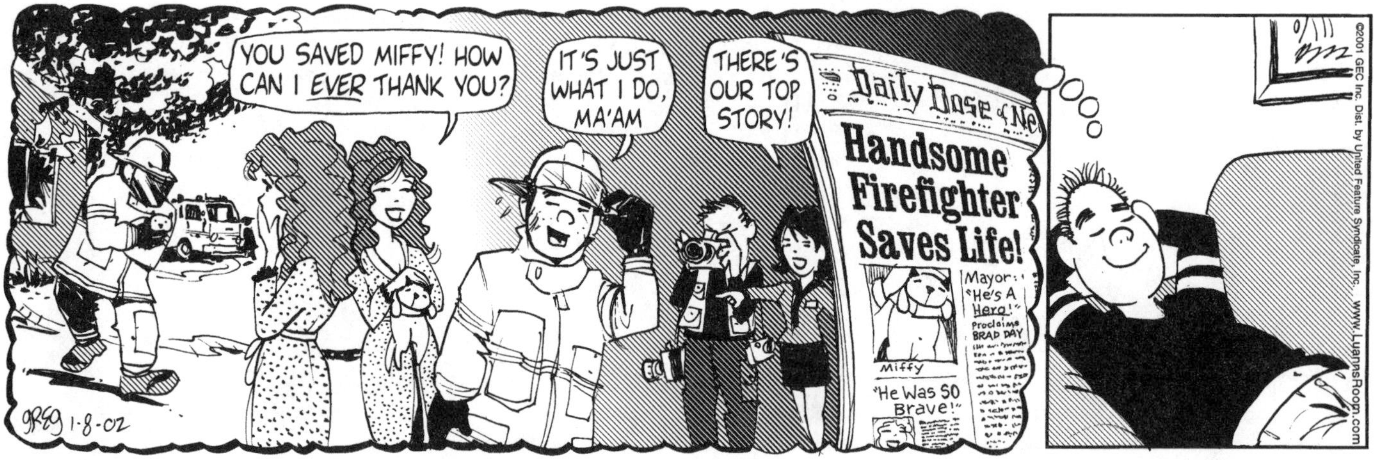
YOU SAVED MIFFY! HOW CAN I EVER THANK YOU?
IT'S JUST WHAT I DO, MA'AM
THERE'S OUR TOP STORY!
Daily Dose of Ne
Handsome Firefighter Saves Life!
Mayor: "He's A Hero!"
Proclaims BRAD DAY
Miffy
"He Was SO Brave!"
GREG 1-8-02
©2001 GEC Inc. Dist. by United Feature Syndicate, Inc. www.LuannsRoom.com

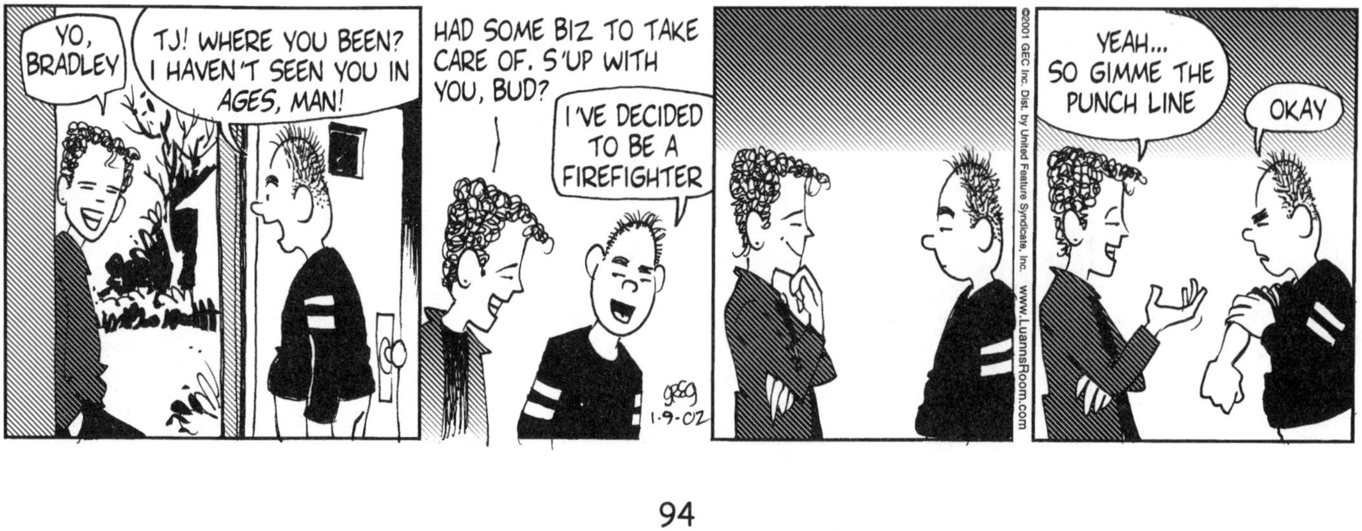
YO, BRADLEY
TJ! WHERE YOU BEEN? I HAVEN'T SEEN YOU IN AGES, MAN!
HAD SOME BIZ TO TAKE CARE OF. S'UP WITH YOU, BUD?
I'VE DECIDED TO BE A FIREFIGHTER
GREG 1-9-02
©2001 GEC Inc. Dist. by United Feature Syndicate, Inc. www.LuannsRoom.com
YEAH... SO GIMME THE PUNCH LINE
OKAY

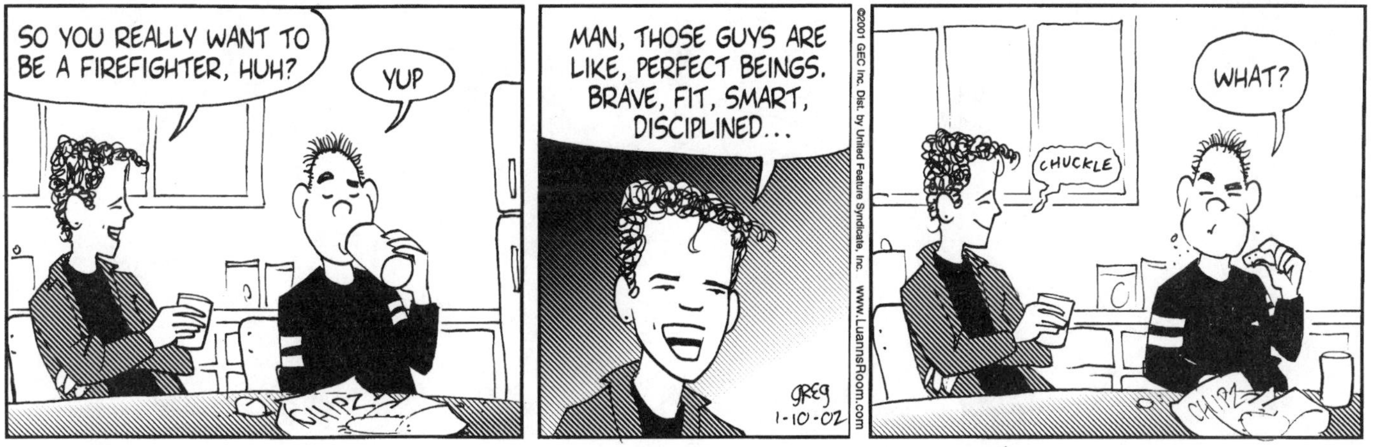
SO YOU REALLY WANT TO BE A FIREFIGHTER, HUH?
YUP
CHIPZ
MAN, THOSE GUYS ARE LIKE, PERFECT BEINGS. BRAVE, FIT, SMART, DISCIPLINED...
GREG 1-10-02
©2001 GEC Inc. Dist. by United Feature Syndicate, Inc. www.LuannsRoom.com
WHAT?
CHUCKLE
CHIPZ

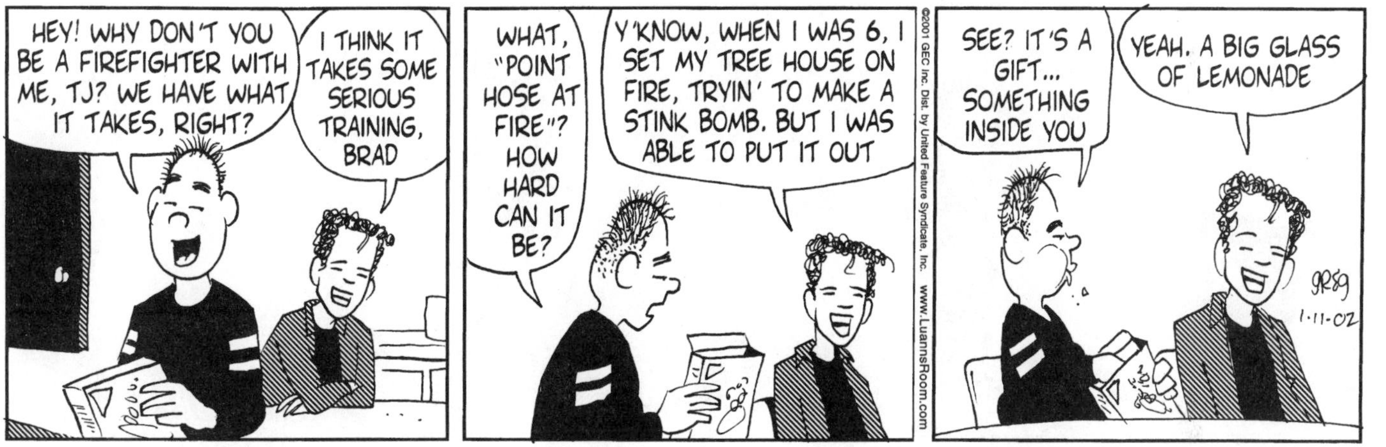
HEY! WHY DON'T YOU BE A FIREFIGHTER WITH ME, TJ? WE HAVE WHAT IT TAKES, RIGHT?
I THINK IT TAKES SOME SERIOUS TRAINING, BRAD
WHAT, "POINT HOSE AT FIRE"? HOW HARD CAN IT BE?
Y'KNOW, WHEN I WAS 6, I SET MY TREE HOUSE ON FIRE, TRYIN' TO MAKE A STINK BOMB. BUT I WAS ABLE TO PUT IT OUT
©2001 GEC Inc. Dist. by United Feature Syndicate, Inc. www.LuannsRoom.com
SEE? IT'S A GIFT... SOMETHING INSIDE YOU
YEAH. A BIG GLASS OF LEMONADE
GREG 1-11-02

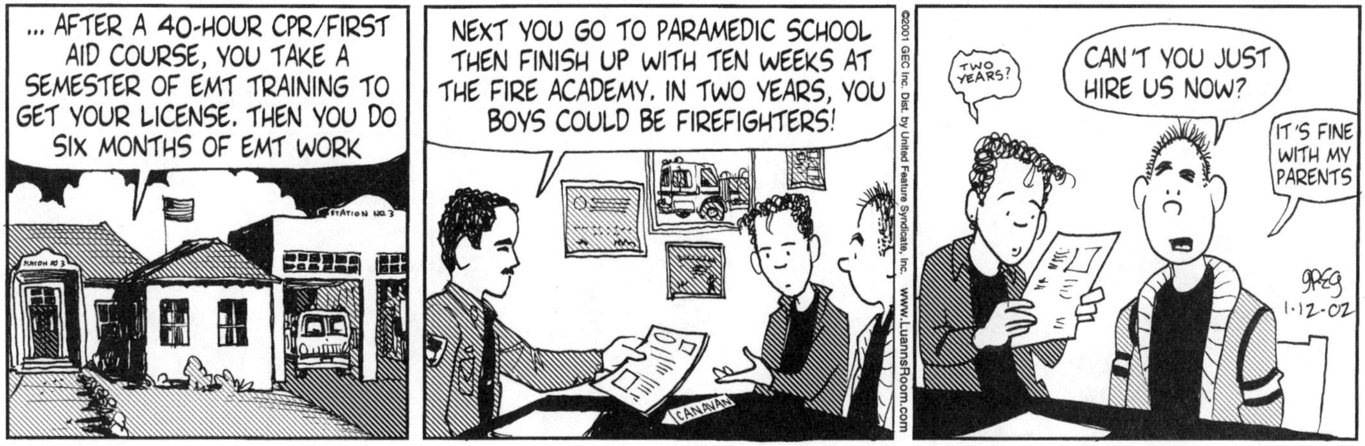
... AFTER A 40-HOUR CPR/FIRST AID COURSE, YOU TAKE A SEMESTER OF EMT TRAINING TO GET YOUR LICENSE. THEN YOU DO SIX MONTHS OF EMT WORK
STATION NO. 3
NEXT YOU GO TO PARAMEDIC SCHOOL THEN FINISH UP WITH TEN WEEKS AT THE FIRE ACADEMY. IN TWO YEARS, YOU BOYS COULD BE FIREFIGHTERS!
CANAVAN
©2001 GEC Inc. Dist. by United Feature Syndicate, Inc. www.LuannsRoom.com
TWO YEARS?
CAN'T YOU JUST HIRE US NOW?
IT'S FINE WITH MY PARENTS
GREG 1-12-02

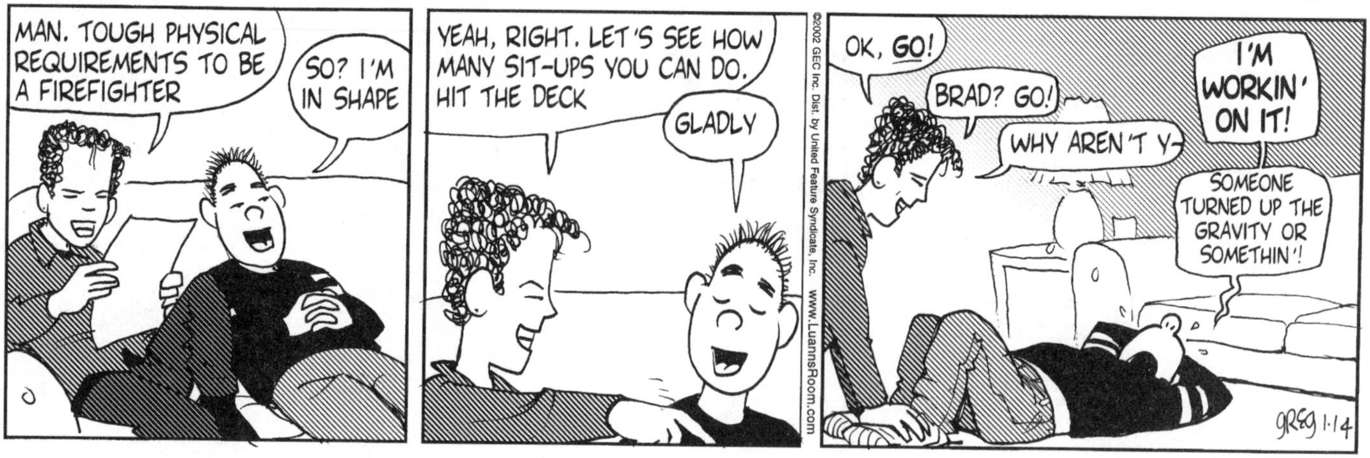
MAN. TOUGH PHYSICAL REQUIREMENTS TO BE A FIREFIGHTER
SO? I'M IN SHAPE
YEAH, RIGHT. LET'S SEE HOW MANY SIT-UPS YOU CAN DO. HIT THE DECK
GLADLY
©2002 GEC Inc. Dist. by United Feature Syndicate, Inc. www.LuannsRoom.com
OK, GO!
BRAD? GO!
WHY AREN'T Y-
I'M WORKIN' ON IT!
SOMEONE TURNED UP THE GRAVITY OR SOMETHIN'!
GREG 1·14

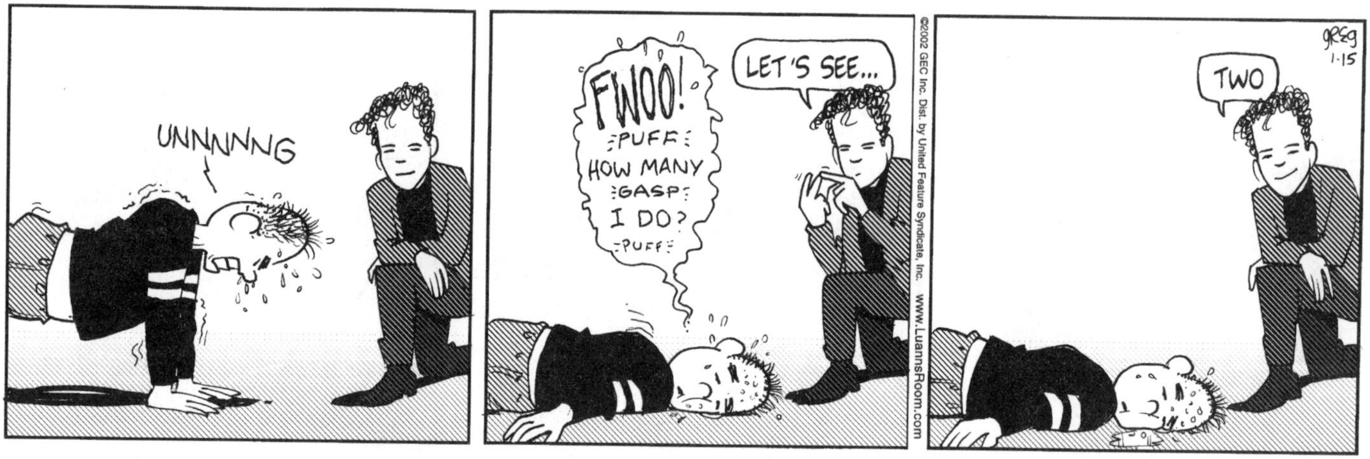
UNNNNNG
FWOO! PUFF HOW MANY GASP I DO? PUFF
LET'S SEE...
©2002 GEC Inc. Dist. by United Feature Syndicate, Inc. www.LuannsRoom.com
GREG 1·15
TWO

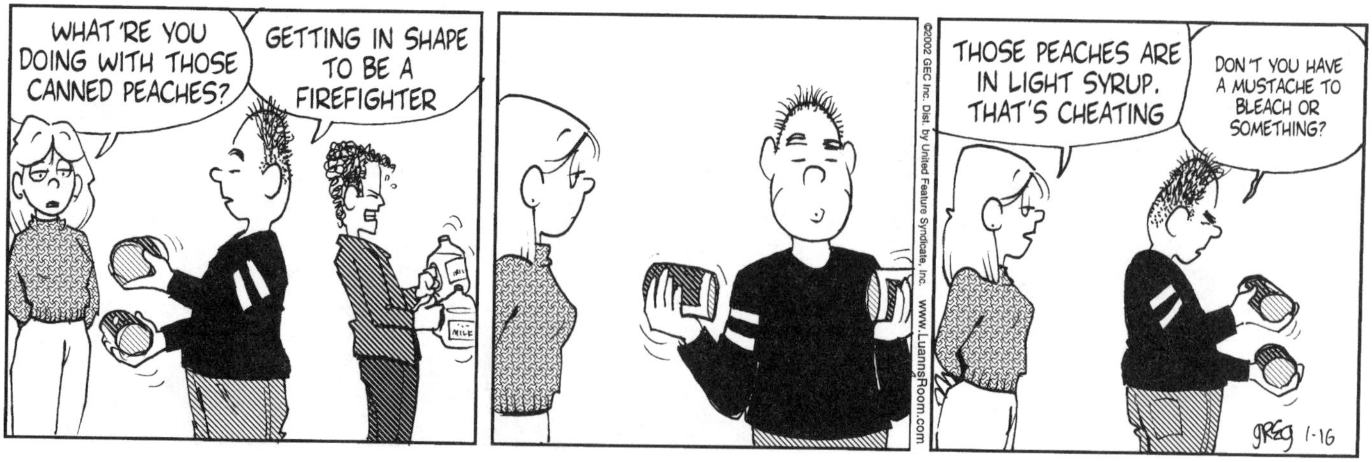
WHAT'RE YOU DOING WITH THOSE CANNED PEACHES?
GETTING IN SHAPE TO BE A FIREFIGHTER
©2002 GEC Inc. Dist. by United Feature Syndicate, Inc. www.LuannsRoom.com
THOSE PEACHES ARE IN LIGHT SYRUP. THAT'S CHEATING
DON'T YOU HAVE A MUSTACHE TO BLEACH OR SOMETHING?
GREG 1·16

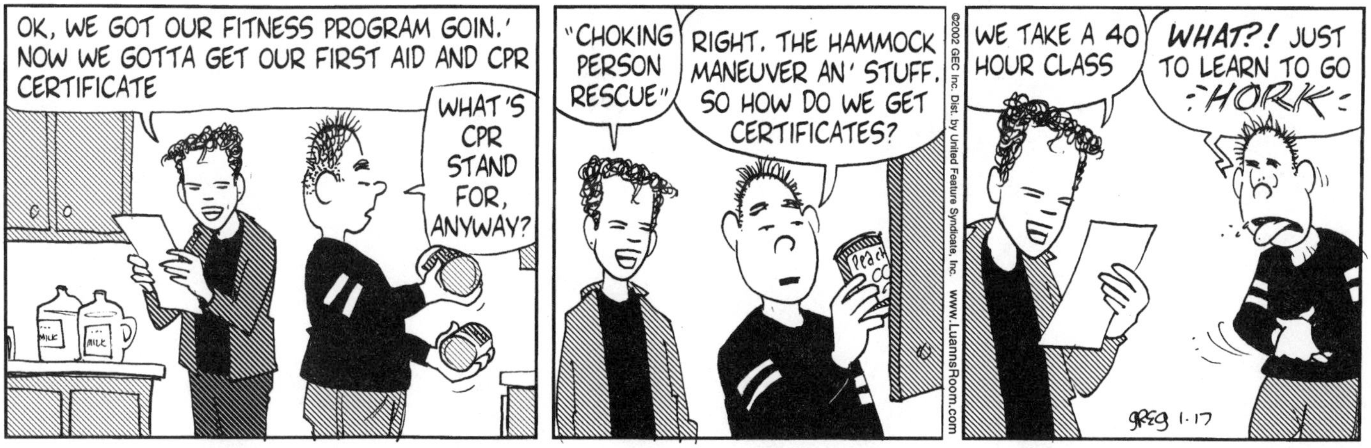
OK, WE GOT OUR FITNESS PROGRAM GOIN.' NOW WE GOTTA GET OUR FIRST AID AND CPR CERTIFICATE
WHAT'S CPR STAND FOR, ANYWAY?
"CHOKING PERSON RESCUE"
RIGHT. THE HAMMOCK MANEUVER AN' STUFF. SO HOW DO WE GET CERTIFICATES?
WE TAKE A 40 HOUR CLASS
WHAT?! JUST TO LEARN TO GO HORK
GREG 1-17
©2002 GEC Inc. Dist. by United Feature Syndicate, Inc. www.LuannsRoom.com

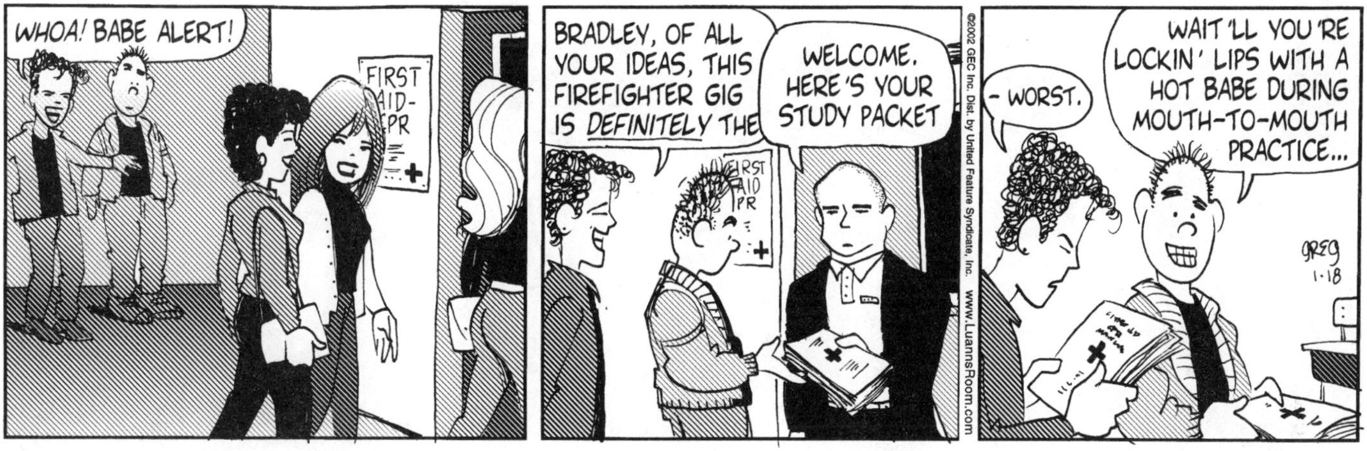
WHOA! BABE ALERT!
FIRST AID-CPR
BRADLEY, OF ALL YOUR IDEAS, THIS FIREFIGHTER GIG IS DEFINITELY THE
WELCOME. HERE'S YOUR STUDY PACKET
-WORST.
WAIT'LL YOU'RE LOCKIN' LIPS WITH A HOT BABE DURING MOUTH-TO-MOUTH PRACTICE...
GREG 1-18
©2002 GEC Inc. Dist. by United Feature Syndicate, Inc. www.LuannsRoom.com

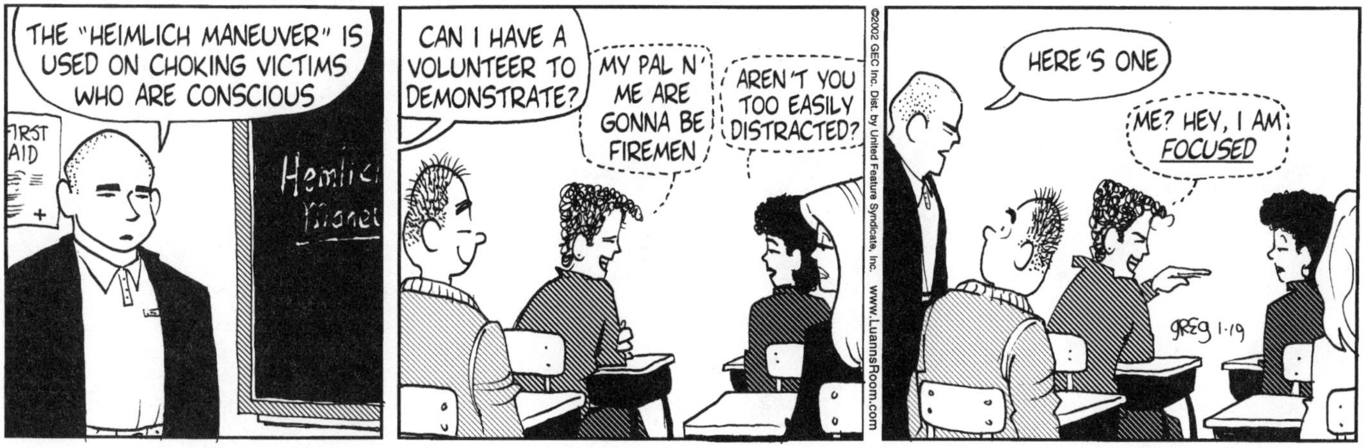
THE "HEIMLICH MANEUVER" IS USED ON CHOKING VICTIMS WHO ARE CONSCIOUS
FIRST AID
CAN I HAVE A VOLUNTEER TO DEMONSTRATE?
MY PAL N' ME ARE GONNA BE FIREMEN
AREN'T YOU TOO EASILY DISTRACTED?
HERE'S ONE
ME? HEY, I AM FOCUSED
GREG 1-19
©2002 GEC Inc. Dist. by United Feature Syndicate, Inc. www.LuannsRoom.com

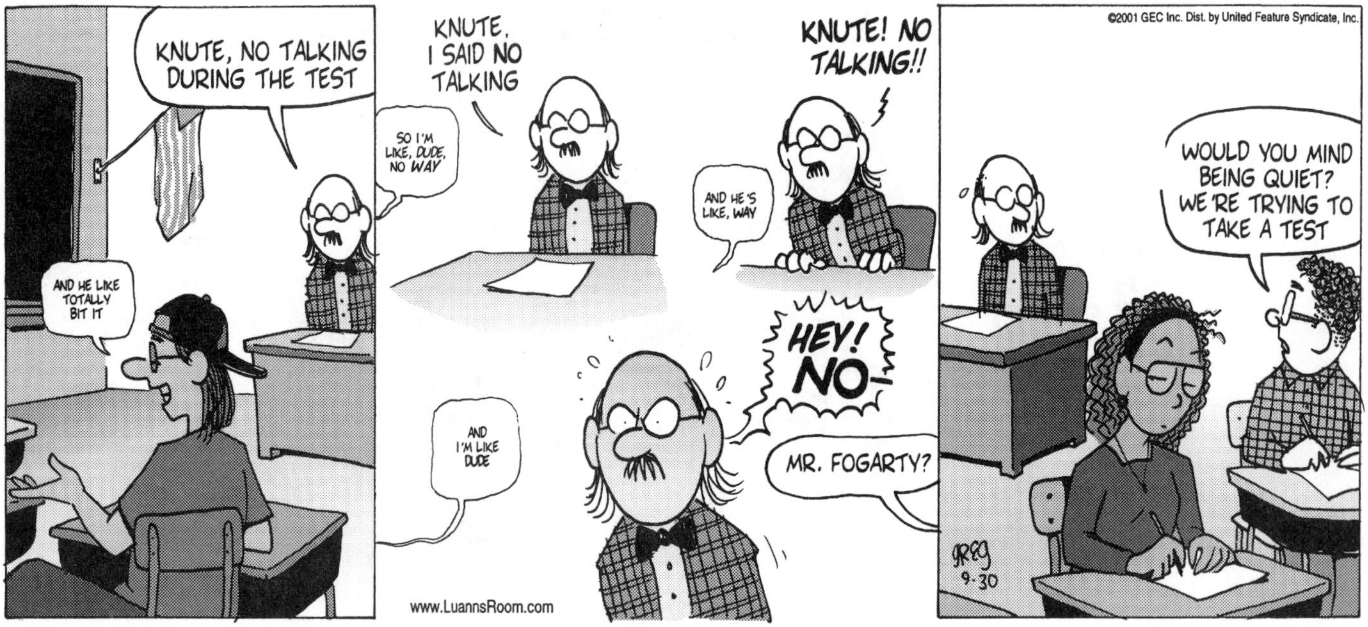
KNUTE, NO TALKING DURING THE TEST
AND HE LIKE TOTALLY BIT IT
SO I'M LIKE, DUDE, NO WAY
KNUTE, I SAID NO TALKING
AND HE'S LIKE, WAY
KNUTE! NO TALKING!!
AND I'M LIKE DUDE
HEY! NO-
MR. FOGARTY?
©2001 GEC Inc. Dist. by United Feature Syndicate, Inc.
WOULD YOU MIND BEING QUIET? WE'RE TRYING TO TAKE A TEST
greg 9-30
www.LuannsRoom.com

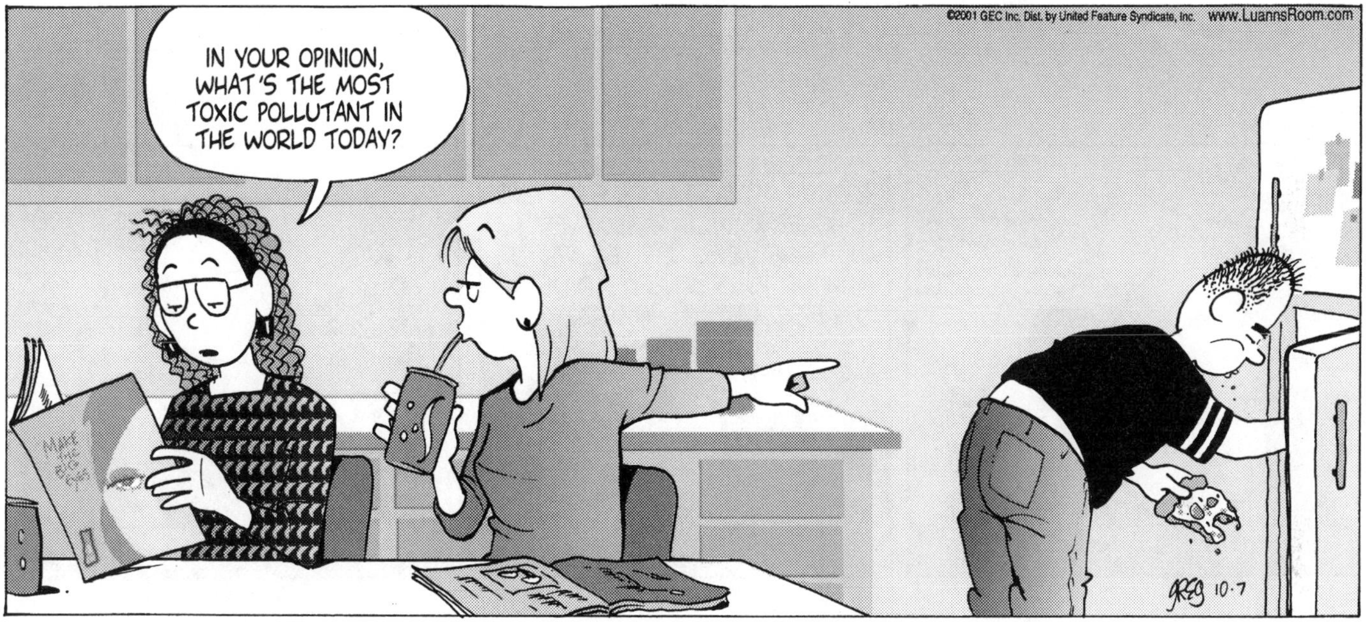
IN YOUR OPINION, WHAT'S THE MOST TOXIC POLLUTANT IN THE WORLD TODAY?
©2001 GEC Inc. Dist. by United Feature Syndicate, Inc. www.LuannsRoom.com
GREG 10·7

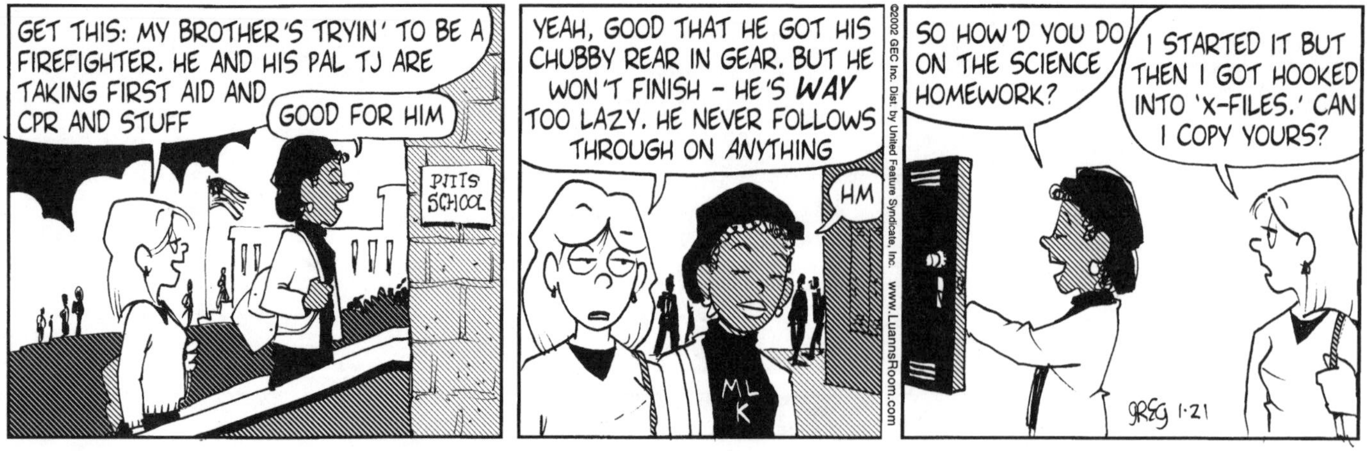
GET THIS: MY BROTHER'S TRYIN' TO BE A FIREFIGHTER. HE AND HIS PAL TJ ARE TAKING FIRST AID AND CPR AND STUFF
GOOD FOR HIM
PITTS SCHOOL
YEAH, GOOD THAT HE GOT HIS CHUBBY REAR IN GEAR. BUT HE WON'T FINISH – HE'S *WAY* TOO LAZY. HE NEVER FOLLOWS THROUGH ON *ANYTHING*
HM
MLK
©2002 GEC Inc. Dist. by United Feature Syndicate, Inc. www.LuannsRoom.com
SO HOW'D YOU DO ON THE SCIENCE HOMEWORK?
I STARTED IT BUT THEN I GOT HOOKED INTO 'X-FILES.' CAN I COPY YOURS?
GREG 1·21

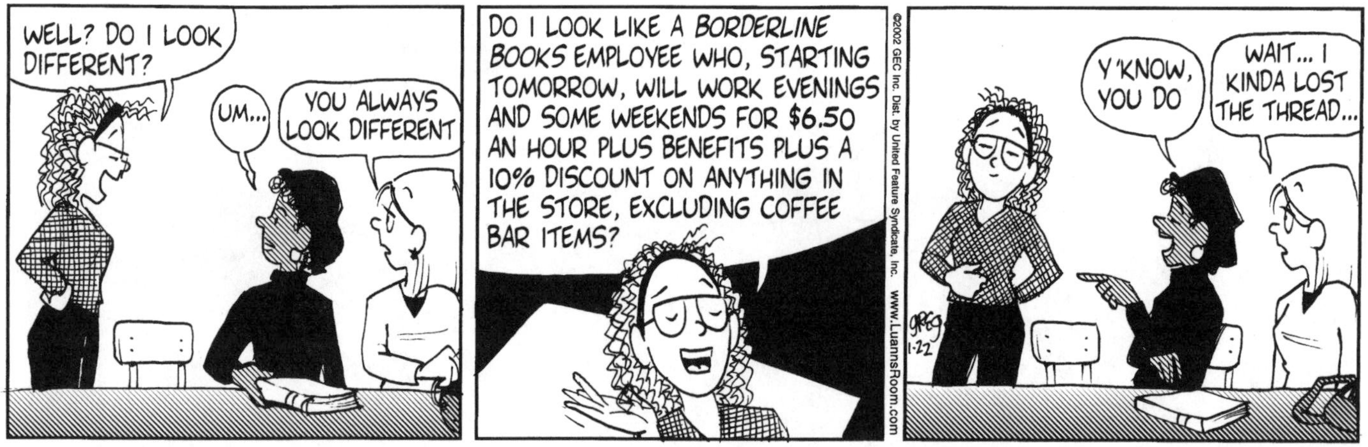
WELL? DO I LOOK DIFFERENT?
UM...
YOU ALWAYS LOOK DIFFERENT
DO I LOOK LIKE A *BORDERLINE BOOKS* EMPLOYEE WHO, STARTING TOMORROW, WILL WORK EVENINGS AND SOME WEEKENDS FOR $6.50 AN HOUR PLUS BENEFITS PLUS A 10% DISCOUNT ON ANYTHING IN THE STORE, EXCLUDING COFFEE BAR ITEMS?
©2002 GEC Inc. Dist. by United Feature Syndicate, Inc. www.LuannsRoom.com
GREG 1·22
Y'KNOW, YOU DO
WAIT... I KINDA LOST THE THREAD...

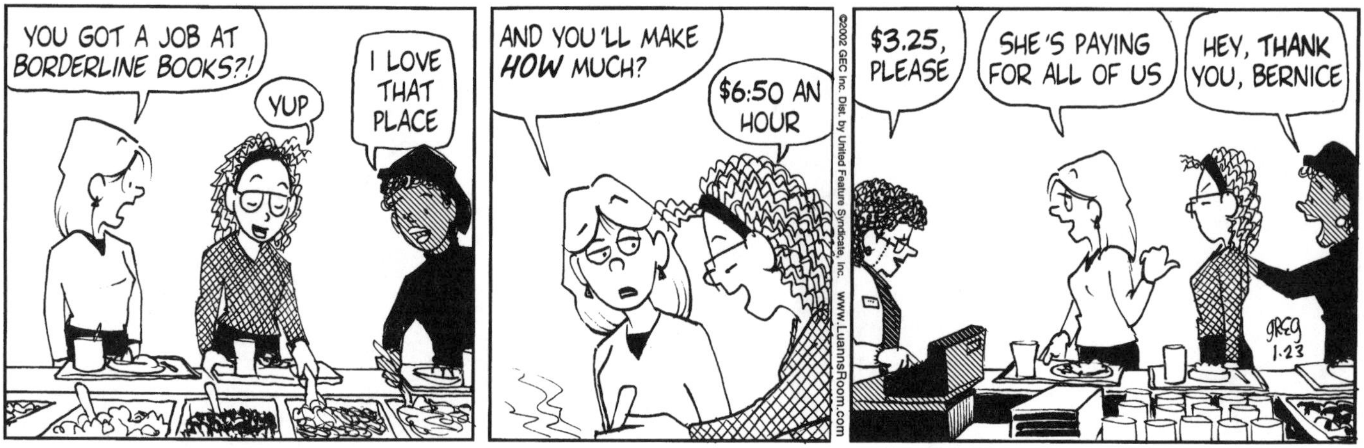
YOU GOT A JOB AT *BORDERLINE BOOKS?!*
YUP
I LOVE THAT PLACE
AND YOU'LL MAKE ***HOW*** MUCH?
$6.50 AN HOUR
©2002 GEC Inc. Dist. by United Feature Syndicate, Inc. www.LuannsRoom.com
$3.25, PLEASE
SHE'S PAYING FOR ALL OF US
HEY, **THANK** YOU, BERNICE
GREG 1·23

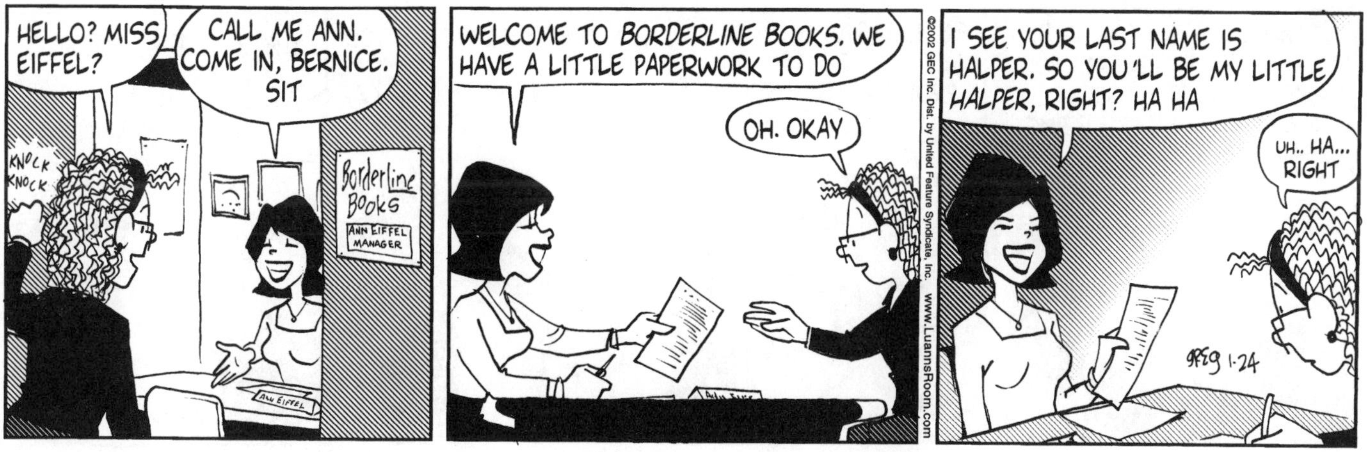
HELLO? MISS EIFFEL?
KNOCK KNOCK
CALL ME ANN. COME IN, BERNICE. SIT
Borderline Books
ANN EIFFEL MANAGER
WELCOME TO *BORDERLINE BOOKS.* WE HAVE A LITTLE PAPERWORK TO DO
OH. OKAY
©2002 GEC Inc. Dist. by United Feature Syndicate, Inc. www.LuannsRoom.com
I SEE YOUR LAST NAME IS HALPER. SO YOU'LL BE MY LITTLE *HALPER,* RIGHT? HA HA
UH.. HA... RIGHT
GREG 1·24

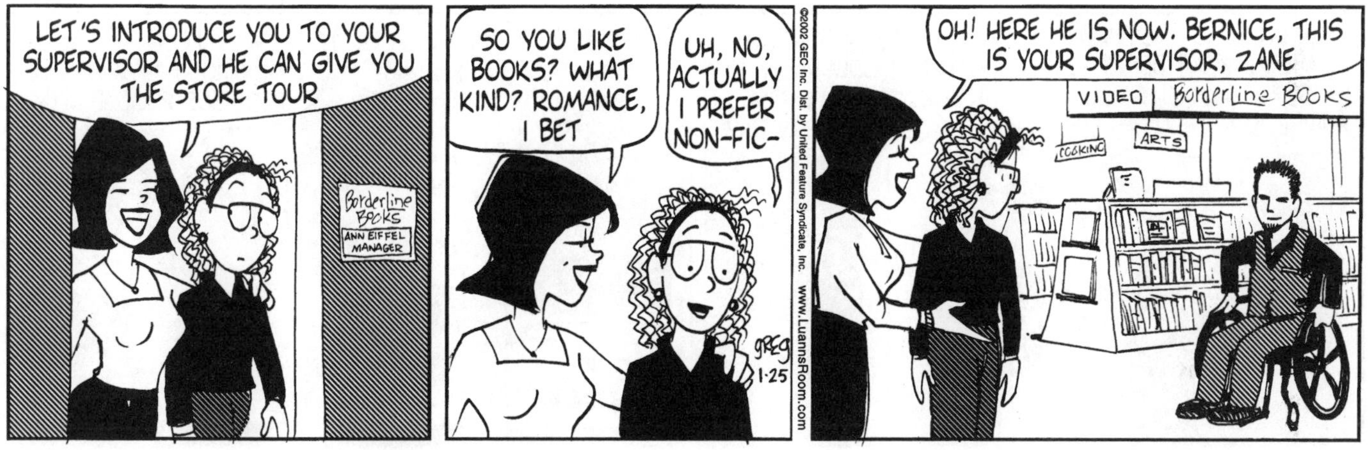
LET'S INTRODUCE YOU TO YOUR SUPERVISOR AND HE CAN GIVE YOU THE STORE TOUR
Borderline Books
ANN EIFFEL MANAGER
SO YOU LIKE BOOKS? WHAT KIND? ROMANCE, I BET
UH, NO, ACTUALLY I PREFER NON-FIC-
GREG 1·25
©2002 GEC Inc. Dist. by United Feature Syndicate, Inc. www.LuannsRoom.com
OH! HERE HE IS NOW. BERNICE, THIS IS YOUR SUPERVISOR, ZANE
VIDEO
Borderline BOOKS
COOKING
ARTS

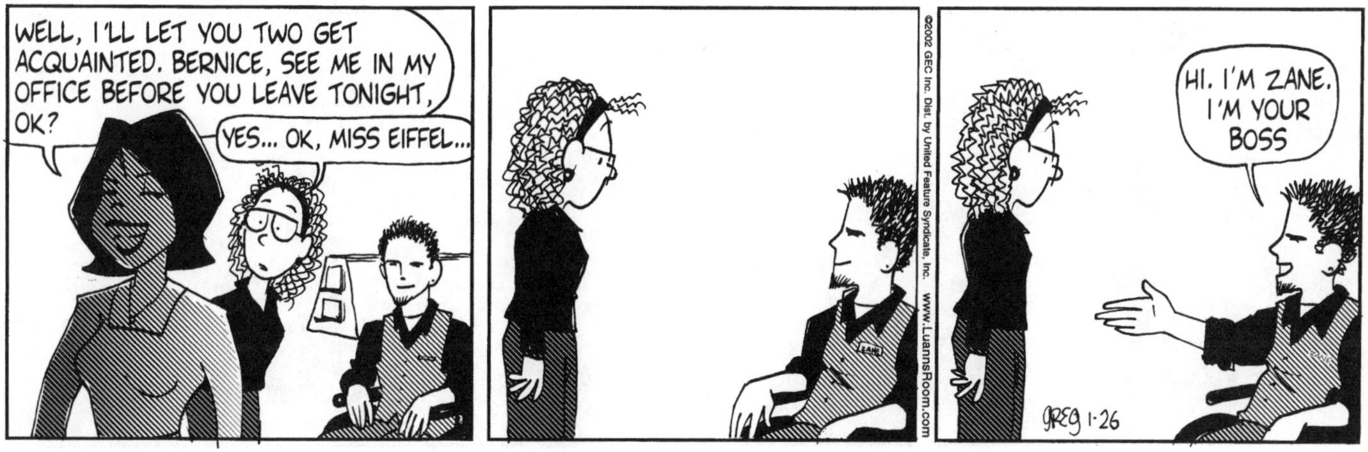
WELL, I'LL LET YOU TWO GET ACQUAINTED. BERNICE, SEE ME IN MY OFFICE BEFORE YOU LEAVE TONIGHT, OK?
YES... OK, MISS EIFFEL...
©2002 GEC Inc. Dist. by United Feature Syndicate, Inc. www.LuannsRoom.com
HI. I'M ZANE. I'M YOUR BOSS
GREG 1·26

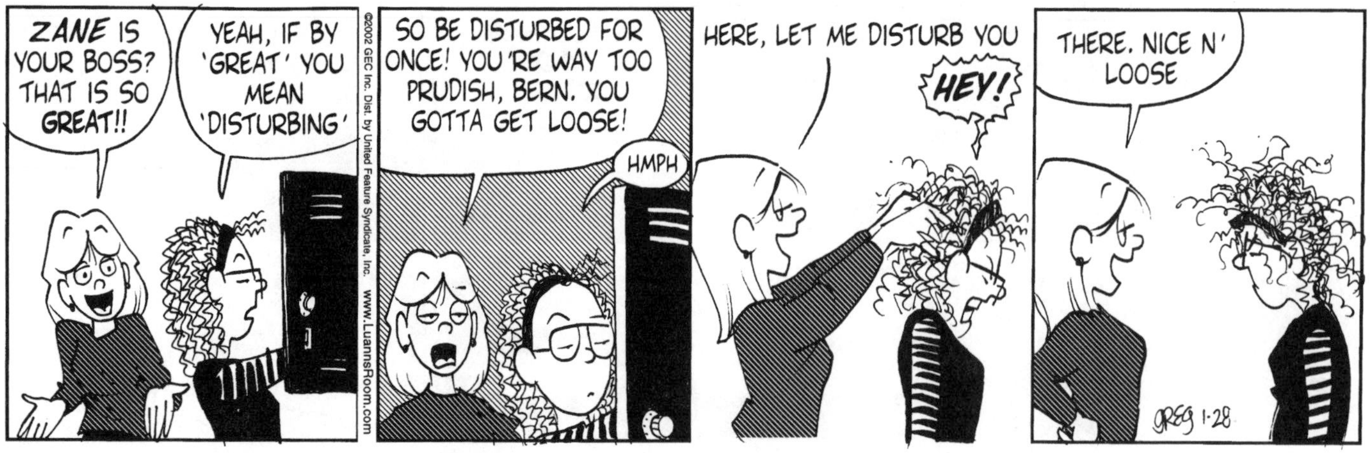
ZANE IS YOUR BOSS? THAT IS SO GREAT!!
YEAH, IF BY 'GREAT' YOU MEAN 'DISTURBING'
©2002 GEC Inc. Dist. by United Feature Syndicate, Inc. www.LuannsRoom.com
SO BE DISTURBED FOR ONCE! YOU'RE WAY TOO PRUDISH, BERN. YOU GOTTA GET LOOSE!
HMPH
HERE, LET ME DISTURB YOU
HEY!
THERE. NICE N' LOOSE
GREG 1·28

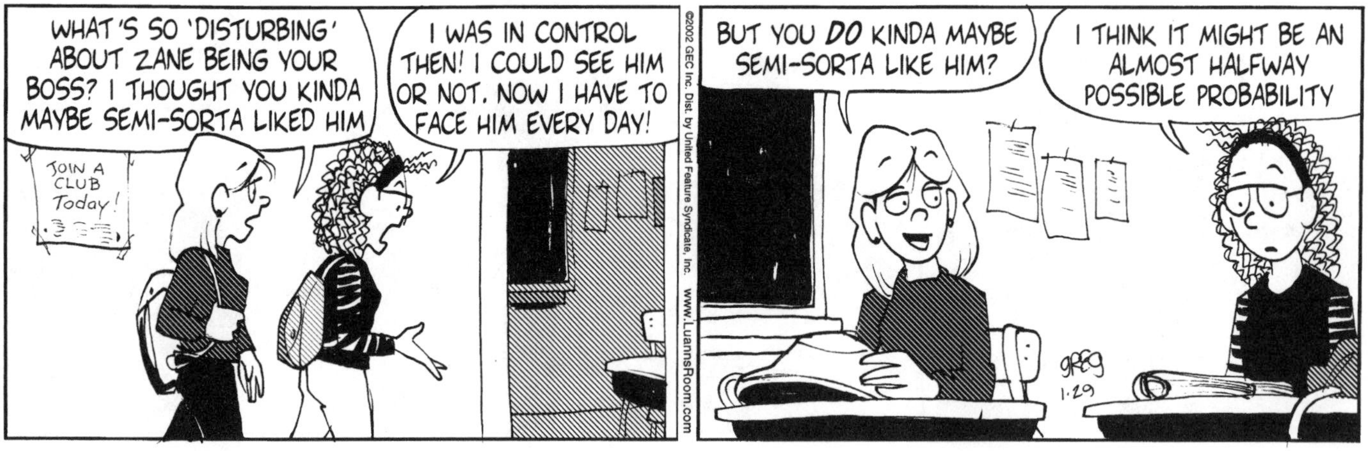
WHAT'S SO 'DISTURBING' ABOUT ZANE BEING YOUR BOSS? I THOUGHT YOU KINDA MAYBE SEMI-SORTA LIKED HIM
I WAS IN CONTROL THEN! I COULD SEE HIM OR NOT. NOW I HAVE TO FACE HIM EVERY DAY!
JOIN A CLUB Today!
©2002 GEC Inc. Dist. by United Feature Syndicate, Inc. www.LuannsRoom.com
BUT YOU DO KINDA MAYBE SEMI-SORTA LIKE HIM?
I THINK IT MIGHT BE AN ALMOST HALFWAY POSSIBLE PROBABILITY
GREG 1·29

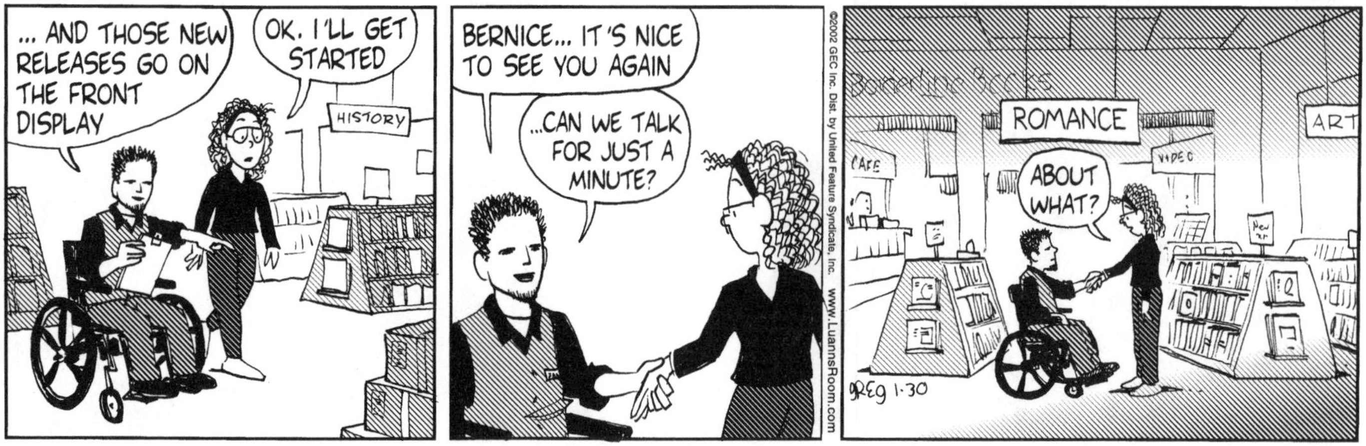
... AND THOSE NEW RELEASES GO ON THE FRONT DISPLAY
OK. I'LL GET STARTED
HISTORY
BERNICE... IT'S NICE TO SEE YOU AGAIN
...CAN WE TALK FOR JUST A MINUTE?
©2002 GEC Inc. Dist. by United Feature Syndicate, Inc. www.LuannsRoom.com
ROMANCE
ART
CAFE
VIDEO
ABOUT WHAT?
GREG 1·30

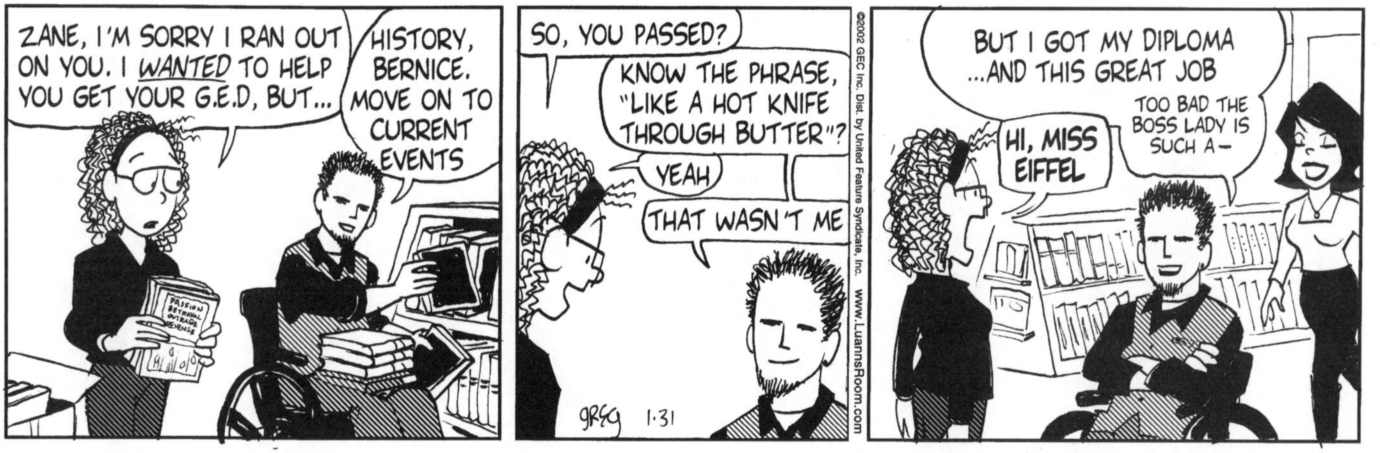
ZANE, I'M SORRY I RAN OUT ON YOU. I WANTED TO HELP YOU GET YOUR G.E.D, BUT...
HISTORY, BERNICE. MOVE ON TO CURRENT EVENTS
PASSION BETRAYAL OUTRAGE REVENGE
SO, YOU PASSED?
KNOW THE PHRASE, "LIKE A HOT KNIFE THROUGH BUTTER"?
YEAH
THAT WASN'T ME
GREG 1·31
©2002 GEC Inc. Dist. by United Feature Syndicate, Inc. www.LuannsRoom.com
BUT I GOT MY DIPLOMA ...AND THIS GREAT JOB
HI, MISS EIFFEL
TOO BAD THE BOSS LADY IS SUCH A—

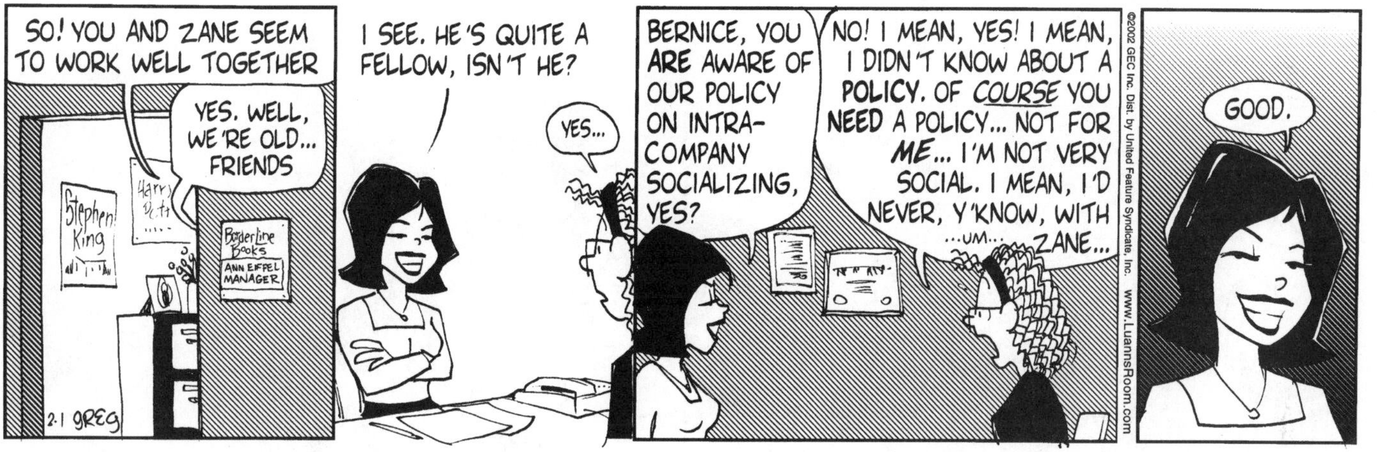
SO! YOU AND ZANE SEEM TO WORK WELL TOGETHER
YES. WELL, WE'RE OLD... FRIENDS
Stephen King
Borderline Books
ANN EIFFEL MANAGER
2·1 GREG
I SEE. HE'S QUITE A FELLOW, ISN'T HE?
YES...
BERNICE, YOU ARE AWARE OF OUR POLICY ON INTRA-COMPANY SOCIALIZING, YES?
NO! I MEAN, YES! I MEAN, I DIDN'T KNOW ABOUT A POLICY. OF COURSE YOU NEED A POLICY... NOT FOR ME... I'M NOT VERY SOCIAL. I MEAN, I'D NEVER, Y'KNOW, WITH ...UM... ZANE...
©2002 GEC Inc. Dist. by United Feature Syndicate, Inc. www.LuannsRoom.com
GOOD.

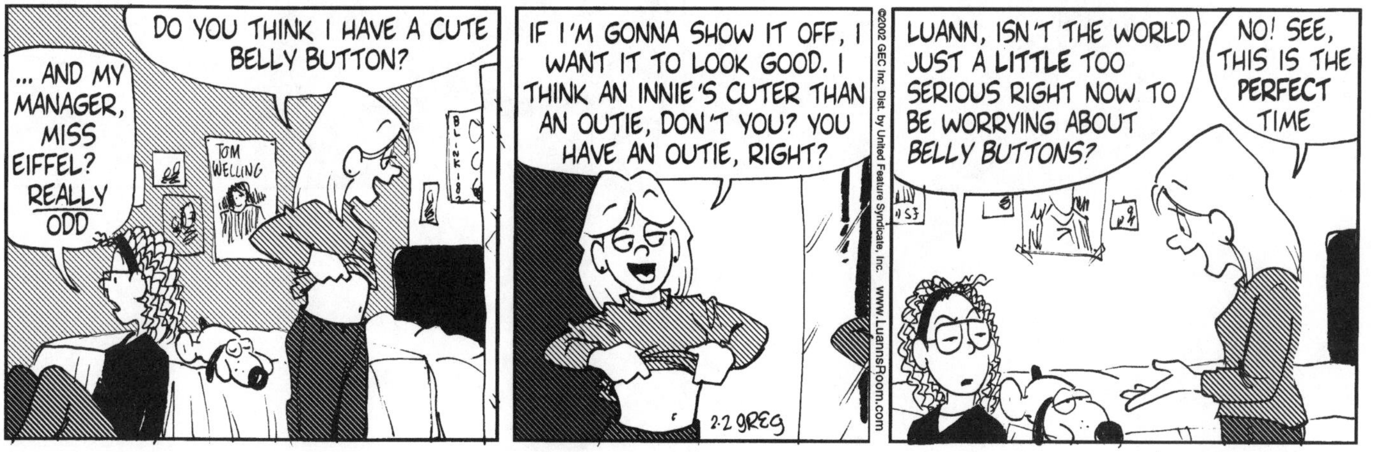
... AND MY MANAGER, MISS EIFFEL? REALLY ODD
DO YOU THINK I HAVE A CUTE BELLY BUTTON?
TOM WELLING
BLINK-182
IF I'M GONNA SHOW IT OFF, I WANT IT TO LOOK GOOD. I THINK AN INNIE'S CUTER THAN AN OUTIE, DON'T YOU? YOU HAVE AN OUTIE, RIGHT?
2·2 GREG
©2002 GEC Inc. Dist. by United Feature Syndicate, Inc. www.LuannsRoom.com
LUANN, ISN'T THE WORLD JUST A LITTLE TOO SERIOUS RIGHT NOW TO BE WORRYING ABOUT BELLY BUTTONS?
NO! SEE, THIS IS THE PERFECT TIME

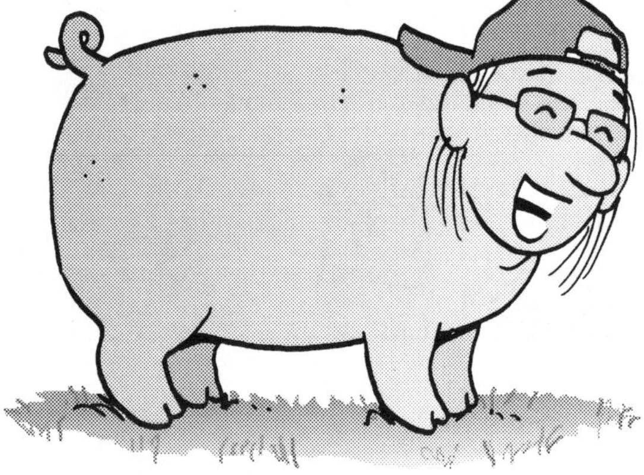

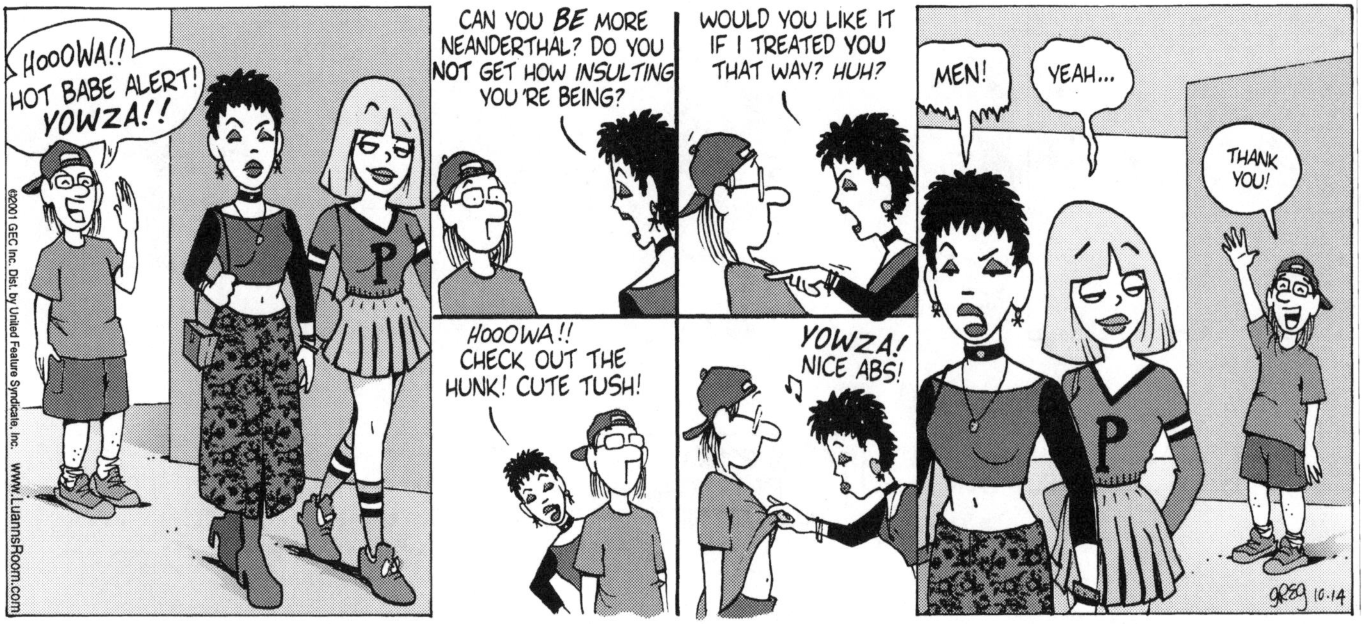
HOOOWA!! HOT BABE ALERT! YOWZA!!
©2001 GEC Inc. Dist. by United Feature Syndicate, Inc.
www.LuannsRoom.com
CAN YOU *BE* MORE NEANDERTHAL? DO YOU NOT GET HOW *INSULTING* YOU'RE BEING?
WOULD YOU LIKE IT IF I TREATED **YOU** THAT WAY? *HUH?*
HOOOWA!! CHECK OUT THE HUNK! CUTE TUSH!
YOWZA! NICE ABS!
MEN!
YEAH...
THANK YOU!
GREG 10·14

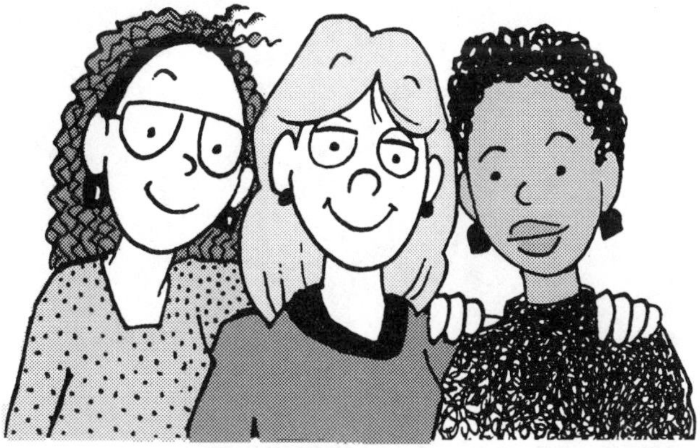

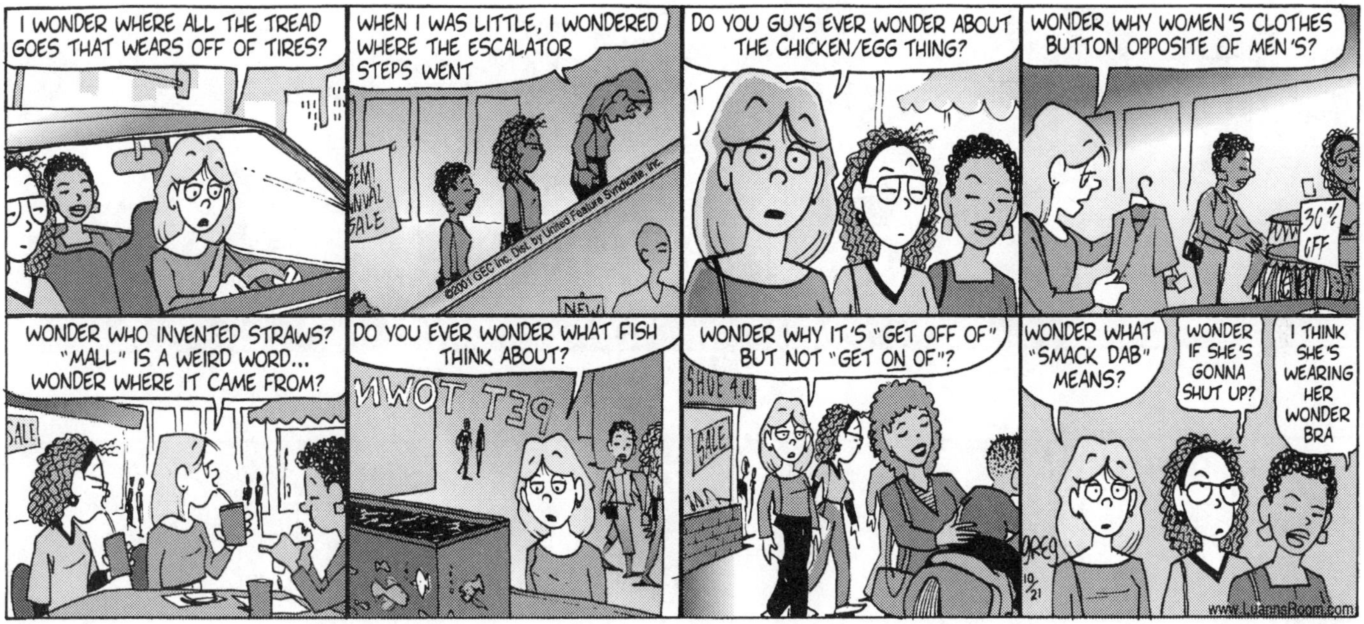
I WONDER WHERE ALL THE TREAD GOES THAT WEARS OFF OF TIRES?
WHEN I WAS LITTLE, I WONDERED WHERE THE ESCALATOR STEPS WENT
©2001 GEC Inc. Dist. by United Feature Syndicate, Inc.
NEW
DO YOU GUYS EVER WONDER ABOUT THE CHICKEN/EGG THING?
WONDER WHY WOMEN'S CLOTHES BUTTON OPPOSITE OF MEN'S?
30% OFF
WONDER WHO INVENTED STRAWS? "MALL" IS A WEIRD WORD... WONDER WHERE IT CAME FROM?
SALE
DO YOU EVER WONDER WHAT FISH THINK ABOUT?
PET TOWN
WONDER WHY IT'S "GET OFF OF" BUT NOT "GET ON OF"?
SHOE 4.U.
SALE
GREG 10/21
WONDER WHAT "SMACK DAB" MEANS?
WONDER IF SHE'S GONNA SHUT UP?
I THINK SHE'S WEARING HER WONDER BRA
www.LuannsRoom.com

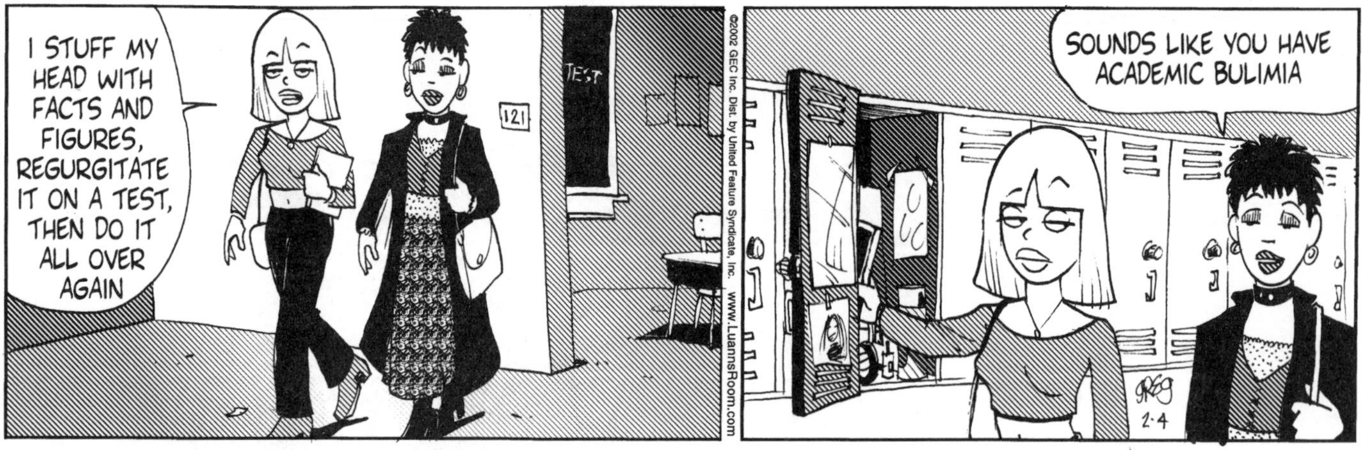
I STUFF MY HEAD WITH FACTS AND FIGURES, REGURGITATE IT ON A TEST, THEN DO IT ALL OVER AGAIN
TEST
121
©2002 GEC Inc. Dist. by United Feature Syndicate, Inc. www.LuannsRoom.com
SOUNDS LIKE YOU HAVE ACADEMIC BULIMIA
GREG 2·4

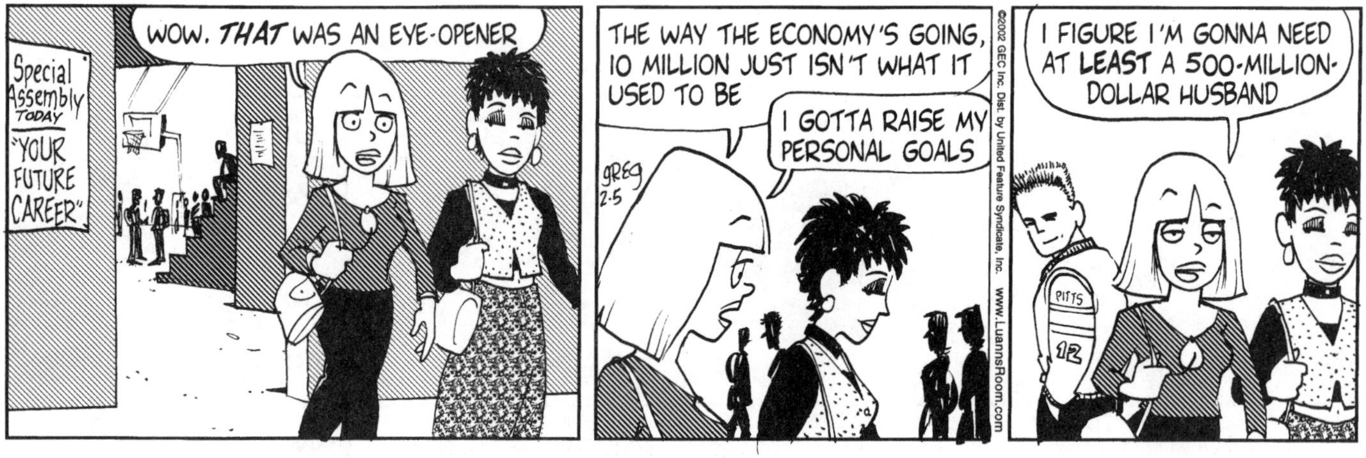
Special Assembly TODAY "YOUR FUTURE CAREER"
WOW. *THAT* WAS AN EYE-OPENER
THE WAY THE ECONOMY'S GOING, 10 MILLION JUST ISN'T WHAT IT USED TO BE
I GOTTA RAISE MY PERSONAL GOALS
GREG 2·5
©2002 GEC Inc. Dist. by United Feature Syndicate, Inc. www.LuannsRoom.com
I FIGURE I'M GONNA NEED AT **LEAST** A 500-MILLION-DOLLAR HUSBAND
PITTS
12

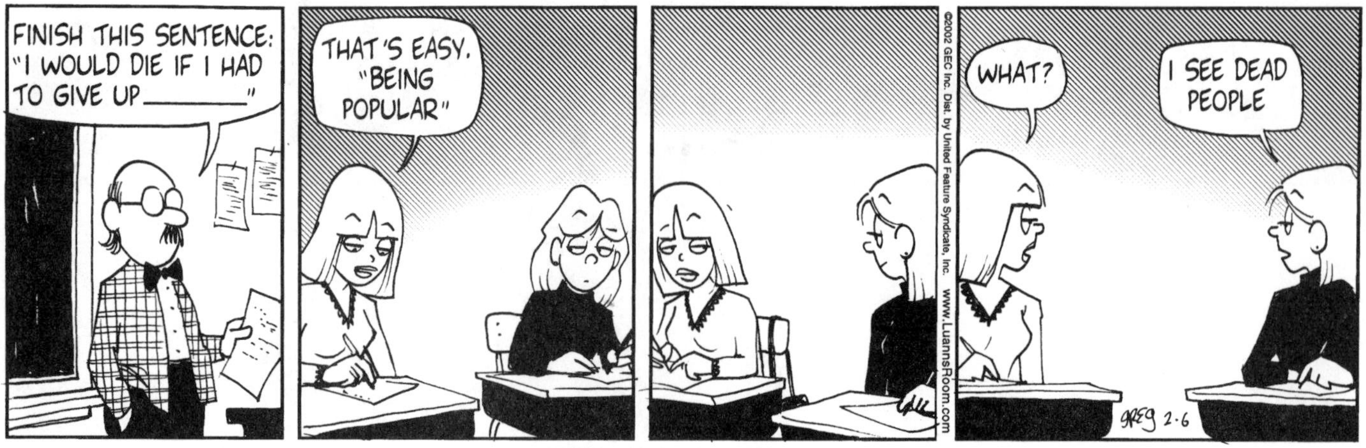
FINISH THIS SENTENCE: "I WOULD DIE IF I HAD TO GIVE UP_______"
THAT'S EASY. "BEING POPULAR"
©2002 GEC Inc. Dist. by United Feature Syndicate, Inc. www.LuannsRoom.com
WHAT?
I SEE DEAD PEOPLE
GREG 2·6

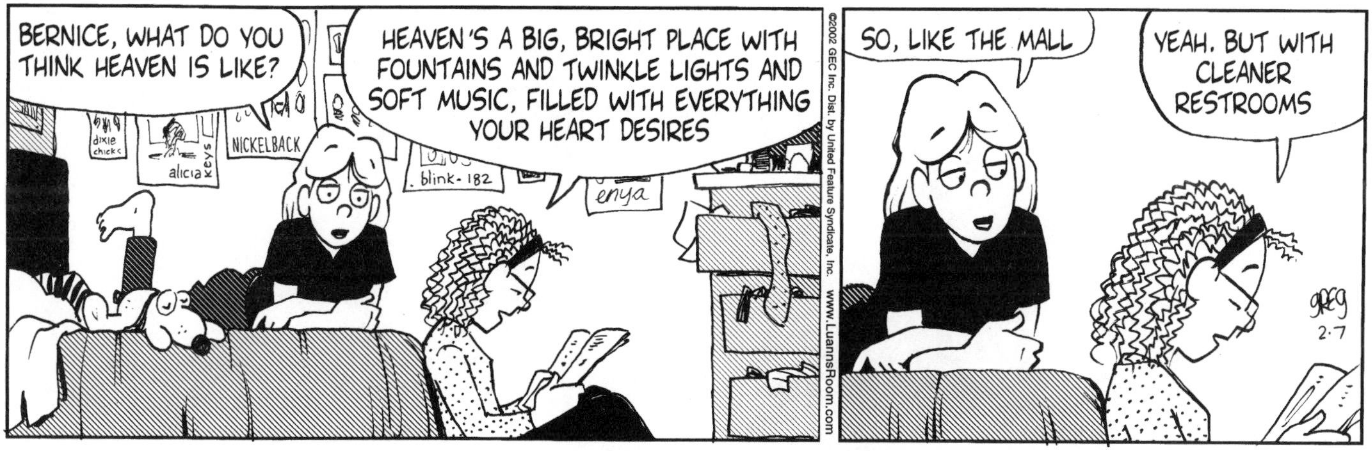
BERNICE, WHAT DO YOU THINK HEAVEN IS LIKE?
HEAVEN'S A BIG, BRIGHT PLACE WITH FOUNTAINS AND TWINKLE LIGHTS AND SOFT MUSIC, FILLED WITH EVERYTHING YOUR HEART DESIRES
dixie chicks
alicia keys
NICKELBACK
blink-182
enya
©2002 GEC Inc. Dist. by United Feature Syndicate, Inc.
www.LuannsRoom.com
SO, LIKE THE MALL
YEAH. BUT WITH CLEANER RESTROOMS
GREG 2·7

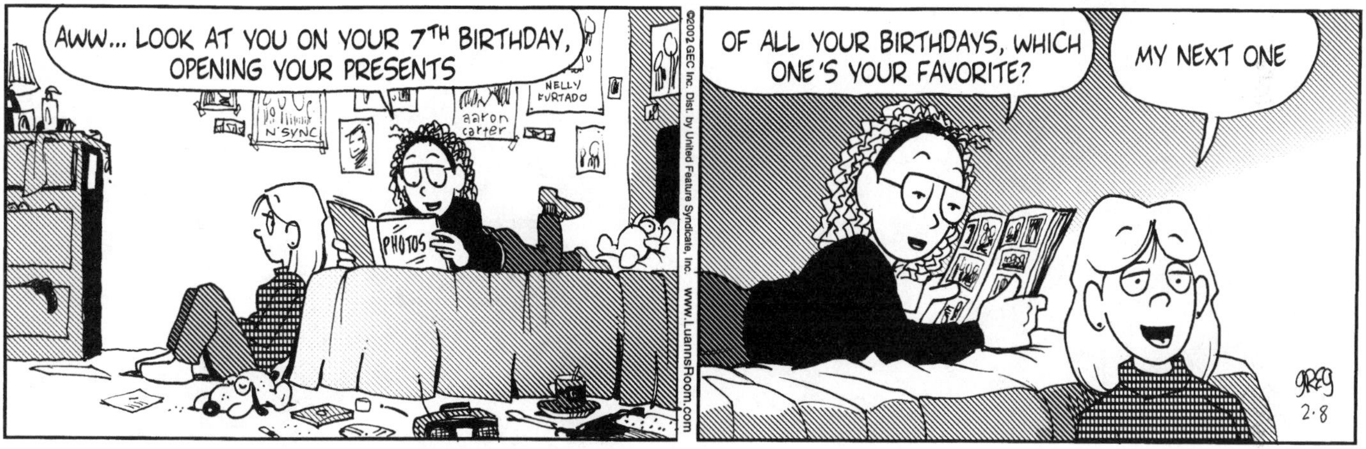
AWW... LOOK AT YOU ON YOUR 7TH BIRTHDAY, OPENING YOUR PRESENTS
NELLY FURTADO
aaron carter
N'SYNC
PHOTOS
©2002 GEC Inc. Dist. by United Feature Syndicate, Inc.
www.LuannsRoom.com
OF ALL YOUR BIRTHDAYS, WHICH ONE'S YOUR FAVORITE?
MY NEXT ONE
GREG 2·8

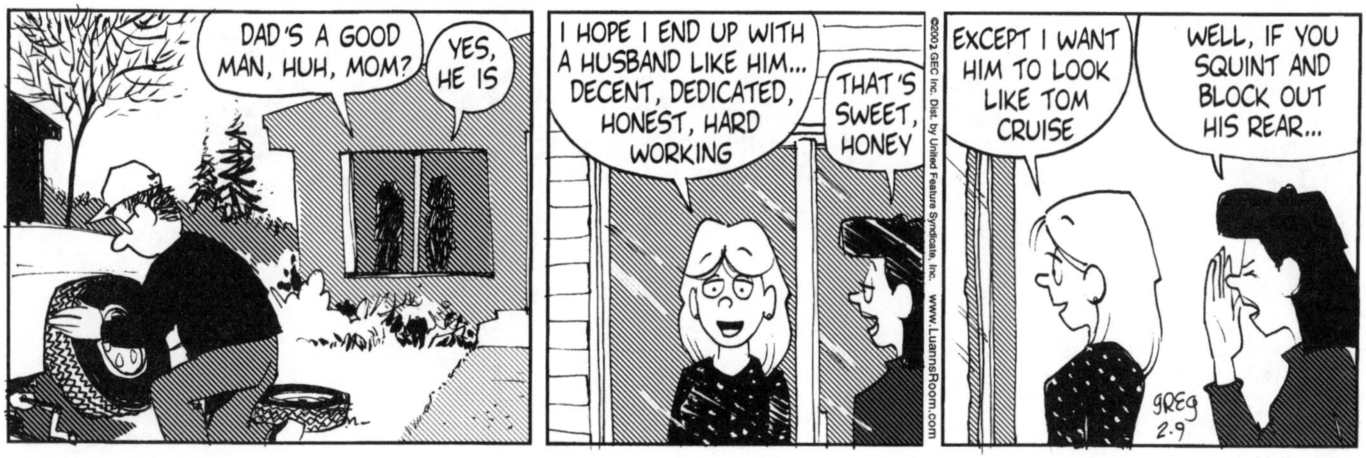
DAD'S A GOOD MAN, HUH, MOM?
YES, HE IS
I HOPE I END UP WITH A HUSBAND LIKE HIM... DECENT, DEDICATED, HONEST, HARD WORKING
THAT'S SWEET, HONEY
©2002 GEC Inc. Dist. by United Feature Syndicate, Inc.
www.LuannsRoom.com
EXCEPT I WANT HIM TO LOOK LIKE TOM CRUISE
WELL, IF YOU SQUINT AND BLOCK OUT HIS REAR...
GREG 2·9

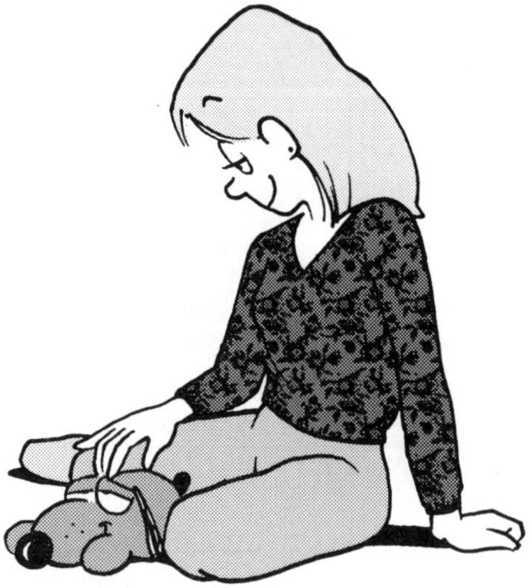

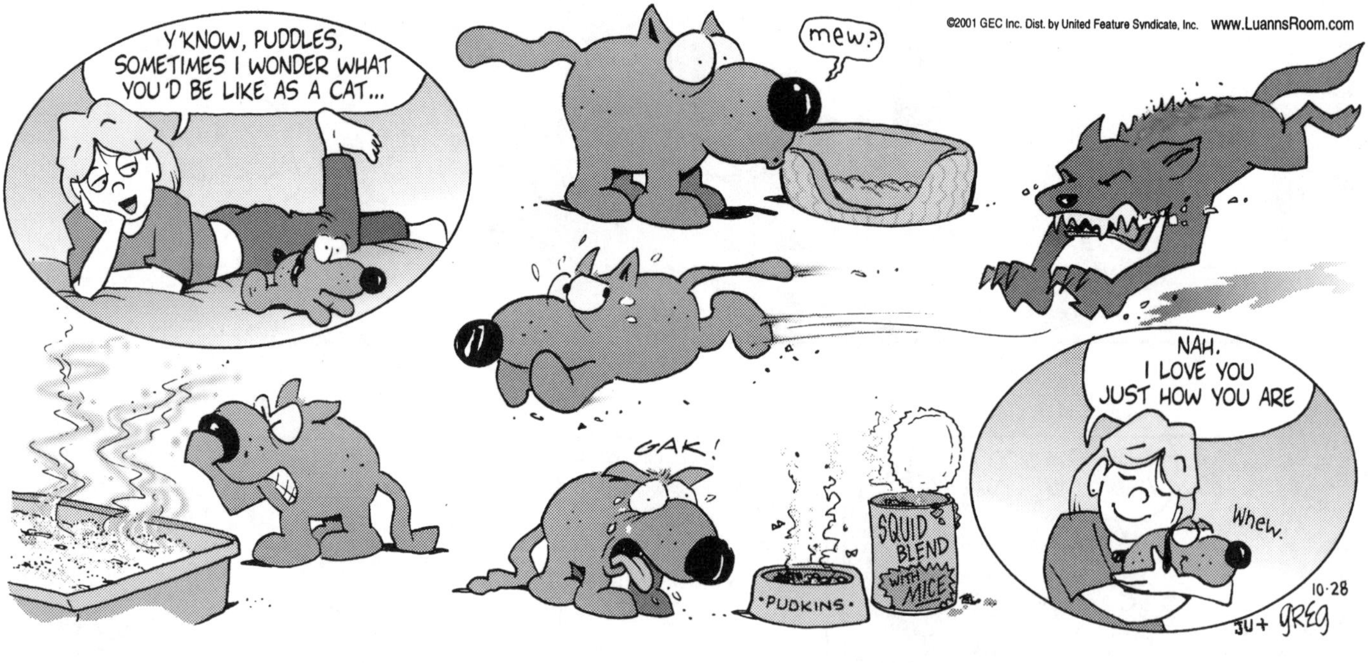

Y'KNOW, PUDDLES, SOMETIMES I WONDER WHAT YOU'D BE LIKE AS A CAT...
mew?
GAK!
PUDKINS
SQUID BLEND WITH MICE
NAH. I LOVE YOU JUST HOW YOU ARE
Whew.
10·28
JU + GREG
©2001 GEC Inc. Dist. by United Feature Syndicate, Inc. www.LuannsRoom.com

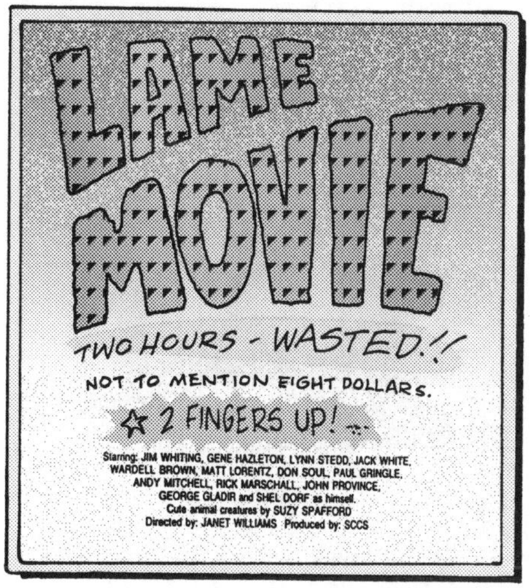
LAME MOVIE
TWO HOURS - WASTED!!
NOT TO MENTION EIGHT DOLLARS.
2 FINGERS UP!
Starring: JIM WHITING, GENE HAZLETON, LYNN STEDD, JACK WHITE, WARDELL BROWN, MATT LORENTZ, DON SOUL, PAUL GRINGLE, ANDY MITCHELL, RICK MARSCHALL, JOHN PROVINCE, GEORGE GLADIR and SHEL DORF as himself.
Cute animal creatures by SUZY SPAFFORD
Directed by: JANET WILLIAMS Produced by: SCCS

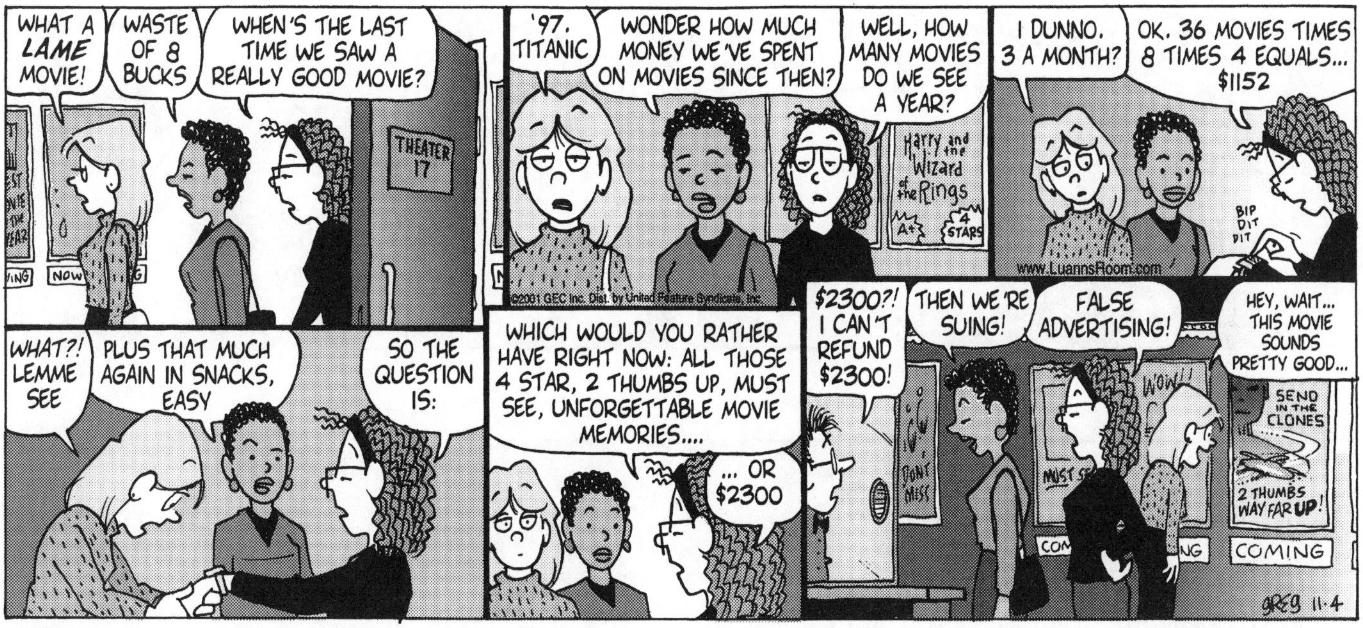
WHAT A *LAME* MOVIE!
WASTE OF 8 BUCKS
WHEN'S THE LAST TIME WE SAW A REALLY GOOD MOVIE?
THEATER 17
'97. TITANIC
WONDER HOW MUCH MONEY WE'VE SPENT ON MOVIES SINCE THEN?
WELL, HOW MANY MOVIES DO WE SEE A YEAR?
Harry and the Wizard of the Rings
A+
4 STARS
©2001 GEC Inc. Dist. by United Feature Syndicate, Inc.
I DUNNO. 3 A MONTH?
OK. 36 MOVIES TIMES 8 TIMES 4 EQUALS... $1152
BIP DIT DIT
www.LuannsRoom.com
WHAT?! LEMME SEE
PLUS THAT MUCH AGAIN IN SNACKS, EASY
SO THE QUESTION IS:
WHICH WOULD YOU RATHER HAVE RIGHT NOW: ALL THOSE 4 STAR, 2 THUMBS UP, MUST SEE, UNFORGETTABLE MOVIE MEMORIES....
... OR $2300
$2300?! I CAN'T REFUND $2300!
THEN WE'RE SUING!
FALSE ADVERTISING!
HEY, WAIT... THIS MOVIE SOUNDS PRETTY GOOD...
DON'T MISS
WOW!!
SEND IN THE CLONES
2 THUMBS WAY FAR **UP**!
COMING
GREG 11·4

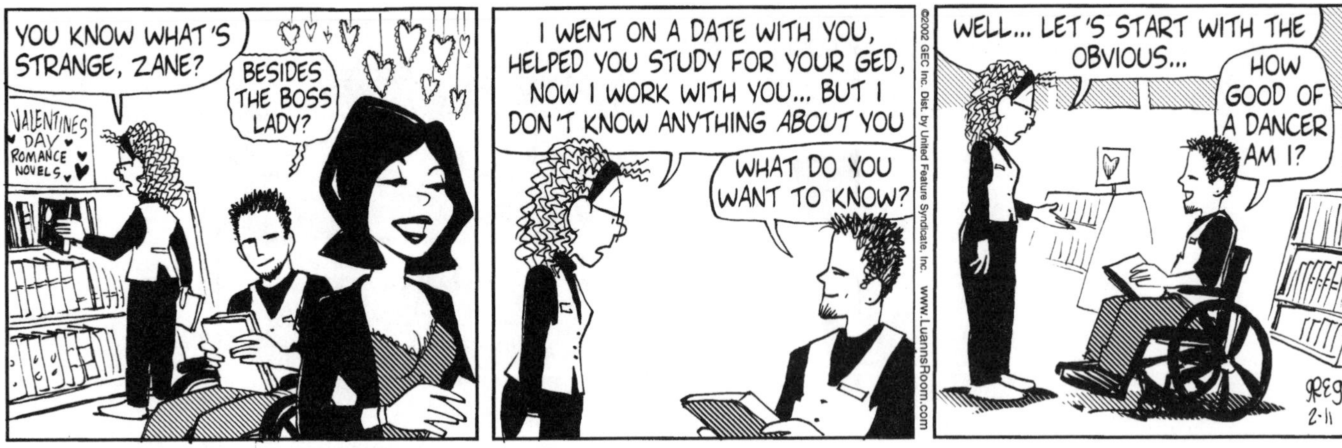
YOU KNOW WHAT'S STRANGE, ZANE?
VALENTINES DAY ROMANCE NOVELS
BESIDES THE BOSS LADY?
I WENT ON A DATE WITH YOU, HELPED YOU STUDY FOR YOUR GED, NOW I WORK WITH YOU... BUT I DON'T KNOW ANYTHING *ABOUT* YOU
WHAT DO YOU WANT TO KNOW?
©2002 GEC Inc. Dist. by United Feature Syndicate, Inc. www.LuannsRoom.com
WELL... LET'S START WITH THE OBVIOUS...
HOW GOOD OF A DANCER AM I?
GREG 2-11

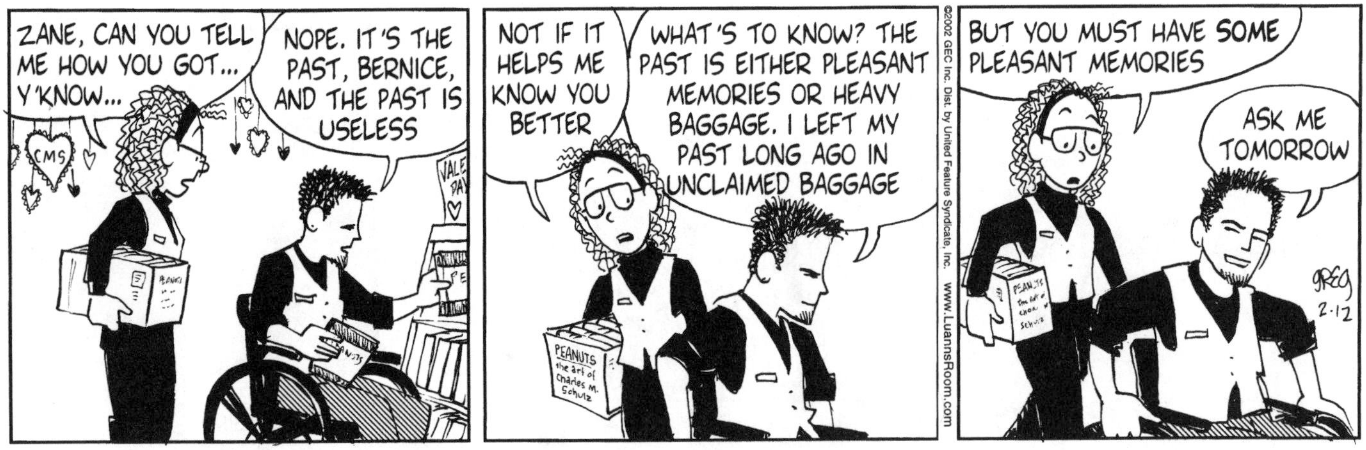
ZANE, CAN YOU TELL ME HOW YOU GOT... Y'KNOW...
NOPE. IT'S THE PAST, BERNICE, AND THE PAST IS USELESS
NOT IF IT HELPS ME KNOW YOU BETTER
WHAT'S TO KNOW? THE PAST IS EITHER PLEASANT MEMORIES OR HEAVY BAGGAGE. I LEFT MY PAST LONG AGO IN UNCLAIMED BAGGAGE
PEANUTS the art of Charles M. Schulz
©2002 GEC Inc. Dist. by United Feature Syndicate, Inc. www.LuannsRoom.com
BUT YOU MUST HAVE **SOME** PLEASANT MEMORIES
ASK ME TOMORROW
GREG 2-12

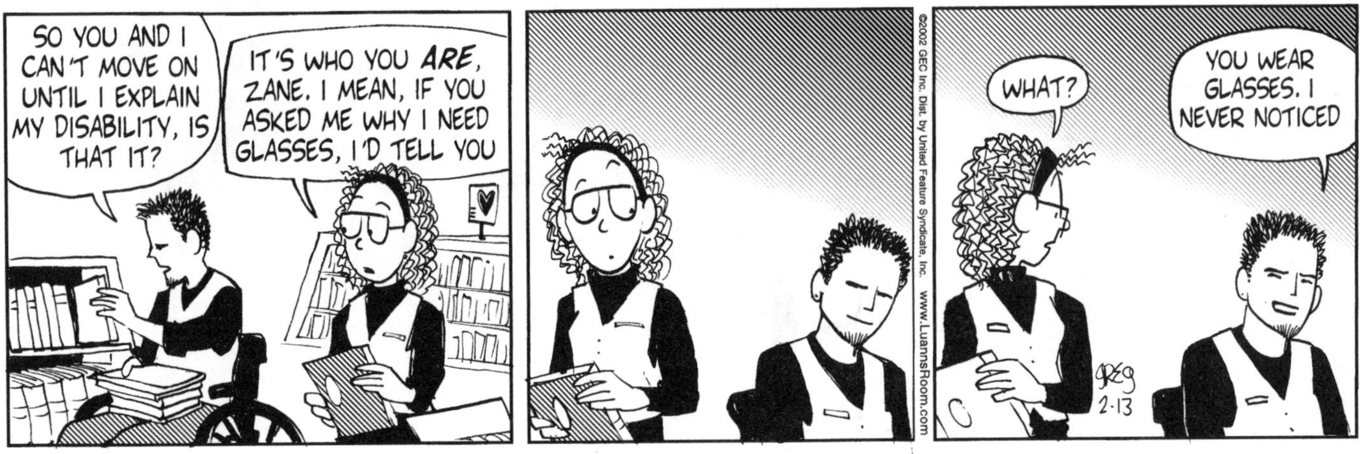
SO YOU AND I CAN'T MOVE ON UNTIL I EXPLAIN MY DISABILITY, IS THAT IT?
IT'S WHO YOU ***ARE***, ZANE. I MEAN, IF YOU ASKED ME WHY I NEED GLASSES, I'D TELL YOU
©2002 GEC Inc. Dist. by United Feature Syndicate, Inc. www.LuannsRoom.com
WHAT?
YOU WEAR GLASSES. I NEVER NOTICED
GREG 2-13

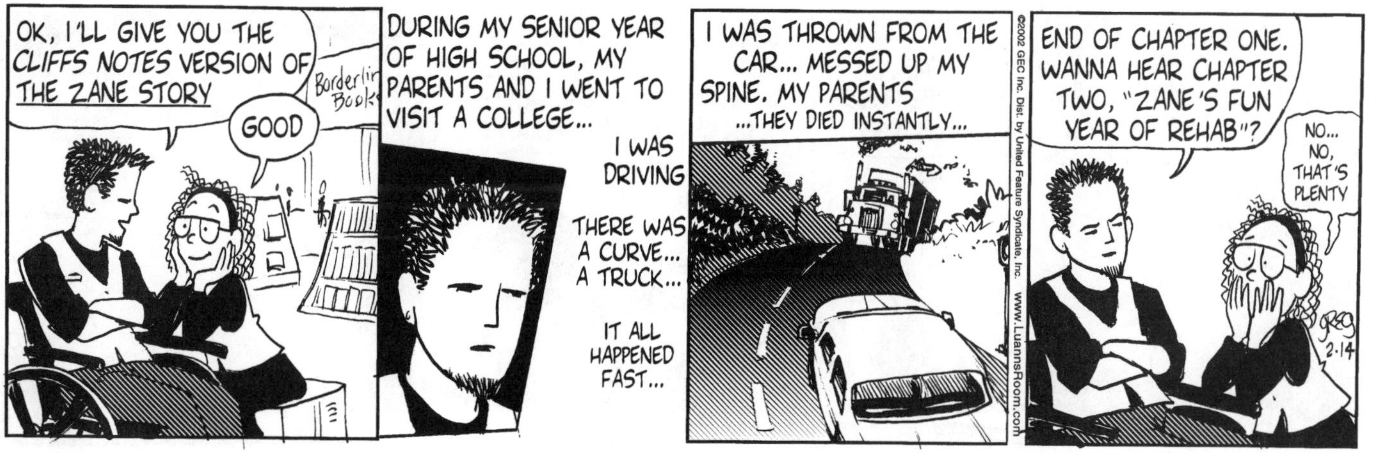
OK, I'LL GIVE YOU THE CLIFFS NOTES VERSION OF THE ZANE STORY
GOOD
Borderline Books
DURING MY SENIOR YEAR OF HIGH SCHOOL, MY PARENTS AND I WENT TO VISIT A COLLEGE...
I WAS DRIVING
THERE WAS A CURVE... A TRUCK...
IT ALL HAPPENED FAST...
I WAS THROWN FROM THE CAR... MESSED UP MY SPINE. MY PARENTS ...THEY DIED INSTANTLY...
©2002 GEC Inc. Dist. by United Feature Syndicate, Inc. www.LuannsRoom.com
END OF CHAPTER ONE. WANNA HEAR CHAPTER TWO, "ZANE'S FUN YEAR OF REHAB"?
NO... NO, THAT'S PLENTY
GREG 2·14

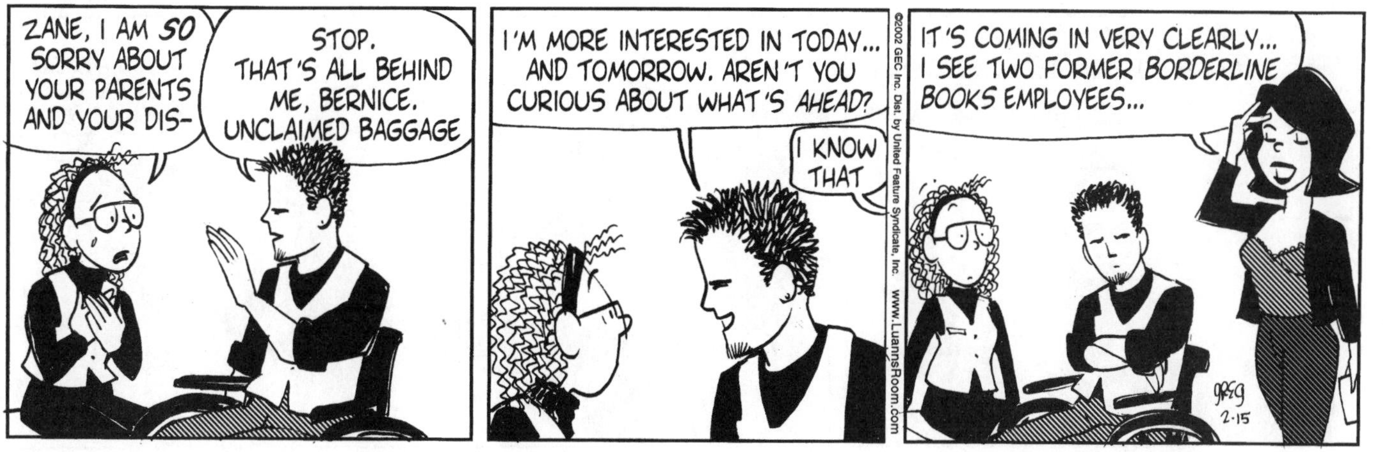
ZANE, I AM SO SORRY ABOUT YOUR PARENTS AND YOUR DIS-
STOP. THAT'S ALL BEHIND ME, BERNICE. UNCLAIMED BAGGAGE
I'M MORE INTERESTED IN TODAY... AND TOMORROW. AREN'T YOU CURIOUS ABOUT WHAT'S AHEAD?
I KNOW THAT
©2002 GEC Inc. Dist. by United Feature Syndicate, Inc. www.LuannsRoom.com
IT'S COMING IN VERY CLEARLY... I SEE TWO FORMER BORDERLINE BOOKS EMPLOYEES...
GREG 2·15

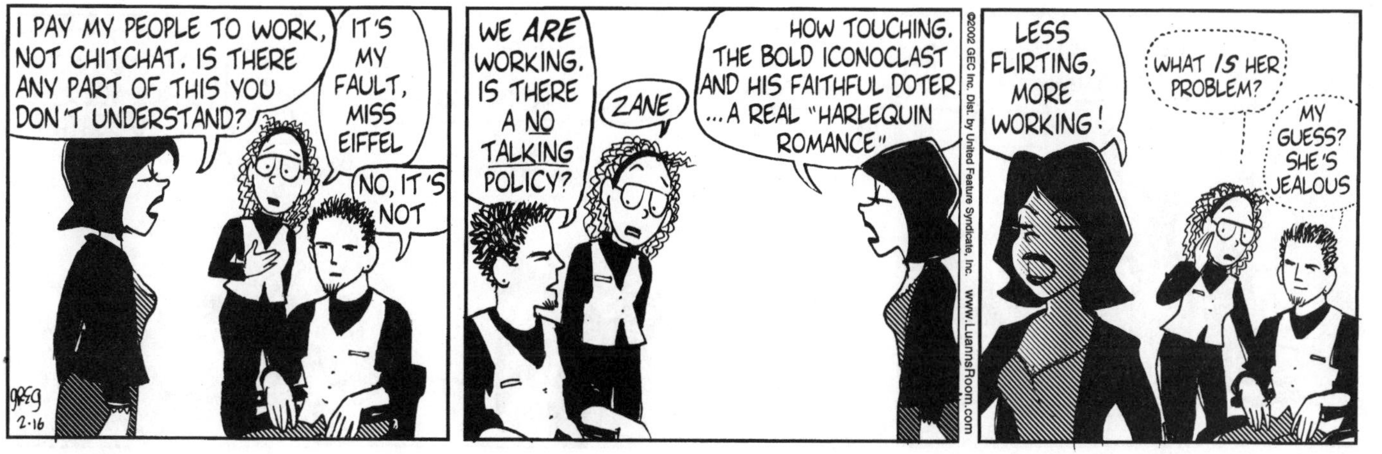
I PAY MY PEOPLE TO WORK, NOT CHITCHAT. IS THERE ANY PART OF THIS YOU DON'T UNDERSTAND?
IT'S MY FAULT, MISS EIFFEL
NO, IT'S NOT
GREG 2·16
WE ARE WORKING. IS THERE A NO TALKING POLICY?
ZANE
HOW TOUCHING. THE BOLD ICONOCLAST AND HIS FAITHFUL DOTER ...A REAL "HARLEQUIN ROMANCE"
©2002 GEC Inc. Dist. by United Feature Syndicate, Inc. www.LuannsRoom.com
LESS FLIRTING, MORE WORKING!
WHAT IS HER PROBLEM?
MY GUESS? SHE'S JEALOUS

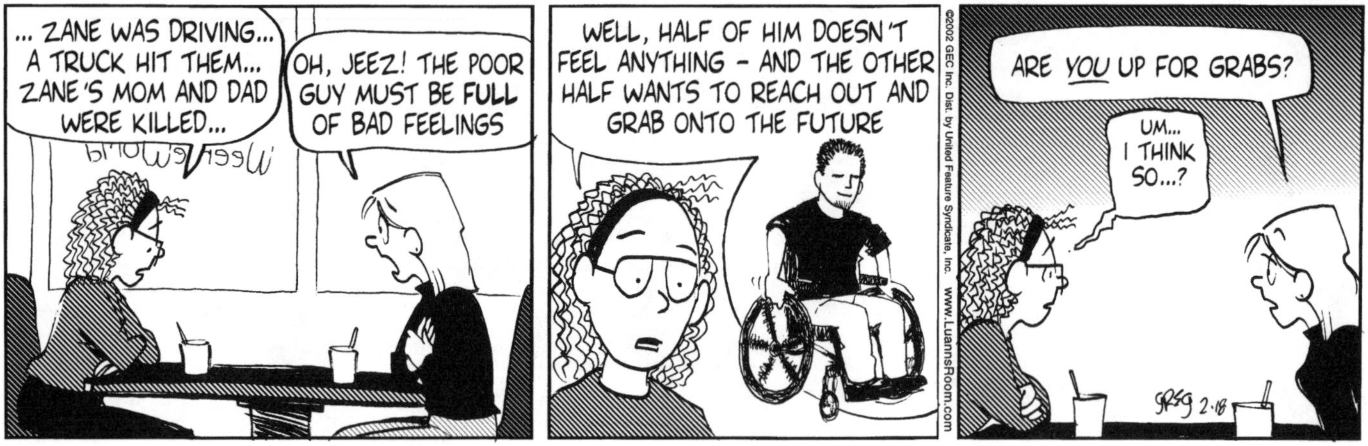
... ZANE WAS DRIVING... A TRUCK HIT THEM... ZANE'S MOM AND DAD WERE KILLED...
OH, JEEZ! THE POOR GUY MUST BE **FULL** OF BAD FEELINGS
WELL, HALF OF HIM DOESN'T FEEL ANYTHING - AND THE OTHER HALF WANTS TO REACH OUT AND GRAB ONTO THE FUTURE
©2002 GEC Inc. Dist. by United Feature Syndicate, Inc. www.LuannsRoom.com
ARE YOU UP FOR GRABS?
UM... I THINK SO...?
GREG 2.18

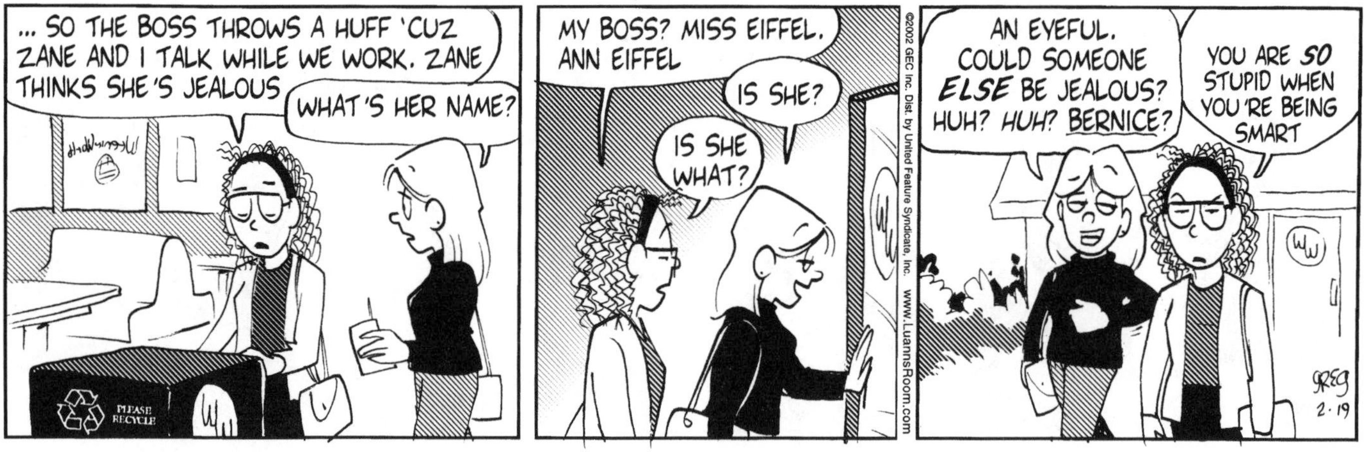
... SO THE BOSS THROWS A HUFF 'CUZ ZANE AND I TALK WHILE WE WORK. ZANE THINKS SHE'S JEALOUS
WHAT'S HER NAME?
PLEASE RECYCLE
MY BOSS? MISS EIFFEL. ANN EIFFEL
IS SHE?
IS SHE WHAT?
©2002 GEC Inc. Dist. by United Feature Syndicate, Inc. www.LuannsRoom.com
AN EYEFUL. COULD SOMEONE ***ELSE*** BE JEALOUS? HUH? *HUH?* BERNICE?
YOU ARE ***SO*** STUPID WHEN YOU'RE BEING SMART
GREG 2.19

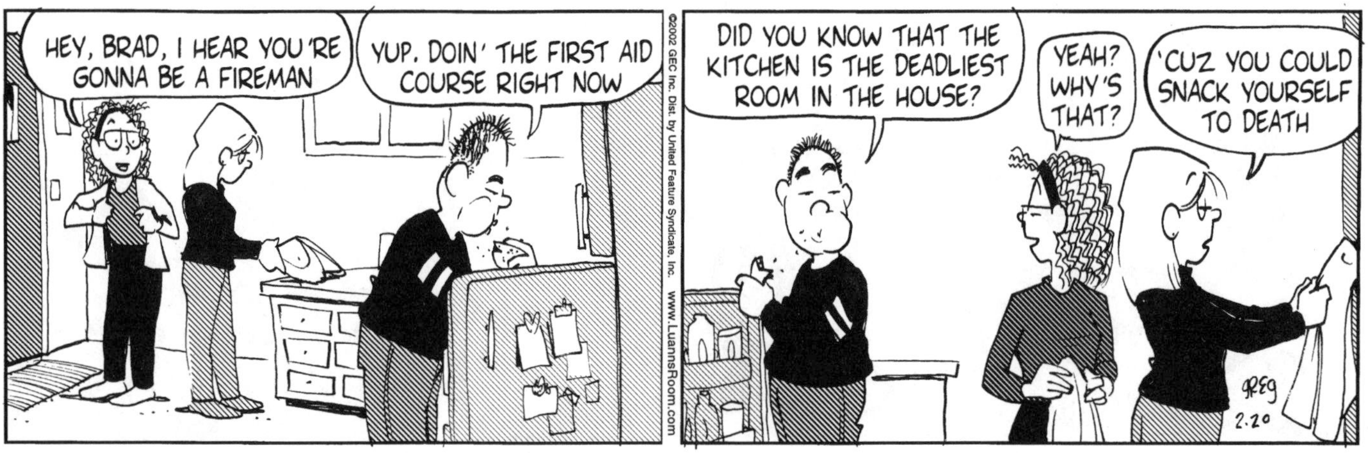
HEY, BRAD, I HEAR YOU'RE GONNA BE A FIREMAN
YUP. DOIN' THE FIRST AID COURSE RIGHT NOW
©2002 GEC Inc. Dist. by United Feature Syndicate, Inc. www.LuannsRoom.com
DID YOU KNOW THAT THE KITCHEN IS THE DEADLIEST ROOM IN THE HOUSE?
YEAH? WHY'S THAT?
'CUZ YOU COULD SNACK YOURSELF TO DEATH
GREG 2.20

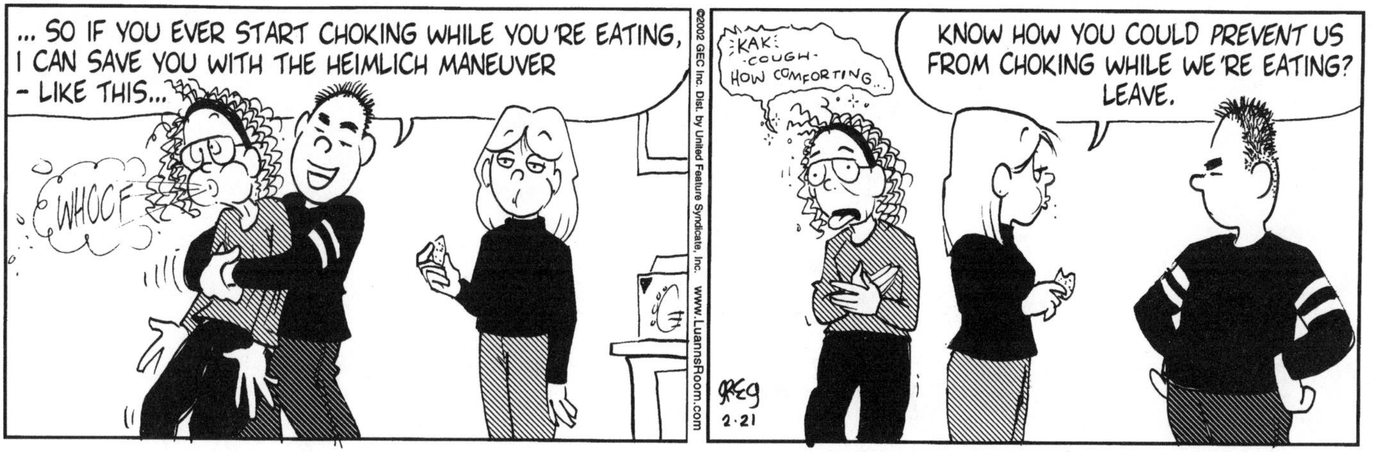
... SO IF YOU EVER START CHOKING WHILE YOU'RE EATING, I CAN SAVE YOU WITH THE HEIMLICH MANEUVER – LIKE THIS...
WHOOF
©2002 GEC Inc. Dist. by United Feature Syndicate, Inc. www.LuannsRoom.com
KAK · COUGH · HOW COMFORTING...
KNOW HOW YOU COULD PREVENT US FROM CHOKING WHILE WE'RE EATING? LEAVE.
GREG 2·21

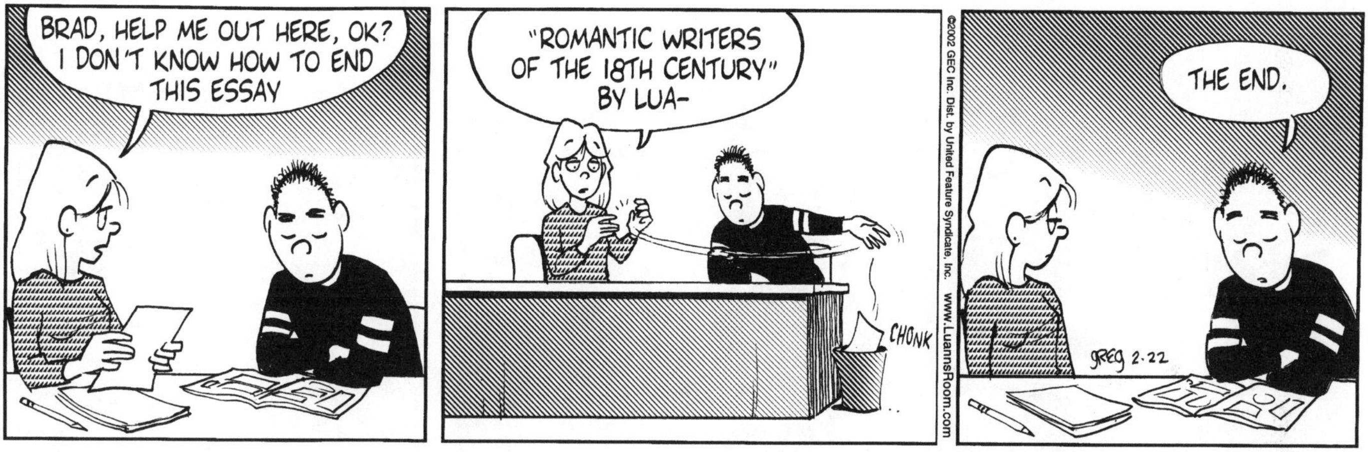
BRAD, HELP ME OUT HERE, OK? I DON'T KNOW HOW TO END THIS ESSAY
"ROMANTIC WRITERS OF THE 18TH CENTURY" BY LUA–
CHONK
©2002 GEC Inc. Dist. by United Feature Syndicate, Inc. www.LuannsRoom.com
THE END.
GREG 2·22

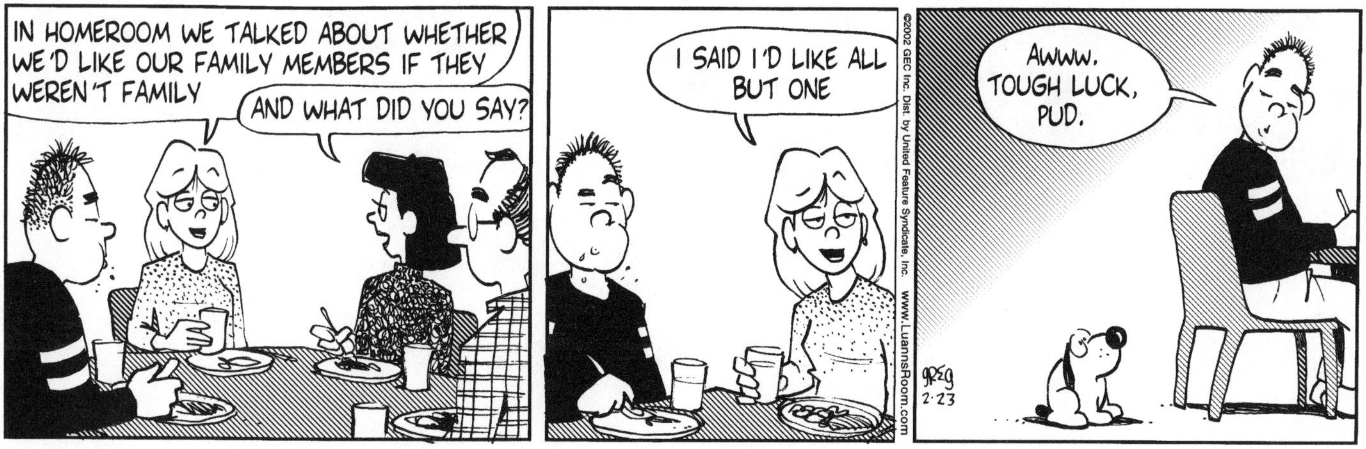
IN HOMEROOM WE TALKED ABOUT WHETHER WE'D LIKE OUR FAMILY MEMBERS IF THEY WEREN'T FAMILY
AND WHAT DID YOU SAY?
I SAID I'D LIKE ALL BUT ONE
©2002 GEC Inc. Dist. by United Feature Syndicate, Inc. www.LuannsRoom.com
GREG 2·23
AWWW. TOUGH LUCK, PUD.

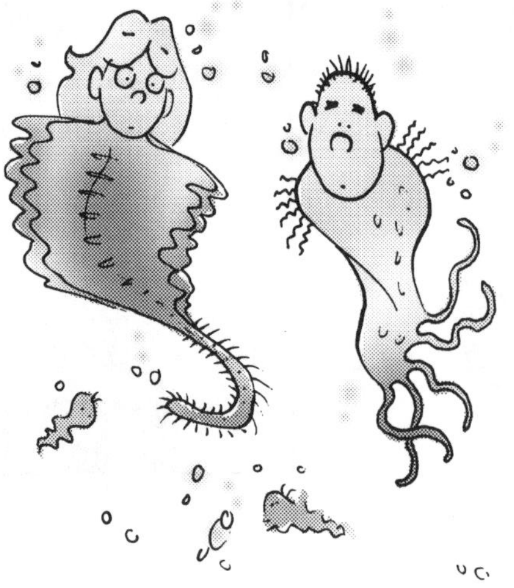

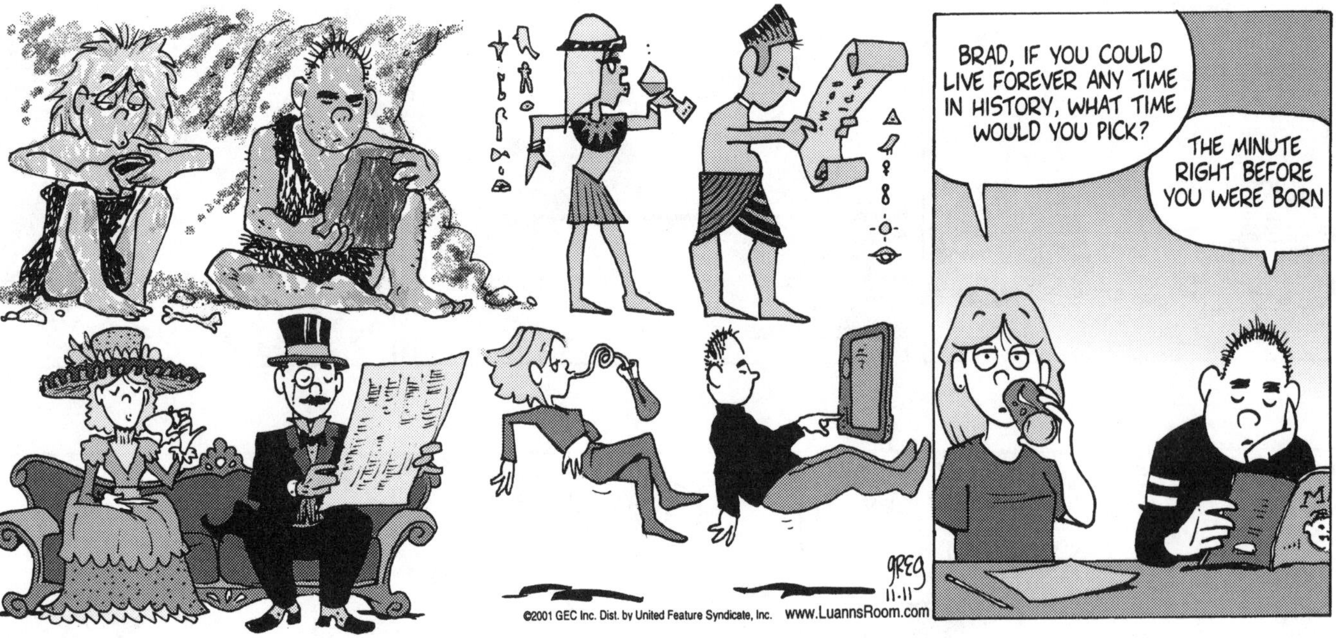
GREG 11-11
©2001 GEC Inc. Dist. by United Feature Syndicate, Inc.
www.LuannsRoom.com
BRAD, IF YOU COULD LIVE FOREVER ANY TIME IN HISTORY, WHAT TIME WOULD YOU PICK?
THE MINUTE RIGHT BEFORE YOU WERE BORN

OOP
BONK
I HOPE NEXT YEAR THE WORLD GETS BACK TO NORMAL
I HAVE A FEELING IT WILL
GREG 12.30
©2001 GEC Inc. Dist. by United Feature Syndicate, Inc.
www.LuannsRoom.com

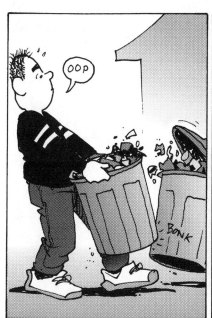

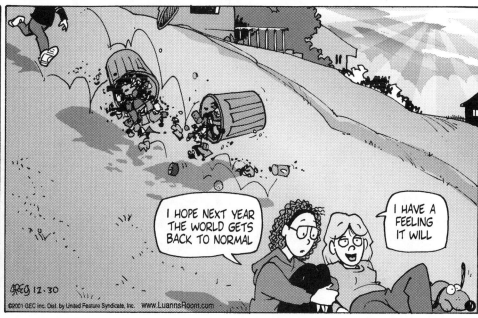

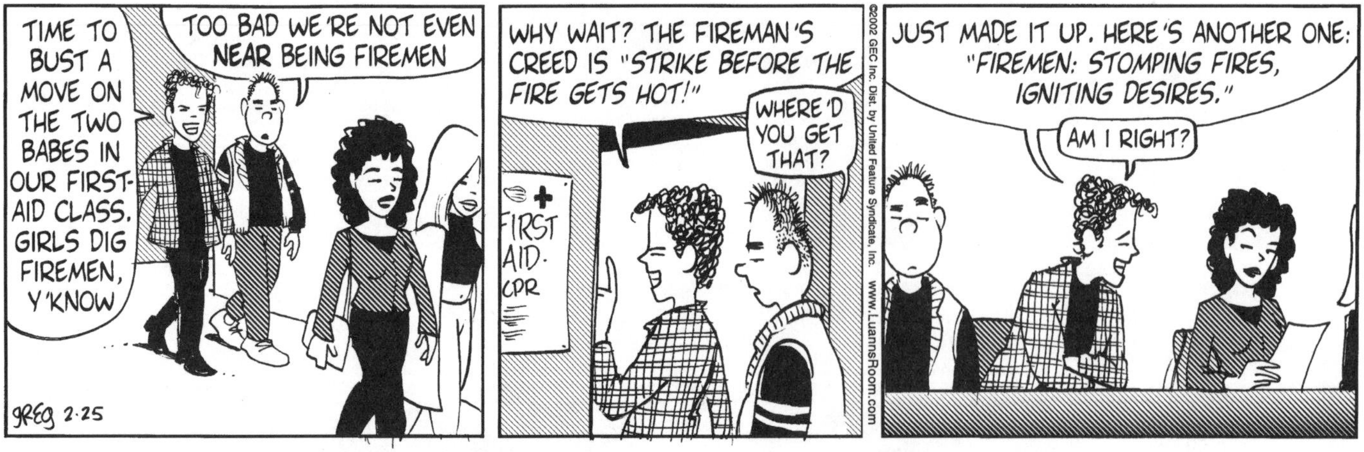
TIME TO BUST A MOVE ON THE TWO BABES IN OUR FIRST-AID CLASS. GIRLS DIG FIREMEN, Y'KNOW
TOO BAD WE'RE NOT EVEN **NEAR** BEING FIREMEN
GREG 2·25
WHY WAIT? THE FIREMAN'S CREED IS *"STRIKE BEFORE THE FIRE GETS HOT!"*
WHERE'D YOU GET THAT?
FIRST AID · CPR
©2002 GEC Inc. Dist. by United Feature Syndicate, Inc. www.LuannsRoom.com
JUST MADE IT UP. HERE'S ANOTHER ONE: *"FIREMEN: STOMPING FIRES, IGNITING DESIRES."*
AM I RIGHT?

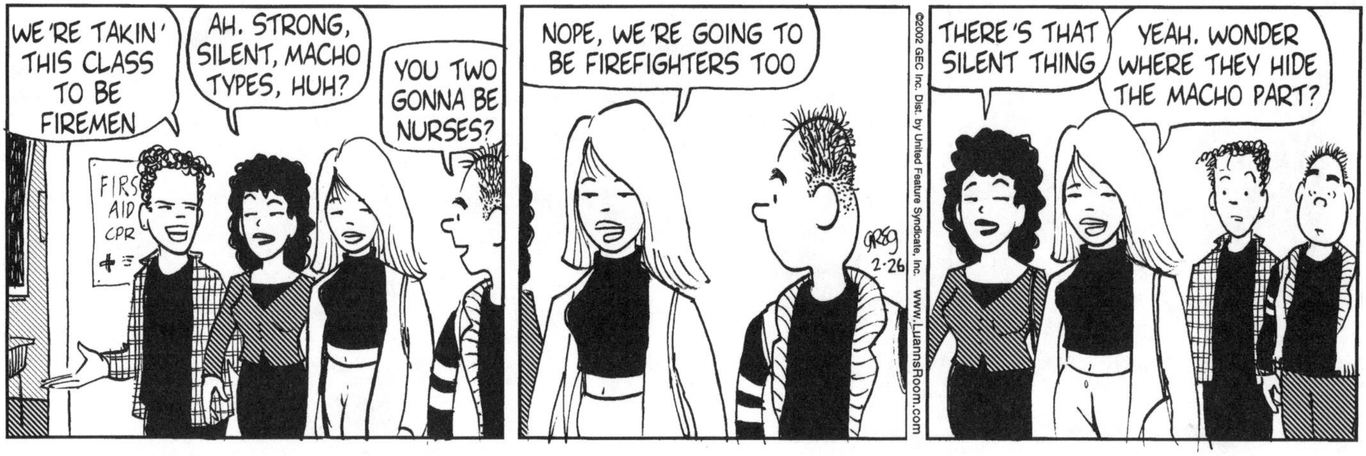
WE'RE TAKIN' THIS CLASS TO BE FIREMEN
AH. STRONG, SILENT, MACHO TYPES, HUH?
YOU TWO GONNA BE NURSES?
FIRS AID CPR
NOPE, WE'RE GOING TO BE FIREFIGHTERS TOO
GREG 2·26
©2002 GEC Inc. Dist. by United Feature Syndicate, Inc. www.LuannsRoom.com
THERE'S THAT SILENT THING
YEAH. WONDER WHERE THEY HIDE THE MACHO PART?

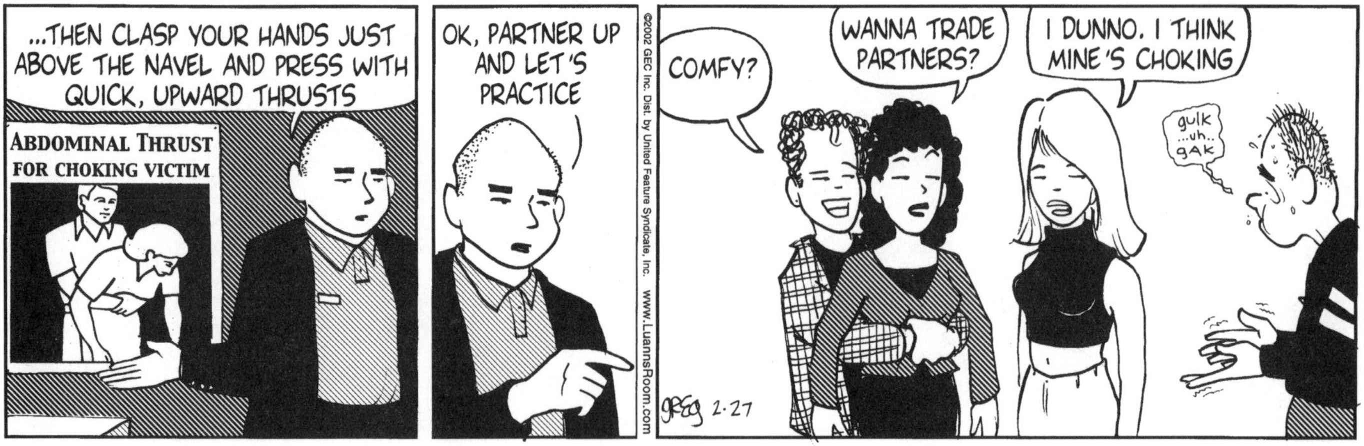
...THEN CLASP YOUR HANDS JUST ABOVE THE NAVEL AND PRESS WITH QUICK, UPWARD THRUSTS
ABDOMINAL THRUST FOR CHOKING VICTIM
OK, PARTNER UP AND LET'S PRACTICE
©2002 GEC Inc. Dist. by United Feature Syndicate, Inc. www.LuannsRoom.com
COMFY?
WANNA TRADE PARTNERS?
I DUNNO. I THINK MINE'S CHOKING
gulk ...uh.. gAk
GREG 2·27

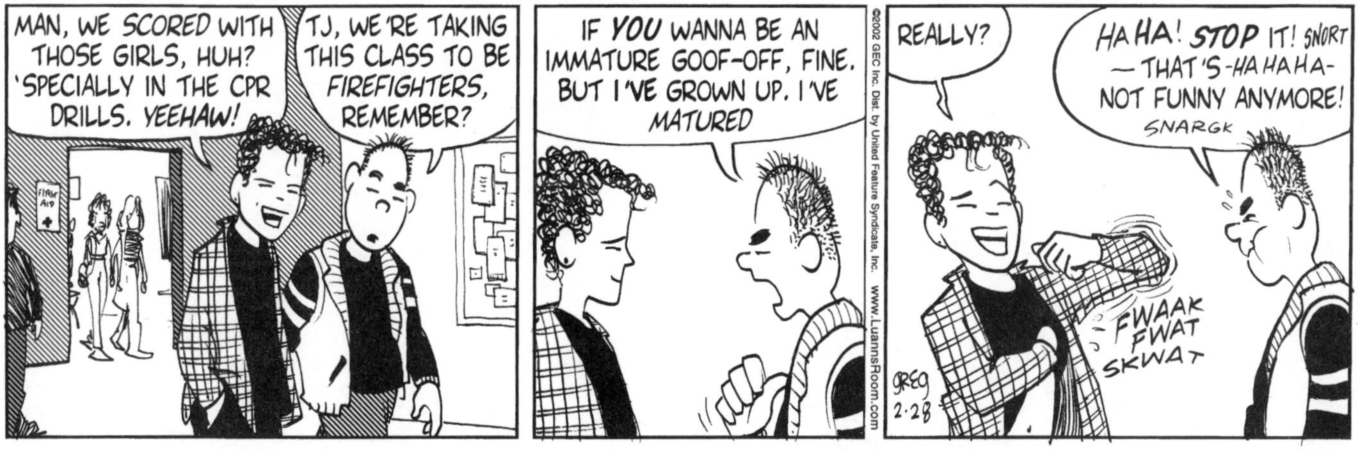
MAN, WE SCORED WITH THOSE GIRLS, HUH? 'SPECIALLY IN THE CPR DRILLS. YEEHAW!
TJ, WE'RE TAKING THIS CLASS TO BE FIREFIGHTERS, REMEMBER?
FIRST AID
IF YOU WANNA BE AN IMMATURE GOOF-OFF, FINE. BUT I'VE GROWN UP. I'VE MATURED
©2002 GEC Inc. Dist. by United Feature Syndicate, Inc. www.LuannsRoom.com
REALLY?
HA HA! STOP IT! SNORT — THAT'S -HA HA HA- NOT FUNNY ANYMORE! SNARGK
FWAAK FWAT SKWAT
GREG 2·28

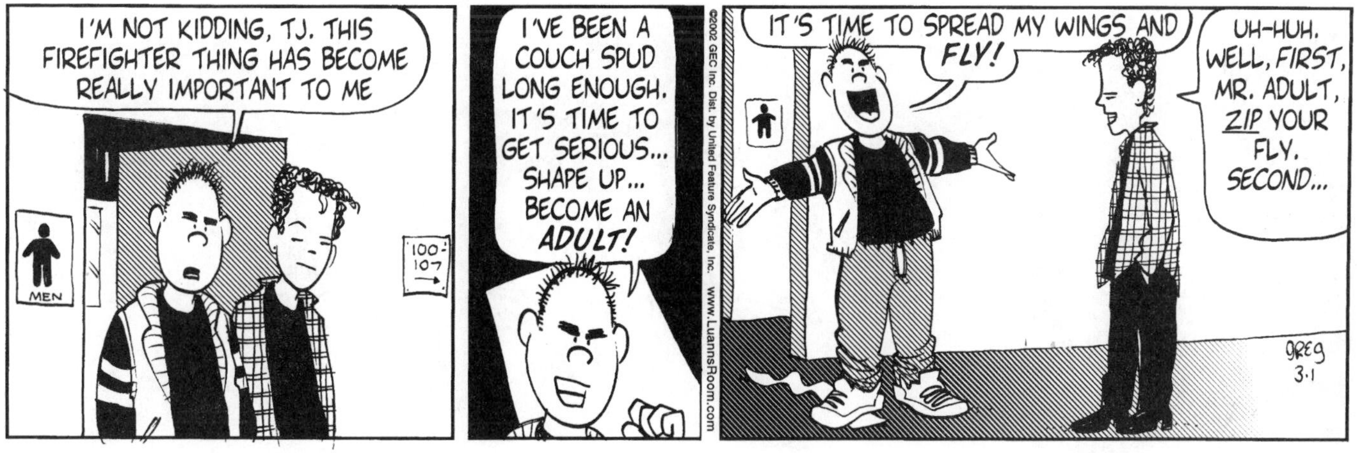
I'M NOT KIDDING, TJ. THIS FIREFIGHTER THING HAS BECOME REALLY IMPORTANT TO ME
MEN
100-107
I'VE BEEN A COUCH SPUD LONG ENOUGH. IT'S TIME TO GET SERIOUS... SHAPE UP... BECOME AN ADULT!
©2002 GEC Inc. Dist. by United Feature Syndicate, Inc. www.LuannsRoom.com
IT'S TIME TO SPREAD MY WINGS AND FLY!
UH-HUH. WELL, FIRST, MR. ADULT, ZIP YOUR FLY. SECOND...
GREG 3·1

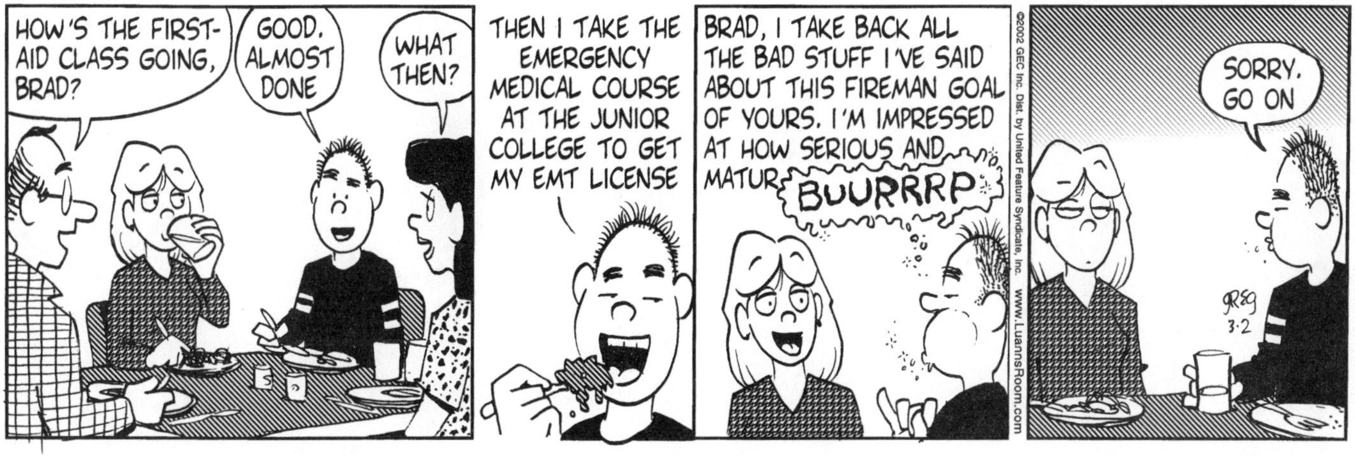
HOW'S THE FIRST-AID CLASS GOING, BRAD?
GOOD. ALMOST DONE
WHAT THEN?
THEN I TAKE THE EMERGENCY MEDICAL COURSE AT THE JUNIOR COLLEGE TO GET MY EMT LICENSE
BRAD, I TAKE BACK ALL THE BAD STUFF I'VE SAID ABOUT THIS FIREMAN GOAL OF YOURS. I'M IMPRESSED AT HOW SERIOUS AND MATUR
BUURRRP
©2002 GEC Inc. Dist. by United Feature Syndicate, Inc. www.LuannsRoom.com
SORRY. GO ON
GREG 3·2

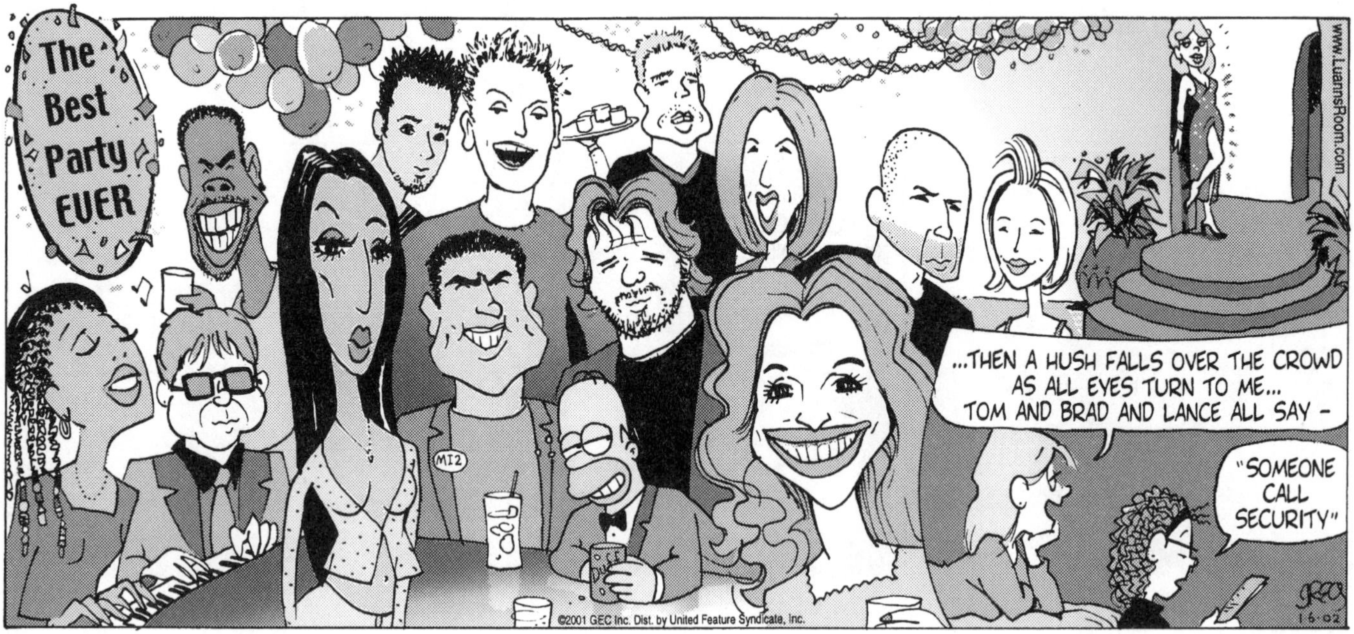
The Best Party EVER
MI2
...THEN A HUSH FALLS OVER THE CROWD AS ALL EYES TURN TO ME... TOM AND BRAD AND LANCE ALL SAY -
"SOMEONE CALL SECURITY"
www.LuannsRoom.com
©2001 GEC Inc. Dist. by United Feature Syndicate, Inc.
GREG 1-6-02

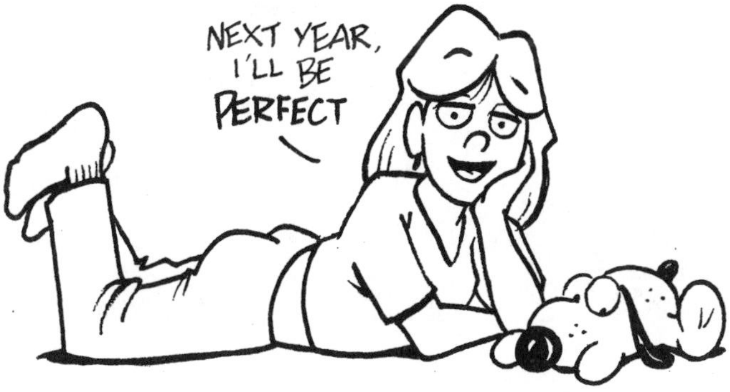
NEXT YEAR, I'LL BE PERFECT

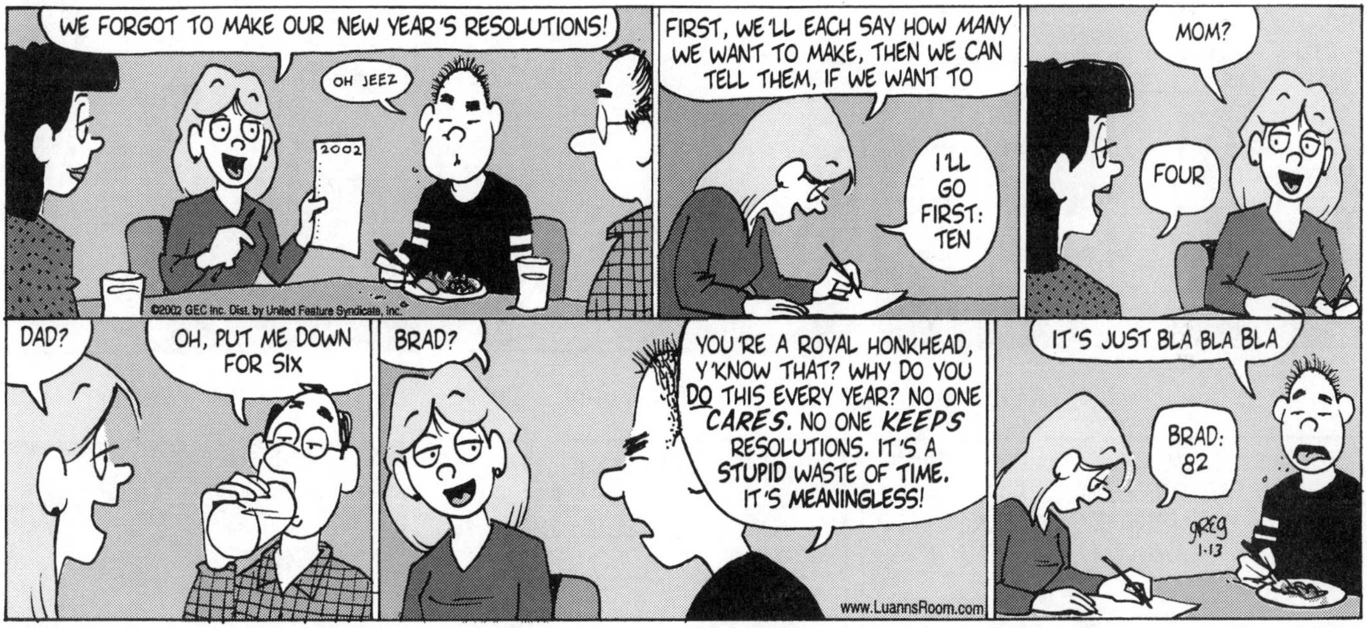
WE FORGOT TO MAKE OUR NEW YEAR'S RESOLUTIONS!
OH JEEZ
2002
©2002 GEC Inc. Dist. by United Feature Syndicate, Inc.
FIRST, WE'LL EACH SAY HOW MANY WE WANT TO MAKE, THEN WE CAN TELL THEM, IF WE WANT TO
I'LL GO FIRST: TEN
MOM?
FOUR
DAD?
OH, PUT ME DOWN FOR SIX
BRAD?
YOU'RE A ROYAL HONKHEAD, Y'KNOW THAT? WHY DO YOU DO THIS EVERY YEAR? NO ONE CARES. NO ONE KEEPS RESOLUTIONS. IT'S A STUPID WASTE OF TIME. IT'S MEANINGLESS!
www.LuannsRoom.com
IT'S JUST BLA BLA BLA
BRAD: 82
GREG 1-13

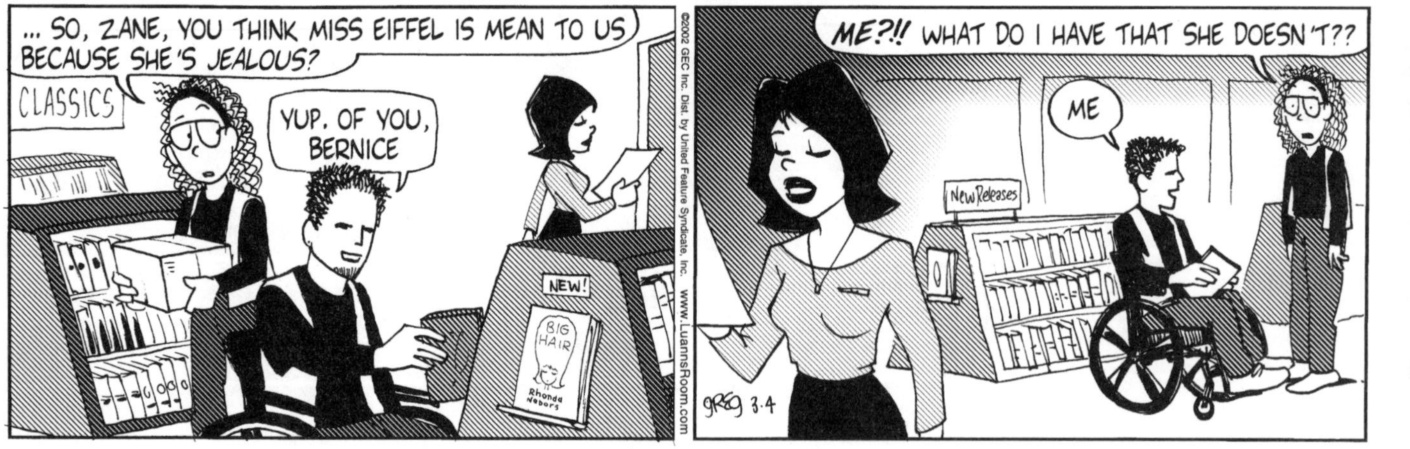
... SO, ZANE, YOU THINK MISS EIFFEL IS MEAN TO US BECAUSE SHE'S JEALOUS?
CLASSICS
YUP. OF YOU, BERNICE
NEW!
BIG HAIR
Rhonda Nebors
©2002 GEC Inc. Dist. by United Feature Syndicate, Inc. www.LuannsRoom.com
ME?!! WHAT DO I HAVE THAT SHE DOESN'T??
ME
New Releases
GREG 3·4

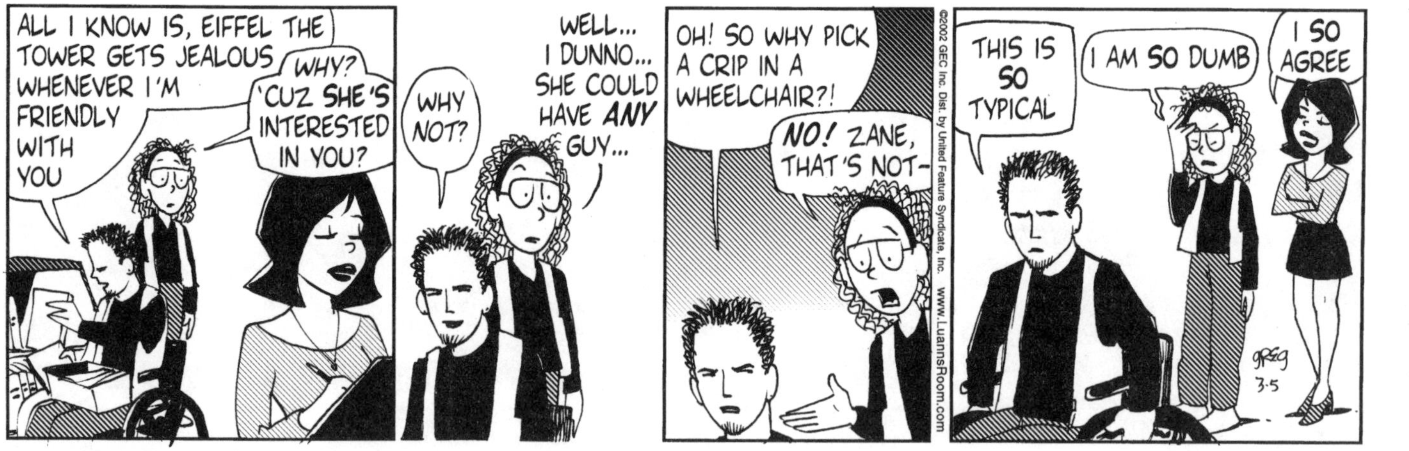
ALL I KNOW IS, EIFFEL THE TOWER GETS JEALOUS WHENEVER I'M FRIENDLY WITH YOU
WHY?
'CUZ SHE'S INTERESTED IN YOU?
WHY NOT?
WELL... I DUNNO... SHE COULD HAVE ANY GUY...
OH! SO WHY PICK A CRIP IN A WHEELCHAIR?!
NO! ZANE, THAT'S NOT-
©2002 GEC Inc. Dist. by United Feature Syndicate, Inc. www.LuannsRoom.com
THIS IS SO TYPICAL
I AM SO DUMB
I SO AGREE
GREG 3·5

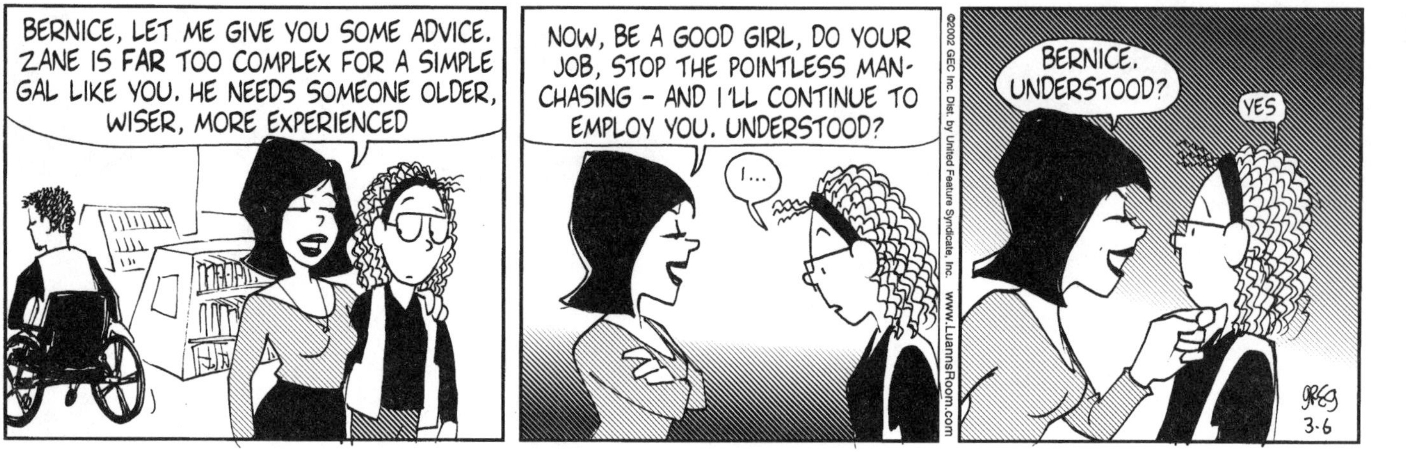
BERNICE, LET ME GIVE YOU SOME ADVICE. ZANE IS FAR TOO COMPLEX FOR A SIMPLE GAL LIKE YOU. HE NEEDS SOMEONE OLDER, WISER, MORE EXPERIENCED
NOW, BE A GOOD GIRL, DO YOUR JOB, STOP THE POINTLESS MAN-CHASING – AND I'LL CONTINUE TO EMPLOY YOU. UNDERSTOOD?
I...
©2002 GEC Inc. Dist. by United Feature Syndicate, Inc. www.LuannsRoom.com
BERNICE. UNDERSTOOD?
YES
GREG 3·6

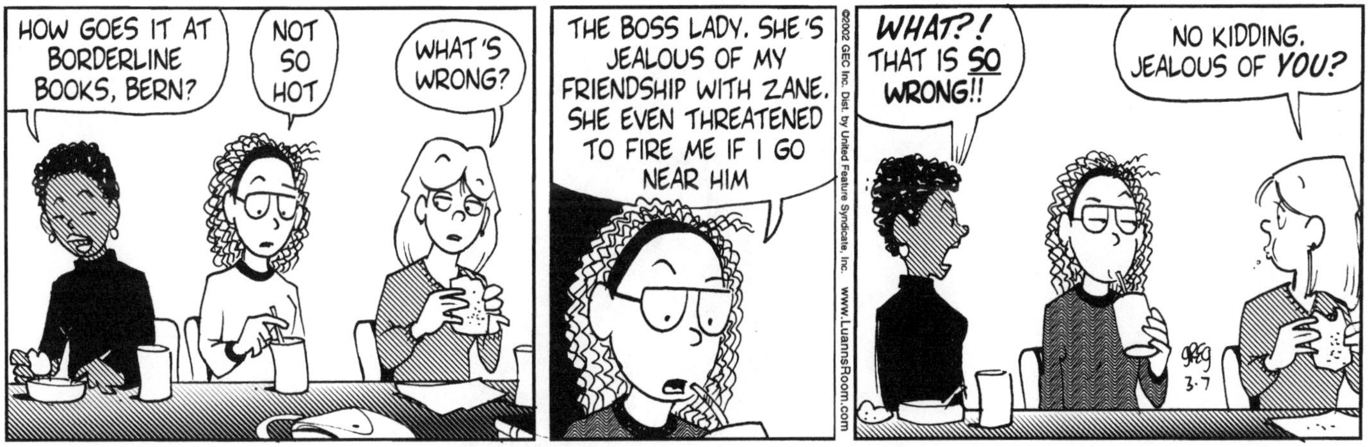
HOW GOES IT AT BORDERLINE BOOKS, BERN?
NOT SO HOT
WHAT'S WRONG?
THE BOSS LADY. SHE'S JEALOUS OF MY FRIENDSHIP WITH ZANE. SHE EVEN THREATENED TO FIRE ME IF I GO NEAR HIM
©2002 GEC Inc. Dist. by United Feature Syndicate, Inc. www.LuannsRoom.com
WHAT?! THAT IS SO WRONG!!
NO KIDDING. JEALOUS OF YOU?
GREG 3-7
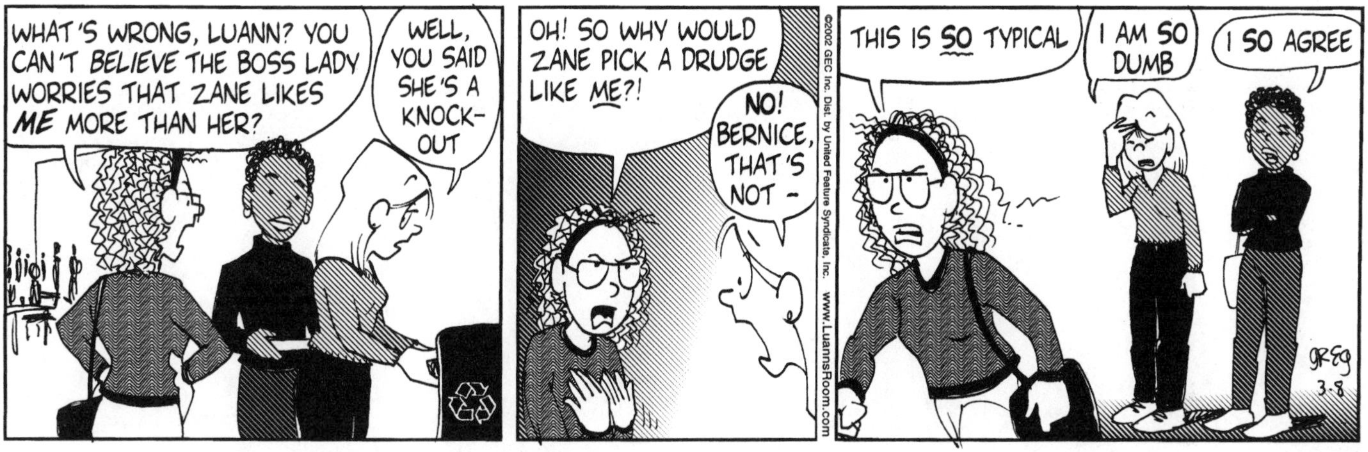
WHAT'S WRONG, LUANN? YOU CAN'T BELIEVE THE BOSS LADY WORRIES THAT ZANE LIKES ME MORE THAN HER?
WELL, YOU SAID SHE'S A KNOCK-OUT
OH! SO WHY WOULD ZANE PICK A DRUDGE LIKE ME?!
NO! BERNICE, THAT'S NOT -
©2002 GEC Inc. Dist. by United Feature Syndicate, Inc. www.LuannsRoom.com
THIS IS SO TYPICAL
I AM SO DUMB
I SO AGREE
GREG 3-8
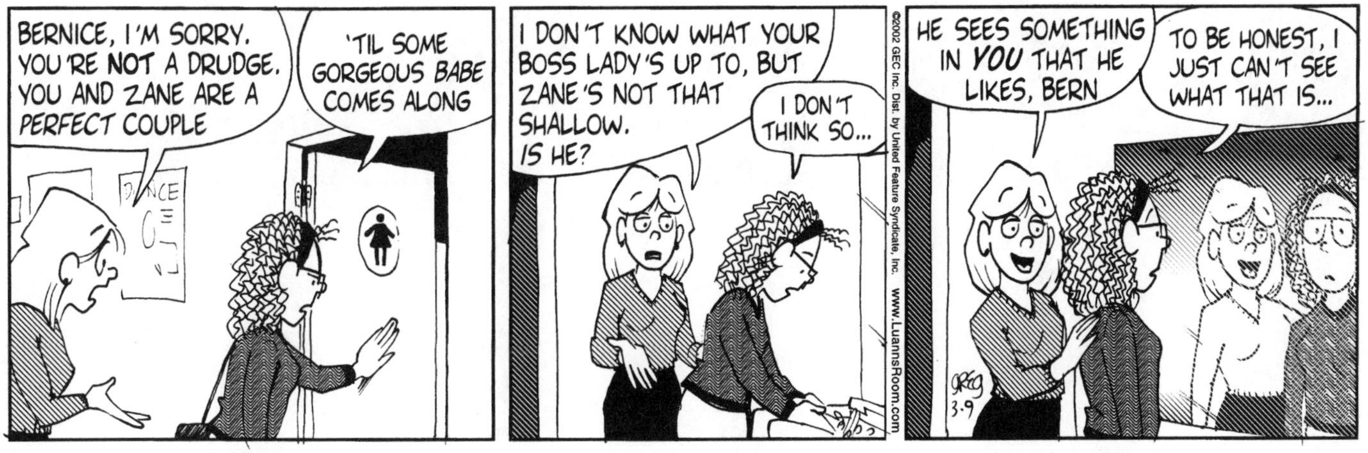
BERNICE, I'M SORRY. YOU'RE NOT A DRUDGE. YOU AND ZANE ARE A PERFECT COUPLE
'TIL SOME GORGEOUS BABE COMES ALONG
I DON'T KNOW WHAT YOUR BOSS LADY'S UP TO, BUT ZANE'S NOT THAT SHALLOW. IS HE?
I DON'T THINK SO...
©2002 GEC Inc. Dist. by United Feature Syndicate, Inc. www.LuannsRoom.com
HE SEES SOMETHING IN YOU THAT HE LIKES, BERN
TO BE HONEST, I JUST CAN'T SEE WHAT THAT IS...
GREG 3-9

THE CAR'S ACTING FUNNY
FUNNY?
©2002 GEC Inc. Dist. by United Feature Syndicate, Inc. www.LuannsRoom.com
IT STUTTERS AND STALLS
HM. POSSIBLE FUEL PROBLEM
OR ELECTRICAL
WELL, IT'S NICE TO HAVE CAR EXPERTS HERE. SO WHAT SHOULD WE DO?
I'M THINKING CLOGGED FUEL FILTER. OR A BAD PUMP. COULD BE A FUEL INJECTOR...
I'D CHECK THE SPARK. MIGHT BE WIRING... OR A COMPUTER MALFUNCTION
TAKE IT TO ALLEN'S CAR REPAIR
GREG 1·20

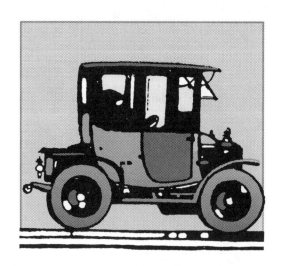

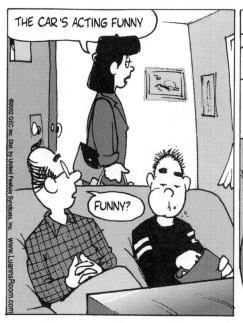

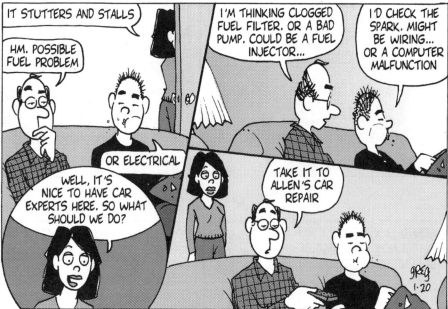

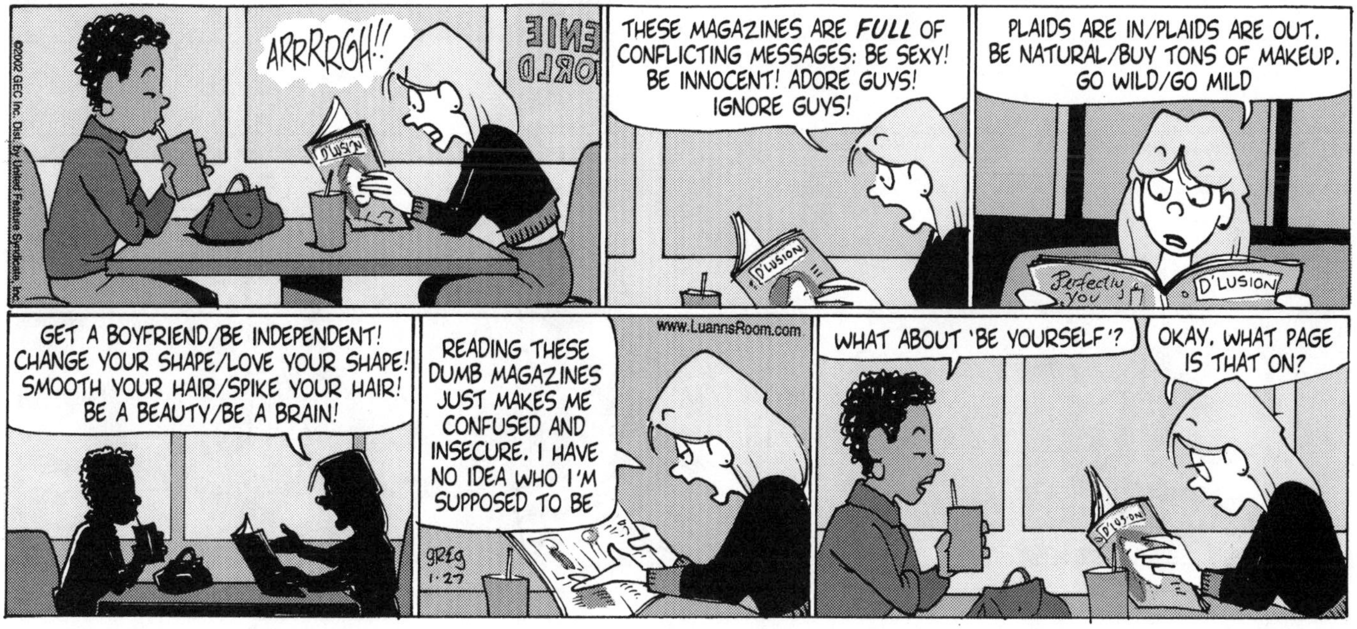
©2002 GEC Inc. Dist. by United Feature Syndicate, Inc.
ARRRRGH!!
D'LUSION
THESE MAGAZINES ARE ***FULL*** OF CONFLICTING MESSAGES: BE SEXY! BE INNOCENT! ADORE GUYS! IGNORE GUYS!
D'LUSION
PLAIDS ARE IN/PLAIDS ARE OUT. BE NATURAL/BUY TONS OF MAKEUP. GO WILD/GO MILD
Perfectly You
D'LUSION
GET A BOYFRIEND/BE INDEPENDENT! CHANGE YOUR SHAPE/LOVE YOUR SHAPE! SMOOTH YOUR HAIR/SPIKE YOUR HAIR! BE A BEAUTY/BE A BRAIN!
www.LuannsRoom.com
READING THESE DUMB MAGAZINES JUST MAKES ME CONFUSED AND INSECURE. I HAVE NO IDEA WHO I'M SUPPOSED TO BE
GREG 1·27
WHAT ABOUT 'BE YOURSELF'?
OKAY. WHAT PAGE IS THAT ON?
D'LUSION

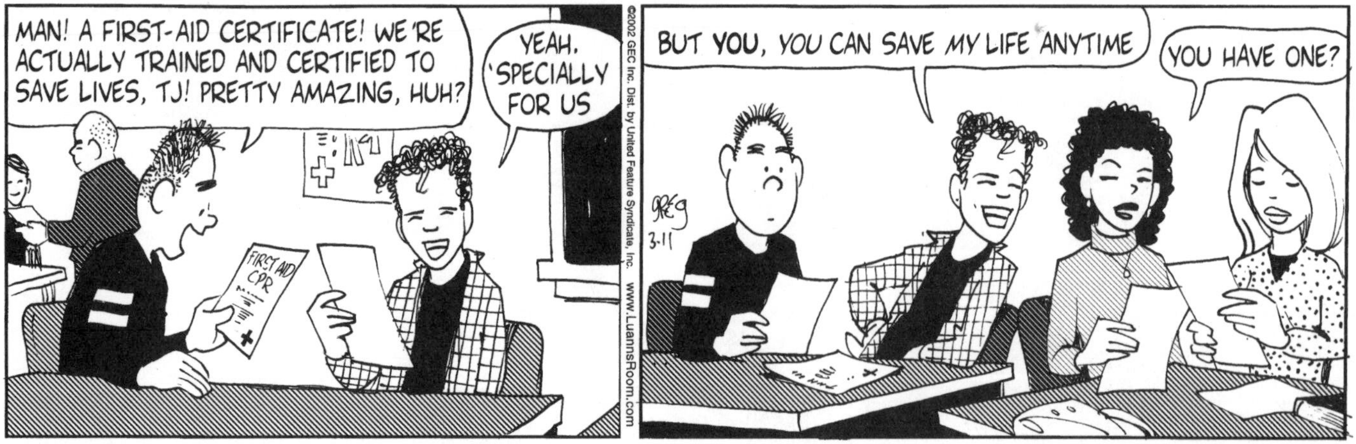
MAN! A FIRST-AID CERTIFICATE! WE'RE ACTUALLY TRAINED AND CERTIFIED TO SAVE LIVES, TJ! PRETTY AMAZING, HUH?
YEAH. 'SPECIALLY FOR US
FIRST AID CPR
©2002 GEC Inc. Dist. by United Feature Syndicate, Inc. www.LuannsRoom.com
BUT YOU, YOU CAN SAVE MY LIFE ANYTIME
YOU HAVE ONE?
GREG 3-11

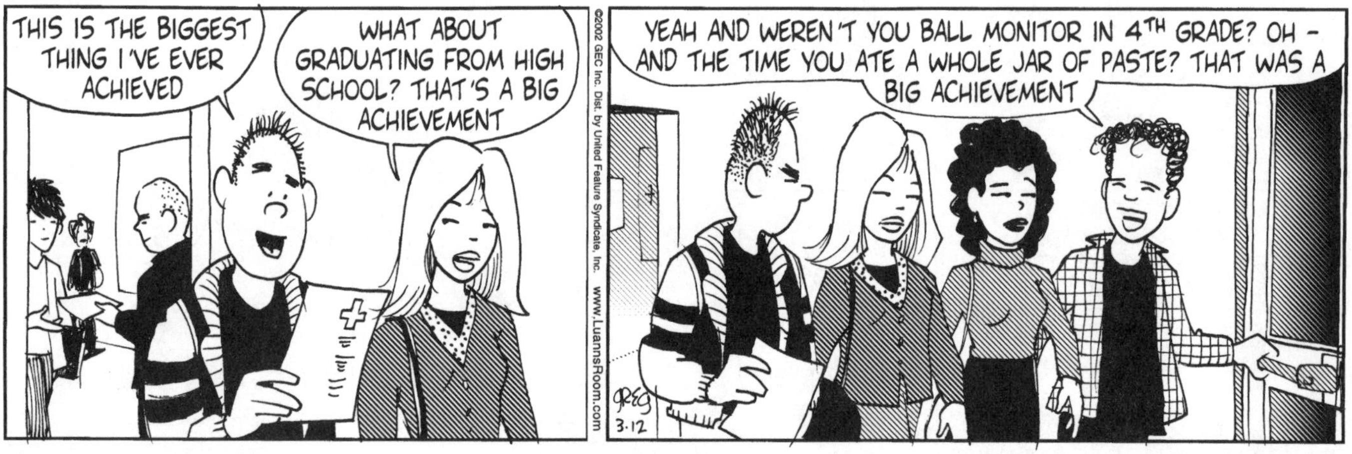
THIS IS THE BIGGEST THING I'VE EVER ACHIEVED
WHAT ABOUT GRADUATING FROM HIGH SCHOOL? THAT'S A BIG ACHIEVEMENT
©2002 GEC Inc. Dist. by United Feature Syndicate, Inc. www.LuannsRoom.com
YEAH AND WEREN'T YOU BALL MONITOR IN 4TH GRADE? OH - AND THE TIME YOU ATE A WHOLE JAR OF PASTE? THAT WAS A BIG ACHIEVEMENT
GREG 3-12

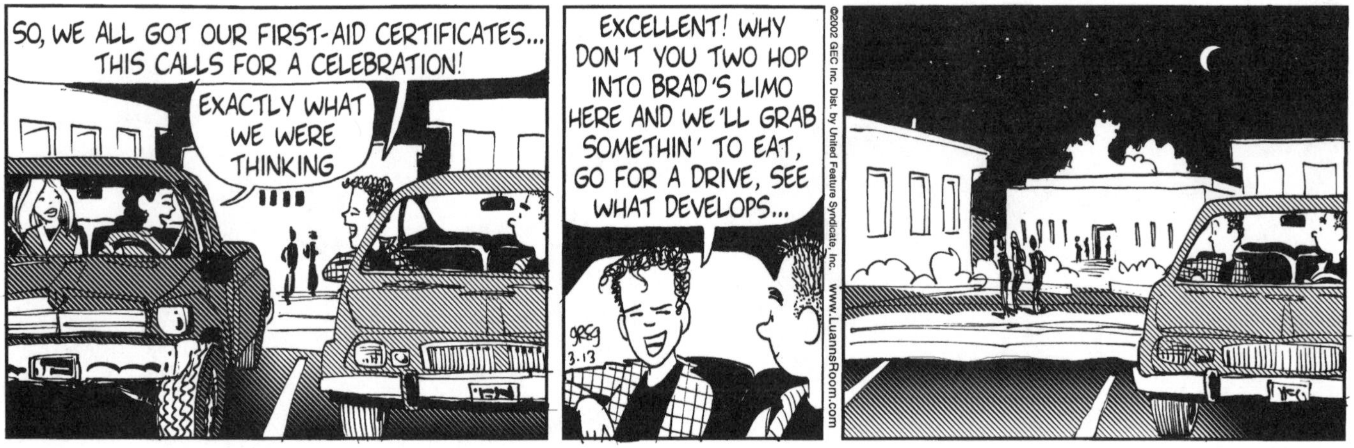
SO, WE ALL GOT OUR FIRST-AID CERTIFICATES... THIS CALLS FOR A CELEBRATION!
EXACTLY WHAT WE WERE THINKING
EXCELLENT! WHY DON'T YOU TWO HOP INTO BRAD'S LIMO HERE AND WE'LL GRAB SOMETHIN' TO EAT, GO FOR A DRIVE, SEE WHAT DEVELOPS...
GREG 3-13
©2002 GEC Inc. Dist. by United Feature Syndicate, Inc. www.LuannsRoom.com

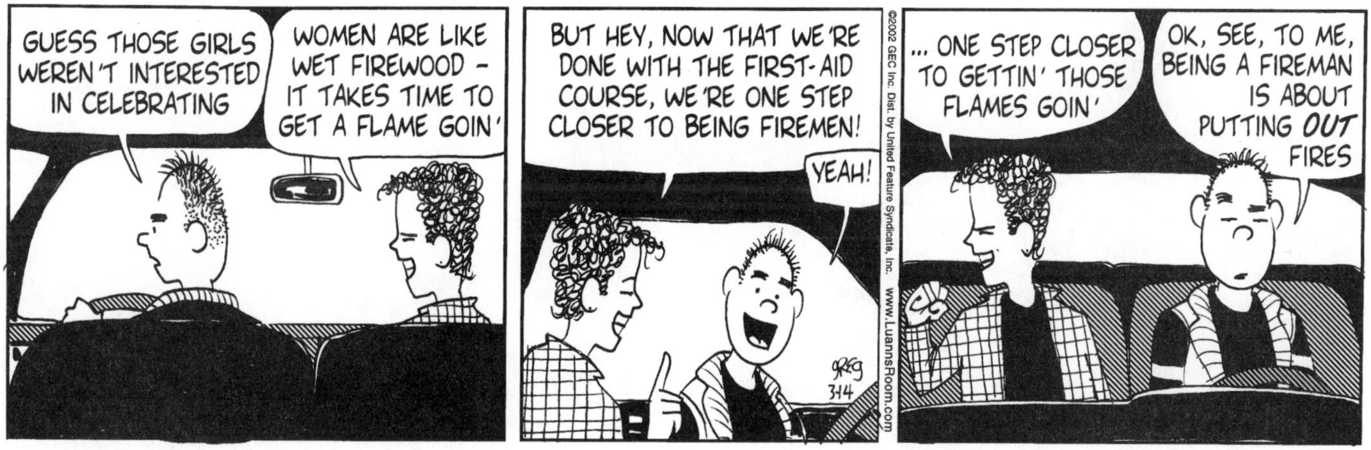
GUESS THOSE GIRLS WEREN'T INTERESTED IN CELEBRATING
WOMEN ARE LIKE WET FIREWOOD – IT TAKES TIME TO GET A FLAME GOIN'
BUT HEY, NOW THAT WE'RE DONE WITH THE FIRST-AID COURSE, WE'RE ONE STEP CLOSER TO BEING FIREMEN!
YEAH!
GREG 3-14
©2002 GEC Inc. Dist. by United Feature Syndicate, Inc. www.LuannsRoom.com
... ONE STEP CLOSER TO GETTIN' THOSE FLAMES GOIN'
OK, SEE, TO ME, BEING A FIREMAN IS ABOUT PUTTING *OUT* FIRES

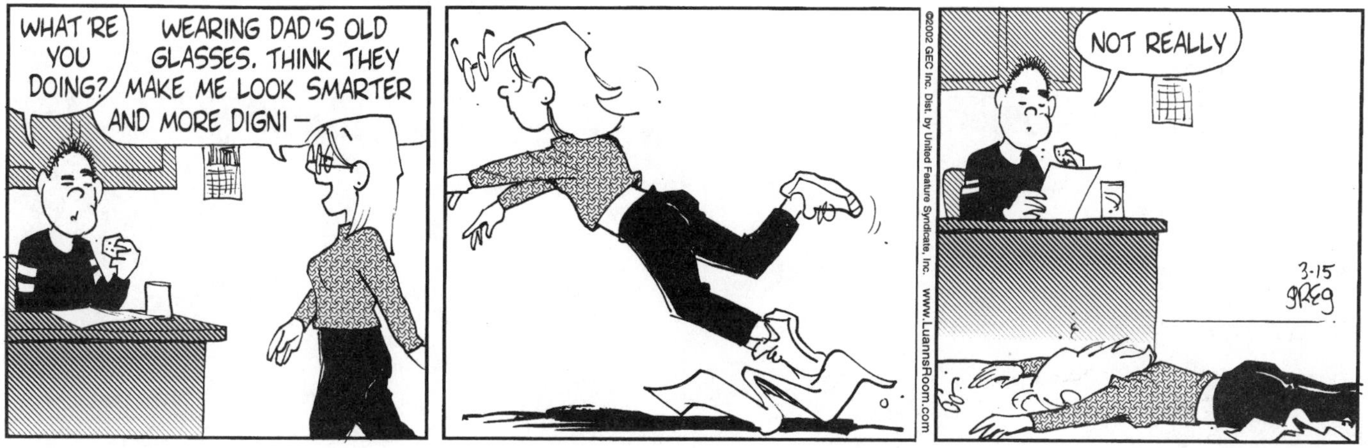
WHAT'RE YOU DOING?
WEARING DAD'S OLD GLASSES. THINK THEY MAKE ME LOOK SMARTER AND MORE DIGNI–
©2002 GEC Inc. Dist. by United Feature Syndicate, Inc. www.LuannsRoom.com
NOT REALLY
3-15 GREG

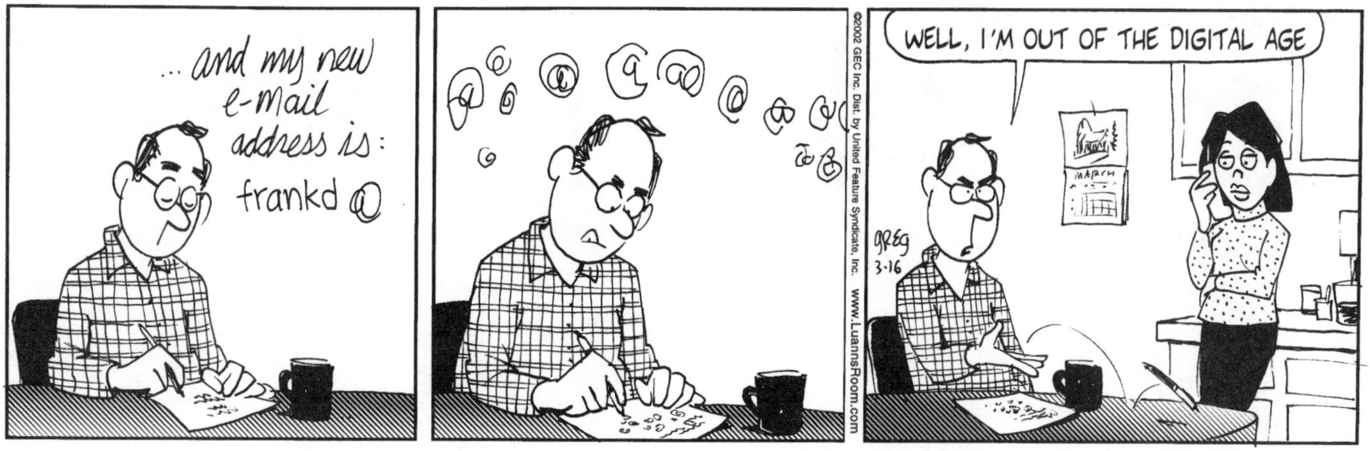
... and my new e-mail address is:
frankd @
©2002 GEC Inc. Dist. by United Feature Syndicate, Inc. www.LuannsRoom.com
GREG 3-16
WELL, I'M OUT OF THE DIGITAL AGE

D'LUSION
HELPING YOU BE SOMEONE ELSE

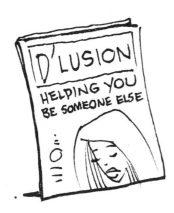

Men Working Together
IN?
YEP
©2002 GEC Inc. Dist. by United Feature Syndicate, Inc.
www.LuannsRoom.com
Women Working Together
... I STEPPED ON AARON'S FOOT AND TIFFANY YELLED, "GEEZ, WHAT A KLUTZ!" SO AT LUNCHTIME, I POKED A LITTLE HOLE IN HER MILK CARTON. WHEN SHE OPENED IT, MILK LEAKED OUT ONTO THE FLOOR. TONY BANCROFT, MR. FOOTBALL-TEAM-CAPTAIN, SLIPPED IN THE MILK AND FELL ON TIFFANY, KNOCKING HER INTO A CART OF DIRTY DISHES. SO I YELLED, "GEE, GLAD I'M ONLY A KLUTZ!"
THE FIRST DATE YOUR DAD AND I WENT ON, IT WAS JULY AND I WORE A SUMMER DRESS CUT LOW IN THE BACK. HE TOOK ME TO AN ICE CREAM PLACE AND WE ORDERED A HUGE SUNDAE. WHEN THE WAITER BROUGHT IT, HE TRIPPED ON DAD'S FOOT AND DROPPED THE ENTIRE SUNDAE DOWN MY BACK. I BET PEOPLE IN CHINA HEARD MY SCREAM
GREG
2·3

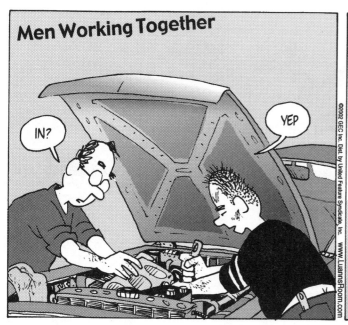

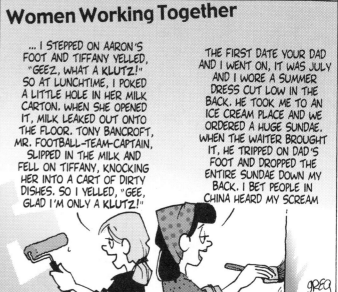

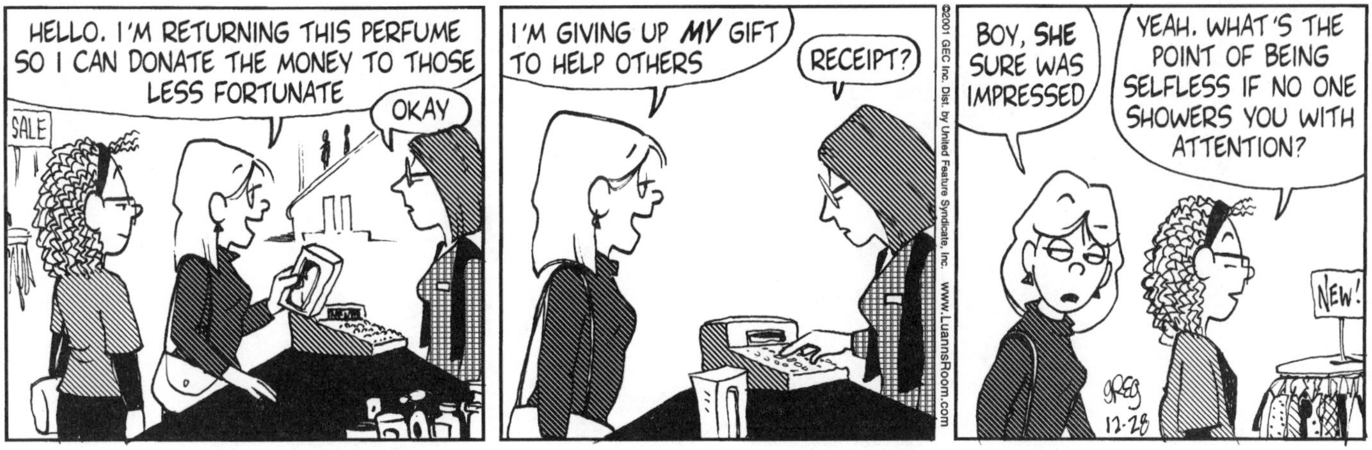
HELLO. I'M RETURNING THIS PERFUME SO I CAN DONATE THE MONEY TO THOSE LESS FORTUNATE
OKAY
SALE
I'M GIVING UP **MY** GIFT TO HELP OTHERS
RECEIPT?
©2001 GEC Inc. Dist. by United Feature Syndicate, Inc. www.LuannsRoom.com
BOY, **SHE** SURE WAS IMPRESSED
YEAH. WHAT'S THE POINT OF BEING SELFLESS IF NO ONE SHOWERS YOU WITH ATTENTION?
NEW!
GREG
12-28

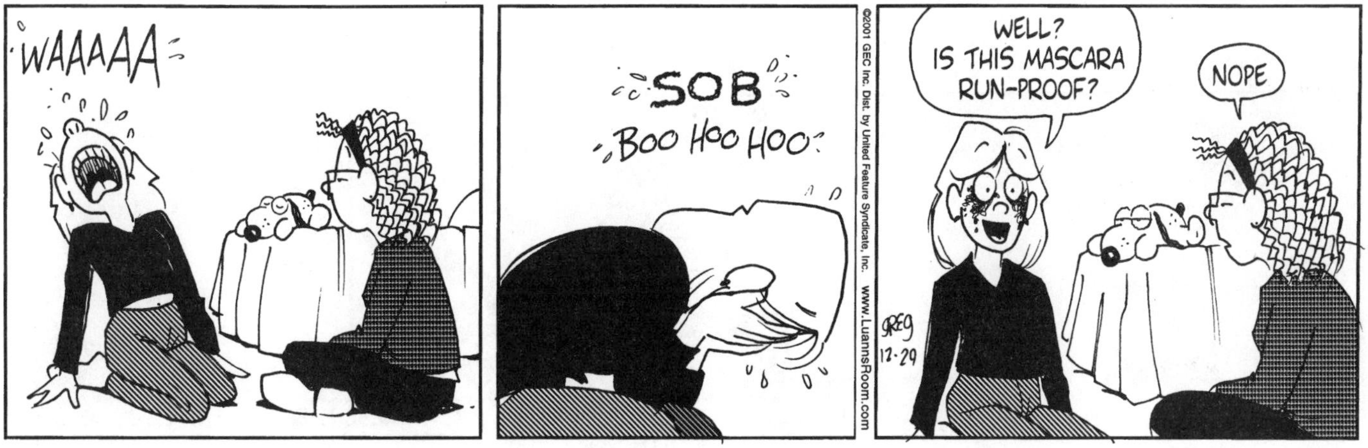
WAAAAA
SOB
BOO HOO HOO
©2001 GEC Inc. Dist. by United Feature Syndicate, Inc. www.LuannsRoom.com
WELL? IS THIS MASCARA RUN-PROOF?
NOPE
GREG
12-29

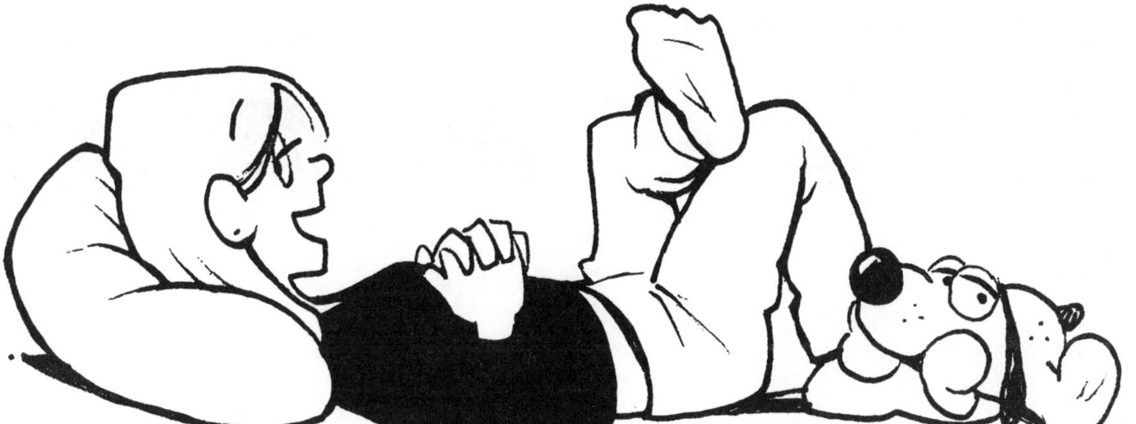

©2002 GEC Inc. Dist. by United Feature Syndicate, Inc.
www.LuannsRoom.com
I'D LOVE TO GET MARRIED ON A BEACH. HOW ROMANTIC...
BRIDE
A BEACH?! YOU KIDDIN'?
SAND WOULD GET EVERYWHERE, SHOES N' STUFF WOULD GET ALL SOGGY, YOU'D GET SUNBURNED...
Mulch mulch
SEAGULLS WOULD PLOP ON PEOPLE, BIG SMELLY PILES OF SEAWEED AND DEAD FISH WOULD DRAW FLIES...
BURP
NO THANKS. NO BEACH WEDDIN' FOR ME
GLUK GLUK
BELIEVE ME, YOU DON'T NEED TO WORRY
GREG 2-10

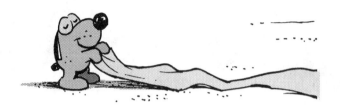

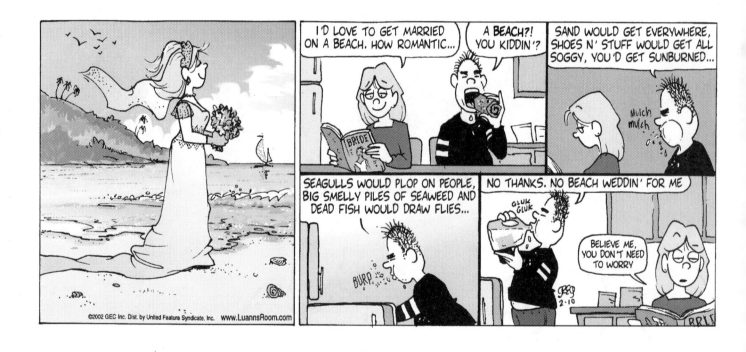